GIVING PSYCHOLOGY AWAY

Giving Psychology Away

Duane M. Belcher

Bakersfield College
Bakersfield, California

Canfield Press ⟁ **San Francisco**
A Department of Harper & Row, Publishers, Inc.
New York   Evanston   London

GIVING PSYCHOLOGY AWAY

Copyright © 1973 by Duane M. Belcher

Printed in United States of America
All rights reserved.
No part of this book may be used or reproduced in any manner
whatsoever without written permission except in the case of
brief quotations embodied in critical articles and reviews.
For information address Harper & Row, Publishers, Inc.,
10 East 53rd Street, New York, N.Y. 10022

International Standard Book Number: 0–06–380455–7

Library of Congress Catalog Card Number: 73–1189

73 74 75 10 9 8 7 6 5 4 3 2 1

Editor: Theodore Ricks
Editorial and design supervision: Ken Burke
Design: Joe Fay
Illustrations: Doug Luna
Copyediting: Brian Williams

Preface

As a student, I remember, I was told I had "no right" to expect any practical benefits from taking a psychology course. In those days an academic was supposed to withdraw into an ivory tower and toil away at "pure" research. I felt only slightly uneasy with these attitudes: surely the university knew what was best for me and, in any case, my peers seemed to accept these views without noticeable protest.

The title of this book, *Giving Psychology Away*, suggests a rejection of the ivory tower approach. As George A. Miller stated, in his 1969 presidential address to the American Psychological Association, psychology must be made more relevant to the real world; we must provide people with the behavioral tools to solve their problems. Psychology has much to offer, as Miller notes, that can enlarge our view of what is humanly possible and desirable and help us to live, love, and work together more harmoniously.

Giving Psychology Away is "humanistic behaviorism"—a selection of topics that I believe are relevant to student concerns in the 1970s, drawn chiefly from social and clinical psychology and learning, motivation, and personality. I have tried to convey to the student some of the excitement associated with psychology's rapidly expanding frontiers. The concerns of women are discussed in at least four chapters, of blacks in five chapters, and of the environment in two chapters. In handling the factual data of psychology I have tried to respect the attitudes of students and their interest in those psychological topics that can be applied to their own concerns. Thus, the discussion constantly shifts back and forth from basic psychology to applications relevant to the student. Many traditional topics, therefore, such as experimental method and design, physiology, sensation, and statistics, are left out entirely.

I have also tried to respect the fields of psychological science, research and practice, presenting findings as accurately as possible, compatible with the interests of students who are not psychology majors. While research findings are often presented in considerable detail, no effort has been made to explain the fine points of research.

This book has been designed for the general reader who has had no previous exposure to psychology instruction. Excessively technical jargon has been avoided whenever possible. Such technical vocabulary as is necessary is explained in the "Terms and Concepts" section at the end of each chapter. A student workbook is available from the publisher at the option of the instructor.

I have used the manuscript in its various forms in my classes at Bakersfield College for several years. The material has benefitted from feedback by students in the 18 to 21-years-old range and older, both daytime and night school students, and I owe all of these students a debt for their many useful ideas and comments.

Thanks are also in order to my colleagues at Bakersfield College who read portions of the manuscript and provided me with useful criticism, especially James Whitehouse, Sally Hill, Ray Chism, Marion Axford, Elbert Stewart, and Clyde Verhine. Thanks too are due to Victor Halling, chairman of the Department of Psychology, who encouraged me to write the book in the first place. The criticism of Ed Poindexter at San Jose City College and Richard Maslow at the College of the Sequoias also encouraged me. The editorial assistance of David Willard of Bakersfield College was invaluable. My editors at Canfield Press, Ted Ricks and Ken Burke, have been patient and understanding in assisting the manuscript along. A last, special thanks must go to Suzanne Adams of Merritt College in Oakland, who criticized the entire manuscript in each stage of its production, and without whose helpful criticism, suggestions, and encouragement it would never have come to completion. Thanks also to Brian Lewis who assisted with research and Daisy Hickman who typed the entire manuscript several times. Most of all I appreciate the understanding of my wife, Chloe, and my children, Sean and Megan, who for too long a time did not see much of me.

Duane M. Belcher

Bakersfield
March 1973

CONTENTS   Preface   v

GIVING PSYCHOLOGY AWAY

Men can starve from a lack of self-realization as much as they can from a lack of bread.

Richard Wright, Native Son

Freedom and constraint are two aspects of the same necessity, the necessity of being the man you are and not another. You are free to be that man, but not free to be another.

Antoine de Saint Exupéry, The Wisdom of the Sands

The Development of Personality

PERSONALITY has been defined as "a set of organized ways of perceiving the environment, including the self, which determine the individual's unique ways of adjusting to the environment" (Stagner, 1961, p. 73). Personality consists of attitudes and values, motives and emotions, intelligence and talent, ways of coping and adjusting and other enduring traits which we will consider in later chapters. Personality development, according to one writer, "is the name given to the gradual transformation from biological organism to biosocial person" (Cameron, 1963, p. 26).

The theme of this chapter is that a child's personality does not spring forth in full bloom but is developed gradually as a result of many forces—his heredity, early experiences, identifications, and cultural training. The family, of course, provides the earliest and most important influence, for it is usually in the family that children learn most of what it is to be human.

The development of personality has been studied in different ways. Here we will use the descriptive framework of a modern psychoanalyst, Erik Erikson, who postulates that all children pass through a series of universal crises produced by the growth demands of different ages. In later chapters we will deal with a behaviorist approach to personality, which requires an understanding of the basic data from studies of learning. Here we will consider personality in terms of the acquisition of social roles and values, such as an appropriate sex role and a healthy value system or philosophy of life. This has been termed a cultural conditioning approach.

THE TASKS OF DEVELOPMENT

Human strength, then, depends on a total process which regulates at the same time the sequence of generations and the structure of society. The ego is the regulator of this process in the individual.

Erik Erikson, Insight and Responsibility

Sigmund Freud, who created the first theory of personality development, and the early psychoanalysts thought of the development of personality as being a progression from infantile to mature sexuality. The modern psychoanalytic view is perhaps best explained by Erik H. Erikson in his *Childhood and Society* (1950) and *Insight and Responsibility* (1964). Erikson believes the progression is from infantile to mature *social* behavior (of which sexual behavior is only a part) and that it proceeds through eight more or less universal stages of psychosocial development. As a person grows more mature, Erikson says, he progresses through these stages by solving the problems typical of each age. When everything proceeds normally, the person succeeds in dealing with the problems or tasks of each stage, and moves on to the succeeding one. If he has difficulty, he may spend a longer time working through a stage. If he fails to master the tasks of a stage, thereafter he remains preoccupied with its problems, bringing them to the later life-tasks he is expected to handle. Thus, Erikson believes that each stage is a dimension of possible solutions, ranging from growth to decline and regression. The eight stages are described below (see Figure 1-1).

Figure 1-1.   Widening circle of concern for others with successive stages of psychosocial development.

The First Stage: Trust versus Mistrust

This stage occurs during a child's first year, when he is very dependent on his mother for satisfaction of his simple though basic needs. Typically, the infant discovers that somebody is there, eager to feed him, cuddle him, and change his wet diapers. He counts on her and she is dependable. Her predictability gradually develops in him a sense of security, or a sense of *trust* in people. If all goes well during this stage, he develops faith in his social environment, but if he is neglected or deprived, he may become frustrated, angry, and distrustful. Later he will feel unable to count on others and he will be cold and distant.

Lack of basic trust is a feature of psychological disorders such

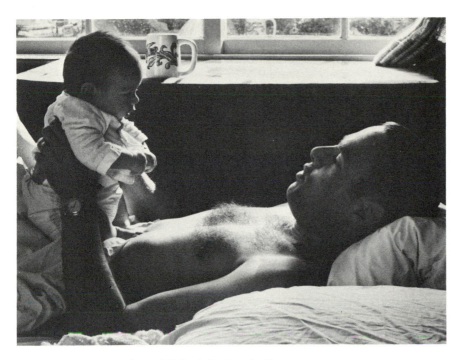

Trust versus mistrust is established during the first year.

as infantile autism (schizophrenia), paranoia, and depressive character. "The reestablishment of a state of trust," says Erikson, "has been found to be the basic requirement for therapy in these cases" (1963, p. 248). The sense of trust, however, is shaped not by the *quantities* of food or affection, but by the overall *quality* of the mother's care.

The Second Stage: Autonomy versus Shame and Doubt

This stage, which lasts from 1 to 4 years of age, is the development of a sense of *autonomy*. Once the child has achieved a sense of trust, he begins to move away from total dependence on his parents and to assert himself. Such moving away, however, may cause him anxiety; he may become frightened and wonder if this step toward being more independent might not anger his mother enough to change her behavior. She is, after all, the chief source of his security.

The methods of discipline and control used by the parents at this stage may either encourage autonomy or foster feelings of shame and doubt. The parents need to reassure the child that his base of security is not threatened by his desire to assert himself. Erikson believes that when the child's will is frustrated at this stage it leads to anger or rage, which if turned inward becomes shame. A person who experiences shame feels exposed; he is conscious of being looked at and wishes the world would look away. Shame stifles a child's move toward autonomy.

The Third Stage: Initiative versus Guilt

Between ages 4 and 5 the child develops a sense of initiative. In this stage there is a conflict between his natural strivings and his developing some inner controls based on the teachings of his parents and society. If he masters the problems of this stage, he will emerge with a kind of balance in which he is able to test reality (evaluate correctly his perception and thinking) and yet accommodate its demands.

There is some danger that control will be too forceful and interfere with the child's natural spontaneity. A curious child may get into things as he expresses himself and draw a good deal of parental criticism. Such criticism may eventually stifle his natural curiosity, if he learns to equate curiosity with undesirable consequences. Discipline that is too rigid may produce a child whose guilt over his natural desires overwhelms him. A result may be that the child gives up on his own desires and rigidly conforms to parental demands.

The Fourth Stage: Industry versus Inferiority

From 6 to 11 a child usually develops a sense of *industry*. As Erikson says, he "learns to win recognition by producing things," relying less on fantasy and more on solid accomplishment for satisfaction. During this time he also begins to relate to, compare himself to, and become part of a peer group.

The danger of this stage is that a child may develop feelings of inferiority because he is unable to compete successfully in talent or status with his friends. He must also adjust to the challenge offered by school. According to Erikson: "Many a child's development is disrupted when family life has failed to prepare him for school life, or when school life fails to sustain the promises of earlier stages" (1963, p. 260). It is during this stage that a child begins to learn something of the meaningful adult roles he is to play later.

Developing a sense of identity is an important part of adolescence.

The Fifth Stage: Identity versus Identity Diffusion

During adolescence, ages 12 to 15, a person achieves a sense of *identity*. By this point his skills and talents have begun to flower, he is almost sexually mature, he is able to play more social roles, and he has become part of a semi-independent peer group and is less dominated by his parents. Even his feelings about the opposite sex are a part of this self definition. As Erikson points out, "to a considerable extent adolescent love is an attempt to arrive at a definition of one's identity by projecting one's diffused ego image on one another and by seeing it thus reflected and gradually clarified" (1963, p. 262).

In most societies young people assume adult roles at younger ages than they do in ours. Our society has greatly prolonged the period of adolescence, partly because complex roles in an industrial society require extensive education and partly because there are arbitrary cultural limitations on the behavior of adolescents in the areas of sex, work, group leadership, politics, and so on. Adults have been hesitant to admit youth to full participation until they are sure that adult roles will be "responsibly" enacted. Young people, on the other hand, find it difficult to "responsibly" relate to adult roles until they can fit into the economic world.

It is normal for young people to be drawn away from the exclusive domination of parental values, to turn to their peer group for support, and (sometimes overenthusiastically) to identify with folk heroes and peer group values. They may, however, spread themselves too thin trying out the various roles open to them, roles that may or may not become a permanent part of self. Such difficulties in adjustment (which may be made more painful by doubts left over from earlier stages) are examples of *role diffusion*, confusion about identity. Two major types of role diffusion are, as Erikson puts it, "the inability to settle on an occupational identity" and the difficulty of achieving an adult view of oneself as male or female. Erikson's explanation, it should be noted, is centered on male identity; most psychoanalysts, in fact, can be faulted for failing to give feminine identity careful consideration.

The Sixth Stage: Intimacy versus Isolation

The last three of Erikson's stages occur in adult life—if they occur at all: some people do not resolve the adolescent crisis and thus remain fixated there, always searching, always trying to discover who they are. As Erikson says, "It is only as young people emerge from their identity struggles that their egos can master the sixth stage, that of intimacy" (1950, p. 229). *Intimacy* involves a widening of concern beyond the self, extending it to another person, one who can be loved. Whereas the adolescent uses love and his relationships with the opposite sex to clarify who he is, the adult already knows who he is and is thus able to commit himself more successfully to another person.

Intimacy with another human being is both a rewarding experience and a potential source of anxiety. Sexual intimacy calls for a kind of abandon that can be threatening. Some people avoid such experience because of fear and become preoccupied with themselves, or isolated. Erikson believes that if sexual expression is to be of *lasting social significance* it should include:

1. mutuality of orgasm
2. with a loved partner
3. of the other sex
4. with whom one is able and willing to share a mutual trust
5. and with whom one is able and willing to regulate the cycles of
   a. work
   b. procreation
   c. recreation
6. so as to secure to the offspring, too, all the stages of a satisfactory development (1963, p. 266).

The Seventh Stage: Generativity versus Isolation

Generativity means a further widening of concern, a gradual expansion of ego interests, which may occur when one becomes a parent. For instance, a parent might get excited when his child is criticized. It also implies a creative and productive urge that may be invested in work or other activities. Generativity, as Erikson defines it, is the "power behind various forms of selfless 'caring' [and] potentially extends to whatever a man generates and leaves behind. . . . I refer to man's *love for his works and his ideas as well as for his children*, and the necessary self-verification which adult man's ego receives, and must receive, from his labor's challenge" (1964, p. 131). Failure in this stage, says Erikson, leads to stagnation, regression to compulsive sexuality, and a sense of interpersonal impoverishment.

The Eighth Stage: Integrity versus Disgust, Despair

In this last stage, a person expands his concern beyond his own children to the community, the nation, and perhaps even mankind. *Integrity* appears to be a kind of maturity in which the person "finds meaning to his existence" and reconciles himself to life as it is. He accepts himself for what he is. He achieves perspective on his parents and the values they taught him. He recognizes the validity of his own life-style. Still, he sees other ways of life in perspective as providing meaning too.

The last of Erikson's ego values, integrity, comes full circle to the first, trust. Webster's defines trust as "the assumed reliance on another's integrity." Thus we see that the developmental process provides for the sequence of generations on which society depends.

Development in Middle Age and Later Life

We talk of development rather than of child psychology to emphasize that growth does not cease with the passing of childhood. Just as the body changes with age, so does personality. The roles we are expected to play change as we progress from one life stage to another. No sooner have we emerged with youthful enthusiasm from the crises

If we speak of a cycle of life we really mean two cycles in one: the cycle of one generation concluding itself in the next, and the cycle of individual life coming to a conclusion.

Erik H. Erikson, Insight and Responsibility

Box 1-1   Developmental Tasks

Early Childhood 0–6 Years	Acquiring a sense of trust in self and others. Developing healthy concept of self. Learning to give and receive affection. Identifying with own sex. Achieving skills in motor coordination. Learning to be member of family group. Beginning to learn physical and social realities. Beginning to distinguish right and wrong and to respect rules and authority. Learning to understand and use language. Learning personal care.
Middle Childhood 6–12 Years	Gaining wider knowledge and understanding of physical and social world. Building wholesome attitudes toward self. Learning appropriate masculine or feminine social role. Developing conscience, morality, a scale of values. Learning to read, write, calculate, other intellectual skills. Learning physical skills. Learning to win and maintain place among age-mates. Learning to give and take, and to share responsibility.
Adolescence 12–18 Years	Developing clear sense of identity and self-confidence. Adjusting to body changes. Developing new, more mature relations with age-mates. Achieving emotional independence from parents. Selecting and preparing for an occupation. Achieving mature values and social responsibility. Preparing for marriage and family life. Developing concern beyond self.
Early Adulthood 18–35 Years	Seeing meaning in one's life. Getting started in an occupation. Selecting and learning to live with a mate. Starting a family and supplying children's material and psychological needs. Managing a home. Finding a congenial social group. Taking on civic responsibility.
Middle Age 35–60 Years	Achieving full civic and social responsibility. Relating oneself to one's spouse as a person. Establishing adequate financial security for remaining years. Developing adult leisure-time activities, extending interests. Helping teen-age children become responsible and happy adults. Adjusting to aging parents. Adjusting to physiological changes of middle age.
Later Life	Adjusting to decreasing physical strength. Adjusting to retirement and reduced income. Adjusting to death of spouse and friends. Meeting social and civic obligations within one's ability. Establishing an explicit affiliation with age group. Maintaining interests, concern beyond self.
Tasks At All Periods	Developing and using one's capacities. Accepting oneself and developing basic self-confidence. Accepting reality and building valid attitudes and values. Participating creatively and responsibly in family and other groups. Building rich linkages with one's world.

From —Coleman, James C., *Psychology and Effective Behavior,* Scott, Foresman and Company, 1969, p. 80.

of childhood and adolescence than we must face those of adulthood. We must not only achieve identity in a paired relationship, but provide for, as Erikson puts it, "the sequence of generations." We recognize this switching of roles in William Wordsworth's line, "the child is father of the man."

In maturity a person faces new opportunities and responsibilities. A man must adjust to earning a living and finding whatever satisfaction and meaning he can in work. A woman will probably be engrossed in home and family during the early part of her married life, but she may also work outside the home. Both men and women must also establish adult leisure-time interests and activities. During these prime years of adulthood a person should achieve full civic and social responsibility. More and more interests turn away from narrow self-interest, if a person has been successful in achieving the kind of integrity Erikson observes.

The problems of old age are rarely mentioned in elementary psychology books, perhaps because our culture is so youth oriented. Yet, because of better health conditions and longer life expectancy, most of us can expect to finish out our lives in that stage.

Old age is a time not only for the display of integrity but also for adjusting to declining income, strength, and influence. One's family is grown and communication is strained between the generations, perhaps aggravated by the modern tendency to segregate the elderly away from other age groups. Older people need contact with other age groups in order to feel integrated into the sequence of generations, to stimulate concerns beyond the self. They have something valuable to give young people too—an example of maturity and wisdom presently beyond youth's grasp. This wisdom, as Erikson says,

> . . . *is detached concern with life itself, in the face of death itself.* It maintains and conveys the integrity of experience, in spite of the decline of bodily and mental functions. It responds to the need of the on-coming generation for an integrated heritage and yet remains aware of the relativity of all knowledge (1964, p. 133).

We turn away now from Erikson's discussion of personality development in terms of the crises of development and consider how one learns his social roles, especially the sex role. This learning is largely governed by the process of cultural conditioning.

SEX ROLE TRAINING

> *What are little boys made of, made of?*
> *What are little boys made of?*
> *Toads and snails, and puppy-dogs' tails;*
> *That's what little boys are made of.*
> *What are little girls made of, made of?*
> *What are little girls made of?*
> *Sugar and spice, and all that's nice;*
> *That's what little girls are made of.*

—Nursery rhyme

Cultural Conditioning

What are the differences between men and women? Some are biological, of course, and involve size, strength, glands, and hormones. However, other differences are actually culturally conditioned. Which differences are most influenced by cultural learning may be suggested by studies of sex roles in various cultures, such as anthropologist Margaret Mead's famous 1949 study of sex and temperament in three primitive societies of New Guinea. Among the *Arapesh*, both sexes were trained to be gentle, cooperative, and noncompetitive—emotional qualities commonly thought in our culture to be feminine. By contrast, the *Mundugumor* trained both sexes to be violent, aggressive, and competitive. In the *Tchambuli* tribe the sex roles (as we know them) were reversed: the men stayed home and were concerned with fashion, decoration, and the arts; the women did the important work, such as fishing, and held power and leadership roles. Women were described as practical and efficient, while the men were timid, graceful, subservient, and concerned about the others. Clearly, none of these three cultures had a pattern like our own.

Many other studies also show that Western ideals of appropriate sex roles are not universal among mankind and thus hardly biologically determined. Though in our culture men are supposed to be sexually aggressive, among many Africans and American Indians it is the women who are more preoccupied and motivated by sex. Among the Zuñi Indians, for instance, there are stories of how nervous the *bridegroom* is on the wedding night; indeed, a man is expected to approach his bride in a state of fear.

Although most people in our culture assume that men are better suited to heavy manual labor, in eastern Europe, the Soviet Union, most peasant cultures, and Africa it is women who do such labor (see Figure 1-2). In central Africa, for example, it is commonly believed that

> . . . men are not suited by nature for heavy work, that women are stronger and better workers. Men drink too much and do not eat enough to keep up their strength; they are more tense and travel about too much to develop the habits or the muscles needed to sustained work on the farms (Albert, 1963, p. 110).

This society, unlike the Tchambuli, is an old-fashioned, male-dominated, feudal culture, where equality of the sexes has never been considered.

In our culture, men are supposed to be more emotionally stable. Men are, in fact, more *in control* of their emotions. It may be that we train men to express their emotions differently, more physically. In Iran, however, which is also a male-dominated culture, the men are expected to be emotional, intuitive, and sensitive, while the women are practical and self-directing. Even in many parts of Europe, notably Italy, men are more emotional and expressive than in America or northern Europe. As one observer puts it:

> What is believed to be true of the nature of males and females influences significantly the content of ideal models constructed for the formation of character. Within a given society, there is a statistical tendency to develop according to socially defined ideals of appropriate behavior. But viewing humanity on a world-wide scale, we find no consensus. Again, nature makes us male or female, but the beliefs and values of our society make us the kind

Figure 1-2.   These two photographs show how our stereotypes of women and work are defied in other cultures. *Top,* Bulgarian peasant women working with crude tools in the fields. *Bottom,* women in Katamandu crush rocks.

of men or women we become. . . . However, in no society is there a demand for complete conformity (Albert, p. 111).

Let us now consider the roles commonly expected in our culture.

Masculine and Feminine Stereotypes

A stereotype (defined, Chapter 8) is a belief about members of a group which serves as a basis for anticipating their behavior. A sex-role stereotype is a kind of crude cultural expectation, a prescription for behavior. Stereotypes about masculinity and femininity are relatively easy to elicit from most people in our culture: men are described as being aggressive, dominant, strong, independent, and confident; women are described as being weak, emotional, soft, affectionate, and sensitive. The information in Table 1-1 is based on an unpublished study by the author; the results are substantially in agreement with other studies (Sherriffs & McKee, 1958).

Table 1-1   Masculine and Feminine Stereotypes, as Revealed by Self-descriptions of 50 Male and 50 Female Community College Students

Masculine Stereotype	*Feminine Stereotype*
Aggressive	Submissive, dependent
Active, driving, ambitious, competitive	Modest, timid, weak
Dominant	Sociable, poised
Independent, adventurous	Emotional, neurotic
Resourceful, shrewd	Soft, warm, kind, affectionate, lovable
Stolid, stern, quarrelsome	Comforting, nurturant, well-mannered
Strong, hard, tough, rugged	Tactful, sympathetic
Self-confident	Fearful, inhibited
Wise, intelligent	Sensitive, sentimental

The stereotypes are, of course, extreme statements of what men and women are supposed to be. Not every person adheres entirely to such stereotypes, but most people are unable to ignore them when thinking about themselves, their spouses, and their children. Conflict in the family may develop as a result of a person's failure to develop in accord with the stereotype. A boy with too many of the supposedly feminine characteristics may cause his family a great deal of worry, as may a girl whose behavior is described as dominant, adventurous, or aggressive. There is evidence, however, that stereotypes are changing and that today's younger people are less concerned with achieving an inflexibly proper masculine or feminine pattern of behavior. This youth culture may be the quiet cultural revolution of this century.

Most adults are probably unaware of how carefully they "teach" appropriate sex roles to their children. The case of Frankie (see Box 1-2) illustrates how totally compelling such learning can be, even when the identification is biologically wrong. Let us now consider some of the situations in which children are socialized.

Box 1-2   Frankie: A Case of Cultural Conditioning of the Wrong Sex Role

The importance of social learning of sex roles is most sharply illustrated in Frankie's case, where an inappropriate sex role was learned. As reported by Lindesmith and Strauss (1968), Frankie was a girl who, because of an abnormally large clitoris at birth, had been mistakenly pronounced a boy, and was therefore raised for her first five years as a boy. During a routine surgical examination at age 5 the error was uncovered and she subsequently began to be treated as a girl. A nurse described the difficulties involved in the change:

> This didn't sound too difficult—until we tried it. Frankie simply didn't give the right cues. It is amazing how much your response to a child depends on that child's behavior toward you. It was extremely difficult to keep from responding to Frankie's typically little boy behavior in the same way that I responded to other boys in the ward. And to treat Frankie as a girl was jarringly out of key. It was something we all had to continually remind ourselves to do. Yet the doing of it left all of us feeling vaguely uneasy as if we had committed an error. Even remembering to say "her" instead of "him" was difficult. One of the interns just flatly stated that he couldn't do it and referred to Frankie either by name or as "it." After the surgical examination Frankie was in bed and for a few days was satisfied with the more peaceful entertainment which we furnished and in which we vainly hoped she would become interested. But after a few days she began to demand trains, wagons and guns. About the same time Frankie became increasingly aware of the change in our attitude toward her. She seemed to realize that behavior which had always before brought forth approval was no longer approved. It must have been far more confusing to her than it was to us and certainly it was bad enough for us. Her reaction was strong and violent. She became extremely belligerent and even less willing to accept crayons, color books and games, which she simply called "sissy" and threw on the floor. She talked constantly of the wagon she had been promised for Christmas and what she and the other little boys with whom she played would do when she was well and home again. She also objected strenuously to the hospital gown she wore, insisting that it was too "sissy" and that she would wear pajamas or nothing. Her departure from the hospital created a disturbance: her mother had brought a dress and Frankie took one look and sent up a howl. Her mother finally got her dressed, stepped out of the room to the nurses' station and went back to find a completely nude Frankie. Frankie went home in a pair of hospital coveralls.

Reprinted with permission from *Social Psychology*, 3rd edition, by A. R. Lindesmith & A. L. Strauss, 3rd ed. (New York: Holt, Rinehart and Winston, 1968), p. 339.

Play

Boys and girls are trained early in life for the respective sex roles they will play. The play and toys of children are obviously sex-typed. Boys "like" trucks, cars, and guns; girls like dolls and household items. Boys engage in vigorous and energetic sports, which give them a chance to shine and earn status. Girls engage in pretend baby care, playing house and school. Boys chase, run, jump, and hit; girls play games that are quieter and cleaner. Boys are expected to get dirty; girls are supposed to be dainty and delicate. A father is likely to be upset if he sees his son pick up a doll and chide him for being a sissy. A daughter, on the other hand, will cause her parents anxiety if she wants to play with her brother's race-car set or if she acts too much like a "tomboy."

School

School provides many other opportunities for the conditioning of sex roles. Girls are supposed to excel at art, spelling, and literature, boys at mathematics and science. Girls are expected to be neat, clean, and nicely dressed, boys less so. Doing jobs for the teacher, currying favor, and tattling about misbehavior are expected of girls; boys are expected to challenge the authority of school and teacher more. The teacher may be only half complaining when she says, "He is all boy." Girls are punished less because their offenses, such as passing notes, whispering, and giggling, are all considered less serious than the more strident misbehavior of boys. Boys are more likely "to be made examples of"; indeed, a boy may even gain status among his peers for defiance of authority.

Work

The fact that father's work is called "work," while what mother does is called "staying at home," with the implication that her work is not very important, is not lost on either boys or girls. To a child, work means *going* somewhere and *doing* something. Dad dresses up for his job and leaves home in the morning. His coming and going occur according to a strict schedule and are the occasion of the comment, "Daddy is home." The implication is clear that men and their work are important.

The books children read seldom show mother doing anything interesting. She is never pictured fixing things (even in her own province, the home). She never has serious adventures. However, unmarried women are usually portrayed as working. Boys' playthings and games (fireman, soldier, cowboys and Indians) all emphasize active, enterprising male roles. Girls are given dolls, dishes, and clothes to play with. Their play seems designed to teach them that hearth and home are their only future.

Home Supervision

The aggression of children is socialized. Boys are told, "Boys don't hit girls." Girls are told, "That is not ladylike," and "It is not nice to be too aggressive."

As children, boys and girls are taught to react differently when they are injured. At first, little boys cry just as hard as the girls, and mother's lesson that "big boys don't cry" takes a while to sink in. But by the age of 10 or 11 most boys feel embarrassed when they cry, and a year or two later they will have ceased crying altogether.

As children grow older, different standards are used for disciplining them, especially during adolescence. Boys are encouraged to become independent and self-sufficient, girls to be docile and dependent. The behavior of girls is more strictly controlled; adolescent boys are trusted to set their own hours for coming and going, but girls' hours still tend to be regulated. Parents may say that too much freedom for their daughters will lead to sex, while of their sons, they may say simply "Boys will be boys."

Fate Control

Boys are taught to admire the independent, active, and, aggressive aspects of the masculine role. A boy is taught to respect his intelligence and to value achievement in the wider world. He is much more likely than a girl to come to the conclusion that he is actively in control of his own future. When he reaches the age of dating, he takes the initiative, it is up to him whether he chooses to court or ignore a particular girl. She, however, is taught to be ready and expectant; if she is lucky, some boy will choose to pay attention to her. She is selected, he chooses—that is the fundamental difference. Adolescent girls, therefore, become very conscious of their physical appearance as a means of enhancing desirability, while simultaneously they tend to de-emphasize intelligence, since adults and peers pay little or no attention to these qualities.

Desirability of Male and Female Characteristics

Research shows that both sexes admire the supposedly "masculine" characteristics more than supposedly "feminine" ones (Sherriffs & McKee, 1958). Boys tend to have more positive self-images than girls. Girls tend to describe themselves and other women in negative, neurotic terms. It is almost as if both sexes agree that the most important aspects of a *definite identity* are masculine. This viewpoint is not a failure to appreciate the warm, loving, caring, sensitive aspects of the feminine role, because both sexes admire these characteristics. Rather it is probably a trend of our culture to value publicly those aspects of the masculine role which contribute to materialistic success, while privately admitting the need for someone to soften the blows of life through feminine supportive behavior.

Modification of Basic Characteristics

Some basic personality differences between the sexes, such as the dominant-submissive dimension, can be modified. To be sure, some aspects of male dominance can be accounted for as biological differences. Greater male size and strength and effects of male hormones have probably contributed to the male's typically dominating the female throughout history. But it is becoming clear from research that many animals can be trained to be more dominant or submissive in spite of their original inclinations (Murphy *et al.*, 1955). There are also indications that human dominance-submissiveness can be similarly modified. Indeed, some psychotherapists are having success in modifying it. The "assertive therapy" of J. Wolpe, for instance, teaches patients, both men and women, to be more assertive in their relationships with others (Wolpe, 1969, pp. 61–71).

Role Models

Each child is exposed to role models of his or her sex, usually a parent, whose behavior provides vital information about how the child is supposed to behave. (Chapter 9 discusses observational learning, which is basically produced by the emotional identification between parent and child.) The child may also be directly instructed in appropriate standards of behavior for his sex and age. Even children who lack a parent of the same sex are exposed to role models in friends, relatives, teachers, and sports and entertainment figures. In their case, direct instruction by the parent of the opposite sex may play an unusually important role.

Segregation and Discrimination by Sex

Although there are class and background differences in attitude and behavior, many kinds of activity are heavily sex-segregated. Many Americans feel that there is a *man's world* of serious work, politics and public affairs, sports and outdoor activity which women participate in only indirectly or not at all. Such people also tend to feel that "a woman's place is in the home." Certain occupations are considered masculine. Women who work find that they are discriminated against in hiring, training, and promotion. Once hired, they are paid less than men. On the average, women in the United States earn only two-thirds as much as men (1960 census). It is not generally recognized how some of our major social problems, such as poverty, are based on sexual discrimination. Nearly half (47 percent) of families with children headed by women in 1970 were below the poverty line, according to the U.S. Department of Labor statistics.

By now the ironic significance of the nursery rhyme at the beginning of this section should be apparent. The nice, cute, and lovable qualities of little girls, although admirable, seem inadequate to establish a self-sufficient adult identity, at least in a society which consistently ranks them low on its hierarchy of values.

PHILOSOPHY OF LIFE

It is thus with most of us; we are what other people say we are. We know ourselves chiefly by hearsay.

Eric Hoffer, The Passionate State of Mind

One important aspect of personality is the set of values, or personal philosophy of life, which emerges most clearly in adolescence from experience and socialization. *Socialization* refers primarily to training in informal situations directed toward creating a child who is a social being aware of the pressures and obligations of group life. These values are guiding principles that influence behavior in most, if not all, situations. Values may be considered high-level motives that have the effect of channeling behavior. A common example of a value in our society is the orientation toward materialism: in one family, children are taught to value money, property, and status; in another to "serve humanity" rather than to make money.

The socialization of values is primarily the function of home, school, and church. When the person reaches adolescence, the peer group becomes more important, and the values he has been taught are called into question. Carl Rogers (1964) points out that the adolescent usually emerges from this critical examination much surer of himself; he has tested the values he was taught, discarded some, and retained others. A mature conscience, Rogers believes, cannot be achieved until one "makes his own" what he has been taught. Various disorders, such as many neuroses, can be traced to the fact that a child's conscience has incorporated untested values or values that do not really reflect his genuine desires. As an instance of this, Rogers cites the case of a boy who discovers, perhaps not consciously, that he is loved and prized more when he expresses a desire to become a doctor than when he talks of being an artist. Eventually he learns to want what his parents want and introjects the values attached to being a doctor. Later in college he is puzzled by the fact that, although he has the ability to do well in his pre-med course, he repeatedly fails chemistry. In counseling he comes to realize how he had lost touch with his own valuing process. In other words, values must reflect the genuine needs, interests, and integrity of the person.

Rogers observes that psychotherapists see many people whose trouble is not lack of control but rather joyless conformity to values they never really believed in. Such people often talk about wanting "to taste forbidden fruit" and regret not having "sowed their wild oats."

Although we cannot say which values are best, because there is, of course, no *scientific* way of deciding between the various contending systems, we can talk about the *process* of achieving a mature value system. Being more positive about oneself after psychotherapy is one measure that has been used as a rough guide to improved mental health.

Rogers has discussed some characteristics of patients—or "clients," as he calls them—who get well in client-centered psychotherapy. These ideas seem particularly relevant to our discussion of the normal development of a meaningful "philosophy of life" or value system. Rogers' clients who get well move in the direction of growth and maturity.

They tend to move away from façades. Pretense, defensiveness, putting up a front, tend to be negatively valued.

They tend to move away from "oughts." The compelling feeling of "I ought to do or be thus and so" is negatively valued. The client moves away from being what he "ought to be," no matter who has set that imperative.

They tend to move away from meeting the expectations of others. Pleasing others, as a goal in itself, is negatively valued.

Being real is positively valued. The client tends to move toward being himself, being his real feelings, being what he is. This seems to be a very deep preference.

Self-direction is positively valued. The client discovers an increasing pride and confidence in making his own choices, guiding his own life.

One's self, one's own feelings come to be positively valued. From a point where he looks upon himself with contempt and despair, the client comes to value himself and his reactions as being of worth.

Being a process is positively valued. From desiring some fixed goal, clients come to prefer the excitement of being a process of potentialities being born.

Sensitivity to others and acceptance of others is positively valued. The client comes to appreciate others for what they are, just as he has come to appreciate himself for what he is.

Deep relationships are positively valued. To achieve a close, intimate, real, fully communicative relationship with another person seems to meet a deep need in every individual, and is very highly valued.

Perhaps more than all else, the client comes to value an openness to all of his inner and outer experience. To be open to and sensitive to his own *inner* reactions and feelings, the reactions and feelings of others, and the realities of the objective world—this is a direction which he clearly prefers. This openness becomes the client's most valued resource.*

This picture of emerging freedom does not imply that a person becomes less social, more selfish, or more inconsiderate of others. In such a climate of freedom, it is not true, Rogers finds, "that one person comes to value fraud and murder and thievery, while another values a life of self-sacrifice, and another values only money." Instead, when people have genuine freedom to choose, Rogers believes, they choose that which not only makes for their own survival and growth but also for the survival and growth of others. Rogers believes these growth trends are universal to mankind so long as one is exposed to a growth-promoting environment.

*Reprinted from Carl R. Rogers, "Toward a Modern Approach to Values: The Valuing Process in the Mature Person," *Journal of Abnormal and Social Psychology, 68* (1964): 166. Copyright 1964 by the American Psychological Association, and reproduced by permission.

MARK HARRIS

One American Woman:
A Speculation upon Disbelief

NORMA Jean Mortenson, known also as Norma Jean Baker, was born June 1, 1926, in or near Los Angeles under circumstances whose mysteries, after discommoding her childhood, would aggravate her mature anxieties. Of her father it was sometimes said that he died by automobile, sometimes that he died by motorcycle. Perhaps he was a baker. In any case, from the beginning he was effectively gone. The little girl dreamed of a father who looked like Clark Gable.

Of her mother more is known, but it is not encouraging. A film cutter at RKO, she was reputed beautiful, but no claim was made for her peace of mind: betrayed and abandoned, penultimately widowed, and finally insane, she in turn abandoned Norma Jean to a sequence of orphanages and foster homes. Norma Jean, who lost count, later estimated that she had lived with twelve families, each receiving, in those Depression days, $20 a month in public money for her care. Her first home, she recalled, was a "semi-rural semi-slum." She could turn a phrase.

Photographs show a lovely child, but the childhood wasn't. At the age of two she was almost smothered to death by an hysterical neighbor and at six almost raped by "a friend of the family." One family taught her to recite.

> I promise, God helping me, not to buy, drink,
>   sell, or give
> Alcoholic liquor while I live.
> From all tobaccos I'll abstain
> And never take God's name in vain

but at the hearth of another her playthings were whiskey bottles.

At nine, in the Los Angeles Orphans' Home, her first big money was a nickel a month for pantry labor, of which a penny a Sunday went into the church basket. With the surplus penny she bought a hair ribbon. So runs the legend. She stuttered, she heard noises in her head, and she contemplated suicide.

At sixteen, working in a wartime aircraft plant, she was photographed by an Army publicity man who thought that the distribution of her picture among the fighting forces would serve an inspirational end. Indeed, one unit soon named her Miss Flamethrower, soldiers in the Aleutians voted her the girl most likely to thaw Alaska, and the Seventh Division Medical Corps elected her the girl they would most like to examine.

Then she married, perhaps to avoid being returned to an orphanage. She called him Daddy, and he called her Baby. For a while they lived with his parents, later in "a little fold-up-bed place." It was a marriage which brought her, she afterward said, neither happiness nor pain, just an aimless silence. He entered military service. She modeled.

By the time of their divorce, in October, 1946, her face and figure had appeared upon several magazine covers and been seen by, among others, 20th Century-Fox, who signed her to a one-year contract at $125 a week and changed her name to Marilyn Monroe. A cameraman said, "Her natural beauty plus her inferiority complex give her a look of mystery." She was twenty years old, and she must have believed, in her youth and relative innocence, that she was headed somewhere, like Up, like Success. She knew by her mirror that she was radiant, and she knew by her history that she had a nimble, preserving intelligence: had she not thus far survived neglect, poverty, and a mistaken marriage? She thought, too, putting radiance and intelligence together, that she had a talent for acting. She studied acting at The Actors' Lab in Hollywood and literature at U.C.L.A. downtown, and she lived frugally. She would afterward play in a moving picture called *How to Marry a Millionaire*, but in the life that was her own she was unmoved by millionaires. "I was never kept, to be blunt about it. I always kept myself. I have always had a pride in the fact that I was on my own." She owned 200 books (Schweitzer, Tolstoy, Emerson, Whitman, Rilke, Milton, Lincoln Steffens, and Arthur Miller) and records of Beethoven and Jelly Roll Morton.

It is not difficult to see, especially in retrospect, that she was uncommon, though to 20th Century-Fox, which paid a great many young ladies $125 a week, she was only one blonde girl in a world of blonde girls where even here or there an uncommon blonde was common enough. After a year, for lack of a clear motivation to renew, the studio allowed her contract to lapse.

Still she modeled. Once, for $50, she modeled anonymously nude on red velvet for a photographer named Tom Kelley, who was afterward proud of the fact that no matter how you turned the photograph its composition was impeccably symmetrical. The photograph, turned calendar, brought him $900 from a printer who sold it in quantity for 3/4 million dollars to barber shops, gasoline stations, ship's galleys and soldiers' barracks, wherever men mark time across the world. Several years later, when her proprietors feared that the revelation of the calendar would damage her career, she refused to disclaim it. "Sure I posed. I was hungry." As a child she had had persistent dreams of walking naked in church over the prostrate forms of her friends, neighbors, and foster parents, "being careful not to step on anyone."

In 1950, in a pair of lounging pajamas, she played a small part in a motion picture called *The Asphalt Jungle*. She had auditioned for the director, John Huston. "I remember she was nervous," Huston remembered. "But she knew what she wanted. She insisted on reading for the role sprawled on the floor. She wasn't

satisfied. She asked if she could do it again. But she had the part the first time. . . ." Joseph Mankiewicz, watching her in *The Asphalt Jungle*, wanted her for a picture called *All About Eve*, and Zanuck, watching her in *All About Eve*, reclaimed her for 20th Century-Fox, this time with a seven-year contract beginning at $500 a week.

So much money resounds with authority. But it was less than star money, and Hollywood above all is stars—names and faces capable of magically drawing the public into movie houses in spite of the force of such competing attractions as television, bowling, motoring, and bed rest. Miss Monroe was not yet a star.

Of course, she was soon to become one, and she must have believed, at twenty-five years and $500 a week, that the choices and decisions of her life had thus far been more right than wrong. Almost everything her culture had ever taught her and all that she had ever known or seen or heard must have impressed upon her mind the American fact that More is Up: Success. Or even if she doubted this, alone of an evening with Schweitzer or Tolstoy (she took little pleasure in night life, felt no necessity to be seen), who in Hollywood could possibly have corroborated or encouraged her skepticism, or explored its implications with her, or really seriously persuaded her or anyone that the shape of death might early appear even in the indisputably happy form of a moving picture invitingly entitled *Don't Bother to Knock*, which grossed $26,000 in its first week in New York in spite of bad movie-going weather and bad newspaper reviews?

The pictures *Niagara* and *Gentlemen Prefer Blondes* quickly followed. In the first she showered in silhouette, in the latter she danced à la burlesque, bumps and grinds pruriently denatured to satisfy a code which, forbidding nakedness, provides the basic material from which interested persons may labor independently upon their own fantasies. ("American culture," Isaac Rosenfeld has written, "is contradictory with respect to sex, urging its members on in a riot of stimulation, while it upholds conventional and moral restraints and taboos.")

For Marilyn Monroe a formula had been found. Henceforth she would be compelled to perform according to the formula so long as the profit flowed. The very titles of the moving pictures with which she was associated during the early 1950s suggest the restrictions of that formula—*Ladies of the Chorus, Love Happy,*

Let's Make It Legal, Love Nest, Pink Tights.

By 1954 she was a star. In that year she made *The Seven-year Itch* and after the shooting attended a supper in her honor, arriving an hour late in a red chiffon gown borrowed from the studio. She had never owned an evening gown. Now for the first time she met Clark Gable, once the fantasy father of the fatherless child. She was twenty-eight years old, and she danced in his arms.

How is 20th Century-Fox like a little girl in a borrowed blue sweater?

In West Los Angeles, when Norma Jean was twelve years old, she went to school one day in a borrowed blue sweater. The boys of her class "suddenly began screaming and groaning and throwing themselves on the floor." After school they went to her house. "For the first time in my life I had friends. I prayed that they wouldn't go away." But there was a way of keeping them even more effective than prayer, and so she wore the blue sweater again. This she learned.

Marilyn Monroe and 20th Century-Fox produced happiness by formula. In a decade of crisis in Hollywood she was one answer to the single question the industry asked: what sells? It no longer even pretended to be serious. (In 1820 an Englishman asked, "In the four quarters of the globe, who reads an American book?" Now one might ask, "Who sees an American movie?") Its principal function had become its exclusive function—to respect the ultimate consumer's sacred whimsy. What's good for Hollywood is good for the U.S.A. Profit and democracy are sisters under the skin.

Having learned to produce happiness by formula, what would happen to Marilyn Monroe if what she became should disgust her and poison her with self-contempt? The course of her career had received its first impetus from the odd penchant of large numbers of men for photographs—pin-ups—to be hung upon walls for the purpose of study. If claim may pass as fact, Miss Monroe, by the end of 1951, hung upon more walls than any other American woman; 20th Century-Fox was soon receiving, says one report, "thousands of letters a month" requesting her photograph.

Why Marilyn Monroe? Few of her admirers had ever seen her act in a movie, and to most of them her name was unknown. Why not any of a hundred or a thousand young ladies who had contrived to appear upon the cover of a magazine?

My first inclination is to search for publicity machinery behind a phenomenon so irrational. But no, whatever it was, Miss Monroe had it. It was hers. It came through. It was felt. It defied imitation, like the syrup of Coca-Cola.

And her very namelessness may have been chief among her charms. Was this not the simplest and purest and least menacing relationship most of her admirers had known? Perfectly sexual, she was also absolutely silent. So long as she was only a picture on the wall she could never outwit or outsmart her partner, while, like the paper doll of the song, she was always waiting, she could never be stolen. A relationship with her was therefore effortless, without mess or obligation, totally uncomplicated. Above all, she provided that highest of all selfish pleasure, for she demanded no equality of pleasure, no exchange, no collaboration, no mutuality.

In the film *The Seven-year Itch* the pin-up turned to flesh. Marilyn Monroe played The Girl upstairs whom Tom Ewell downstairs more or less hopes to seduce while his wife's away. But he doesn't really dare, or can't, or won't. Like the red-blooded Americans peeping at pin-ups in gas stations and ships' galleys, he can't relate with sufficient grace to a live and superior beauty. Such a relationship would force him to grant all her humanity, as if he believed not only in her tape-measure dimensions (finally paper-thin for safety's sake) but in the dimensions of her mind and spirit.

As the success of her formula increasingly bored her, Marilyn Monroe more and more expressed her desire to become an actress, thus to employ the larger range of her womanhood. This desire was generally viewed as amusing but impractical. *Life* magazine called this ambition "irrational," and *Time* said that "her acting talents, if any, run a needless second" to her truest virtues—"her moist 'come-on' look . . . moist, half-closed eyes and moist, half-opened mouth." The journalists, incapable of believing in motivations not their own —believing in fame and gross receipts and the easiest popular expectations of women—could never imagine what more Miss Monroe might have wished to be. Didn't she, after all, fulfill *their* idea of a woman? "You know, journalists," said Arthur Miller—the playwright, her third husband—"usually come around with an angle. They *have* to. They simply never get the time or the opportunity to hang around long enough to decide anything. Over the years that angle becomes the easiest thing to do."

Above all, the danger lies in the thinking that makes it so. Sufficiently propagandized, the innocent believes in his guilt, as Marilyn Monroe learned to believe in her limitations, and as women in general perhaps do. Of course we freely say, "I don't care what anybody thinks," but of course we care. At the time of her marriage to Joe DiMaggio in 1954 she must herself have capitulated to a public image of herself which had overwhelmed her private conviction. His life was his body, his power was his power. It must have seemed to her a proper wedding because a proper definition of herself. Within a year it ended. Mrs. Joe DiMaggio she wasn't. That she knew. Nor The Girl upstairs. Nor a pin-up. At this time of her life, said a friend, she was engaged in "an absolute desperate attempt to find out what she was and what she wanted."

One thing she didn't want was 20th Century-Fox's film, *How to Be Very Very Popular*. She walked out, announcing the formation of an independent company to be known as Marilyn Monroe Productions, Inc. More money? Perhaps so. But she had been "drowning in Hollywood" (Eli Wallach's phrase), and she was determined, he said, not to spend the rest of her life "just wiggling [her] behind."

"I want to expand," said Miss Monroe, "to get into other fields, to broaden my scope. . . . People have scope, you know, they *really* do." She declared herself, at this time, with a remark which was to plague her. She said, "I want to play strong dramatic parts, like Grushenka," an assertion which was to be hurled mockingly back at her, quite as if her experiences as waif and queen among peasants and lechers rich and poor in Southern California necessarily deprived her of a Dostoevskian outlook.

Hollywood minimized her by laughing at her. Director Billy Wilder, cynically reducing her new hope to the old focus, cheerfully said he would be pleased to direct her not only in *The Brothers Karamazov* but in a series of *Karamazov* sequels, such as *The Brothers Karamazov Meet Abbott and Costello*, etc. Disputing her claim that she needed training in acting, Wilder expressed in a breath the ruling conviction of both commercial Hollywood and an America gaping at pin-ups: "God gave her everything. The first day a photographer took a picture of her she was a genius." Her employer summed it up more formally. "20th Century-Fox," said 20th Century-Fox, "is very satisfied with both the artistic and financial results from the pictures in which Miss Monroe has appeared."

For a year, in New York, she led a private life. She studied acting with Lee and Paula Strasberg at The Actors Studio. I say *studied*, implying teachers, though I suspect that the Strasbergs served mainly as counselors, cheerleaders, psychologists whose task was perhaps less instruction than a demonstration of faith. All teachers of adults have had the experience of the woman touching thirty who has come to realize that she has for some time known what exists to be known but who needs an outer voice to confirm the inner. "For the first time I felt accepted, not as a freak, but as myself." Praised for her acting, her health improved. Here her circle of friends also included Arthur Miller.

Miller's interior, like hers, baffled the press. The marriage of Miller and Miss Monroe was described by one reporter as "the most unlikely . . . since the Owl and the Pussycat"—the familiar insistence, in the language of American disbelief, upon the imagined incongruity between brains and beauty, love and intellect, flesh and sensibility. Owning no matching veil for her beige wedding dress, she dyed one in coffee. The groom, though he was wealthy enough, owned only two suits—"the one he was married in," the bride said, "and the other one." Miller posed for photographers awkwardly, perhaps because grudgingly, resisting the insolence of the expectation that a man married to Marilyn Monroe must necessarily embrace her during every waking moment. Nor did Miller ever answer the question most often asked by obsessed reporters, "What does Marilyn wear to bed?" On the back of a wedding picture the bride wrote, "Hope, Hope, Hope."

He spoke of her always as actress, person; as mind, never as freak. Of her acting he said, "I took her as a serious actress before I ever met her. I think she's an adroit comedienne, but I also think that she might turn into the greatest tragic actress that can be imagined." His own arduous habits of labor enabled him to share her distress at moments when others viewed her as merely petulant. "In a whole picture," he said, "there may be only two scenes of which she is really proud. She has great respect for the idea of acting, so great that some part of her is always put to shame by the distance between what she achieves and the goal she has set for herself."

It was a noble strategy and a clearheaded loyalty, too late. Nor is it irrelevant that at the time of their marriage Miller's dispute with the Congressional Un-American Activities Committee centered about the question of loyalty—his refusal to implicate associates of his political past. "The only real territory left," he said in another connection, "is relationship to other people. There really never was any other territory. . . ."

Miller said once, "Marilyn identifies powerfully with all living things, but her extraordinary embrace of life is intermingled with great sadness." This conception of her he carried into a short story, *Please Don't Kill Anything*, in which a girl with a "startling shape" laments fish dying upon a beach. She wants to throw them back. Her less anguished escort—her husband—points out that there are twenty-five miles of beach alive with dying fish. "He did not bend to pick them up because she seemed prepared to sacrifice them and he went back to her, feeling, somehow, that if he let those two die on the beach she might come to terms with this kind of waste." Once, during her first marriage, she had tried to bring a cow indoors out of the rain; as Rosalyn, in Miller's screenplay *The Misfits*, she would oppose the killing of horses.

In the autumn of 1956 the Millers went to England, where she made *The Prince and the Showgirl* with Sir Laurence Olivier—another "unlikely" match said the very magazine (*Life*) with the very word it had used to describe her marriage to Miller. The British newspapermen asked her what she wore to bed.

The picture was made, though not without friction among the principals. When it was done, Miss Monroe apologized to the acting company for having been "so beastly," writing: "I hope you will all forgive me. It wasn't my fault. I've been very sick all through the picture. Please, please don't hold it against me." To some commentators such a note, from a lady so wealthy, so famous, so well married, and with so little apparent reason to be difficult, had a whining sound.

Two miscarriages and gynecological surgery during the months that followed were perhaps more convincing. There were also two pictures—a lively comedy called *Some Like It Hot*; and *Let's Make Love*, with Yves Montand, whose expressions of admiration for her "professional conscience" tended to be lost among newspaper rumors that he and she were in love.

In Nevada, in the summer of 1960, she began *The Misfits*. It would be her last film. It was also Clark Gable's last film. In September her exhaustion forced an interruption, but the work was soon resumed and completed. The following February, divorced from Miller, she entered a clinic in New York for rest and psychiatric treatment. Fourteen months later she began work upon a film called *Something's Got to Give*, but she answered less than half her calls, and the shooting schedule fell impossibly behind. "She was sick, she insisted," according to *Life*. "She was reneging on her contract, said 20th Century-Fox. . . . Fox blew the whistle. They fired the star and filed a $750,000 lawsuit against her. . . ." To the cast and crew she had wired a message echoing her message to the company of *The Prince and the Showgirl* six years before: "Please believe me, it was not my doing. . . . I so looked forward to working with you." Four months later she was found dead in her bed.

Whatever it was that worked its poisons upon her—three dead marriages, two miscarriages, an absent father, an insane mother, a forlorn childhood, a devouring press, the revelations of psychiatry—disbelief in herself was an obvious fact and perhaps a first factor. It so deeply undercut her belief in her own potentiality that she was equally unable to believe in Miller's belief in her. Who was Arthur Miller that he knew more than the whole world knew? "You know, journalists," said Arthur Miller, "over the years that angle becomes the easiest thing to do, and it's gotten, in Marilyn's case, to be very fruitful in terms of copy. And they keep pounding her all the time until that thing becomes reality. By that time, it's impossible to imagine anything else."

First reports of the death of Marilyn Monroe said she died nude, later reports corrected the first, and a panting world knew at last what Marilyn Monroe wore to bed. But would anybody believe her, even now? "It can't be, it can't be," cried a Hollywood agent, "she couldn't have killed herself, she had three deals going."

Summarizing Statements

1. "Personality" refers to the unique way a person adjusts to his environment, based on a set of organized ways of perceiving the environment. A child's personality is developed out of the tension

and challenge of his experience. Personality develops gradually as a result of many forces, such as physical endowment, attachment to others, and cultural training.

2. The family is the earliest and most powerful agent involved in socializing the child.

3. Historically, personality has been discussed in terms of (a) psychosocial stages, (b) learning mechanisms, and (c) social roles and values. In this chapter we considered Erikson's stage theory and some aspects of cultural conditioning.

4. Erikson's theory asserts that children pass through a series of universal crises in growing up which are caused by the growth demands of different ages.

5. The infant's personality learning begins when a basic trust in people is achieved because of a satisfactory relationship with the mother. In developing a *sense of autonomy*, he begins to move away from dependency. With a *sense of initiative* his autonomy is moderated in terms of what is realistic and possible. He moves in these early stages away from dependency to increasing self direction. Later he will develop his capacity for concern for others. Since the tasks of life demand complicated skills as well as guiding attitudes and values, the child masters only pieces of the puzzle—giving rise to noticeable "stages" of preoccupation and choice of activity.

6. During the middle childhood years, 6 to 11, a child should develop a *sense of industry*, winning recognition by substantial achievement in the real world and beginning to understand and play adult-like roles. In adolescence, 12 to 15, he should achieve a *sense of identity*, definite sense of individuality based on successful integration of (a) his identifications, (b) his training and occupational aspirations, and (c) his developing sexuality. Since a number of problems converge here, it is no surprise that some people do not pass this stage.

7. The last three are adult stages of development, in which one should move away from self-preoccupation to a concern for others. In the *sense of intimacy* one should learn to love and be concerned with a spouse and achieve sexual adequacy. In the parental sense, *generativity*, one should be concerned for his offspring and the younger generation. In the *sense of integrity*, one should be concerned with finding meaning in his existence.

8. Cultural conditioning is responsible for many of our ideas of what is appropriate masculinity and femininity. The study of different cultures reveals that our present standards are by no means universal among mankind.

9. In some cultures women are more sexually aggressive than men. In others they, not men, perform heavy manual labor. And in still others they, not men, are supposed emotionally more stable.

10. In our culture the stereotype of appropriate masculine personality is that it is aggressive, dominant, independent, active, competitive, hard, rugged, and intelligent. The stereotype of femininity is that

it is modest, submissive, dependent, emotional, soft, inhibited, weak, affectionate, and sensitive. However, today's youth seem to be less concerned with achieving such an inflexible masculine or feminine pattern of behavior.

11. Play is one way children are socialized into "appropriate" sex roles, and school continues the pattern. Work roles teach how each sex values its work, with the work of men being defined as being more important and rewarded with status by the culture.

12. Aggression is socialized differently, with boys being taught to control their emotions carefully. Boys are also encouraged to be more self-sufficient and are given greater freedom of movement.

13. A boy is taught to be master of his own fate, to be able to determine what his life will be, whom he will marry, etc. A girl is taught to rely on luck, to be attractive to the "right" boy and to expect her future to be shaped by men.

14. Both sexes value male personality characteristics more than female ones, apparently because the former contribute to success in a materialistic culture.

15. Fundamental personality characteristics such as dominance or submissiveness have been modified both among humans and in the animal laboratory.

16. Many kinds of activity have been heavily sex-segregated. Women are restricted in occupational opportunities and are discriminated against in hiring, training, and promotion.

17. Adolescence is a time in which the values taught by home, school, and church are questioned, but one usually emerges from this critical examination much surer of himself.

18. Science cannot tell us which values are best because there is no scientific way of deciding between contending systems. The process of achieving a mature system, however, can be described according to criteria of psychological health.

19. Carl Rogers observes that patients who get well in psychotherapy show certain changes in values. They stop adopting masks and phony poses, move away from "oughts" imposed on them by others, and away from excessive dependence on others' approval. They learn to value and trust themselves and to become more complex and open to experience. They also value close, meaningful relationships with others and are concerned about their welfare.

READING SELECTION

20. The case study of Marilyn Monroe observes that she was orphaned by her mother's emotional breakdown, and while growing up was shifted about between twelve different foster families.

21. As a young woman, she married and divorced, got into modeling, and later got into the movies as a contract player. At 20, she felt "she was headed somewhere, like Up." She had, it is reported "a nimble, preserving intelligence; had she not thus far survived neglect, poverty and a mistaken marriage?" And she knew she was beautiful.

22.   At 25, "almost everything her culture had ever taught her and all that she had ever known or seen or heard MUST have impressed upon her mind the American fact that More is Up; Success." She was packaged as a sex symbol in a highly profitable formula for movie success. As long as she lived she was compelled to perform according to the formula.

23.   "What would happen to Marilyn Monroe if what she became should disturb her and poison her with self-contempt?" Her aspirations to become a serious actress were met with laughter and disbelief by the industry and the press. "Didn't she, after all, fulfill *their* idea of a woman?" Her marriage to one of America's most famous and serious playwrights, Arthur Miller, also astounded them. Miller spoke of her always as a serious actress, a real person, a mind, not as some kind of sexual freak.

24.   "Whatever it was that worked its poisons upon her—three dead marriages, two miscarriages, an absent father, an insane mother, a forlorn childhood, a devouring press, the revelations of psychiatry—disbelief in herself was an obvious fact and perhaps a first factor. It so deeply undercut her belief in her own potentiality that she was equally unable to believe in Miller's belief in her."

25.   Her suicide, like her life, also evoked disbelief. "It can't be, it can't be," cried a Hollywood agent, "she couldn't have killed herself, she had three deals going."

Terms and Concepts

Autonomy: a stage of development in which the child begins to move away from total dependency. He asserts himself willfully. Erikson's second stage of psychosocial development.

Fate control: a sense of being able to actively shape one's own future; as contrasted to being a pawn of fate. A person who has a low sense of fate control relies on luck.

Identity: a stage of development in adolescence in which the person achieves his unique individuality. In Erikson's thinking, identity involves integration of (1) childhood identifications, (2) aptitudes developed out of endowment, (3) opportunities offered from social roles, and (4) confidence that one is perceived as one perceives one's self.

Industry: a stage of development in which the child learns to win recognition by producing things. He achieves things in the real world.

Initiative: a stage of development in which the child's autonomy will come in conflict with the control of parents and society.

Integrity: the last stage of development in which an adult finds meaning to his existence and reconciles himself to life as it is.

Intimacy: an adult developmental stage in which there is a widening of concern beyond the self, to another person who can be loved.

Generativity: a stage in which there is further widening of concern to include one's children and one's creative works.

Neurosis: a learned pattern of self-defeating behavior, characterized by feelings of inferiority and various physical and psychological symptoms. Neurotic behavior is developed as a means of coping with anxiety.

Personality: "A set of organized ways of perceiving the environment, including the self, which determine the individual's unique ways of adjusting to the environment." Stagner.

Psychoanalysis, psychoanalysts: a particular type of psychotherapy, characterized by both its method and theory. Pioneered by Sigmund Freud.

Psychosocial development: the development of a child's social attitudes and behavior, as it takes place in the socialization process. The theory of Erikson postulates that maturity emerges out of the various problems which are encountered and solved at each age.

Role models: people after which a child may model his behavior. A social role is based on status, such as fatherhood, and contains a blueprint of expected behavior for those playing that role.

Sex role stereotype: a kind of crude cultural expectation about what is appropriately masculine or feminine behavior. Example: men are aggressive, dominant, independent, strong, and self-directing. See also the definition of stereotype in Chapter 8.

Socialization: the process by which a person becomes a social being as he grows up and learns about the pressures and obligations of group life; child training in the home concerned with values and morals. A well-socialized child has a firm sense of right and wrong and an internalized conscience.

Trust: a faith and security in the external world, achieved through the satisfaction of the infant's most basic need, such as hunger, warmth, and affection in his first year.

Value, value system: high-level motives that (1) regulate a person's conduct, often without his awareness, and (2) are consciously accepted by a person or a social group. These two meanings are quite divergent. Adapted from English and English.

*Where there is no love
there is no sense either.*

Fyodor Dostoevski, Notes from
Underground

Identity through Love and Work

2 WHEN Sigmund Freud, the founder of modern psychoanalysis, was asked what he thought a normal person should be able to do he replied curtly, "love and work." The last chapter ended with a reading selection about one woman's lonely and shattering search for a more meaningful identity. This chapter expands on the place of love and work in establishing a person's identity.

The infant develops love only after being exposed to it. His love is rooted in dependency. He is grateful to mother because she gratifies his physical needs. Later in childhood he begins to relate to others as playmates and friends. During his middle childhood years, friendships are almost always limited to his own sex. In adolescence his awakening sexual maturity spurs him on to a fresh discovery and appreciation of the opposite sex. Adolescent dating is oriented toward self-discovery. The relationship is used at first like a mirror held up to discover the full reality of self. Only when a person has developed a firm sense of identity is he ready to relate to the opposite sex in an adult manner.

THE FORMS OF LOVE

Friendship

Think for a moment about friendship. What is your best friend of the same sex like? How do you spend your time together? What is the essence of friendship? The most common answers students have given me are:

A friend is someone you like and trust . . .

Someone you spend a lot of time with . . .

Someone in whom you can confide and share your secrets . . .

A friend provides a sounding board, and he will listen and provide help when needed.

How does one form a friend? We can learn much about the significance of friendship by considering briefly the process of its formation. If a stranger were to walk up to you and just begin to talk about serious things, you might feel somewhat uneasy. Most of us would not think of discussing serious matters with strangers; it seems to violate unwritten rules about the way most of us function. Usually people size up one another in terms of social background characteristics before they engage in serious conversation much beyond the weather. If someone is similar to you, you are more likely to go ahead with conversation and perhaps disclose things about yourself. If the person knows and likes people and things that you know and like, the chances are pretty good you will like him. The reasons we are attracted toward and come to like someone are not fully understood. A great deal of research in progress makes it only too clear that the acquaintanceship process is more complicated than one might suppose. For now, it is enough to say that encounters with a stranger usually lack the fundamental *liking* and *rapport* (close, harmonious relations) needed for significant communication. With friends you assume that what you say will be perceived as you mean it, although often this assumption is not met. Encounters with strangers also lack the vital element of mutual trust, one of the essential elements of real friendship.

A man cannot be said to succeed in this life who does not satisfy one friend.

Henry David Thoreau, Journal

This communicating of a man's self to a friend works two contrary effects; for it redoubleth joys, and cutteth griefs in half.

Francis Bacon, "Of Friendship," Essays

When you first begin to form a relationship with another person—which may or may not develop into friendship—you probably do not "invest" your confidence all at once. A relationship of trust is built up slowly. Two people are involved. One person starts it off by "investing" a small confidence in the other. The other reciprocates by both keeping that secret and by offering a confidence in return.

Thus, trust is gradually established. That is part of what students mean when they say, "a friend is someone you can talk to." A friend may not be able to do anything definite to help you solve your problems, but he is there to listen to you and understand your point of view. There is undoubtedly an element of identification in friendship. You may sympathize with the hopes and fears of your friend and feel, to some extent, similar emotions about his life adjustment problems.

Dating, Romance, and Love

The glow of romantic love, of course, differs from the feelings in friendship. The feelings are more intense and the relationship is more involved in offering the excitement and possibility of sexual fulfillment.

Dating has many purposes. Having fun and enjoying the company of another person are usually important. There is also the opportunity dating offers to size up the other person. In many ways this process is essentially the same as in friendship. But questions may be asked too about the suitability of the other for a permanent relationship, such as: Are our interests similar? Are we compatible? Could we get along day in and day out? Depending on the goals and expectations of the individuals involved, the relationship may be continued or ended. The dating may be formal or informal. A structured date is just one possibility. Obviously, students also meet, have fun, size one another up, and make judgments in very informal situations, too, such as over coffee. The value of these informal encounters lies in the potential which they offer to broaden the student's experience in a safe environment with little risk of premature commitment. Many such near dates occur between individuals informally that would never occur at all if they depended on having a formal invitation offered and accepted.

Steady dating indicates to one and all the possibility of a permanent relationship. Kerckhoff & Davis (1962) have concluded that there are three stages in moving toward marital commitment which filter selectively or screen out potential mates. The first stage is one involving selection based on similarity of social and cultural background. This filter automatically eliminates many potential spouses. Many studies show that (1) people tend to select a mate on the basis of similar social class, education, religion, and ethnic background, and that (2) marriages contracted between people so selected have a much better than average chance of success. In many cases this first stage operates even before dating has had a chance to take place.

The second filter, according to Kerckhoff & Davis, involves a mutual exploration of each person's value system. If the partners remain serious about one another, there is usually, but not always, agreement on major values, such as family planning. Furthermore, most couples who do not make progress toward marital commitment do not agree on major values. Some couples who do not agree, however, do make progress. These couples are generally those with marked complementary needs as measured by personality tests. The third filter, then, is progress based on complementary needs. This is similar to the old idea that opposites attract.

These filters do not necessarily operate in strict order. Many other studies support the utility of the value-exploration process. The

Love is that condition in which the happiness of another person is essential to your own.

Robert A. Heinlein,
Stranger in a Strange Land

Love does not cause suffering; what causes it is the sense of ownership, which is love's opposite.

Antoine de Saint Exupéry,
The Wisdom of the Sands

We are not the same persons this year as last; nor are those we love. It is a happy chance if we, changing, continue to love a changed person.

W. Somerset Maugham,
The Summing Up

evidence for attraction between people who have complementary needs is less firm. Kerckhoff & Davis give us a theory which could account for the ambiguous research findings on this score. The mutual assessment of needs is usually made late in a relationship. Early in courtship the partners are too much involved in idealization and perceptual distortion (seeing through rose-colored glasses).

Romance and Infatuation

Oscar Wilde said that love was a mutual misunderstanding. In psychological terms, this means each love partner shows a tendency (1) to project his fantasies on the other, and (2) to play a romantic but deceptive role during courtship. Romantic infatuation involves elements both of narcissism and of need. (Narcissus was a mythical Greek who fell in love with his own reflection in a spring.) If a man thinks he needs an ultra-feminine, clinging-vine woman to enhance his ego, then the vigorous and independent American beauty he is dating may be reshaped or transformed into his fantasy ideal. This reshaping is not only in his head; it is also, at least momentarily, in reality. That is, in learning terms, he may reinforce her clinging-vine behavior, thus getting more of it and confirming in turn his stereotype of her. The more intense (and unfulfilled) his physical attraction toward the loved one, the less likely he will notice departures from what he hopes she is.

Besides engaging in this kind of fantasy, most dating partners also try to impress one another. Each tries to project an image of a romantic self (or public self) that exaggerates what he feels are his best

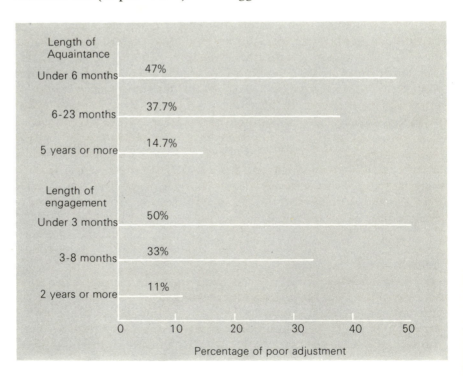

Figure 2-1. "Marry in haste . . . repent at leisure." The shorter the time of acquaintance and courtship, the greater the chance of poor marital adjustment. (Data from Burgess & Cottrell, 1939, pp. 164–165, 167–168.)

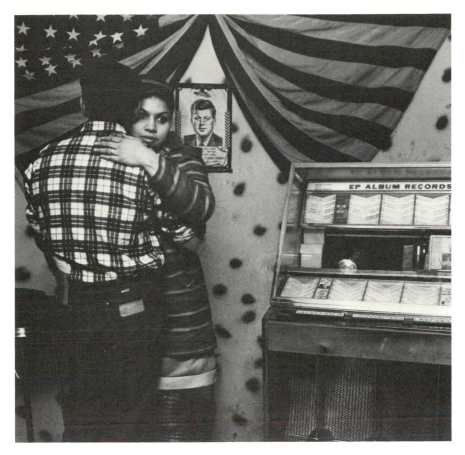

qualities. The projected image is given a big assist through play acting, through a kind of personal public relations.

Eventually the rose-colored glasses mysteriously turn clear and one is face to face with the reality that one's love is only human. Hopefully, by the time this infatuation has passed, as it must, the other person has been seen and appreciated at work, at play, when angry, when sad, and so on. A relationship needs more than just romantic love if it is to survive. There is evidence that romantic love is declining as the principal reason for choosing a mate in the United States. Students cite a growing emphasis on companionship and compatibility as reasons for marriage. Perhaps, instead of "Is this love?", one should ask, "Is this the kind of love on which I can build a lasting marriage?"

Three Concepts of Love

Freud believed that the capacity for *lieben* and *arbeiten*, loving and working, were the defining aspects of sound mental health. An impaired ability to love, either through loss of ability or failure to develop it in the first place, is universally recognized as a sign of failing mental health.

Jourard: love as promoting another's happiness.   Sidney Jourard (1963) defines love in terms of interpersonal behavior toward a loved one: *"Loving behavior refers to all action which a person undertakes to promote*

Box 2-1   The Meaning of Love: Definitions of College Students

Feeling or Attraction

"Love represents a magnetic attraction between two persons."

"Love is a feeling of high emotional affiliation . . . which sends a person's ego into dizzying heights."

"Love is the emotional feeling two people receive when they both have sexual and Platonic love in the proper proportions."   40%

Companionship and Compatibility

"Love is the physical and mental compatibility of two people."

"Love is the end result of a mature union of two compatible personalities."

"Love . . . is helping the other person whenever he needs it . . . being his companion. It's having common goals, dreams, and ambitions."

"Love . . . is doing things together and liking it."   20%

Giving

"Love is giving—time, understanding, yourself."

"Love is to give of oneself to another."

"Love is giving trust."

"Love is a give and take relationship—and mostly 'give.'"   20%

Security

"Love is having security in being wanted and knowing you have someone to rely on."

"When a person is in love the world is right and a person has security."
17%

Realistic or Practical

"Love for the girl is cooking for him, washing his clothes and keeping the home in order. For the man it is providing security, safety, and helping his wife."

"Love to me is faithfulness to my mate and caring for our children."   3%

Total   100%

From Udry (1971), p. 159.

---

the happiness and growth of the being he loves" (p. 367). The lover doesn't do this for any ulterior motive, but as an end in itself. Giving is a near-synonym for loving. When we love another, we identify with him and empathize or feel with him. We share his joys and sorrows. Love is also a need; as Jourard notes: "Humans *need* to be loved, *and they need to* love actively *if they are to become and remain healthy personalities"* (p. 394).

A number of investigators, both clinical and experimental, have shown that insufficient affection during childhood can produce

Box 2-2   Impaired Ability to Love: the Con Man

Many people seem to believe that interpersonal relations can be reduced to formula or technique. Sidney Jourard tells of a case of a young man who consulted with him.

> A nineteen-year-old male student once consulted with the writer, seeking help at improving his relations with people. He stated that he had studied Dale Carnegie's book, *How to Win Friends and Influence People,* and found the advice given there extremely helpful to him in "conning" others, especially girls. He was very successful as a campus lover, and had up to six of the most attractive coeds in love with him at the time of seeking help. The help he sought was any suggestions that psychology might offer to him in his campaign to win over the affections of the campus queen, who rejected him, telling him he was a "phony." This rejection upset him very much, and he wondered if there were some new gimmicks he might learn in order to convince her that he was desirable. Parenthetically, he mentioned that, once he won over the affections of a girl, "it's like a book you've just read; you don't want to have anything more to do with her." The author refused to help the student learn new manipulative methods, but it was possible, through more prolonged personality therapy, to help the young man gain some insight into his motives and background, such that he became a more sincere person and less the unscrupulous user of other people.
>
> Reprinted from Sidney M. Jourard, *Personal Adjustment* (New York: Macmillan, 1963), pp. 288–289.

an adult who is emotionally crippled, perhaps unable to give or receive love. All love is rooted in certain dependencies on others. Mature love means the lovers mutually satisfy each other's needs. Jourard cautions, however, that excessive dependency may interfere with the establishment of a healthy love relationship. "Dependency in a love relationship," he says, "is compatible with personality health when it does not involve undue suppression of the real self in either partner and when each partner does not use the other's dependency as a means of controlling his life" (p. 383).

Fromm: love as overcoming separation.   Erich Fromm has written extensively, in his 1963 book *The Art of Loving,* about the meaning of love. He sees love as developing fundamentally out of man's feeling of separation. When a person is born, he is torn from the security he has known and placed in a world he never made. The result is:

> . . . the awareness of his aloneness and separateness, of his helplessness before the faces of nature and of society, all this makes his separate, disunited existence an unbearable prison. He would become insane could he not liberate himself from this prison and reach out, unite himself in some form or other with men, with the world outside (p. 8).

Sometimes to overcome loneliness we form unhealthy love relationships (dependencies of a masochistic or sadistic sort) in which the integrity of the other is sacrificed. However, mature love, Fromm says, is

> . . . *union under the condition of preserving* one's integrity, one's individuality. *Love is an active power in man*; a power which breaks through the walls which separate man from his fellow men, which unites him with others; love makes him overcome the sense of isolation and separateness, yet it permits him to be himself, to retain his integrity. In love the paradox occurs that two beings become one yet remain two (pp. 20–21).

Love involves a giving of one's self to another. Giving love depends on having, as Fromm puts it, a *productive orientation* toward life, which means one must be free to actively use his powers to fulfill his potential. Being productive also means one must have overcome excessive dependencies and not wish to exploit others. There is both mutual giving and mutual taking, mutual needing and mutual willingness to provide the other with what he needs. We need another for gratification, as a stimulus for growth, and for confirmation of our own self-esteem.

In addition to giving of oneself, the active character of love involves caring for the other, taking responsibility for him, respecting him, and encouraging his uniqueness. These aspects of love all depend on developing enough sound knowledge about the other person.

Maslow: love as self-actualization. The third concept of love is that of A. H. Maslow, as developed in his book *Motivation and Personality* (1954, 1970). Maslow studied the personalities of exceptionally healthy and effective persons, whom he calls *self-actualizing*. By looking at love as it is among self-actualizing pairs of lovers, we look at love as it might be for us if we were to achieve a higher state of maturity.

One of the most significant aspects of love among self-actualizers, Maslow says, is their lack of anxiety, their dropping of defenses and roles, and their ability to give complete trust. As he describes it:

> One of the deepest satisfactions coming from the healthy love relationship reported by my subjects is that such a relationship permits the greatest spontaneity, the greatest naturalness, the greatest dropping of defenses and protection against threat. In such a relationship it is not necessary to be guarded, to conceal, to try to impress, to feel tense, to watch one's words or actions, to suppress or repress. My people report that they can be themselves without feeling that there are demands or expectations upon them; they can feel psychologically (as well as physically) naked and still feel loved and wanted and secure (1970, p. 185).

In this state there is less maintenance of distance, mystery, and glamour, less reserve, concealment, and secrecy, and less tendency to always put the best foot forward. Unlike infatuation and other less mature kinds of love, love among self-actualizers seems to deepen and improve the longer it exists.

Honesty and freedom of self-expression accompany a growing sense of intimacy. Also, sex and love become perfectly fused. Maslow writes: "These people do not need sensuality; they simply enjoy it when it occurs."

Self-actualizers encourage their loved one to grow, to be unique, to be individual. They are not threatened by growth in loved ones. They avoid the "use" or manipulation of others. They are less influenced in choice of a loved one by superficial, exterior attractiveness

Box 2-3 Impaired Ability to Love: the Dynamics of Rejection

If a person has a self-image that is insecure, fearful, and lacking in self-assurance, he may anticipate that he will be rejected by potential lovers, believe that he is rejectable. He needs desperately to be loved, but his need may overwhelm the other. Excessive needs are often the result of extreme deprivation early in life, and love hunger in an adult may represent a fixation on a childhood deprivation. Such a person might receive a great deal of love, but he would still be unsatisfied, for this hunger is nearly insatiable. His response to this need is to make excessive demands for love on the other. Fear of loss breeds suspicion and jealousy.

The other partner may want, and try at first, to give love freely, but eventually "love on demand" becomes constricting, manipulating, and tiresome. Besides, the hunger is like a bottomless pit, and cannot be filled up. A vicious circle is established in which the fear of rejection and the hunger for affection becomes oppressive and produce exactly the anticipated outcome. The loved one feels smothered by love, and for his own integrity, must escape. Thus, the fear of rejection, combined with neurotic, self-defeating behavior, results in rejection. The loved one departs from the relationship sadder but wiser. Next time he will probably select someone less complicated and easier to love.

and are drawn to deeper aspects of character. They are not threatened by differences or by strangeness.

MARRIAGE AND ITS PRECONDITIONS

Everything we have discussed so far about love and friendship applies to marriage as well. Most Americans marry thinking it will be fully compatible with romantic love. And people today have very high expectations of marriage; they believe that they have the right to expect happiness from it. As Udry puts it:

> Americans believe in marriage above all. They marry earlier, remain unmarried less often, and remarry after divorce more frequently and more rapidly than people of any other industrialized nation. They look to their marital relationship for their greatest satisfaction in life (1971, p. 2).

The kind of cultural ideal that combines romantic love, sex, and marriage is a fairly recent cultural innovation. In some societies a person's interests in love and sex are not expected to coincide. In other societies love is not expected as a prerequisite for marriage, and even in our own culture love was not always so regarded. In twelfth-century Europe, people did not believe that marriage and romance were compatible: romantic love was always sought outside of marriage, and marriages were made for other reasons and were primarily institutional and financial arrangements. Even today, many sociologists agree with the definition of marriage as "an institution or complex of social norms that sanctions the relationship of a man and woman and binds them in a system of mutual obligations and rights essential to the functioning of family life" (Theodorson & Theodorson, 1969).

Marriage thus must be seen as a social institution that accomplishes many goals other than just providing a setting in which love occurs. Marriage provides a bridge for age roles. An adolescent is not considered an adult in our society until he assumes adult roles, especially in marriage and work. Society is maintained through family life. The family provides a setting in which children are born, socialized, and taught the values of their various reference groups. In some social classes, marriage is still to some extent a system for nourishing wealth, status, and prestige.

Liking and Approval

In a successful marriage the partners should, of course, have a firm liking for and approval of each other. One need not like everything about the other, but on balance the qualities liked should outweigh those disliked. Marriages based on romantic love alone, in which liking and approval are lacking, are highly unstable and likely to lead to divorce.

Common Interests and Values

Successful marriage is based on the partners having a common core of shared interests and values. The research indicates, however, that it is not the number of shared interests which is important, but the type. A few unshared interests probably enrich the relationship, but it is essential that the partners share interests and values about family life, home and children, and demonstrations of love (Benson, 1952, 1955; Frumkin, 1954). In addition, they should agree on their respective roles and obligations, and on how they are going to spend their time.

"We're not living happily ever after."

Sharing

One value about which there must be agreement is the willingness to share time in recreation and family activities. Erikson noted that if mature love was to be of lasting social significance, it should include mutual trust and the sharing of the cycles of work, procreation, and recreation. If these activities are not shared emotionally, the relationship is unlikely to continue.

Eventually, most couples find that romantic love begins to diminish. Certainly the demands of family life are unromantic; the relentless routines constantly undermine romantic love. De Rougement (1959) states this view well:

> Romance is by its very nature incompatible with marriage even if the one has led to the other, for it is the very essence of romance to thrive on obstacles, delays, separations, and dreams, whereas it is the basic function of marriage daily to reduce and obliterate these obstacles . . . (pp. 451–453).

Communication and Accommodation

Problems are bound to arise in marriage. Their significance, however, lies in how they are handled. Jourard notes that unhealthy marriage relationships are characterized by an inability of the partners to resolve *impasses*. Problems or conflicts develop in which neither partner will "give in" a little or accommodate the other.

Basically this is a problem of communication and attitudes. As an attitude, healthy accommodation indicates a willingness to talk things over, to work things out to the mutual satisfaction of both partners. Neither one should have to feel that he is the one who must always give in. This kind of resolution does not imply a sacrifice of one's integrity. Accommodation implies honesty, respect, and liking and support of the other as a matter of course.

Good communication is based on fundamental attitudes of trust and trustworthiness. In communicating fully about problems in the marriage, one demonstrates trust, honesty, and openness. The other demonstrates that he is trustworthy by respecting confidence, by caring and being supportive. The capacity to trust seems to depend largely on being secure and confident about oneself.

Resources for Achieving Marital Success

There are a number of resources to help one achieve success in marriage. Psychological literature contains a good deal of practical information about marriage and family, which one may learn about in high school and college courses. A person may discover, for example, how others have dealt with a particular problem that seems so oppressive to him. Such knowledge may provide a better perspective and lessen anxiety. Developing the ability to cope with problems is another

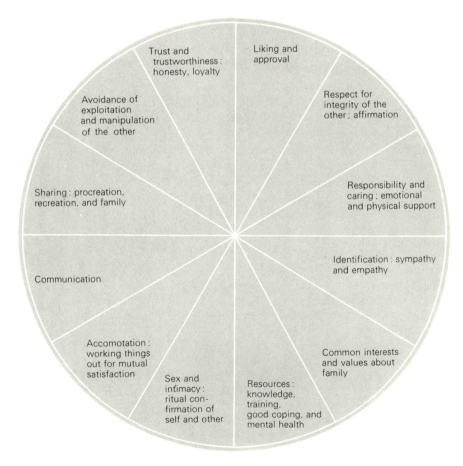

Figure 2-2.   Some factors involved in happy and successful marriages. Successful and happy marriages involve open communication, acceptance of realistic dependencies but avoidance of unhealthy ones, acceptance of growth of self and of the other partner, caring and respect, having an egalitarian attitude, being genuine.

valuable resource; if one feels he copes somewhat ineffectively, he may want to seek the help of a psychologist. Marriage counselors also provide help for many people.

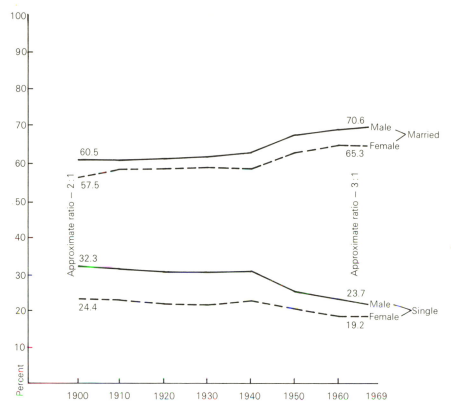

Figure 2-3. Percentage of U.S. population 14 years or older that was married and single (excluding divorced and widowed) from 1900 to 1969. Standardized for age. (Source: Department of Commerce, Bureau of the Census, U.S. Census of Population.)

Marriage and Divorce

Marriage has never been more popular in the United States than it is today. That may seem like a curious statement because of the well-known statistics on divorce and family break-up, which indicate that approximately one out of four marriages is destined to end up in divorce. These trends obscure the *marriage* rates themselves, as the census analysts Wattenberg & Scammon (1965) point out. The proportion of married persons to single persons has never been higher. As Figure 2-3 shows, in 1969 the percentage of people 14 years or older who were single had declined almost by half from what it was in 1900. In the same period, the ratio of married to single persons had increased from about 2 to 1 to 3 to 1. Further, many people who have been divorced only once are today happily married. Among those getting *first* divorces, 2 out of 3 remarry, and 9 out of 10 of those stay remarried (p. 36).

Wattenburg & Scammon sum up by quoting Dr. Paul Glick, the U.S. Census Bureau expert on marriage, who says:

The more I study the subject, the more apparent it becomes: marriage is regarded as . . . the happiest, healthiest, and most desired state of human existence. We get divorced not because we don't like marriage, but to find a better marriage partner. We live longer and are healthier if we are married. More of us are getting married, more of us are staying married longer and we are getting married younger. Marriage is the central fact of our lives (p. 35).

Divorce has been slandered and misunderstood. Many men and women accept the common belief that the divorce rates constitute a threat to the stability of our country. It is widely believed that the rates are continually rising, but the rates are much lower today than they were at the end of World War II. Every women's rights movement in the world has generally been accompanied by agitation for divorce legislation. In countries not allowing divorce, public morality is usually characterized by hypocrisy. The "double standard" permits a male, but not a female, to escape psychologically from an unsuccessful marriage. A dissatisfied man who can afford to do so takes a mistress. Divorce is rightly seen by feminists the world over as a progressive development which gives them more freedom and choice. Paradoxically, it probably results in a higher proportion of married people reporting that they are happily married. In societies that do not permit divorce, women bear almost the entire responsibility for making marriage work. When divorce becomes a possibility, the male also must try to make the marriage work; otherwise his spouse may press for a divorce. Marriage becomes a mutual enterprise. Before divorce became possible, many people remained married and together although insufferably unhappy because there simply was no readily acceptable alternative.

The existence of divorce as a possibility has probably contributed to the increase in marriages that are based on a relationship of equality. According to Landis (1968), democratic marriages in which neither the husband nor the wife is clearly dominant are the happiest marriages.

Easier divorce is not the only change in the institution of marriage. There has been a great deal of talk recently about the so-called sexual revolution. Many young people—and some not so young—are experimenting with different relationships and marriage forms. This may not involve great numbers of people in terms of absolute numbers, but certainly tradition is being questioned. In a recent poll of 20,000 *Psychology Today* readers (July 1970), 78 percent of those responding thought *extramarital sex* was permissible, depending on various circumstances. As for *group marriage*, 25 percent thought either that it was acceptable or that they "might be interested." A third of the sample thought that they "might be interested" in *wife* (or husband) *swapping*, although only 5 percent admitted they had tried it. Perhaps this is an unusual sample.

Much of this so-called revolution is just talk at this stage, as indicated by the discrepancy between thought and behavior in the wife-swapping statistics, and yet there are genuine shifts taking place in public opinion and legislation. Pollster Louis Harris found in a representative, nationwide poll (*Time*, 1969) that the "double standard" of sexual morality was declining, and that "most American parents are now willing to concede girls as much sexual freedom as boys," although, surprisingly, women remain more inclined to protect the female than men. Harris found that 59 percent of men but only 38 percent of women thought "unmarried women should be as free sexually as bachelors."

Two-Step Marriage

Anthropologist Margaret Mead in 1966 proposed an innovation in marriage which would reconcile the needs of youth with the needs of society. Miss Mead recognized that the pressures of today are all in the direction of permitting younger and younger marriages—as a way of allowing legitimate sex. But youth marriages are unsatisfactory, for many reasons. Many young people feel trapped into marriage before they are ready; often, in fact, pregnancy is the only reason for the marriage in the first place. Divorce is not always an adequate answer, since divorce is a painful process that usually leaves scars and the children of such a marriage are usually forced to give up one parent permanently. Furthermore, the increase in youthful marriages has not lessened the rates of illegitimacy nor the numbers of unwanted children being brought into the world.

Mead believes, therefore, that what is needed are two new types of marriage which separate the functions of marriage. The first type, called *individual marriage*, would be a legally sanctioned relationship with serious but limited commitment. The marriage would be based on love and companionship, but the partners would not be permitted to have children. The obligations would be minimal—for instance, the man would not have to support the woman, although either partner might choose to support the other (just as in some student marriages today). If the marriage was terminated, there would be no alimony or continuing responsibility of any sort. The second type, called a *parental marriage,* would start with an individual marriage but progress to parenthood only after the partners had carefully considered all the responsibilities involved and had demonstrated to civil authorities and to themselves their economic and emotional capacity to care for children. Unlike the individual marriage—which would be easy to get in and out of—the parental marriage would be hard to contract and dissolve.

By instituting the individual marriage choice, says Mead, we would "invest with new dignity a multitude of deeply meaningful relationships of choice throughout life." We would place a special emphasis on parenthood but still give strong support to marriage as a working relationship of still-growing people.

Trial Marriage

Actually, some young people today are already entering into relationships much like Mead's type of marriage, although such "living together" is not legally sanctioned, of course. This practice raises a number of issues. First, the trial relationship may be entered into casually, with little or no commitment to establishing a sound relationship. This practice may or may not be good, depending on whether it permits the growth of the partners.

Second, the relationship offers little or no protection to the woman, either as wife or mother. Many women may not feel they want protection, however, if a woman feels vulnerable in such a relationship, she will not be able to relate equally to her partner. If the couple have children, there can be legal complications in many states. In California, for example, the law does not assume that the man in a common-law marriage is necessarily the father of any of the children, which means that if the couple breaks up, the woman might have to sue to establish paternity or to get child support. Moreover, the woman does not have any rights under the community property law; her contracts may be legally voidable and she may not be able to inherit property or insurance benefits. In addition, people in common-law relationships meet a good deal of discrimination in buying homes, insurance, and getting eligibility for federal programs of various sorts. There is also a law against co-habitation, although today prosecutions are rare under its provisions. In states where common-law relationships become legal after a set period of time (usually 5 to 7 years), the wife is much better protected.

A third issue is that society does not approve of casual relation-ships. None of us is free from the effects of others' opinions; to a greater extent than most of us imagine, our self-esteem depends on the attitudes of approval of others. Perhaps an exceptionally self-actualized person can ignore the opinions of society, but the question arises how he became self-actualized in the first place: was it not through general approval by others of his behavior?

Contract Marriage

Life-long marriage is not the only form of marriage contract; in some societies marriage contracts, like other contracts, have been made for various periods of time. In ancient China it was not unknown for a legal marriage to be contracted for brief periods, sometimes even as short as *one* day. And any child born of such a union was as legitimate as any other. There is no compelling reason why marriage could not be altered so that it would be for a relatively short, specified period.

How would husband and wife react if they knew that at the end of the third year their marriage contract would expire automatically? Perhaps at the contracting stage people would include agreements covering separation, disposition of property, alimony, and child support, so that if either party was dissatisfied he could simply allow the contract to expire. Quite probably, the effect would be electric! Each partner would become more aware of the possibility that he might not be holding up his end of the bargain.

The possibility of divorce, however, does not have the same effect. Hilsdale (1962) observes that four out of five couples waiting to get married do not even consider the idea of divorce. Moreover, divorces are relatively hard to get (compared to getting married) and decidedly unpleasant to go through, and it is often impossible for the former partners to remain on friendly terms. In a contract marriage, each partner would be constantly reminded that he has a responsibility to make the marriage work. Such a contract would tend to strengthen 50-50 partnerships and provide the freedom for each partner to grow.

A bill to permit 3-year contract marriages with the option to renew was introduced in 1971 in the Maryland House of Delegates. One of the authors of the bill, Mrs. Hildagarde Boswell of Baltimore, argued that "with the 18-year-old vote coming in, I think the youngsters will look upon this as a totally new approach toward marriage and a family situation." Set against the positive arguments for contract marriage, however, are the adverse effects of one's always feeling he is "on trial"— a feeling to which many people in our society are very vulnerable.

WORK AND IDENTITY

As already mentioned, an adolescent is not considered an adult until he assumes adult work and family roles. Since education often determines *when* these roles will be assumed, we see some young people assuming them early, perhaps in their late teens, and others much later, sometimes in their thirties.

Belief in the value of work is deeply rooted in our society, and most people still think that paid employment is more important for males than for females. Although today's youth are increasingly questioning the value of work, it is still possible to outline the importance of work to most people's personalities.

It was noted in discussing the ideas of Erikson in Chapter 1 that children begin a stage of development (6 to 11 years) in which a sense of *industry and accomplishment* is created. During adolescence, a youth must reconcile his developing sense of identity and "the dreams, idiosyncrasies, roles, and skills cultivated earlier with the occupational and sexual prototypes of the day" (Erikson, 1963, p. 307). The danger says Erikson, is that of role diffusion: the youth feels he cannot take hold of a definite direction in life. The most serious problem probably occurs when one is so confused over his sexual identity that it interferes with his search for a meaningful work role.

When adolescents actually enter the world of work, a number of useful changes occur. From case studies, McCandless (1970) summarizes a number of these gains:

1. There is a gain in autonomy in becoming both responsible and

more independent of parents. Work assists in the process of weaning away from the exclusive influence of the home.

2. Earnings give youth both a feeling of independence and real independence.

3. The work environment may broaden young people's social lives, contributing to their becoming independent of their school crowd.

4. Work may contribute to young people's becoming more flexible. They have to learn to get along with people who may be very different from themselves.

5. As part of this flexibility, they may have to learn manners and social skills used by adults to get along with others—whom they may not like.

6. They may have to learn to adjust to (or at least put up with) tiresome work routines, schedules, and the power hierarchy of the working world. These may not be happy adjustments, but to some extent they are necessary.

7. Work *at this age* may or may not contribute to future careers. But it may provide money, which makes further education or other gratifications possible.

8. Work may contribute to enhancing the individual's self-concept. Being successful at work makes a person more confident in every other activity.

9. Work during adolescence provides youth with a time for taking stock—a time free of the irrevocable commitments of adult life, time during which direction can be attained (pp. 326–329).

The definite choice of an occupation seems more crucial for a boy than for a girl. As a boy grows older, he begins to sense more and more how seriously men take their work. *Society Today* (1971) puts it well:

Entry into an occupation and the contracting of marriage form two of the individual's strongest bonds to the society's institutional structure. For the young man, his occupational position will be an important factor in determining his social class position; the content of his daily activity, the identity of his friends, the degree of his power and prestige, and the level of his monetary income (pp. 54–55).

Women who plan to play traditional marriage roles will have their social status, friends, prestige, and income determined by their husband's achievement. Even working women find this to be true, since, if they are married, their own achievements are largely ignored; their status, unfortunately, is still determined by their husband's achievement.

The following reading examines critically the role of work in the formation of a woman's identity. The big question today for women is how they can satisfy the identity needs which in men are satisfied through the work role. Here the authors evaluate the many changes in our society that have made it necessary to rethink the traditional wisdom in this area.

Box 2-4   A Woman's Life

The following essay by Ellen and Kenneth Keniston makes clear that a woman today faces a much different life after raising her children than did women in former times. What to do with one's later years was not much of a problem when life expectancy was only 35 or 40 years. As the illustration shows however, the average woman now has about half of her life ahead of her after she has finished raising the children. The Kenistons analyze the options open to her.

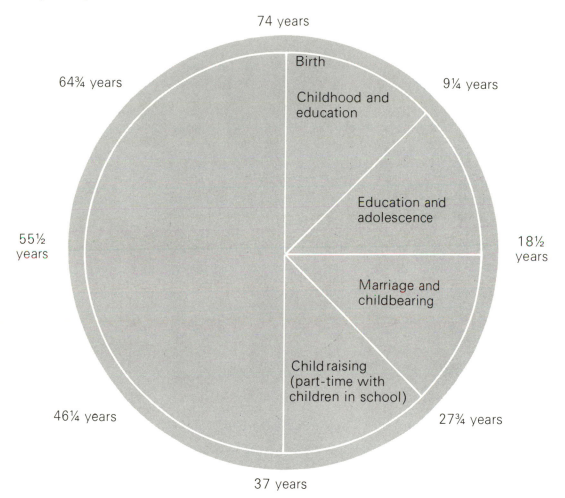

(Source: **Women: Report of the National Advisory Commission on the Status of Women, State of California Documents Section, 1971.**)

ELLEN AND KENNETH KENISTON

An American Anachronism:
The Image of Women and Work

Ellen Keniston received her Ph.D. in clinical psychology from Harvard in 1960. She has done clinical work with children and adults. Kenneth Keniston is Associate Professor in the Department of Psychiatry in the Yale Medical School. A former Rhodes Scholar and Junior Fellow at Harvard, he is engaged in studies of alienation from American society.

THE most effective forms of oppression are those with which the victim covertly cooperates. So long as coercion is exercised from without and experienced as such by the coerced, revolt is possible and ultimately probable. As the rulers of Chinese thought-reform centers know, coercion is truly effective only when its targets assent to its justice, and, more than that, accept their servitude as a part of their view of themselves. As long as American Negroes consciously or unconsciously saw themselves as an inferior race, they inevitably collaborated in their own exploitation; only the awareness of their unwitting connivance with oppression has released their energies toward relieving their second-class citizenship.

The past few years have seen renewed concern about the problems, the continuing "oppression" and the "incomplete emancipation" of American women. We have been reminded

that women attend college in smaller ratio to men than thirty years ago; that sex-linked wage differentials persist in most occupations; that other industrialized countries make far better provision for working mothers; that our mass media extol the virtues of home, family and children while deprecating the working woman; that feminism in America exhausted itself with the achievement of the vote for women. Although women work in greater numbers than ever before, many professions remain closed to any but the most resolute women, and most women's jobs are concentrated in underpaid and menial positions. Compared, say, with Russian society, ours makes little use of the extrafamilial talents of women, and seems to "oppress" them by pushing them simultaneously away from work and toward home and family.

In seeking to explain this apparent backwardness of our society, two interpretations are frequently given. One is largely conspiratorial: in its most extreme form, it holds that women are kept oppressed by a sinister junta of reactionary psychoanalysts, Madison Avenue hucksters, and insecure husbands; in more moderate statement, it stresses the role of men's vanity, weakness, or need for an "Other." The second common explanation of the "problem" of American women emphasizes the absence of "objective opportunities," such as equal employment regulations, subsidies for women's education, maternity benefits, community supported day-care centers for children, more adequate domestic help, *et cetera*. Were such opportunities available, this argument runs, women would move easily outside the confines of kitchen, kaffee-klatsch and kindergarten.

Each of these explanations has something to be said for it. Advertisers clearly do have a vested interest in keeping women at home buying their products; psychoanalysts have often advanced theories of universal feminine "masochism" and "passivity" (which made it difficult to explain the undeniable intellectual talents and careers of many women psychoanalysts); insecure men do frequently stand between their wives and "fulfillment" outside the home; and a majority of American (male) congressmen have shown little interest in legislation to equalize women's inferior economic position. So, too, the lack of adequate institutional support for women is clear, and clearly needs correction: the lot of working women, and especially of working mothers, could be vastly improved by changes in employment laws, by added social security benefits for maternity and by better facilities for child care. And the absence of such institutional support does indeed discourage women who might otherwise want to do something outside their own homes.

But both these interpretations overlook what seems to us the central "problem" for most American women: namely, that most not only accept but largely desire a homebound position, and the obstacles on which they founder are less often external conditions than internal ambivalences. The vast majority of women in this country—even the vast majority of middle-class college graduates—give love, marriage and family supreme priority over "career." If they are indignant or resentful, it is most often over the social or personal situation that requires them to work, and far more rarely over either the pressures that impede their working or the injustices of their situation in work. Whether they work to supplement their husbands' incomes (the reason given by most working-class women), to relieve the boredom of empty houses once children are in school, or, as widowed, divorced, separated or unmarried women, simply to earn a living, most women work because they must, and would gladly exchange their "careers" for the life of a happily-married, financially-secure wife-and-mother. If working-class high school girls are asked about their ideal life, they tell of a dream-cottage with successful husband and many children: there is no mention of work. And even in elite women's colleges, many, and perhaps most, girls consider any pressure to plan seriously for a career an unwanted distraction from their main emotional concern—finding husbands and beginning their lives as wives-and-mothers. Despite the fact that eight or nine out of every ten American women will be employed at some time during their lives, probably the same proportion in some part of themselves dislikes, even detests, the thought of working.

Resentment and indignation at the social barriers to complete emancipation are not widespread. They tend to be concentrated among a relatively small group of highly educated professional women, many of whom have succeeded in overcoming these real barriers and in finding interesting and even "fulfilling" jobs because they were unambivalently determined to do so. Indeed, if anything like a majority of American women felt a small part of their resentment and indignation, the social barriers would soon crumble before the pressure. If even a quarter of the electorate (half of the women) was willing to vote with some selectivity for candidates who favored equal employment opportunities for women, subsidies for women's education, maternity benefits, women's employment rights and community-supported child-care centers, it would take but a decade before these easily envisioned goals were attained. But there is no consistent demand; these are rarely live political issues; most women "fulfill their potential" outside the home reluctantly, if at all. If there is a "problem" for women in America today, it is that they work only of necessity or by default; if women remain unemancipated, theirs is a largely voluntary servitude.

It is therefore an oversimplification to trace the causes of women's homebound situation solely to masculine prejudice and to seek a solution of the problem only in improvements in social opportunities. Behind both masculine prejudice and women's homebound situation lie enormous historical changes that have pushed the American woman into an unprecedented social and human situation; and behind the inability of American women to create better social conditions for themselves lie anachronistic images of womanliness and work, defensively reasserted by women themselves. How has the situation of American women changed in the past generations? And why do outmoded definitions of womanliness and work persist despite these radical changes?

THE UNPRECEDENTED SITUATION OF AMERICAN WOMEN

Consider the life-situation of the average woman in all societies two hundred years ago, and in most nonindustrial societies today. None of the "problems of modern woman" could possibly arise: to survive, society had no choice but to require women to spend their lives as guardians of the home and of the next generation. In any community where the average life-span is thirty to forty years and infant mortality approaches fifty percent, mere maintenance of the population requires that adult women devote all of their time to bearing children. Moreover, what to do with "the later years" is hardly a problem: most women are dead long before they reach the end of their fertility, and those few who survive are usually so exhausted from child-bearing that they have little energy available for "a later career." And even if a singular woman wanted to have only a few children, knowledge of contraception was so limited that she had no way of doing it short of refusing all men.

Furthermore, high birth and death rates have usually gone hand in hand with a kind of family organization that gave a woman more than enough to do *within* her family. In most societies, the family, not the individual, was the basic unit of the economy, and women have had to work for and within families in order to survive. The peasant wife must share the tasks of the land with her husband; the wife of the hunter must clean and store her husband's game; the shepherd's wife must help to guard the herds. Even today on old-fashioned farms a wife is essential to care for domestic animals, can and store food for the winter, and maintain the domestic side of farm life. In a few complex and highly differentiated societies, of course, small groups of leisured aristocratic women have existed; but these women have often become, as Veblen pointed out, status symbols for their husbands; and much of their energy has traditionally gone toward maintaining the visible signs of leisure and affluence that would provide continual reminders of their husbands' wealth and power. Historically, then, women have always worked, but at the tasks of the family economy, not outside it.

The industrial revolution, however, brought a series of changes that created a "problem" where none could have existed before. Advances in medicine and public health have decreased the infant mortality rate and lengthened the life-span; changes in economic organization have all but destroyed the family as an economic unit. Women began to work outside the home primarily in response to these economic and social changes. Thoughts of self-fulfillment, always an aristocratic ideal, were

far from the minds of the first women in the mills of England and Germany in the eighteenth and nineteenth centuries; for them factory labor was an unwanted economic necessity. To be sure, the physical conditions of life were probably better in the new mill towns than they had been for the peasantry; but the "alienated" labor of the woman factory worker was psychologically far more arduous than tilling fields that had been tended by the same family for generations. Working women in the early industrial period must have looked back with nostalgia to the lives of their own peasant mothers, for whom work and family were part of an unfragmented whole. For the vast majority of working women, work outside the family began as a deprivation, as a necessity, as part of the loss of peasant family life; and these meanings of work persist to the present.

The medical and technological advances made possible by the industrial revolution have of course borne full fruit only in the past two generations. Only now has infant mortality been sufficiently lowered and the life-span enough increased so that social survival is fully compatible with widespread family limitation. A modern American woman can rightly anticipate that her children will survive into adulthood, and that she herself will live into her mid-seventies. Modern medical care makes bearing children less dangerous, and modern conveniences make caring for them less onerous. Furthermore, any woman who wants to limit the size of her family has available a variety of contraceptive techniques; and the population explosion suggests that family limitation, formerly the route to social suicide, has on the contrary become a prerequisite for social survival. Technological advances have both freed and deprived women of the need to devote their lives to procreation and child care.

The impact on women of these technological advances has been shaped by equally unprecedented changes in the family. Consider the family's increasing sociological "isolation." Formerly, husband, wife and their children were embedded in a network of extended family relationships—cousins, aunts, uncles, grandparents and grandchildren who lived together and functioned as a social and economic unit. Now, increasingly, parents and their offspring live apart and separate, isolated both geographically and psychologically from wider family ties. In societies with extended family systems, surviving older women can be socially useful by caring for their grandchildren, nieces and nephews. But in our society a woman must anticipate that her adult children will leave her to establish new homes of their own, often far from her; and any older woman who assumes a maternal role with anyone but her own children is usually told, subtly or directly, that she is neither wanted nor needed. Furthermore, the isolation and the small size of American families mean that all emotional ties within the family are inevitably concentrated on a smaller number of people and, in that measure, intensified. The absence of aunts, grandmothers, female cousins and the like within the immediate family gives the mother an added centrality as the *only* female model available to her daughters during their early years—a point to which we will return.

In addition, the family's functions have been drastically reduced in the last century. The family is no longer the chief productive unit of society: only in a declining number of old-style farms or small retail stores do husband and wife share a family economic task; instead, for the vast majority of Americans of all classes, the "isolated" family is tied to the economic system solely through its breadwinner's work. To be sure, the older notion of husband and wife working "side by side" in a common task often recurs as a dream or hope; but for most women it is a practical impossibility. Even those rare couples today who manage to work as a team usually do so outside the home; and most can testify how hard it is to maintain such a husband-wife team in a society that normally considers their marriage relationship detrimental to their objectivity, performance and achievement on the job. Work is no longer a family affair; the "home workshop" has become a place to play; both women and men sharply separate family and work.

What is left for a woman is of course her role as "homemaker," "wife-and-mother," nurturer and upbringer of her children. But even here her job has been drastically reduced. Labor-saving devices and modern homes, advances in the packaging and processing of food, the introduction of electricity, running water, bathrooms, refrigeration and telephones into American life, all mean that a woman's housework can be quickly done unless she is truly determined to make a full-time job of housecleaning and cooking. Nor can bringing up children be counted on to occupy a woman's life, for in the past two centuries the family has relinquished many of its child-rearing functions to schools. In a technological society,

teaching children adult skills is too complex and essential a task to leave to idiosyncratic families, we therefore remove children from their parents for the better part of the day and "socialize" them in schools where more standardized learning is guaranteed. This approach again both frees women and deprives them of their traditional role as those who teach children the complex skills of adulthood; it leaves mothers responsible for the full-time care of their children for only five or six years.

Finally, new demands on men in their work directly increase the pressures on women. Over the past few generations, men's jobs have become increasingly specialized, increasingly distant from any visible relationship to a useful finished product, more and more demanding of technical skill, expertise, "rationality" and the suppression of emotion, fantasy and passion on the job. More and more, men work "to earn a living," and the real "living" for which they work is increasingly sought within the family, kept separate from the working world by physical distance and social convention. After marriage, the average woman sees nothing of her husband during the working-and-commuting day; and middle-class wives with "successful" husbands often do without their spouses evenings and weekends as well. To make a "career" of marriage is psychologically difficult when one's husband is away for eighty percent of one's waking hours.

And when men are with their wives, they usually need them to make up for what is lacking in their jobs. Like our ideals of recreation, our ideals of family life are defined by contrast with the demands of our working day. In home or recreation, women are expected to fill the emotional lacunae in their husbands' jobs and to relieve the pressures and tensions they come home with. In family or fun, the good wife should be spontaneous, warm, caring, emotionally responsive, not too practical or intellectual and somewhat passive, yet at the same time consoling and supportive when necessary. Above all, she should not be aggressive, initiating, intellectual, analytic, ambitious or in any other way encourage talents or qualities in herself that might remind her husband of the working world he comes home to forget.

In every nation with an advanced industrial technology, similar changes in medical care, family life and the demands of work have, as in America, begun to alter the situation of women and to create a "problem" where none could have existed two generations ago. But in most other industrial nations the impact of these social changes on women has been attenuated by strong centers of opposition to the new industrial order. Most often, opposition has sprung from traditional institutions and values that long antedated industrialism: in France, the Church and the peasantry; in Japan, "feudal" patterns of familial and social interdependence; in England, an entrenched class system. In each case, these traditional institutions have preserved competing models of family and woman, so that women who remained loyal to the Church, the extended family, or their social class could often be relatively unaffected by the new demands of industrialism. But in America, a nation without a "feudal" past, without an entrenched class system, without an established church or an aristocratic tradition, the impact of industrial society on women has been unusually thoroughgoing and intense.

The lack of an aristocratic tradition in this country is especially important in explaining the special stresses on American women. Traditionally, in Europe, women of the upper classes have had enough leisure and freedom from family needs to permit them, if they chose, to "work" outside their homes. Those who did choose to work gradually developed a positive definition of woman's work, at first concerned with matters charitable and educational, then artistic and intellectual, and finally even scientific or political—a model that in part counterbalanced the negative images of prostitutes, servants and factory workers. But in this country, where aristocratic traditions were weak and highly suspect and where most upper-class women devoted themselves not to intellectual attainment but to ostentatious display, no countervailing image of woman's work could develop. Most American women continue to view work as at best a necessity, to be avoided if possible and borne with resignation if required.

Countless other factors contribute to the special stresses on American women. Industrialization and specialization have been more thoroughgoing here than abroad, and the resulting pressures on the family, on women, and on men's demands on women have been correspondingly more intense. Our national reverence for youth helps make it difficult for women (or men) to plan realistically for a time in life when neither they nor their children will be young. So, too, our traditional distrust of grand ideologies has inoculated most Ameri-

cans against that continuing enthusiasm for feminist ideals that exist in other nations. Together these factors have cooperated to push American women into the vanguard of social change; and it may always be the lot of they who must face an unprecedented historical situation without signposts, models or maps to suffer the most intensely and to blame themselves for their "problems." Without adequate signposts a vanguard inevitably falls back on outdated guides. In this case definitions of family, conceptions of womanliness and images of work left over from an era when they were necessary for social survival and congruent with family function have persisted into an era in which they are no longer viable. The result of this cultural lag is the "problem" of American women.

FROM GENERATION TO GENERATION

"Cultural lag" is of course not so much an explanation as a description, and only by examining the reasons why archaic definitions of womanliness have persisted can we understand the ambivalence and reluctance with which most American women confront the need for life outside the family. We cannot hope to deal here with all of the social, cultural and historical factors that have contributed to preserve more traditional ideals of woman's role, nor can we consider the enormous variety of outlooks on womanliness in different sectors of American society. Instead we will concentrate on the transmission of images of femininity and masculinity from generation to generation within the family.

The fundamental processes involved in learning the lessons of gender are fairly constant in American society. An American girl first learns what it means to be a woman at her mother's knee. She may decide to be like her mother, not to be like her mother, to be like her in some ways and not in other ways; or she may even believe she has completely forgotten her mother and set out on a new path of her own; but in the background her conscious and unconscious assessment of her mother's life, of its joys, satisfactions, virtues and failings, almost always remains central. In determining this assessment, the mother's conception of her own adequacy as a woman is of enormous importance, but equally momentous is the father's conscious and unconscious conception of his wife. In most stable marriages, these two judgments are (or soon become) complementary; and in our small and "related" families where mother and father are the only two adults present to a small girl, their consensus is especially decisive in forming the daughter's view of her sex. So, too, from their parents American girls also learn the meanings of masculinity and, by repeated admonition and example, the precise boundaries between what is desirably "ladylike" and what is undesirably "boyish." Again, if the parents feel and act in concert, these early lessons become so deeply ingrained that they persist unconsciously even for adult women who consciously deny their validity.

Beyond these commonplaces of the learning of sex roles, there are vast differences among American families, differences related to individual idiosyncracy, to ethnicity and social class, to region and religion. But, despite these differences, we know enough of how our society has changed in the last two generations to reconstruct a more or less "typical" pattern of development. Very few of the grandmothers of today's young women worked outside their families; rather, as did ninety percent of the Victorian women of all classes in America, they devoted themselves to the care of children, home and husband. In such a family, a daughter was likely to inherit from both mother and father an unambivalent definition of womanliness, which glorified domestic virtues and saw outside work as an unequivocal "fall" to menial status, factory exploitation, or—the ultimate fall—prostitution. The "outside world" was quintessentially masculine, and the sharp lines that separated male and female partly served to protect "innocent" women from a side of life and of themselves seen as potentially dangerous, wild and promiscuous.

In our grandparents' day, this splitting of existence into a dangerous, masculine outside world and a sheltered, protected feminine domestic world was still workable. But for a woman born at the turn of the century and married in the 1920's, the situation began to change. Although she herself may have initially accepted her parents' view of womanhood, the rapid change in the objective conditions of women's lives—the dissipation of the extended family, the lengthening of the life-span, the introduction of laborsaving devices—all these meant that the definition of womanhood that satisfied her mother was less likely to satisfy her. New economic pressures, new job opportunities for women and her own lengthening life-span made it more likely that she would work at some point in her life—either to supplement the family income or to relieve her boredom in a spotless but empty house.

But the fact of working rarely meant joy in working. Given their upbringing, few women were psychologically prepared to enter a "man's world" without inner conflict. In the absence of any positive image of women's work, all ways of construing a job were fraught with difficulty; to find satisfaction in a job inevitably meant to find something heretofore defined as a malprerogative, and often resulted in a feeling of loss of womanliness; not to find satisfaction in one's work—and still to work—meant to risk reduction to the role of a menial in one's own eyes. In either case, working seemed to mean not being as good as one's mother, who had "made a go" of a purely domestic life.

Furthermore, husbands of the last generation were rarely happy about wives who moved outside the family. Remembering their own mothers (who had stayed at home), they could seldom confront their wives' outside jobs without feelings of inadequacy. And should the wife work—whether as volunteer or as paid employee—in order to relieve her own frustration and boredom within an empty home, then the husband's guilt and fear would usually be even greater, for this suggested that he, compared to his father, was less able to "satisfy" his wife, to "provide for her" a marriage within which she felt "fulfilled"—with all the myriad sexual and economic implications of these terms. Men, like women, tended to see work as an exclusively male prerogative; and they felt easily unmanned by wives who entered any but a small number of traditionally feminine jobs, such as nursing.

Nor should we overlook the real elements of masculine identification and rivalry in women which were fostered by Victorian definitions of sex roles. The "outside world" of the Victorian male was seen as not only dangerous and wild, but intensely interesting, free and exciting; and the protected "inside world" of Victorian women had its custodial and even imprisoning side. Many a daughter of a Victorian family covertly scorned the domestic docility of her mother and, in her own quest for freedom and excitement, secretly envied and identified with men. Those few who acted on their envy had to accept society's explicit judgment that their demeanor was "mannish" and its unstated suspicion that their behavior was "loose." But most women guiltily suppressed whatever "mannish" and "loose" aspirations they had, and, by compulsive conscious attachment to a "homely" role, denied—even to themselves— the existence of these aspirations.

A young woman of today is most likely to have grown up in a family in which her mother, if she worked, felt at some level inadequate or guilty about it, and if she did not work, felt frustration and resentment at the boredom of her homebound life. Her father was usually made subtly uneasy by whatever domestic discontents or career aspirations his wife had, and appreciated her most in her homely role. Such attitudes are of course rarely stated as such, but they are nonetheless expressed in countless indirect ways, and are the more powerful because, unstated, they are the harder to confront or oppose. A mother's look of remorse as she leaves for work, her fear of "neglecting" her children, her resentment of her need to work, her failure to discuss her work at home—these are far more expressive than any open discussion of her ambivalence. And a father's deprecation of "mannish" women, his praise for the "truly feminine," and his dislike of women in his own work more effectively tell his daughter what he desires from her than any lecture could. Most fathers and mothers of the last generation implicitly agreed in blaming women for their inability to be happy in a narrowly defined wife-and-mother role, and in seeing women who wanted to work as really wanting to wear the pants.

As often happens, the assumptions and conflicts of parents form the unconscious substratum of inner conflict in their children; the stage was thus set for a continuing, although often unconscious, ambivalence about the relationship between work and womanliness in this generation. But, ironically, both emulation of one's mother and rivalry with her have often led in practice to the same determination to excel in a homely role. The woman who strongly identifies with the best in her mother has usually come unconsciously to define the best as the domestic; the woman who seeks to avoid her mother's failings has usually learned to attribute women's failings to their inability to find fulfillment within the family. And not least of all, many women who naturally enough envy and identify themselves with men's work and freedom cannot admit this envy to themselves because it seems a denial of their femininity; and they often devote themselves to home

and family with a passion born partly from fear of their latent discontents.

These same psychological themes can of course lead to very different outcomes in behavior. But it is a rare working woman in whom inner conflict does *not* complicate the practical problems of combining marriage and career, for whom working is not accompanied by silent questions about her adequacy and by implicit apprehension about her "envy" of men, and who does *not* at some level consider a career a denial rather than an expression of femininity. On the other hand, few women are able to make a full and lifetime job from reduced family roles—and to remain satisfied and content in their later years. Not surprisingly, those who have escaped inner conflict have been most often recruited from atypical circumstances— from upper-class families or from European backgrounds where a more positive conception of women's work prevails.

A woman's sense of what it is to be a woman, although founded on her relationships with her parents, is of course much more than this. But for most American girls the familistic lessons of their childhoods are merely reinforced by their later education. The curriculum of American schools is primarily oriented toward what are thought to be the special talents of boys, and this emphasis convinces girls that they are not "really good" at the things that matter in the world of men. So, too, girls soon learn that "popularity"—that peculiar American ecstasy from which all other goods flow—accrues to her who hides any intelligence she may have, flatters the often precarious maleness of adolescent boys, and devotes herself to activities that can in no way challenge their sex. The popular girls in high schools are seldom the brilliant girls; or if they are, it is only because they are so brilliant they can hide their brilliance from less brilliant boys. Any girl whose parents support her in an early commitment to a career outside those few that are deemed unthreateningly feminine often spends many miserable years in a public school system. Indeed, most American public schools (like many private schools) make a girl with passionate intellectual interests feel a strong sense of her own inadequacy as a woman, feel guilty about these "masculine" outlooks, perhaps even wonder about her own normality.

At best, adolescence should provide a second chance in life, an opportunity to reassess childhood self-definitions, envies and identifications and to seek out new models of selfhood more appropriate to capacities and opportunities. But as we argued earlier, American society provides few models adequate to the situation of modern women. On the whole, mass media and popular fiction continue to portray career women as mannish, loose, or both; and the happy ending for working girls still involves abandoning work, marrying and having many children—and there the story ends. So, too, many of the potential models have been systematically debunked by the misapplication of psychiatric judgments; thus, few outstanding women have been spared the implication that their achievements spring primarily from neurosis. And the most immediate models of working women available to girls during adolescence—their teachers—are too often unmarried women who have had to pay a high human price for their work. Thus, the selective reorganization and redefinition of childhood images of womanhood that *could* take place during adolescence rarely occur; and during her late teens and early twenties, many a girl who might otherwise be capable of more merely confirms her surrender to the pressures for popularity. Adequate models of adult identification can sustain one against strong internal and social pressure; when they are absent, one surrenders at the first push.

Paradoxically, then, the effect of new technology, of changes in family structure and function, has been to make many—probably most—women even *more* determined to make a go of a wife-and-mother role which objective conditions daily undermine more completely. Most young women in this country still cherish the fantasy of a marriage that will totally and automatically fulfill all emotional and intellectual needs, a fantasy that sets the stage for colossal disappointment, guilt and self-castigation when—as increasingly happens—marriage alone is not enough. So, too, most remain enormously ambivalent about the thought of working, to say nothing of finding a "vocation" in work; and even those who secretly enjoy their jobs often find it easier to blame their extrafamilial life on financial need than to admit, even to themselves, that they want or enjoy it. Although the dream-cottage with the built-in totally fulfilling wife-and-mother role has been destroyed by a changing society, most women cling tenaciously and sometimes defensively to this older image and blame themselves for cracks in the picture window.

WOMANLINESS AND WORK

Assuming that our characterization is adequate, what can be done? Or, indeed, need anything be done? One rejoinder would be to argue that by freely choosing to devote themselves entirely to their husbands and families, women are merely expressing a deeply feminine outlook. But against this, recall that any American woman who has had a family of three children by the time she is thirty years old and who lives to the age of seventy-five will have forty years of her adult life that can*not* under any circumstances be spent primarily in child care. Furthermore, the disappearance of the family as a productive unit means that a woman has few economic functions to perform within the home. Cleaning, cooking, and caring for older children are, even for the most compulsive housewife and conscientious mother, at best part-time occupations. For a girl to dream only of being a happy wife-and-mother thus is a gross denial of reality, a motivated refusal to confront the kind of life she will actually lead.

Furthermore, the choice most women make can hardly be said to be "free" in the psychological sense. We have argued that identification, rivalry, emulation, fear and guilt often make it psychologically impossible for women to respond to changed social conditions, to seize the opportunities that do occur or to fight for those that do not. Thus we return to the proposition from which we began: the failure of most American women to exploit the potentials open to them or to struggle to create new opportunities stems in large part from their own inner conflicts, from archaic images of womanhood and from family patterns that subtly but effectively discourage commitment to vocation. If our society has not yet availed itself of the talents of women, it is largely because women themselves feel they must hide their talents under a bushel.

Nor can the choice of the wife-and-mother role to the exclusion of all else be seen as merely a "natural" expression of the "eternal feminine," of woman's biological role as bearer and nurturer of the next generation. To be sure, a woman's capacity for biological creativity is and must be central to many of her fundamental concerns, affecting her life-style, her personal relations, her conceptions of time, even her orientation to space. But women express their womanliness differently in every culture; and in our own culture they often express it in ways less than adequate to meet their unprecedented situation. Women need not abandon their distinguishing womanliness: even now, there are the many exceptions to these remarks who are sufficiently free of inner conflict to realize their womanliness both within their families and in useful work outside their homes. The problem is how to open this option to all women.

What, then, can be done to alter the prevailing outmoded definitions of the good life for women? We have already mentioned one major line of improvement—the development of social institutions to support and encourage those women who want or need to work. But if our analysis is correct, an even deeper problem than the lack of opportunities is the lack of unambivalent motivation. And the processes of generational identification, emulation and rivalry upon which such lack of motivation is based are difficult to change by direct social intervention. What parents communicate to their daughters about womanhood, work and femininity can only be affected indirectly, by changing other social agencies, ideologies and models, which may in turn affect patterns of family influence, interaction and identification.

This is not a small or simple task, but some of the ways it might be done can be anticipated. For one, the facts we have here emphasized should be continually reiterated to both young men and young women: that most women *will* work, that society has changed so as to make *impossible* the kind of fulfillment within the family that earlier generations found; that unless they work most women—single or married —will find themselves during the greater part of their adulthood with nothing to do. Educational authorities, mass media, schools, all can cooperate in emphasizing the difficulties in an older conception of womanhood and the objective possibilities open to women today.

Women's conceptions of their potentials might also be changed by altering the demands that men—their fathers and husbands—make upon them. Unlike all other "oppressed" groups, women live on terms of intimate interdependence with their alleged oppressors, and this interdependence means that if the lives of men are grossly lacking in some crucial quality, their women will be impelled to develop compensating and opposite qualities. Thus, as we argued earlier, many of the pressures that men exert on their wives and daughters ultimately spring from the lacks in their own work. Could we but make work more humane and more

challenging for men, asking less of their patience and more of their imagination, it would be less necessary for women to compensate for what is missing on the job by being passively "feminine" in the home. As it is, a man whose work is essentially dull, monotonous and *un*fulfilling can only be threatened when his wife seeks "self-fulfillment" in her work.

But perhaps the greatest leverage for changing the image of women and their potential could be gained by providing more viable models of womanhood to girls in adolescence. In every community, there are some women who feel little inner conflict between their commitments to their families and their vocations, who manage both with equal womanliness. The existence of such women must be brought to the attention of adolescent girls searching for models for the future. At present, most adolescent girls are confronted with two equally unsatisfactory models—spinster teachers, sometimes embittered, mannish and overly intellectual, and women like their mothers, who usually have the many conflicts about work and womanliness we have discussed. If a third model could be available as well—as housemothers, teachers, advisors and friends— a model that epitomizes marriage *and* career instead of marriage or career, more adolescent girls and young women might break out of these sterile alternatives. We Americans are not an ideological people, and our pragmatism demands visible proof of the possibility of what we advocate. Such proof exists in every community, and were it consistently brought to the attention of girls in the process of defining their future lives as women, they might be better able to avoid the literally impossible alternatives in whose terms many now shape their futures.

All this implies a vision of the possibilities available to women for the first time in history. We would hopefully envisage a society that was not an androgenous world in which men and women were similar as anatomically possible, but one in which women could make what Erik Erikson calls their "inner space" and their attitude toward their inner creativity felt in the outer world as well—and men could learn to enjoy it. We would hope that women who saw the need to extend their life-space beyond the family would become not less but more womanly in consequence; that in time they would evolve new ways of expressing, rather than denying, their womanliness in their work; and that the result would be a betterment of work for both men and women. We would hope that Americans of both sexes could gradually abandon outdated images of masculinity and femininity without ceasing to rejoice in the difference. And we would hope that women who were emancipated from voluntary servitude to anachronistic images of "femininity" could abandon outmoded alternatives for more appropriate alternations between the traditional inner world of children and family and new efforts to realize the virtues of this inner world outside the home. Thus, we would hope, the fruitful mutuality and interdependence of men and women that has always existed in love might be extended in the works of society.

Summarizing Statements

1. Friendship is based on liking, trust, confidence, and mutual support. There is also an element of identification involved, since we empathize and sympathize with the life problems of our friends.

2. Among the purposes of dating are having fun, getting to know someone, broadening your own experience, and experiencing romance.

3. There is evidence that long-term dating (going steady, engagement) involves a series of "filters" or tests through which potential spouses must pass as they move toward marital commitment. These filters are selection based on (a) similarity of social and cultural background, (b) agreement on important values, and (c) complementary needs and motives.

4. In romantic love, one's love is distorted by fantasy and play acting. This infatuation, although pleasant, is not usually enough to sustain a pair in marriage. The favorable relationship that exists in friendship and some degree of compatibility are needed in marriage too. As a sole basis for selection of a spouse, romantic love appears to be declining.

5. Jourard defines love in terms of action taken to promote the happiness and growth of one's love. Loving is mutual giving and mutual receiving. Love is rooted in need.

6. Fromm says that mature love is union under the condition of preserving one's integrity and individuality. Love involves caring, taking responsibility, and respecting and encouraging one's love.

7. Maslow studied love among self-actualizing people. Their love was free of anxiety and defensiveness. They were free and spontaneous. Unlike in romantic love, where there is a great deal of fantasy idealization and deception of the other, their love was based on genuineness and truthfulness. There was less distance, mystery, and glamour. These people were not threatened by growth in their love.

8. The *fear* of being rejected in love can produce exactly that outcome: being rejected. The one who fears rejection becomes aggressive (jealous, demanding) and demands persistently to be reassured that he is loved.

9. Most Americans who marry believe that marriage and romantic love are compatible. Marriage, however, is a social institution that regulates man and woman in a system of mutual obligations and rights essential to the functioning of family life. As such, it requires more than just love: the partners should share: (a) a core of family-oriented interests, (b) the cycles of work, procreation, and recreation, and (c) an accommodating attitude toward resolving whatever problems come up. Resources exist to help the individual solve these problems.

10. Marriage has never been more popular. More people are married than ever before. The divorce rate has leveled off. Most divorcees remarry and are successful the second time around. Divorce exists as an escape valve for unhappy marriages. Its existence probably contributes both to the relatively high rates of marital happiness reported, and the growth of egalitarian attitudes and relationships.

11. Attitudes toward sexuality are beginning to change. The "double standard" is declining. The vast majority of Americans today approve of divorce.

12. Margaret Mead has proposed a new kind of two-step marriage which would separate the companionship features of *individual marriage* from *parent marriage*. Child rearing would be limited to the latter. The purpose is both to legitimize the individual sexual union and to protect children. The obligations of the individual marriage would be minimal.

13. *Trial marriage* is discussed in terms of the depth of commitment likely, the protection it offers to women, and the fact that society does not approve of it.

14. *Contract marriage* is discussed as an innovation that would make divorce obsolete. Marriage would be contracted for a specific period of time and would automatically expire unless renewed. It was suggested that contract marriage would spur each partner on to do his best to make the marriage work.

15. An adolescent is not considered to be an adult until he assumes adult work and family roles. A child begins to develop a *sense of industry* in middle childhood, followed by a *sense of identity*. This sense of identity involves reconciling his sense of self with sex and work roles and sexual and occupational fashions of the day. Two obstacles to developing a firm sense of identity are confusion over sex identity and finding a meaningful work role.

16. When adolescents go to work, a number of useful changes occur in their lives, including gains in autonomy, flexibility, self-confidence, and realism. However, the occupations of men will be primary in determining the social class of their families, their circle of friends, and the degree of their power and prestige.

READING SELECTION

17. Our society makes little use of women's talents and seems to

oppress them by simultaneously pushing them away from work and toward marriage, home, and family. Our backwardness compared to other societies has been inadequately explained as being (a) a conspiracy of reactionary psychoanalysts, Madison Avenue hucksters, and insecure husbands, and (b) an absence of objective occupational opportunities, such as equal-employment laws, job maternity benefits, and community-supported day-care centers.

18. These interpretations overlook the central problem, which is that most American women not only accept but largely desire a home-bound position. What keeps them back is internal ambivalence. For most women, love, marriage, and family have priority over career. Resentment of the lack of full emancipation is not widespread. If even half of the women voters voted selectively for candidates who promised to dismantle the remaining obstacles to complete equality, the barriers would soon come down.

19. Beyond masculine prejudice and women's home-bound situation lie outmoded images of womanliness and work, defensively reinforced by women themselves.

20. The industrial revolution brought changes. Advances in medicine lowered infant mortality and lengthened the life span. Economic changes destroyed the family as an economic unit in production. Women worked in the factories at first out of necessity. The family became increasingly isolated with the decline of the extended family system. And the women's role in the family became reduced to homemaker, wife and mother. All of these functions, even the job of socializing the children, have continued to decline in modern times, leaving women with much less to do.

21. Women in this country have not had positive models of successful, happy working women. Their role training has subtly taught them that to be feminine is to be domestic. The school curriculum is primarily oriented toward what are thought to be the special talents of boys. Girls become convinced that they are not good at those things that matter in the world of men.

22. Popularity comes to those girls who conceal their intellect, play up to the maleness of adolescent boys, and do not challenge them. Outstanding women have been undermined by psychiatric theories that imply their success was due to neurosis.

23. Today a woman who raises her children to school age has by 35 *half her life remaining* that cannot be spent primarily in child care. House care is no longer an occupation that requires much time of anyone.

24. What is needed? (a) The creation of social institutions to support and encourage those women who want and need to work, and (b) motivation. The reality that most women will work needs to be constantly restated. The kind of society that permitted a fully developed identity within the traditional feminine role is gone forever. Unless women work, they will find themselves with nothing to do for half their lives. Girls need successful models who combine marriage and work roles.

Terms and Concepts

Common law marriage: a free union in which two people live together for a long period of time. Such unions are legally recognized in some states after a set period of time, usually 5–7 years.

Contract marriage: a form of divorce, or rather a form of marriage which makes divorce unnecessary, since it is for a fixed interval of time.

Fixation: an attachment developed in infancy or early childhood, which persists in an immature or neurotic form; an inability to form normal attachments; arrested development.—English & English

Friendship: a relationship of trust with another person involving liking and rapport.

Individual marriage: the first step in Mead's two-step marriage proposal in which a legal marriage of limited commitment would be recognized although children would not be permitted.

Love: According to Jourard, it is an action a person undertakes to promote the happiness and growth of the being he loves. According to Fromm, as a love between equals, it is a union under the condition of preserving one's integrity and individuality; involves knowing, caring for, respecting, and encouraging the loved one. According to Maslow, a self-actualizing person is able to be natural, honest, and unguarded in a love relationship, and secure enough to encourage the growth (change) of the other.

Marriage: an institution or complex of social norms that sanctions the relationship of a man and woman and binds them in a system of mutual obligations and rights essential to the functioning of family life. —*A Modern Dictionary of Sociology*—Theoderson and Theoderson

Romantic love: an intense feeling of love based on physical attraction and projection of the person's own need, also tending to involve play acting and deception; infatuation.

Trial marriage: a marriage without sanction by law, with no defined rights and obligations; a free union, with protection of parties not assured and no necessary lasting commitment involved.

Two-step marriage: a proposal by Margaret Mead to separate the sexual, companionship aspects of marriage from the right to parenthood and to establish separate ceremonies for each.

*Approval given to
intelligence, beauty, and
valor enhances and
perfects them and makes
them produce finer
results than they could
have done by
themselves.*

Francois, Duc de la Rochefoucauld

Personality: Intelligence and Creativity

3 MANY people still think of personality and intelligence as separate, distinct aspects of our behavior. Here we are classifying intelligence as an aspect of personality because intelligence is influenced, modified, and controlled by the same factors that affect other aspects of personality. Intelligence, it has been observed (Combs, 1951), is limited or enhanced by a sizable number of factors that affect one's perceptual field or conscious awareness: nutrition and health, sensory experience, self-image, and motivational condition. The following discussion is based on this premise.

INTELLIGENCE TESTING: THE HISTORICAL BACKGROUND

Intelligence testing has been a major activity of psychologists since the beginning of their profession. The rapid growth of psychology between World Wars I and II was, in large part, due to the need for trained personnel to administer and interpret intelligence tests.

Although the term "intelligence" was used in ancient times, psychologists have been studying and measuring this ability only since the turn of the century. A number of attempts to construct tests were made in the nineteenth century, but they were largely unsuccessful. In 1904, the Minister of Public Instruction of France appointed a commission to study mental retardation in the schools. An objective means was needed to identify retarded youngsters in order to provide them with special classrooms in which instruction could be better adjusted to their learning rates. As a result of this study, Binet and Simon constructed the first practical intelligence test. By 1908 this test had been revised and the items age-graded.

Items placed at the 3-year age level were those which it was found the normal 3-year-old could answer. The child's score was

Box 3-1   A Case of Pseudo-feeblemindedness

During his clinical training the author tested a most interesting case of apparent feeblemindedness. A 35-year-old man was referred by a psychiatrist for intelligence testing to assess the degree of mental retardation. The psychiatrist estimated informally that the patient's IQ was in the neighborhood of 40 or 50, which is in the bottom 1 percent of the general population. There was concern whether he was bright enough to profit from psychotherapy.

The Wechsler Adult Intelligence Scale (WAIS) was administered. The WAIS has a number of subtests that can be scored separately, so that the psychologist can determine both a verbal and a performance IQ. The scores on the patient's individual subtests were within the normal limits, although somewhat low.

The most significant difficulty he had was with arithmetic. He did fine on addition and subtraction, but when asked a multiplication question, "What is 3 times 4?", he hesitated, looked puzzled, and replied, "That is not multiplication, is it?" The author, not suspecting the significance of the question, answered, "Yes, it is." He sighed and blurted out, "Oh, well, I don't do multiplication!" The response was so astonishing that after the testing session was over, the author attempted to teach the patient then and there the principle of successive addition, a disguised form of multiplication. He learned it quickly and proceeded to apply it without error—as long as one did not mention the offending word "multiplication."

Later it developed that this man had been reared by a mother who apparently had a *need* to have a mentally deficient son. She never encouraged him to be independent, and she undermined any feelings of competence he might have developed. Since he was of normal intelligence, he picked up the role fairly easily and became convinced himself that he was of very limited ability. When one mentioned something like the signal "multiplication" it was as if a steel door rolled down in his mind. His concept of self did not include being capable of multiplication. He would not even try.

---

expressed in terms of mental age. A child with a mental age of 3 years, 6 months, for example, answered all of the 3-year items and half of the 4-year items. (See Box 3-2)

As a result of Binet's success, interest in the use of such tests spread rapidly. Binet's test was an *individual* test, in that only one person at a time could be tested. During World War I, both sides in the conflict developed *group tests* (objective, paper-and-pencil tests) to screen military recruits quickly so they could be assigned duties in line with their talents. In the United States more than one million men were tested with an intelligence test constructed just for Army use—the Army Alpha.

After World War I, American schools, impressed by the military's successful use of the tests, adopted them enthusiastically. By the time of World War II, almost all American schools had become enthusiastic, if perhaps uncritical, users of these tests. Their popularity rests on the undeniable fact that an intelligence test is one of the best indications of a student's probable academic success.

Box 3-2   Binet Scales: Some Items from Two of the
Age Scales of Binet's Original Test

Age 7	Age 9
1. Shows right hand and left ear	1. Makes change from twenty sous
2. Gives description of pictures	2. Defines names of familiar objects in terms superior to use
3. Executes three commissions given simultaneously	3. Recognizes all nine (French) coins
4. Gives values of three single and three double sous	4. Gives months of the year in correct order
5. Names four colors: red, green, yellow, blue	5. Comprehends and answers easy problem questions

Reprinted from F. S. Freeman, *Theory and Practice of Psychological Testing,* 3rd ed. (New York: Holt, Rinehart and Winston, 1962), p. 110.

THE NATURE-NURTURE CONTROVERSY

You can't make a silk purse out of a sow's ear.

As the twig is bent, so grows the tree.

Johnny is a bright boy. His mother believes that his talent can be explained in terms of traits that "run in her family." His father, on the other hand, believes that Johnny's talent is due to the supportive environment of the home. Does it matter who is right?

The nature of intelligence has been somewhat obscured by the controversy between those who, like Johnny's mother, believe that hereditary factors are responsible for intellectual differences, and those who, like Johnny's father, hold that environment is the primary factor. The hereditarians tend to use tests to *select* people for training, or to fill certain jobs, whereas the environmentalists emphasize creating favorable learning opportunities. The two camps have very different ideas about what the proper role of education should be. The environmentalists tend to favor the view that "intelligence can be perfected through training." The hereditarians seek to measure some kind of "innate potential" and determine by tests who would best profit from training.

The behaviorists insisted on rejecting the kind of psychological emphasis which dealt with the mind in favor of concentrating on what could be observed directly, thus the emphasis on the study of behavior. Early behavioral psychologists such as John B. Watson unwittingly undermined the environmental position by overzealous claims. Watson once said, "Give me a baby and I'll make practically anything out of it, butcher, baker, or candlestick maker," apparently ignoring genetics altogether. It was not long before that view was seen as being much too simple. There *are* limitations on training imposed by

heredity, though in any individual case we may not be able to identify them. During the time of psychology's great expansion in the United States, between World Wars I and II, intelligence testing was dominated by experts who favored the hereditarian view of fixed intelligence. The reaction against the environmental position was such that the views of Alfred Binet, the father of the intelligence test, were ignored. Binet believed that intelligence could be improved through education. He even developed a system of intelligence training which he called *mental orthopedics* (1909), a carefully graded series of exercises designed to "cultivate and strenghten the attention, memory, perception, judgment, and will" (see Box 3-3).

Another example of the effects of the nature-nurture controversy may be seen in the somewhat less than open-minded reception given to the Montessori nursery school movement in America. When Dr. Maria Montessori's successful and popular methods for preschool education were brought from Italy to this country in 1913, her findings and theory were dismissed by experts here as outmoded. Montessori's method employed a kind of *sensory-perceptual training* of the child's mental abilities. This involved materials designed to elicit understanding by use. It gave the child a great deal of freedom to learn, but in a carefully prepared environment. The method was developed to prepare disadvantaged 2- through 5-year-old Italian children for school. The methods were apparently quite successful and became popular in

Box 3-3 The Education of Intelligence:
The Mental Orthopedics of Alfred Binet (1909)

Binet thought of intelligence as a combination of all the functions of discrimination, observation, perception, and retention. He thought that "anyone's intelligence is susceptible of being developed; with practice, training, and above all, with method one arrives at augmenting attention, memory, and judgment, and in becoming literally more intelligent than before; that improvement will continue until one reaches one's limit."

Binet and his co-workers attempted to apply his knowledge of intelligence to the practical task of training mentally retarded youngsters. In the school they started, they developed their system of "mental orthopedics" to cultivate and strengthen "attention, memory, perception, judgment, and will." The system included, for example, the following:

1. *"Statues."* This game was used to teach children to bring all their faculties into play in becoming absolutely motionless, thus helping them gain attention, will, and a measure of self-control.
2. *Pressure exercises.* Using a dynamometer, which measures handgrip strength, the child kept a record and competed with his own previous scores, thus measuring his growth in strength.
3. *Speed tests.* Here the child made as many dots as possible on a sheet of paper in a certain period of time, the idea being to get him to make an intense effort and provide him with encouragement (feedback).

4. *Development of motor skills.* Games were used, such as requiring a pupil to transport a bowl of water without spilling it, for training of both skill and will.
5. *Perceptual training.* Children were trained in observation, by asking them to perceive at a glance a large number of objects. The children were trained "to respond to questions about what they had seen in the street, in the court, or in class."
6. *Memory training.* Memory exercises were also employed with perceptual training. Pupils were asked to recall a series of words, digits, or sentences, which was gradually increased in length.
7. There were also exercises for training imagination, ingenuity, analysis, and judgment.

The proof of the training was illustrated dramatically one day to members of the French House of Deputies, who came to observe the facility before voting on the law regarding the retarded. After observing the perceptual-memory training, some deputies became fascinated and asked to try the exercises themselves. Then they performed less well than the retarded youngsters who had been trained. "The results," says Binet, "were astonishment, laughter, jokes of their colleagues, and all comments imaginable." The deputies were very much impressed to be outpaced by retarded children.

"We may say," Binet noted, that "the intelligence of these children has been increased. We have increased what constitutes the intelligence of the pupil, the capacity for learning and the capacity for assimilating instruction."

Europe. According to Hunt (1964), these methods seemed old-fashioned to American experts in 1914, because her views seemed out of step with the times. Specifically, two of the reasons they were rejected were, first, her notions of sensory-perceptual training appeared to conflict with the then dominant idea that a child's development was merely an orderly unfolding of inherited potentials and, second, the idea of fixed intelligence was then becoming entrenched in the United States and, indeed, would hold sway for nearly a half century. Although Montessori's method and theory seemed old fashioned to the experts of 1914, it seems modern and totally relevant today in light of what has been learned about the problems of educating disadvantaged children.

Historically, the controversy between hereditarians and environmentalists has produced more heat than light. More often than not, times during which scientific progress is slow are times during which scientists are asking essentially the wrong questions. The questions that stirred psychological debate for half a century about whether heredity or environment is more important in determining intelligence, or which factor has the greater relative influence, are still being debated today. Currently the debate centers around the assertions of Arthur Jensen (1969) about the extent to which intelligence is inherited. In summarizing the research literature on individual differences in IQ, Jensen concludes that, on the average, heredity accounts for about 80 percent of the individual differences. He notes, however, that intelligence has been traditionally defined rather narrowly and really only constitutes a limited pattern of the total range of mental abilities. When it comes to other mental abilities, such as rote learning ability, the environment plays a more important role. Studies of twins show that differences between individuals in school performance, for example, are determined only about half as much by heredity as are the differences in IQ.

Jensen goes on to speculate about the possibility of racial differences in IQ (again narrowly defined in terms of test scores). He believes that compensatory education has failed—a fact that is itself disputable—and failed largely because it has been used in an attempt to raise this narrowly defined intelligence, which is largely inherited. He argues for a strategy of compensatory education that stresses those mental abilities at which disadvantaged children excel.

It is probably true that heredity has greater relative influence than environment on a person's intelligence—at least that is the most popular view among psychologists at the moment. But environment is very influential, too, and, most important, *it is something we can do something about*. The mental potentialities we inherit still require environmental stimulation and opportunities in order to be developed. Thus, our intelligence is a product of the continuous interaction of these two sets of influences, and both are completely relevant. As Hebb says,

> . . . trying to determine the contribution of either heredity or environment to intelligence is like asking how much the width of a field contributes to its area and how much the length contributes. Neither can contribute anything without the other (1969, p. 26).

THE NATURE OF INTELLIGENCE

Everyone knows what intelligence is—that is what the intelligence test tests.

It is easier to say what intelligence is not than what it is.

If someone asks you how intelligent your best friend is, you are immediately able to give some kind of answer ("Oh, he can think up a million things to do, but he's stupid about money"). This fact indicates that we all have some kind of theory about intelligence, although we may not agree on what it includes. Psychologists have been measuring or testing intelligence for almost 70 years, but they too have not agreed completely on what is meant by the concept. Each test measures a pattern of abilities, but just what pattern depends on the particular test author's definition of intelligence. Some early definitions of intelligence are that it is:

> "Judgment, good sense, initiative, the ability to comprehend and to reason well and to adapt one's self to circumstance."
> "The ability to carry out abstract thinking."
> "The ability of the individual to adapt himself adequately to relatively new situations."
> "The ability to learn."

These definitions suggest the many different approaches taken by different intelligence-test constructors. Today some textbooks avoid the problem by simply concluding that "intelligence is what intelligence tests test."

Basic Components

What *do* the tests measure? In general, they measure a pattern of complex mental activities, the most important of which are several types of verbal skills, numerical ability, and memory; some perceptual and space factors; and the ability to reason abstractly.

Thus, as commonly measured by intelligence tests, intelligence may be defined as *a pattern of complex mental abilities*, including (1) *learning ability*, (2) *ability to comprehend and use abstract language*, and (3) *the ability to apply knowledge to new situations*. A test may also emphasize some factors that are minimized on another test, such as if intelligence is defined solely as learning ability.

(1) Learning ability. Most tests include items designed to measure aspects of learning ability. The person being tested is exposed to some sort of *novel learning task*, such as the rapid learning of a code, to demonstrate the speed and power of his learning ability. The *learning task* must be novel so that no child can have an advantage because he has already practiced it. The assumption is made that differences in performance on the task are due to differences in learning ability and not in experience. Over the years, psychologists have devoted a great deal of time and effort to attempts to rule out all possible effects of prior experience, first by constructing so-called "culture-free" tests, and then, when that proved impossible, "culture-fair" tests.

All these attempts were essentially fruitless because culture is a part of the situation in which intelligent behavior takes place. The assumption that performance differences on a given task are due to differences in learning ability and not experience can only be justified if the people tested are from similar cultural backgrounds, and the materials used in testing are common to the experience of the whole culture. If items, for example, are based on the number system, if they use only very common vocabulary, or information which everyone should be expected to know, they should be acceptable.

In the following example, cited in Pressey (1933), violation of this assumption could lead to a mistaken interpretation of a person's response. Some "poor white" children in Kentucky were being tested. One boy was asked, "if you went to the store and bought 6 cents worth of candy and gave the clerk 10 cents, what change would you get?" This seems to be a simple item designed to test ability to subtract, but to this child it was so lacking in relevance to his experience that it might as well have been in a foreign language. He replied: "I never had 10 cents, and if I had I wouldn't spend it for candy, and anyway candy is what your mother makes."

The tester tried again. Question: "If you had taken 10 cows to pasture and 6 strayed away, how many would you have left to drive home?" Answer: "I wouldn't dare go home." Question: "If there were 10 children in a school, and 6 were out with the measles, how many would there be in school?" Answer: "None, because the rest would be afraid of catching it too" (pp. 237–238).

But from these answers, of course, we do not really know anything about this boy's ability to compute. When we score his answers wrong, as we must, we only point up the difference between his culture and that of the test maker.

In most cases, however, we are correct in assuming a common background of experience, and in those cases different scores do actually reflect a difference in learning ability.

(2) Ability to comprehend and use abstract language.   Tests that measure vocabulary, reasoning, interpreting, and analyzing language measure the comprehension and use of abstract language. (See the similarities and vocabulary items in Box 3-4.) The ability to reason logically is also measured by tests such as verbal absurdities.

Box 3-4   Some Illustrative Items from The Stanford-Binet Test

The sample items below should be passed, on the average, at the ages indicated.

Age	Type of Item	Examples or Description
2	Three-hole form board	Places form (e.g., circle) in correct hole.
	Block building	Builds tower from model after demonstration.
3	Identifying parts of the body	Points out hair, mouth, etc., on large paper doll.
4	Naming objects from memory	One of three objects (e.g., toy dog or shoe) is covered after child has seen them but is not looking; child then names object from memory.
	Picture identification	Points to correct pictures of objects on a card when asked, "Show me what we cook on," or "What do we carry when it is raining?"
7	Similarities	Answers such questions as, "in what way are coal and wood alike? Ship and automobile?"
	Copying a diamond	Copies a diamond in the record booklet.
8	Vocabulary	Defines eight words from a list.
9	Verbal absurdities	"I saw a well-dressed young man who was walking down the street with his hands in his pockets and twirling a brand new cane. What is foolish about that?"
	Digit reversal	Must repeat five digits backward.
	Vocabulary	Defines twenty words from a list.
Average adult	Proverbs	Explains in own words the meaning of two or more common proverbs.
	Orientation	"Which direction would you have to face so your right hand would be toward the north?"

Reprinted from L. M. Terman & M. A. Merrill, *Measuring Intelligence* (Boston: Houghton Mifflin, 1937), pp. 96, 168.

(3) Ability to apply knowledge to new situations. Tests that call for solving problems by using logic and previously acquired knowledge may be said to measure the ability to apply knowledge to new situations. (See the proverbs and orientation items in Box 3-4.)

It may begin to be apparent that definitions of intelligence depend on the cultural background of the person who constructed the intelligence test. Thus, intelligence is a *pattern* of abilities which is socially recognized and valued. Consequently, not all abilities are included in the pattern *we* may call intelligence; some observable mental abilities—for example, many creative abilities—are usually left out. The observation that "intelligence is what the tests test" can now be seen to mean that definitions of intelligence are relative to culture, and that intelligence is neither more nor less than what the experts say it is.

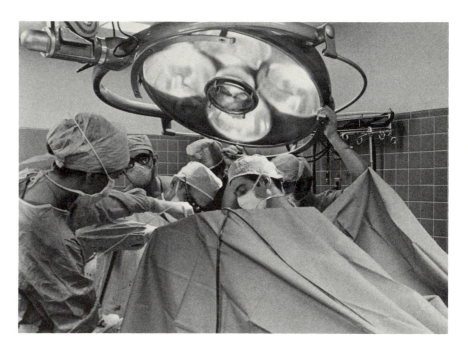

Ethnic Differences in Intelligence

Some differences in *test scores* may be correlated with background factors. Children from families of higher social class do better, in general, than those from lower-class backgrounds. In general, some ethnic groups score better, some worse, than the white, Anglo-Saxon, Protestant (WASP) majority. These differences do not necessarily reflect any inherited differences in intellectual ability. In fact, there is a good deal of evidence that they are due to particular factors in environmental experience.

Children from Jewish culture or Oriental backgrounds tend to get *higher* average IQ scores than do WASPs. Children of Negro, Mexican-American, Puerto Rican, or Indian background tend to get *lower* average IQ scores than do WASPs. There is a relationship between the general subcultural attitude toward education and average IQ scores. Ethnic groups that organize their family life and goals around encouraging the education of children attain the highest average IQ scores and have also progressed most in American society.

The case of the Orientals is instructive. Prejudice and discrimination against most Asians persisted to mid-century. One only has to remember the mass hysteria against the Japanese (and Japanese-Americans) that resulted in their removal from the Western states during World War II, and their loss of civil rights and property, to realize how far they have come since then.

Today the percentage of college-age Asian-Americans going to college is much higher than that of the majority. Like other successful groups in our society, they have emphasized the importance of education. The schools have been their passport to better jobs, housing, and an increasing share of this country's affluence. Today they hardly constitute a disadvantaged minority.

Geographical and Racial Differences in Intelligence

Selective Service data obtained during World Wars I and II revealed that the *average* IQ of people living in different geographic regions varied a good deal. In general, the average scores on the tests were highest for recruits from the North and West and lowest from the South, Southeast, and Southwest. Interestingly, there was a gross relationship between the amounts of money spent per child on public education and how well the entire population did on the test. States that spent the least on public education were also the same states with the lowest average test scores and the highest Selective Service rejection rates. Another finding: although blacks scored generally lower than whites in each region, the average scores of blacks in the North and West *were higher* than the average of whites in the South. The test rankings by region were (1) Northern and Western whites, (2) Northern and Western blacks, (3) Southern whites, and (4) Southern blacks. These findings make it clear that we are dealing with general cultural differences (correlated with education) rather than with racial differences.

Another line of evidence makes it clear that the test scores of blacks tend to improve markedly when they move from the rural South to the urban North. In a 1935 study, Klineberg found that the intelligence test scores of black youngsters increased with length of residence in New York. Children who had been in New York for a number of years attained average scores almost as high as blacks who had always lived in the urban North. Klineberg interprets this finding in terms of the degree to which children have learned the general cultural background that the test takes for granted.

Lee (1951) duplicated Klineberg's study in Philadelphia and found essentially the same results. The fact that the scores went up does not imply that the potential of the youngsters has changed. Rather, living in the city may be seen to reduce the cultural handicap that normally prevents them from demonstrating their true ability. Intelligence tests are biased against both rural children and those from ethnic minorities. Thus, cultural bias can be expected to reduce their scores if they are not as familiar as other children with the objects used in the test, if they lack interest in these objects, or if they lack motivation to perform well on the test.

One study showed that the racial identity of the tester also

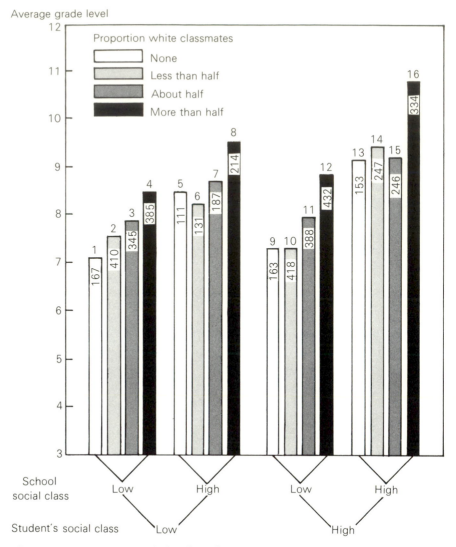

Average grade level

Figure 3-1. Average grade-level performance of twelfth-grade Negro students by individual social-class origin, social-class level of school, and proportion of white classmates last year; metropolitan Northeast. The numbers in the bars represent the number of cases. (Source: U.S. Commission on Civil Rights analysis of Office of Education Survey data, 1966—Coleman Report.)

affects how well children score. Forrester & Klaus (1964) found that a group of black children got average scores six points higher when tested by a black examiner than by a white.

The Coleman Report, *Equality of Educational Opportunity* (1966), is probably the best and most conclusive study yet conducted by social scientists about the achievement of blacks. The study of 600,000 young-sters in 4000 schools shows that the school achievement of black children is highly dependent both on social class and on the degree of integration of the schools. Figure 3-1 shows that twelfth-grade Negro youngsters did best when both they and the schools they attended were of higher social status. The difference in achievement was more than *two* full grade levels between children from lower class back-grounds attending lower class schools (column 4) and children from higher class attending higher status schools (column 16)! Furthermore, within each class category it made a tremendous difference whether the school attended was segregated or integrated. Among higher class students attending a higher class school, the difference is nearly two full grade levels, depending on whether they were in totally segregated black schools (column 16). The combined effect is very nearly *four* full grade levels' difference in achievement (column 1 versus column 16)! The Coleman Report concludes that student or "input" factors (e.g., the social class, ethnic background, and motivation of students) are of prime importance. The quality of school and curriculum are less important than most educators suppose. Black youngsters perform better in fully integrated schools because of the importance of peer pressure in molding favorable attitudes and values about education. Achievement is most likely to blossom in a school in which middle-class attitudes about achievement prevail.

Attitudes about fate control (discussed in Chapter 1) are a crucial factor. It was found that black youngsters in fully integrated schools were much more likely to feel that they were in control of their own destinies, whereas those in segregated schools believed that chance ruled their lives, that there was little they could do personally to be successful.

One reason why all-black schools produce much lower levels of average achievement (with some exceptions) is the prevalence of various attitudes such as the dropout mentality. Young people learn a great deal from one another. A potential dropout may associate with other students whose negative social pressure about school achievement reinforce his feelings about dropping out. If they leave, they often try to convert him to their way of thinking, as if that would convince them that they had done the right thing. (This "proselytizing mechanism" is like that of a religious person who may deepen his own faith by trying to convert others or of a member of Alcoholics Anonymous who helps keep himself dry by "being a friend in need" to other alcoholics.) Even when a youngster does not follow suit, this defeatist attitude is infectious and pervades segregated schools.

Nutritional and Health Factors Affecting Intelligence

It should be no surprise that low IQ is associated with poverty. Many people try to explain this fact by saying that "talent rises to the top and lack of it sinks to the bottom" of the social-class structure. One of the most startling discoveries of recent years throws doubt on this simple explanation.

Poor nutrition, especially protein deficiency, can result in a host of complications of pregnancy, such as prematurity, which are associated with low IQ and mental deficiency. A study of the New Orleans Charity Hospital revealed that the diets of 92 percent of impoverished black women and 74 percent of impoverished white women were "poor" or "very poor" in protein, and averaged only 46 grams daily for the whole group. This is only a fraction of the recommended level needed by a pregnant woman for adequate nutrition. But these women had been nourished at this low level during their entire lifetimes. Inadequate protein in the diet results in a level of premature delivery that is 10 times higher than normal. One expert, Aldrich (1963), says that 22 percent of babies born prematurely will be so retarded as to require permanent care in an institution (versus 0.3 percent in the general population). In other words, these hapless infants will be 73 times more likely than typical children to wind up in institutions for the retarded. Retarded intelligence, which results from such factors, can be called *nutritional mental deficiency*.

In addition, the health of these mothers is poor and they have astoundingly high rates of numerous diseases, many of which are correlated with restricted intellectual functioning. The most direct cause of these diseases is lack of money for adequate medical care.

> Nonwhites have death rates, for example, up to more than twice those of whites for the following diseases: meningitis, measles, encephalitis, diphtheria, whooping cough, scarlet fever, nephritis, influenza and pneumonia. Many of these, if not promptly and properly treated, leave their mark upon the survivors in the form of permanent damage to the central nervous system, the apparatus of intelligence (Hurley, 1967, p. 65).

Sex Differences in Intelligence

There are no *overall* differences in intelligence between men and women, at least not as measured by summary IQ scores; but then the items were selected in the first place so as to minimize any such differences. However, in the working world there are enormous differences in achievement, which ought to correlate closely, one would think, with intelligence test scores. Consider the following subtests included in general IQ tests, where we do find some sex differences (based on Anastasi, 1958):

Favoring Males	*Favoring Females*
Numerical ability	Verbal fluency (not reasoning)
Visualizing perceptual spatial tasks	Memory-related tasks
Performance and mechanical tasks	Manual dexterity
Shorter reaction time	Perceptual speed
	Attention to detail

These differences (which cancel each other out overall) suggest that men and women have a different patterning of mental abilities. Eleanor Macoby (1966) concludes that the "two sexes would appear to have somewhat different intellectual strengths and weaknesses, and hence different influences serve to counteract the weaknesses and augment the strengths" (p. 51).

The Intellectual Development of Women

Until the age of puberty, girls achieve better than boys in school; they get consistently higher grades and are better liked by teachers. This edge begins to drop noticeably, however, about the time girls enter high school, although the forces responsible are at work much earlier.

A fascinating study was made by Sontag, Baker, & Nelson (1958) of children showing large IQ gains between the ages of 3 and 12. The researchers measured IQ for the first time at 3, then again at 4.

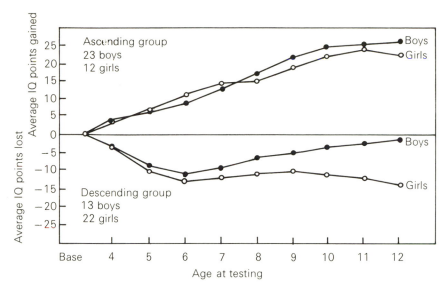

Figure 3-2.   I.Q. gain and loss among boys and girls aged 3 to 12. (Source: Sontag, Baker, and Nelson, 1958.)

Of the 140 children originally studied, they selected for long-range study those 35 children showing the largest IQ *gains* and those 35 showing the largest IQ *losses* between ages 3 and 4. As Figure 3-2 makes clear, the most striking thing about the results is that there are nearly twice as many boys as girls showing gains (23 versus 12) and twice as many girls as boys showing losses (22 versus 13). Even in the amount gained and lost there are impressive differences: the average boy who increased gained 25 IQ points by age 12, whereas the average girl gained only a little over 20 IQ points. The difference among IQ losers is even more significant: the average girl in the decreasing group at 12 years had lost about 15 IQ points, whereas the average boy had lost almost nothing— only 2 IQ points! In other words, the boys who showed the greatest IQ loss at age 4 by age 12 showed only 2 points loss. Evidently they gained back much of what they lost earlier.

Looking beyond IQ, the researchers correlated personality factors to IQ gain and loss, and they discovered that children who gained IQ tended to be aggressive, dominant, independent, active, and competitive. They tended to have conflict with their brothers and sisters and to be very independent about doing what they wanted to do when they wanted to do it. The perceptive reader, noting that these results apply to both sexes, will recognize that *girls who gain intelligence* have personality characteristics that belong to the male stereotype.

Is it any wonder, then, that bright girls enter a time of intense conflict when they begin high school? The pressures to be attractive and popular among the opposite sex are very powerful at adolescence. Have you ever heard anyone say, "Better be careful, don't be too bright, the girls won't like you," to a bright and handsome *boy*? But what about "Its not smart to be smart" directed at a bright girl?

Girls are assailed from all sides with the view that they should not try to compete with boys intellectually, and bright girls tend to perform much better when they are not in direct competition with boys (Horner, 1969). Boys, on the other hand, are given every chance to develop their intelligence, and their performance is, as a group, not undermined by competition.

Girls *are* given free reign in another area: the free expression of their emotionality. But boys are trained from an early age to control rigidly their emotions. Cultural training, then, tends to exaggerate both intellectual and emotional differences between the sexes. The boys are pushed one way and the girls the other.

As with ethnic minorities and IQ, the concept of "fate control" obviously affects the intellectual functioning of women: their attitude of impaired fate control is produced in reaction to unequal life opportunities. Such opportunities, it must be added, are not limited to those commonly noticed, such as employment and professional training. The expectations of others who are parents, teachers, family friends and the like can be seen to be daily opportunities for a child to be noticed for his display of this or that trait. Both girls and children of ethnic minorities are apt to meet repeatedly expectations that they will achieve indifferently.

THE NATURE OF CREATIVITY

Great souls are not those with fewer passions and more virtues than the ordinary run, but simply those with a stronger sense of purpose.

Francois, Duc de La Rochefoucauld

Genius, in truth, means little more than the faculty of perceiving in an unhabitual way.

William James

Intelligence and Creativity

Creativity, like intelligence, may be defined as a complex pattern of mental abilities, but a number of studies make it clear that these two patterns are not the same. In a study using various personality assessment devices designed to tap creativity, Getzels & Jackson (1962) found almost no relationship between tests of intelligence and creativity, although persons scoring high on either one tended to do equally well on standardized tests designed to measure school achievement. Attitudes of school teachers, however, were much less favorable toward the highly creative group, which they tended to label "overachievers" (a negative term), whereas they labeled the highly intelligent group "gifted."

In a further study of the values and aspirations of creative versus intelligent students, Getzels & Jackson discovered that high-IQ students have values and aspirations they believe lead to success in the adult world, whereas highly creative persons have values and aspirations that they themselves value and that are *not* those they feel will lead to conventional success in the adult world. The researchers observe that

. . . it is hardly surprising that our high IQ students are more favored by

teachers than our creative students. The high IQ students value and disvalue the same objects and ideals as they believe their teachers do; the high creativity students do not. And if the motivational impetus represented by a concern with adult success and a desire to emulate their teachers is absent or weak among high creativity students, the observed relationship between creativity and school achievement becomes all the more significant. The results cannot be attributed to some special kind of motivation like "striving for good grades or success" which it is said leads to so-called "overachievement" (p. 36).

One of the largest differences between the two groups was in "sense of humor." High creatives value humor highly and they also actually display more humor and playfulness in their behavior.

When the fantasies (made-up stories) of the two groups were analyzed, it was found that "the high creative adolescents were significantly higher than the *high IQ adolescents in stimulus-free themes, unexpected endings, humor, incongruities,* and *playfulness,* and showed a marked tendency toward more *violence* in their stories" (p. 38).

Fostering High Achievement, Intelligence, and Creativity

The idea of fixed intelligence has been, in the author's opinion, a destructive and limiting factor in deliberate attempts to cultivate achievement, intelligence, and creativity. We now know that there are scores of factors that may depress the effectiveness of a person's behavior. It would appear reasonable to believe that what can be depressed can also be elevated, but we are less sure about just how to accomplish this goal. Below are a number of ideas about how high achievement and intelligence might be fostered.

(1) Perception and experience. We can make sure that children are exposed during the crucial preschool years to a rich variety of perceptual experiences, on which school learning can build. There is already some evidence that exposure to the TV program *Sesame Street* has had a very great effect on children, especially those coming from disadvantaged backgrounds. These are children whose natural life experiences fail to include much that is taken for granted in school. It is significant that preliminary research findings show that disadvantaged youngsters watching the program gained as much as more privileged youngsters. In fact, the gains of Spanish-speaking children and rural children were the greatest of all groups, suggesting that the program content is right "on target," helping those who need help the most (Anonymous, 1971e).

(2) Nutrition and medicine. We can make sure that children are adequately nourished during their childhood so that they can be receptive to school experiences. A hungry child cannot learn. Adequate medical and dental care is also essential. A child in poor health or suffering from a toothache cannot concentrate on his studies. A *universal* school lunch program would ensure every child a basic minimum nutrition. Prospective parents need to be educated to the facts about "nutritional mental deficiency" and how to avoid it. Much of this damage to children can only be avoided if mothers bring to childbearing a healthy body—which has itself had a life-long adequate nutrition. No country can afford senseless damage to its children.

(3) Attitudes. We can teach children to respect learning and see its relevance to their own lives. Families can show their children a good example by providing books and magazines in the home and encouraging children to use them. Children who develop their intelligence to its maximum tend to come from homes in which ideas and issues are taken seriously. Attitudes toward school should be positive. For disadvantaged children, the dropout attitude, mentioned previously, must be countered. The home and school need to work more closely to promote positive attitudes toward school and intellect.

(4) Motivation and personality. As parents and teachers, we can encourage children to be independent and self-reliant. We can help them develop a positive self-image by exposing them to tasks within their developing talents so that they can experience success. We can also be sure to encourage positive accomplishments and provide plenty

of praise when it is due. Although we cannot "give" another person trust in self, we can provide the interpersonal and environmental conditions in which a child repeatedly discovers and confirms his adequacy.

Creativity is even more related to learned personality characteristics than is intelligence or achievement. MacKinnon (1962) has defined creativity in terms of originality, adaptiveness, and realization, taking place over a considerable period of time:

> It involves a response or an idea that is novel or at the very least statistically infrequent. But novelty or originality of thought or action, while a necessary aspect of creativity, is not sufficient. If a response is to lay claim to being a part of the creative process, it must to some extent be adaptive to, or of, reality. It must serve to solve a problem, fit a situation, or accomplish some recognizable goal. And, thirdly, true creativeness involves a sustaining of the original insight, an evaluation and elaboration of it, a developing of it to the full.

According to MacKinnon's study of creativity, the parents of creative children display a remarkable respect for the child and his ability to decide for himself wisely. They succeed in fostering the child's developing sense of autonomy. He notes that creative people come from families in which the mothers were energetic persons who "led active lives with interests and sometimes careers of their own apart from their husbands'." These children were presented with clear standards of conduct, often with a complex set of values promoting integrity. These families also stressed being forthright and honest, respecting others, taking pride in one's work, developing talents, and being ambitious.

DUANE BELCHER

Fixed IQ—A Critical Study

Some 30 years ago in Iowa, a very unusual experiment was conducted with 13 mentally retarded orphans which resulted in spectacular, almost unbelievable, IQ gains over a period of just a few years. At first the scientific community scoffed at these results. Like so many discoveries, this one was inspired by accidental events. Dr. Harold Skeels and his assistant, Dr. Marie Skodak, had tested two baby girls, both a year old, and found them severely retarded with IQs of 46 and 35. Because of severe overcrowding at the orphanage, these children were transferred to an adult institution for the retarded, Woodward State School and Hospital.

About a year later, Dr. Skeels and Dr. Skodak had occasion to visit Woodward, and on making their rounds were surprised to see the two girls, bright and alert, playing happily among the older inmates. They could scarcely believe that these were the same two children. They were tested again and it was found that their IQs had increased to 77 and 87. Although Dr. Skeels was unable to account for what had happened, it was decided to leave the children where they were. A year later the children were tested again. The results were astonishing in a day when the notion of fixed IQ was taken for granted. The girl who first tested at IQ 35, increased to 87 at two years, and 88 by age three. The other girl went from 46 to 77 and then finally to 100, which is the average for the general population.

The investigators decided to find out what had been happening to the girls. Skeels (1966) describes the results:

The two girls had been placed on one of the wards of older, brighter girls and women, ranging in age from 18 to 50 years and in mental age from 5 to 9 years, where they were the only children of preschool age, except for a few hopeless bed patients with gross physical defects. An older girl on the ward had "adopted" each of the two girls, and other older girls served as adoring aunts. Attendants and nurses also showed affection to the two, spending time with them, taking them along on their days off for automobile rides and shopping excursions, and purchasing toys, picture books, and play materials for them in great abundance. The setting seemed to be a homelike one, abundant in affection, rich in wholesome and interesting experiences, and geared to a preschool level of development.

It was recognized that as the children grew older, their developmental needs would be less adequately met in the institution for the mentally retarded. Furthermore, they were now normal and the need for care in such an institution no longer existed. Consequently, they were transferred back to the orphanage and shortly thereafter were placed in adoptive homes.[*]

Dr. Skeels next went to the official in charge of Orphanages and Institutions for the retarded to tell the story of these two girls. He asked permission to repeat this natural experiment with more subjects. Skeels suggested that these orphans had little to lose and everything to gain in the experiment. Typically in that day, when orphans stayed in orphanages they lost IQ. Babies were kept in cribs surrounded with white sheeting, which shut out stimulation. They had few toys and little human contact.

[*]Reprinted from Harold M. Skeels, "Adult Status of Children with Contrasting Early Life Experiences," *Monographs of the Society for Research in Child Development, 31,* Ser. No. 105 (1966): 6, 16–17. By permission of The Society for Research in Child Development, Inc.

We now understand this IQ drop as being primarily a reaction to the lack of a stimulating environment, not due to institutionalization itself.

Skeels wanted to select a new group for transfer to the adult institution. They would be classified as "house guests" rather than as inmates, to make later adoption easier. In the end, eleven children were selected to make up this new experimental group. Skeels explained what happened next:

> As with the first two children, who, by chance, were the first participants in the experiment, the attendants and the older girls became very fond of the children placed on their wards and took great pride in them. In fact, there was considerable competition among wards to see which one would have its "baby" walking or talking first. Not only the girls, but the attendants spent a great deal of time with "their children," playing, talking, and training them in every way. The children received constant attention and were the recipients of gifts; they were taken on excursions and were exposed to special opportunities of all kinds. For example, it was the policy of the matron in charge of the girls' school division to single out certain children who she felt were in need of special individualization and to permit them to spend some time each day visiting her office. This furnished new experiences, such as being singled out, receiving special attention and affection, new play materials, additional language stimulation, and meeting other office callers.
>
> The spacious living rooms of the wards furnished ample space for indoor play and activity. Whenever weather permitted, the children spent some time each day on the playground under the supervision of one or more older girls. Here they were able to interact with other children of similar ages. Outdoor play equipment included tricycles, swings, slides, sand boxes, etc. The children also began to attend the school kindergarten as soon as they could walk. Toddlers remained for only half the morning and 4- and 5-year-olds, the entire morning. Activities carried on in the kindergarten resembled preschool rather than the more formal type of kindergarten.
>
> As part of the school program, the children attended daily 15-minute exercises in the chapel, which included group singing and music by the orchestra. The children also attended the dances, school programs, movies, and Sunday chapel services.
>
> In considering this enriched environment from a dynamic point of view, it must be pointed out that in the case of almost every child, some one adult (older girl or attendant) became particularly attached to him and and figuratively "adopted" him. As a consequence, an intense one-to-one adult-child relationship developed, which was supplemented by the less intense but frequent interactions with the other adults in the environment. Each child had some one person with whom he was identified and who was particularly interested in him and his achievements. This highly stimulating emotional impact was observed to be the unique characteristic and one of the main contributions of the experimental setting [pp. 16–17].

After the study was over it was realized that all the data existed in the files from which a control group—called here a contrast group—could be selected. A dozen children were chosen and they provided a base line against which the experimental group changes could be evaluated.

The results with the original two babies were repeated again with the new "house guest" group of eleven. Before the experiment, their IQs had ranged from 36 to 89, with an average of 64. After the experiment, five exceeded 100, one soared to 113, and the average climbed to 92. These are spectacular gains, and they were made in all cases, except one, within two years or less. The other case increased, but more slowly, and took four years to reach its maximum.

Nine of these children were placed for adoption, as were the original two. Two children were returned to the orphanage, where these gains diminished. Two years after the nine had been adopted, Dr. Skeels evaluated them again. No child who had been adopted had an IQ of less than 90. The average had increased further to 96 (normal).

The fate of the contrast group was sadly different. These children did not have the good fortune of being mothered by the retarded women at Woodward. They were tested, however, at the same times. Over the period when the others were house guests, their average IQ declined from 87 to 66. The brightest child fell from 103 to 49. Less than 1 percent of the population scores as low.

After World War II, an attempt was made

to do a follow-up study on how these two groups had fared a quarter century later. It was possible to track them all down and evaluate the success of their lives in general terms. All of the house guest males had become self-supporting. The average educational level completed was 12 years. Of the three boys, one had become a noncommissioned officer in the Air Force, one was a sales manager, and the third was a vocational counselor. Of the ten girls, eight had married and appeared to be leading satisfying family lives. Among their number was a teacher, a registered nurse, a practical nurse, a beautician, and an office clerk. The two girls who had never been adopted wound up in low-status jobs as domestics. The house guest children had a combined total of 28 children whose average IQ was 104, ranging from 95 to 125.

None of the contrast group children were adopted. The average educational achievement was 4 years. Only two ever married, and one was subsequently divorced. Four remained in state institutions and never held jobs. Of six living on their own, three had jobs as dish-washers. One had a job folding napkins in a cafeteria. One male was classified as a floater. Only one of this entire group was successful in the conventional sense, working as a skilled linotype operator for a newspaper. Even this case seems to be the exception that proves the rule because this man as a child suffered from a hearing problem, which resulted in his being placed in a resident school for the deaf, where he got plenty of love and attention—much like the house guest children.

It has been calculated that the contrast group had spent an aggregate total of 273 years in institutions at a cost of $138,000 in public funds. The house guest group had all become productive members of society and paid taxes during one year alone, ranging from $38 to $848.

Although this study has been criticized, chiefly because of method, it is now recognized as a classic, casting new doubt on the theory of fixed intelligence. It has tremendous contemporary relevance in terms of the current interest in compensatory education.

Summarizing Statements

1. Intelligence is an aspect of personality that is influenced, modified, and controlled by the same factors that affect other aspects of personality.

2. The first successful intelligence test was developed by Binet in France in 1904. An intelligence test is one of the best indicators of a student's probable school success.

3. Environmentalists have favored the view that intelligence could be improved through training. Hereditarians have used tests to measure what they believed was innate potential, mostly for selection purposes. The idea of fixed intelligence was accepted by most psychologists in this country for nearly 50 years, although the father of the IQ test, Binet, believed that intelligence was educable. Binet developed a system of "mental orthopedics" to train the intelligence of retarded children.

4. Although heredity has a relatively greater influence than does environment in determining intelligence, the environment is very important and is often all we can do anything about. Neither factor contributes anything without the other.

5. Intelligence is a complex pattern of mental abilities. An IQ test measures a particular pattern that is valued culturally. Definitions of intelligence are relative to culture. What we call intelligence leaves out many mental abilities—for example, many of those measured by tests of creativity.

6. Different ethnic groups get different average IQs, depending chiefly on the general subcultural attitude toward education and achievement. These scores may decline or increase, depending on exposure to the common culture, social class, and extent of integration in the schools the children attend. There are also geographical differences in intelligence favoring Northerners and Westerners over Southerners. Urban children also outscore rural children. Black children get higher scores (a) in the North, (b) in urban areas, (c) when they are in integrated schools, and (d) when they are tested by Negro examiners. There is no real evidence that ethnic differences in IQ are due to anything other than the effect of environmental disadvantage.

7. Fate control is a crucial factor in the school achievement of black children. It is more common in well-integrated schools than segregated ones. Achievement motivation is promoted by positive peer pressure in middle-class schools and families. Segregated schools promote negative motives such as that of the "dropout mentality."

8. Mental retardation is associated with poverty. Poor nutrition, especially lack of sufficient protein, results in high rates of premature birth among pregnant women. Prematurity is associated with high rates of mental retardation. This condition may be called "nutritional mental deficiency." Numerous diseases common among the poor are also associated with damage to the nervous system (affecting intelligence).

9. There seems to be a different patterning of mental abilities among women compared to men, although there are no overall differences in general IQ. Girls achieve better in school up until the time that they get to high school. Bright girls are observed to experience a decline in tested IQ more often than boys. Growth in intelligence is associated with masculine personality characteristics such as aggressiveness, dominance, independence, activity, and competiveness. Apparently, the culture conditions women to believe that intellectual achievement is unladylike. Women suffer from lack of ability to control their fate, just as do many ethnic minorities.

10. Pseudo-feeblemindedness is a condition in which a normal person has been trained to play the role of a mentally retarded person. The condition appears to be related to an overprotective style of childrearing.

11. Creativity is a complex pattern of mental abilities different from intelligence. Creative persons tend to be independent and nonconforming to the values of the school. Creative persons do just as well as intelligent persons on achievement tests but are less liked by teachers.

12. Creative behavior is novel and original behavior applied appropriately to a practical situation; it involves a "sustaining of the original insight, an evaluation and elaboration of it, a developing of it to the full." An acute sense of humor is also characteristic of creative people.

13. The author believes that achievement, intelligence, and creativity can all be fostered by appropriate support of positive strivings in children. Specific reference was made to improvements affecting (a) perception and experience, (b) nutrition and medical/dental care, (c) attitudes, and (d) motivation and personality.

READING SELECTION

14. The reading about fixed IQ examines a classic study, which demonstrated that large IQ gains and losses among children could take place. These changes were found to be associated with characteristics of the early childhood environment—specifically, love and attention.

15. A group of orphans was placed in an adult institution for the retarded as "house guests," where they were adopted by the women inmates. A contrast group remained in the orphanage. The average IQ of the house guest group rose 40 points over a period of years, while the contrast group declined 20 points.

16. A follow-up study 25 years later demonstrated that these effects were real, producing success for the house guest group. They were well educated, had successful marriages and careers, and had all become self sufficient. Nearly half the contrast group never left state institutions. Only two married, one of those was subsequently divorced. Those who did become self sufficient held low-paying, low-status jobs.

Terms and Concepts

Achievement motive: "an internalized standard of excellence motivating the person to do well in any achievement-oriented situation involving intelligence and leadership ability."—Horner

Creativity: a complex pattern of mental abilities characterized by originality, adaptiveness, and realization.

Cultural bias of IQ tests: the fact that IQ tests favor persons from an urban environment who understand and share the core culture. Most ethnic groups are affected, as are white children from rural backgrounds.

Ethnic group: a group that is seen and sees itself as different from the majority. Often a religious, racial, or nationality group.

Intelligence: a pattern of complex mental abilities, commonly measured by intelligence tests, including (1) learning ability, (2) ability to comprehend and use abstract language, and (3) the ability to apply knowledge to new situations.

Mental orthopedics: a system designed by Binet to cultivate and strengthen attention, memory, perception, judgment, and will and thus develop intelligence.

Nutritional mental deficiency: low IQ produced by inadequate nutrition, especially lack of protein during crucial development.

Pseudo-feeblemindedness: a rare condition in which the person has learned to play the role of a mentally retarded person.

Stanford-Binet: the most famous individual intelligence test. Developed by Terman at Stanford University from the original Binet scale.

WASP: White, Anglo-Saxon Protestant; used in reference to the majority culture.

WAIS: Wechsler Adult Intelligence Scale.

Every man takes the limits of his field of vision for the limits of the world.

Arthur Schopenhauer, "Further Psychological Observations," Parerga and Paralipomena (tr. T. Bailey Saunders)

All seems infected that th' infected spy
As all looks yellow to the jaundic'd eye.

Alexander Pope, An Essay on Criticism

There are no ugly loves nor handsome prisons.

Benjamin Franklin, Poor Richard's Almanac

Attitudes and Values

4 UNDERSTANDING, predicting, and modifying behavior are often said to be the three major goals of psychology. The expression "modifying behavior" sometimes produces confusion or anxiety, but what we mean by it is that, when applied to a person, it will help him achieve new or better self-control over behavior that has been a problem for him. However, before we can modify behavior—our own or anyone else's—we must, of course, know enough to be able to predict it. And, obviously, we cannot predict behavior without a good understanding of it.

One way to really understand a person is to look at his *attitudes* and *values*, concepts that indicate one's behavior tend to be organized consistently over a long period of time. Likewise, the basic psychological processes of learning, perception, and motivation (discussed in the next few chapters) are also ways of understanding his organization, each a slightly different way of "cutting the pie." When we know enough about a person's attitudes and values we can begin to relate to him with more understanding because we can anticipate (predict) his behavior.

Consider David, 17, an "A" student who is about to begin college. While growing up, he, like all of us, has developed many different attitudes and values about people and the world and his place in the scheme of things. In what follows, David talks about a job he once had and one of the families he observed while working.

I worked for a summer cutting lawns with a fellow who had his own business. We cut one lawn that was like a putting green. The shrubs around the house would have run about four to five thousand dollars, and new ones were appearing every week. The house itself would have sold for at least ninety thousand dollars; they had two cars, a Mark III and a Corvette Coupe. Up front, out where you could see it, a hundred thousand was invested in presenting his image. But there was only a kitchen table inside the house. The living room was bare, same with the dining room. The bedroom windows had curtains that were always drawn. The owner always gave us a beer and then paid the boss off from this roll of bills about the size of your fist. The lawn job cost twenty-five dollars, always a twenty and a five. There is this other part of suburban greed, these people all had riding lawn mowers which cost in the neighborhood of twelve hundred dollars. But they never used them. The paint was still fresh except for the dust settled on it. They looked like relics from a past age. The excuse for the bare rooms was that the house was being redecorated, but I doubt if it takes four or five months for any furniture to arrive.

I wonder about the relationships these people have with each other. What sort of relationship is it that it can become so twisted and bent? (Thorp & Blake, 1971, p. 67.)

In wondering about the quality of this couple's relationship, David reveals something of his own attitudes and values. Like the man in the empty $100,000 house, David values hard work, achievement, and status. However, the motivation is different: whereas the home owner works hard for prestige and status because it apparently gives him something he lacks, David works hard because his self-respect is based in part on doing a good job; he does not value prestige and status above human happiness.

From what we know of David so far, we are not able to anticipate very much of his future behavior. We can predict much more, however, if we learn that he (1) values "doing his own thing," so long as it does not hurt anyone else; (2) is opposed to the draft, war, and killing in general, because he is "struggling to be a civilized man"; and (3) does not, in his own words, "want to hurt anyone, even for the greater good, for the common good, or for their own good. And it would be a double evil if I hurt them for a good that they couldn't perceive at the moment. I think a lot of people hurt other people for no other reason but the fact that they have been wronged." (Thorp & Blake, pp. 69–76)

As we gain more information about David's attitudes and values, we begin to expect certain trends in his behavior. For example, in terms of motivation, we might expect David to assert himself, if at all possible, nonaggressively—to cultivate gentleness and to be considerate of the feelings of others. In terms of learning, we might expect him to be most receptive to teachers who are also nonaggressive. In terms of perception, we might predict he would "tune in" more fully to people displaying attitudes he valued, such as being considerate, gentle, and nonaggressive, while attending only marginally to others.

As David's case shows, many of a person's most important attitudes relate to himself. In the short run, he organizes his perceptions, thoughts, feelings, and behavior around goals, best explained in terms of motivation. But in the long run, the concepts of attitude and value best describe and predict the organization of a person's behavior (Newcomb, 1965, p. 20).

ATTITUDES

An attitude is a learned readiness to behave consistently toward a class of things, people, or ideas. It is generally composed of three components: beliefs, feelings, and actions. Our attitudes are concerned not only with facts but with evaluations; when we act on our attitudes, we act on what we believe to be true, not on what is actually true.

Attitude Toward Self

The way subjective reality can be distorted in a person's attitude toward himself is illustrated in the following case. Harold, a 35-year-old army veteran, was referred by the court to a Veterans Administration hospital. He had committed a senseless crime, apparently as a plea to society for punishment. I gave him some tests, one of which called for free responses to incomplete sentences. To the statement, "I could hate . . . ," he wrote, ". . . someone like me." His attitude toward himself was completely negative; he hated himself and those with whom he had identified, such as his father.

The relationship of the three components of belief, feeling, and action was consistent. Harold *believed* he was following in his

alcoholic father's footsteps; his father had abused his mother and he believed he was in danger of repeating the pattern with his own family. He *felt* disgust at himself for being the way he was, yet he felt unable to change. For these reasons, he *acted* in a consistently self-punishing way toward himself. His crime, the latest in a long series of apparently meaningless incidents, consisted of wheeling a shopping cart of groceries out to his car without going through the supermarket checkstand. He had calmly unloaded the cart, fully expecting to be apprehended, but when after waiting anxiously for some time he saw that no one had noticed, he returned to the store and did it again—in effect giving the store employees another chance to catch him, which they did. Since it seemed obvious that he wanted to be caught and punished, the apparently senseless crime had meaning. One could describe Harold's clinical problems with a label, but labels frequently hinder our understanding, for sometimes we believe that they explain more than they do. To really understand Harold, we would need to know more about him, his life history, his personality, and the way he has characteristically attempted to cope with his life problems. What is important in beginning to understand Harold is to see how his negative belief about himself (dislike), his negative feeling (disgust), and his negative action (self-punishment) all combine in a consistent whole.

Attitude Toward Others

The way our lives are lived out is determined not only by our attitudes toward self, but also by our attitudes toward others. And these attitudes are most often governed by differences based on sex, race, and class.

The most obvious classification of people is, of course, in terms of sex. Men and women have attitudes that vary on many, if not most, subjects. There are more-or-less masculine as well as feminine points of view. We tend to identify with our gender, with our sex roles, and with certain social norms generally expected of members of our sex in our culture. This attitude may bias our relations with the opposite sex. In its mild form this bias is a kind of misunderstanding of the reality—and the potential reality—of the opposite sex; in its extreme form it is sexism, a kind of prejudice that cannot be corrected by better information, facts, or logic. For example, a man with a traditional attitude toward women might dismiss his girl friend's views on politics because he believes women don't know much about the subject—which could be bias or prejudice depending on how rigidly it is held. Her view, however, may be different—indeed, she may feel it is irresponsible of women not to participate in public affairs. A person's attitudes toward self, then, are related to his attitudes toward others.

We also have various attitudes toward different racial, national, religious, class, and social divisions of people. When realistic, these attitudes may be called *intergroup attitudes*; when unrealistic, they are called *stereotypes* (discussed more fully in Chapter 8). These attitudes are important factors in determining how we define ourselves and others and how we behave toward others. It is difficult for us to be objective about group characteristics, because our beliefs are usually the results of cultural conditioning and hence are accepted uncritically.

"The Board of Education requires me to give you some basic information on sex, reproduction and other disgusting filth."

Moreover, as folk beliefs, they are not based on facts but instead represent theories about reality that are often wrong. When extreme enough to be considered prejudices, they greatly interfere with our ability to know other people as they really are.

Balance and Imbalance

In a balanced attitude, the three components of belief, feeling, and action are all fully developed and in an imbalanced attitude they are not. An example of one kind of imbalance is when one holds prejudiced beliefs but does not act in a discriminatory manner, when someone says he does not like blacks but he does not go out of his way to avoid them. Somewhat similar is the nonprejudiced person who does discriminate against people of another group. In both cases, the action is inconsistent with the belief and feeling.

A person whose attitudes are imbalanced often experiences pressures to change. A nonprejudiced white person who discriminates against blacks may do several things defensively to avoid changing his attitude. He may deny that his behavior is discrimination, compartmentalizing his thinking to avoid the inconsistency. He may rationalize his behavior by saying that discrimination is just what blacks want and expect. If the inconsistency is forcefully pointed out to him he will probably either change his behavior—or his attitude.

In the case of Harold, his attitude toward himself was fairly well balanced—but negative. The goal of psychotherapy would have been to encourage attitude imbalance in order to make him become more positive in his belief and feeling about himself and thus probably change his behavior toward himself.

Dissonance

The idea of imbalance is similar to Festinger's theory of dissonance (1957). According to this theory, a state of dissonance exists in one's thinking whenever his attitude and belief are not in agreement with his behavior. This dissonance creates a motivational conflict, which one can resolve only by (1) changing either the behavior or the belief, (2) denying that a conflict exists at all, or (3) adopting some other kind of defensive behavior. To illustrate dissonance, Festinger has used the example of how a cigarette smoker copes with the argument that smoking causes cancer. Since this belief is dissonant with continued smoking, the smoker can, of course, quit smoking. Or he can change his belief—reject the supposed relationship between smoking and cancer. Or he can avoid being reminded of the inconsistency by trying to avoid further information about the subject.

Attitude Simplicity and Complexity

A person with simple political *beliefs* (or other kinds of beliefs as well) understands his own position but lumps all other positions together. A person with complex political beliefs understands the

"If I read one more blasted study about the link between smoking and cancer, I'm going to give up . . . reading."

Box 4-1   Dissonance Reduction

Would spies be more loyal if they were paid a lot or a little?

The old saying that "the grass is always greener on the other side of the fence" may not be true. The simple experiment of showing a 4- or 5-year-old child two equally attractive toys and then giving him one demonstrates that he will usually come to prefer the toy that he has been allowed to keep. Festinger (1962) reasons that "some psychological process comes into play immediately after the making of a choice that colors one's attitude, either favorably or unfavorably, toward the decision."

In a classic experiment, Festinger & Carlsmith (1959) asked students who had just finished a rather dull experiment to serve temporarily as assistants and prepare some new subjects waiting in the next room by telling them that it was a *very interesting task* and would be enjoyable. This was supposed to make them more receptive to the experiment, which seemed to involve the measurement of motor performance. Actually, the task was the dullest task the experimenters could devise: turning blocks a quarter turn for an hour's time. The students were instructed to tell a lie, and were offered money to do so. One group of students was offered $1 for the lie and the other $20.

What the researchers really wanted to find out was if there would be greater attitude change in those students who were paid a lot, or those who were paid a little. Common sense might seem to indicate that those who were paid $20 would show greater change. Festinger's theory of dissonance suggests the opposite: those who were paid the least ($1) would experience the most dissonance, and therefore the most attitude change. In their case, the motivation to lie would be inadequate; since they had already said the experiment was interesting, which was untrue, something had to give way. The experimental results supported Festinger's prediction. Those who were paid only $1 to lie did indeed change their private belief more to conform with the fact that they had said publicly that the experiment was interesting. After a while they came to believe what they had said.

The idea of dissonance reduction can be used to explain many examples of defensive behavior in human beings. Rogers (1964) maintains that defensive measures are especially likely when the dissonant information "thwarts the adequacy and worth of the self." In many cases, successful reduction of dissonance results in an increasing loss of contact with reality, as more and more threatening information is ignored, misinterpreted, or transformed.

Applying this discussion to the question of spies, it might be assumed, if dissonance theory holds true, that the loyalty of spies might best be assured by a policy of paying them poorly. People seem to hold most strongly those beliefs for which they have had to suffer.

distinctions between various positions, regardless of what he himself believes. A conservative with complex political beliefs might understand the essential distinctions between conservative, moderate, liberal, socialist, and communist positions. He might even recognize a crucial difference between the forms of democratic and totalitarian socialism. All this is likely to make his attitude much more discriminating with respect to action than that of a fellow conservative with a simpler belief.

Similarly, a young man may have simple or complex *feelings* about the girl he loves. He may feel simple attraction. Or he may feel friendship, tenderness, respect, love, and passion—and even irritation and hostility—toward her.

The *action* component may also be simple or complex. A person opposed to the war in Southeast Asia may simply approve passively of the actions of others or he may talk to others about the war, collect signatures on petitions, work for antiwar political candidates, and participate in demonstrations.

There is evidence that attitudinal complexity-simplicity is a general aspect of a person's thinking (Bieri, 1956). That is, people who tend toward simplicity are simple in *all* their attitudes about a variety of people and processes, whereas those with complex attitudes in, say, politics hold similarly complex attitudes in other matters as well.

Flexibility and Rigidity

What happens to a person's attitudes when they are contradicted by facts? By way of answering, let us consider the case of Jim, a high school senior, and his sports car. Those who believe that cars are simply vehicles to get from place to place wouldn't understand Jim's feelings about his car; it is, in fact, almost an extension of his personality. When Jim goes off to college, however, he won't be able to take his car, since the administration does not permit freshmen to keep cars at the school. Whereas at home Jim went to social and athletic events in his car and generally centered his social life—especially with girls—around his machine, at college he will have to adjust to a new social reality, potentially disturbing, in which he can't depend on his car for respect and status. What can he do?

The concepts of flexibility and rigidity help to explain what might happen. If Jim's attitudes tend to be rigidly held, he may (1) experience psychological depression at the loss of his car, which represents a loss of status, respect, and sex appeal; or he may (2) develop defensive reactions such as withdrawal. But if his attitudes are less rigidly held, he may try to adjust through compensatory strivings, such as improving his scholarship, learning new social skills, or losing himself in athletic activities, thus coming to rely more on himself and realizing that his worth as a person does not depend on owning a car. He may be liked for other reasons. Significantly, he may also change his basis for liking other people.

The nonrigid person is more open to change of his attitude. But if a person's thinking is generally rigid, he will be less likely to adjust—even to his own satisfaction—to the loss of a valued possession.

How Attitudes Are Learned

At first, a person is much more likely to learn his attitudes from his parents than from other sources. *Identification is "the tendency to incorporate or adopt the attitudes and behavior of other individuals or groups"* (Goldenson, 1970, p. 591). The child often admires his parents and their qualities, and tends to take over their attitudes and behavior without reservation. The child's conscience and his sex role are largely developed in this way. It is likely that early identification learning occurs at an unconscious or half-conscious level. As one becomes an adolescent,

he moves away from the exclusive domination of his parents, and begins to identify with the peer group. Attitudes (and values) shaped by the group are integrated into his existing attitudes and developing personality. What is learned at this time is probably more critically evaluated, if only because it must be reconciled with what has already been acquired.

The case of Harold, the self-hating army veteran, can only be understood in terms of his identification with his father. It is fairly obvious that a child will identify with a parent who is loving, warm, and supportive. But he can also identify with a parent (or someone else) who is disliked, despised, or even hated. Usually the identification of a boy with his father occurs because of love and warmth and/or the unequal power relationship between them (Mussen & Distler, 1959). When both factors are operating constructively, the child is likely to develop a positive self-image and a mature conscience. But if identification is based entirely on the power relationship, the likelihood of developing a negative self-image is great. Harold disliked his father, but identified with his goals, attitudes, and values, incorporating not only these attitudes and values into his own sense of self, but also modeling his behavior after that of his father. He seemed to be "a chip off the old block." Like his father, he worked as a chef in a restaurant, an occupation that kept him away from home during the normal family hours; drank excessively to avoid his sorrows; and felt that he neglected his wife and children—all things he held against his father. Thus, when we find Harold repeating the behavior in his own life which he detested in his father, it should be clear why his self-image was totally negative.

The child is also exposed to more deliberate attempts to shape his attitudes. This training is called *socialization* during the early years when his self-image is still forming and as a general process is called *cultural conditioning* (concepts discussed in Chapter 7). The concepts are best distinguished in terms of age and generality: the child is socialized as he learns attitudes, values, and behavior; the adult is culturally conditioned as he learns to play cultural roles, maintain cultural traditions, and accept the myths of his society. Obviously, these two terms are similar and sometimes merge. Both socialization and cultural conditioning are more informal—and probably more difficult to resist—than what we usually regard as *education*. Other "teaching institutions" of society, such as the church, the family, our social class, and the racial and ethnic groups to which we belong are also involved in training.

Changing Sex Roles

As we grow up, perhaps the most fundamental set of attitudes we must acquire concerns our sex roles. We must learn to pattern ourselves after the norms (standards) of masculinity and femininity shared in our culture. By the time a boy is in school, he has begun to model his sex role behavior after his father or some other male. He learns how men and women behave toward each other, and how each tends to play different roles in the home and at work. He observes that one parent is clearly the boss, or perhaps that they share equally in making decisions. What the child learns at this time, and comes to expect, affects every aspect of his life in later years.

The present-day stereotypes of masculinity and femininity, discussed in Chapter 1, are, of course, exaggerated cultural statements of what men and women are supposed to be like. The traditional masculine role places great emphasis on the man as provider, protector, and authority—as the one who goes out into the hardships of the working world, participates in politics and public affairs, and manages the affairs of his family. The traditional feminine role emphasizes marriage, home, and family values. While men are described as aggressive, dominant, independent, strong, and confident, women are described as modest, emotional, soft, affectionate, and sensitive. They are supposed to be more expressive and sociable, whereas men are supposed to be more emotionally controlled and competent in mastering the physical environment.

Although most people do not adhere entirely to these norms, they rely on some of them when thinking about themselves, when coping with their spouses, or when training their children. Conflict may develop within the family when one person fails to adhere to an image of masculinity or femininity that others expect. A boy with too many of the supposedly feminine qualities, for instance, may cause his family a great deal of worry. Or a married woman, tiring of the domestic role, may decide to get a job or go to college, and her new role may cause strong tensions within the marriage.

In America these roles have undergone considerable change in just the last 100 years, and the rate of change seems to be increasing. Certainly the fashions in sex roles today are different from those of 15 or 20 years ago. In general, more women are working outside the home, reflecting a decreased emphasis on the traditional domestic role; family responsibilities are more evenly shared between the sexes than they used to be; and a relationship of equality between husband and wife is increasingly accepted as the norm. Although many people still play the more traditional sex roles, people seem less concerned with playing such stereotyped parts. An important problem facing these young people in this time of change and transition is the choice of a mate with a compatible view of appropriate sex role behavior. Even then, there is bound to be a good deal of unavoidable tension during this period of changing roles and expectations.

VALUES

A value is a belief about what is desirable or undesirable, "good" or "bad." Some examples of value are: "a job worth doing is worth doing well," "honesty is the best policy," and "happiness is the highest human good." We learn values through the process of cultural conditioning.

How do attitudes differ from values? Attitudes are more specific than values. And Rokeach (1968) states that value is a more dynamic concept than attitude; besides, belief, feeling, and action components, it includes a strong motivational element. Attitudes deal with matters of fact and opinion. But to have a value is to believe that a particular way of behaving is better than alternative ways. For example, if you value hard work, thrift, and competition, you are a follower of the so-called Puritan Ethic. In the CBS poll (see Box 4-2) these values

---

Box 4-2   The CBS Poll: Traditional American Values

The following are some traditional American values. Which of them do you believe in? Which do you not believe in?

		Believe	Not Believe
1.	"Hard work will always pay off."	_____	_____
2.	"Everyone should save as much as he can and not have to lean on family and friends the minute he runs into financial problems."	_____	_____
3.	"Depending on how much strength and character a person has, he can pretty well control what happens to him."	_____	_____
4.	"Belonging to some organized religion is important in a person's life."	_____	_____
5.	"Competition encourages excellence."	_____	_____
6.	"The right to private property is sacred."	_____	_____
7.	"Society needs some legally based authority in order to prevent chaos."	_____	_____
8.	"Compromise is essential for progress."	_____	_____

After you have made a choice for each question, turn the page for the poll results (Box 4-3).

---

are measured by questions 1, 2, and 5. Both attitude and value are assumed to affect social behavior, but value, Rokeach says, "is a determinant of attitude as well as of behavior." We possess far fewer values than attitudes. When a person accepts a value, it becomes a high-level motive for him, channeling and directing behavior in a general way in many particular situations. Thus, when we are able to describe a person's values we are able to say more about him—and more economically—than if we were to describe either his attitudes or motives. Finally, unlike an attitude, a value, is a demand for action—for example, "honesty is the best policy," even when no one will find you out. As Rokeach neatly puts it, it is "not only a belief about the preferable, but also a preference for the preferable" (1968, pp. 14–16).

In sum, values and attitudes may be ranged as follows: each value system consists of particular values, each of which in turn consists of several attitudes. An attitude, as stated, has the three components of belief, action and feeling. Each of these components, finally, consists of particular habits.

As mentioned in Chapter 7, a person usually develops a unifying "philosophy of life." This is another phrase for value system, which implies the degree of consistency within the value system and the extent to which the parts of the system are organized into a coherent whole. By the time a person reaches adulthood, he usually has achieved a definite sense of identity, including a unifying system of values, or "philosophy of life."

Box 4-3   The CBS Poll Results: Traditional American Values

This is the way a representative, nationwide sample of young people (1340) answered the eight questions. The figures presented here are a summed average. The results are further broken down by the person's political stance.

	Believe	*Not Believe*
Revolutionaries (1%)	30%	70%
Radical reformers (10%)	72	28
Moderate reformers, Liberals (23%)	73	27
Middle-of-roaders (48%)	84	16
Conservatives (19%)	89	11

As these results show, most youths accept most of these traditional American values. The number of youth rejecting these values increases gradually from a low of 11 percent among conservatives to 27–28 percent among the reformers. There is, however, a tremendous leap from there to the 70 percent rejection of revolutionary youth.

These young people were taken from two samples. One was a college sample of 723, drawn from 30 campuses. The other was a noncollege sample of college-age youth of 617. The noncollege youth were much more conservative politically (*CBS Reports: Generations Apart*, 1969).

Unfortunately, it is not easy to develop a unified value system. We are all subjected to conflicting value messages from the various agents of socialization. They do not speak with one voice.

Value Conflict

Hard work, thrift, and the competitive spirit, core values of the Puritan Ethic, conflict with other values in our culture. The belief in hard work and individual effort, for instance, is undermined by the belief that "pull" and connections are responsible for success. The belief in saving money and being thrifty conflicts with the belief of our "buy now, pay later" consumer society that spending and consuming are the highest goods. It also conflicts with the services of the welfare state, which, in providing security against sickness, old age, and loss of income, has made saving for the future less important.

The competitive spirit—the drive to win at whatever one does—conflicts with the religious values of brotherly love and concern for others. It also conflicts with the widely held value that every child should succeed in his schoolwork, for competition often discourages children and causes them to fail rather than succeed. Further, it conflicts with another widely held value that one should above all be happy, whatever he might do, since, by teaching that one may succeed only by "getting to the top," it causes many people who never rise above modest achievement to be dissatisfied with their lives. This dissatisfaction can be seen as an example of the dissonance which we have already discussed. It can lead to various maladaptive responses, such as taking out one's hostility on family and friends instead of on the genuine source of one's dissatisfaction.

Achieving financial success entails values conflicting with the democratic ideal of social equality. Such success is characterized by status, prestige, and conspicuous material wealth, all of which are the results of inequality. Many people today, however, reject these values, so it may be that financial success as a major value in our culture is decreasing in importance.

Value Change

According to Kluckhohn (1958), decline in the influence of the Puritan Ethic (also called Protestant Ethic) is the best-documented value change that has occurred in the United States during the last generation. There is also considerable evidence that there has been a decline in the inner-directedness of people, that psychological health has become a value, that there is greater prizing of tolerance and diversity, and that there is greater equalization of the roles of the sexes.

Many of these trends find their clearest expression in the development of the so-called "counter-culture," which began to emerge in the late 1960s. So far this has been primarily a youth movement,

but at its very center is a rejection of materialistic values not limited to any particular age group. This counter-culture does not accept any of the core ''Puritan Ethic'' values. It accepts material goods but rejects materialistic values. Basically it is a humanistic philosophy which values human beings and their interrelationships rather than things.

The President's Commission on Campus Unrest: The Causes of Student Protest

OUR purpose in this chapter is to identify the causes of student protest and to ascertain what these causes reveal about its nature. Our subject is primarily the protest of white students, for although they have much in common with Black, Chicano, and other minority student protest movements, these latter are nevertheless fundamentally different in their goals, their intentions, and their sources. . . .

We find that campus unrest has many causes, that several of these are not within the control of individuals or of government, and that some of these causes have worked their influence in obscure or indirect ways. . . .

Race, the war, and the defects of the modern university have contributed to the development of campus unrest, have given it specific focus, and continue to lend it a special intensity. But they are neither the only nor even the most important causes of campus unrest.

Of far greater moment have been the advance of American society into the post-industrial era, the increasing affluence of American society, and the expansion and intergenerational evolution of liberal idealism. Together, these have prompted the formation of a new youth culture that defines itself through a passionate attachment to principle and an equally passionate opposition to the larger society. At the center of this culture is a romantic celebration of human life, of the unencumbered individual, of the senses, and of nature. It rejects what it sees to be the opera-

From *The Report of the President's Commission on Campus Unrest* (*The Scranton Report*) Washington, D.C.: U.S. Gov't. Printing Office, 1970, pp. 51–73.

tional ideals of American society: materialism, competition, rationalism, technology, consumerism, and militarism. This emerging culture is the deeper cause of student protest against war, racial injustice, and the abuses of the multiversity.

During the past decade, this youth culture has developed rapidly. It has become ever more distinct and has acquired an almost religious fervor through a process of advancing personal commitment. This process has been spurred by the emergence within the larger society of opposition both to the youth culture itself and to its demonstrations of political protest. As such opposition became manifest—and occasionally violently manifest—participants in the youth culture felt challenged, and their commitment to that culture and to the political protest it prompts grew stronger and bolder. Over time, more and more students have moved in the direction of an ever deeper and more inclusive sense of opposition to the larger society. As their alienation became more profound, their willingness to use violence increased. . . .

In and of itself, campus unrest is not a "problem" and requires no "solution." The existence of dissenting opinion and voices is simply a social condition, a fact of modern life; the right of such opinion to exist is protected by our Constitution. Protest that is violent or disruptive is, of course, a very real problem, and solutions must be found to end such manifestations of it. But when student protest stays within legal bounds, as it typically does, it is not a problem for government to cope with. It is simply a pattern of opinion and expression.

Campus unrest, then, is not a single or uniform thing. Rather it is the aggregate result, or sum, of hundreds and thousands of individual beliefs and discontents, each of them as unique as the individuals who feel them. These individual feelings reflect in turn a series of choices each person makes about what he will believe, what he will say, and what he will do. In the most immediate and operational sense, then, it is these choices—these *commitments*, to use a word in common usage among students —which are the proximate cause of campus unrest and which are the forces at work behind any physical manifestation of dissent.

These acts of individual commitment to certain values and to certain ways of seeing and acting in the world do not occur in a vacuum. They take place within, and are powerfully affected by, the conditions under which students live. We will call these conditions the contributing causes of campus unrest. Five broad orders of such contributing causes have been suggested in testimony before the Commission.

They are:

The pressing problems of American society, particularly the war in Southeast Asia and conditions of minority groups;

The changing status and attitudes of youth in America;

The distinctive character of the American university during the postwar period;

An escalating spiral of reaction to student protest from public opinion and an escalating spiral of violence; and

Broad evolutionary changes occurring in the culture and structure of modern Western society.

ISSUES AND OPINIONS

The best place to begin any search for the causes of student protest is to consider the [issues] which student protestors themselves offer [as providing reasons] for their activities.
. . .

Both historically and in terms of the relative frequency with which it is the focus of protest, the first great issue is also the central social and political problem of American society: the position of racial minorities, and of black people in particular. It was over this issue that student protest began in 1960. . . .

The second great issue has been the war in Southeast Asia. The war was almost from the beginning a relatively unpopular war, one which college youth on the whole now consider a mistake and which many of them also consider immoral and evil. It has continued now for more than five years, and it has pressed especially on youth. . . .

A third major protest issue has been the university itself. Though at times this issue has been expressed in protests over curriculum and the nonretention of popular teachers, the overwhelming majority of university-related protests have dealt with school regulations affecting students, with the role of students in making those regulations, and more generally with the quality of student life, living facilities, and food services. The same impulse moves students to denounce what they feel to be the general regimentation of American life by large-scale organizations and their by-products —impersonal bureaucracy and the anonymous IBM card. University regulation of political activities—the issue at Berkeley in 1964—has also been a prominent issue. . . .

What students objected to about discrimination against Blacks and other racial minorities was simple and basic: the unfeeling and unjustifiable deprivation of individual rights, dignity, and self-respect. And the targets of protest were those institutions which routinely deprived Blacks of their rights, or which supported and reinforced such deprivation. These two themes—support for the autonomy, personal dignity, individuality, and life of each person, and bitter opposition to institutions, policies, and rationales which seemed to deprive individuals of those things—could also be seen in the other two main issues of the 1960's: the war in Southeast Asia, and university regulation of student life. They may also be seen in the emerging student concern over ecology and environmental pollution.

These three issues—racism, war, and the denial of personal freedoms—unquestionably were and still are contributing causes of student protest. Students have reacted strongly to these issues, speak about them with eloquence and passion, and act on them with great energy.

Moreover, students feel that government, the university, and other American institutions have not responded to their analysis of what should be done, or at least not responded rapidly enough. This has led many students to turn their attacks on the decision-making process itself. Thus, we hear slogans such as "power to the people."

And yet, having noted that these issues

were causes, we must go on to note two further pertinent facts about student protest over race and war. First, excepting black students, it is impossible to attribute student opposition on these issues to cynical or narrow self-interest alone, as do those Americans who believe that students are against the war because they are cowards, afraid to die for a cause. But in fact, few students have been called upon to risk their lives in the present war. It is true that male students have been subject to the draft. But only a small portion of college youth have actually been drafted and sent to fight in Vietnam, and it is reported that, as compared to the nation's previous wars, relatively few college graduates have been killed in this war. It is *noncollege* youth who fight in Vietnam, and yet it is college youth who oppose the war— while noncollege youth tend to support it more than other segments of the population.

It is the same in the case of race. For black and other minority college youth, it hardly needs explanation why they should find the cruel injustice of American racism a compelling issue, or why they should protest over it. Why it became an issue leading to unrest among *white* college students is less obvious. They are not directly victims of it, and, as compared to other major institutions in the society, the university tends to be more open and more willing to reward achievement regardless of race or ethnicity.

Of course, students have a deep personal interest in these issues and believe that the outcome will make their own individual lives better or worse. Yet their beliefs and their protest clearly are founded on principle and ideology, not on self-interest. The war and the race issues did not arise primarily because they actually and materially affected the day-to-day lives of college youth—black students again excepted. The issues were defined in terms not of interest but of principle, and their emergence was based on what we must infer to have been a fundamental change in the attitudes and principles of American students. . . .

Clearly, whatever it is that transforms a condition into an issue lies in the eyes of the beholder—or, more precisely, in his opinions and perceptions. The emergence of these issues was caused by a change in opinions, perceptions, and values—that is, by a change in the culture of students. Students' basic ways of seeing the world became, during the 1960's, less and less tolerant of war, of racism, and of the things these entail. This shift in student culture is a basic—perhaps *the* basic—contributing cause of campus unrest. . . .

THE NEW YOUTH CULTURE

A distinguishing characteristic of young people is their penchant for pure idealism. Society teaches youth to adhere to the basic values of the adult social system—equality, honesty, democracy, or whatever—in absolute terms. Throughout most of American history, the idealism of youth has been formed—and constrained—by the institutions of adult society. But during the 1960's, in response to an accumulation of social changes, the traditional American youth culture developed rapidly in the direction of an oppositional stance toward the institutions and ways of the adult world.

This subculture took its bearings from the notion of the autonomous, self-determining individual whose goal was to live with "authenticity," or in harmony with his inner penchants and instincts. It also found its identity in a rejection of the work ethic, materialism, and conventional social norms and pieties. Indeed, it rejected all institutional disciplines externally imposed upon the individual, and this set it at odds with much in American society.

Its aim was to liberate human consciousness and to enhance the quality of experience; it sought to replace the materialism, the self-denial, and the striving for achievement that characterized the existing society with a new emphasis on the expressive, the creative, the imaginative. The tools of the workaday institutional world—hierarchy, discipline, rules, self-interest, self-defense, power—it considered mad and tyrannical. It proclaimed instead the liberation of the individual to feel, to experience, to express whatever his unique humanity prompted. And its perceptions of the world grew ever more distant from the perceptions of the existing culture: what most called "justice" or "peace" or "accomplishment," the new culture envisioned as "enslavement" or

"hysteria" or "meaninglessness." As this divergence of values and of vision proceeded, the new youth culture became increasingly oppositional.

And yet in its commitment to liberty and equality, it was very much in the mainstream of American tradition; what it doubted was that America had managed to live up to its national ideals. Over time, these doubts grew, and the youth culture became increasingly imbued with a sense of alienation and of opposition to the larger society. . . .

It is not difficult to compose a picture of contemporary America as it looks through the eyes of one whose premises are essentially those just described. Human life is all; but women and children are being killed in Vietnam by American forces. All living things are sacred; but American industry and technology are polluting the air and the streams and killing the birds and the fish. The individual should stand as an individual; but American society is organized into vast structures of unions, corporations, multiversities, and government bureaucracies. Personal regard for each human being and for the absolute equality of every human soul is a categorical imperative; but American society continues to be characterized by racial injustice and discrimination. . . . In this new youth culture's political discussion there are echoes of Marxism, of peasant communalism, of Thoreau, of Rousseau, of the evangelical fervor of the abolitionists, of Gandhi, and of native American populism. . . .

Profoundly opposed to any kind of authority structure from within or without the movement and urgently pressing for direct personal participation by each individual, members of this new youth culture have a difficult time making collective decisions. They reveal a distinct intolerance in their refusal to listen to those outside the new culture and in their willingness to force others to their own views. They even show an elitist streak in their premise that the rest of the society must be brought to the policy positions which they believe are right.

At the same time, they try very hard, and with extraordinary patience, to give each of their fellows an opportunity to be heard and to participate directly in decision-making. The new culture decisional style is founded on the endless mass meeting at which there is no chairman and no agenda, and from which the crowd or parts of the crowd melt away or move off into actions. Such crowds are, of course, subject to easy manipulation by skillful agitators and sometimes become mobs. But it must also be recognized that large, loose, floating crowds represent for participants in the new youth culture the normal, friendly, natural way for human beings to come together equally, to communicate, and to decide what to do. Seen from this perspective, the reader may well imagine the general student response at Kent State to the governor's order that the National Guard disperse all assemblies, peaceful or otherwise.

Practitioners of the new youth culture do not announce their program because, at this time at least, the movement is not primarily concerned with programs; it is concerned with how one ought to live and what one ought to consider important in one's daily life. The new youth culture is still in the process of forming its values, programs, and life style; at this point, therefore, it is primarily a *stance*. . . .

A vast majority of students are not complete adherents. But *no* significant group of students would join older generations in condemning those who are. And almost *all* students will condemn repressive efforts by the larger community to restrict or limit the life style, the art forms, and the nonviolent political manifestations of the new youth culture. . . .

How long this emerging youth culture will last and what course its future development will take are open questions. But it does exist today, and it is the deeper cause of the emergence of the issues of race and war as objects of intense concern on the American campus. . . .

Summarizing Statements

1. Attitudes are predispositions to action which organize a person's long-range behavior. They are concerned with belief, feeling, and action components—not only facts but also evaluation.

2. One's behavior is influenced both by attitudes toward oneself and attitudes toward others. One of the most important parts of the self-image develops out of an identification with one's sex role. When carried to an extreme, this attitude is rigid and inflexible and is referred to as sexist. A sexist attitude may be as irrational as racial prejudice.

3. Realistic attitudes about groups are called intergroup attitudes; unrealistic ones are called stereotypes.

4. Imbalanced or dissonant attitudes set up tension for change. Balance can be achieved by change of attitude or behavior or by screening further information.

5. A person with a complex attitude is aware of many aspects of an issue and is less inclined to distort another person's position.

6. A flexible attitude is one that is tentatively or provisionally held and that can be changed if the person is exposed to new information.

7. Attitudes are primarily learned through identification and cultural conditioning. A small child incorporates into his growing self-image attitudes and behavior. As he grows, he is exposed to a process of cultural conditioning by the various reference groups to which he belongs, especially the family.

8. The most important set of attitudes that boys and girls learn concerns their sex roles. They learn to pattern themselves after the cultural norms of masculinity and femininity. The sex role stereotypes are extreme cultural statements of what men and women are supposed to be like. Conflict may develop when a

person is expected to play a role that does not fit his own self-image.

9. Sex roles have undergone much change in the last century and the extent of change appears to be increasing. The changes which most authorities agree on are (1) an increase in the number of women who work, (b) a more even sharing of family responsibilities, and (c) a greater equality between the sexes. Today equality is accepted by many people as the norm. A most important adjustment problem facing young people today is the choice of a marriage partner with a compatiable attitude toward the changing sex roles.

10. Values are concerned with matters of fact and evaluation. They have to do with preferable ways of behaving. We possess far fewer values than attitudes. Attitudes are organized into values, and values into a value system or philosophy of life. An obstacle to developing a unified value system is posed by conflicting training about values from the various agents of socialization.

11. The traditional values of hard work, thrift, and the competitive spirit (the Puritan Ethic) are declining for a number of reasons. Some other traditional American values are also declining. The value changes that have been occurring during the past century are most clearly evident in youthful members of the counter-culture, which began to appear in the late 1960s.

12. The vast majority of American college students still endorse most, if not all, of the traditional American values. Only a very small percentage of American youth completely reject these values, but many others are sympathetic to their way of thinking.

READING SELECTION

13. The basic cause of campus unrest has been the evolution of a youth culture defining itself through a passionate attachment to idealistic principles. The emergence of American society into a postindustrial era and increasing affluence have made this new culture possible. At its center is a romantic celebration of life and a rejection of materialism, competition, rationalism, technology, consumerism, and militarism. This emerging counter-culture is the deeper cause of student protest against the main issues of the war, racial injustice, and the abuses of the university itself. Many youth are intensely committed to pursuing these values.

14. Students feel that the government, the university, and other American institutions have not responded to lawful protest. Many have turned their attack on the decision-making process itself. But it has not been narrow self-interest that has prompted protest; the protestors have rarely been from among the most disadvantaged. Usually they have come instead from the most privileged classes within our society. It is the idealistic commitment to important American values and a recognition that society has not lived up to what it publicly upholds that has been the basic cause of student unrest.

15. The youth culture or counter-culture, as it is being called, has taken its bearing from the notion of the autonomous, self-determining individual whose goal is to live authentically. It has also rejected the work ethic, materialism, and conventional social norms. It puts a new emphasis on the expressive, the creative, and the imaginative. The tools of the workaday world—hierarchy, discipline, rules, self-interest, self-defense, power—it considers mad and tyrannical.

16. In its commitment to liberty and equality the new culture is very much within the mainstream of American tradition. Its case, as seen through its own eyes, can be summarized: human life is all; men, women, and children are being killed in Vietnam; all living things are sacred, but American industry and technology are polluting the air and streams. The individual should be respected but modern life is organized into countless dehumanizing structures such as unions, corporations, universities, and government bureaucracies. Respect for the person and equality is preached, but racial injustice and discrimination continue.

17. Counter-culture youth are distrustful of conventional, authoritarian organizational structures and tend to form loose, amorphous, leaderless groups. They believe in a political system of direct personal participation by each individual (called participatory democracy). As yet they do not have definite programs. They are primarily concerned with working out how people ought to live, and with developing the stance of a life-style.

Terms and Concepts

Attitude: learned readiness to behave consistently toward a class of things, people, or ideas. It has three components: belief, feeling, and action.

Balanced attitude: an attitude in which the belief, feeling, and action components are in basic agreement.

Belief: an aspect of attitude having to do with what we accept as true. When we act on our attitudes we act on what we *believe* is true, not what is actually true.

Cultural conditioning: training of the younger generation in attitudes, values, and behavior that are related to maintaining cultural roles, traditions, and myths. The church, the family, and reference groups, such as class and ethnic groups, are the agents of this training.

Counter-culture: the emerging youth culture of the 1970s which is passionately dedicated to celebrating life and rejecting materialism, competition racism, consumerism, and militarism.

Dissonance: information or thought not in agreement with previously accepted beliefs, attitudes, and values.

Flexibility: an attitude and personality dimension in which a person is able to assimilate information which is dissonant from that previously accepted.

Identification: a growth mechanism in which a person acquires beliefs, attitudes, values, traits, and behavior of another person.

Imbalanced attitude: an attitude in which either the belief, feeling, or action is dissonant to the others which generally leads to a change of attitude, behavior, or a screening of further information.

Intergroup attitude: a realistic attitude as distinct from a stereotype (unrealistic, false).

Philosophy of life: an organized or coherent set of values; a system of values.

Prejudice: a feeling, favorable or unfavorable, toward a person or thing, prior to or not based on actual experience.—Allport.

Sex roles: the cultural norms (standards) of masculinity and femininity. Boys and girls are taught to pattern themselves after these standards through the process of cultural conditioning.

Value: a belief about what is good or bad, desirable or undesirable. Values are organizations of attitudes. To have a value is to believe that a particular way of behaving is better than some other way.

Johnny is a boy who can't seem to learn anything in school. On the streets, however, he is one of the best young hustlers in his neighborhood. His school is sure that he is dumb, but his friends who look up to him as a leader think that he is clever.

Learning

5
A STUDENT enrolled in a psychology class is likely to think of learning just as knowledge obtained in his formal education. Formal education is important, but so are many other kinds of learning. For example, the student has learned where to go for his psychology class, the appropriate social roles of student and professor, and the meaning of certain "cues" in his instructor's style, such as slowing down and repeating "key" words and concepts. He doesn't actually have to hear, "Now this is important, take it down." The student has learned to drive the car he drove to school, the route or mental "map" from home to school, and the significance of certain internal "cues" such as the rumbling in his stomach at lunch time. He has learned much of his motivation, such as a general desire to succeed or be popular. He has learned how to cope with others, such as being typically submissive (or aggressive) in his interaction with authority figures.

Learning is not just formal education; it is a change in our behavior that enables us to better adapt to our environment.

Of course, there are other changes in behavior—for example, those produced by instinct, fatigue, disease, or sensory adaptation. But they tend to interfere with the kind of performance we ordinarily use as a measure of learning.

INSTINCT VERSUS LEARNING

Sometimes an animal changes its behavior simply because it grows more mature; such behavior is a consequence of instinct—*the term instinct refers to inherited behavior that is complex, unlearned, and universal to the species*. Most scientists agree that humans do not have instinct, although we do display similar but less complex inborn patterns called *reflexes*: when the knee is tapped, it flexes; when light shines in the eye, the pupil constricts; when the infant's lips are stimulated, he sucks.

But instinct is more complex: the complicated nest building of insects, the migration of birds, the mating ritual of Stikelback fish. Such instinctive behavior often requires the help of inborn "releasing stimuli" to set it off—as when cold weather triggers birds to fly south—and when such stimuli are absent, the instinctive behavior may fail to appear.

For many animals, instincts are the means by which they adapt to their environments. Sometimes, in fact, instinctual behavior is so complex and dramatic—as with the tarantula and the giant wasp *Pepsis* (see Box 5-1)—that it may be mistaken for learned, intelligent behavior. Instincts, however, serve animals well only as long as the environment remains relatively stable. When the environment changes—as it did during the Ice Age, when men in northern climates displayed intelligence in adapting—animals often find it impossible to adjust, as the many extinct species unfortunately show. The simplest animals have the greatest number of instincts and the least capacity for modifying behavior through individual learning. Not surprisingly, the higher animals have the greatest learning capacity. Without doubt, man is unique in that, as an individual, he can learn not only from his own experience but also from the experience of others. In fact, man's culture is the accumulation of experience over the centuries through the invention of spoken and written language.

Three other factors that may alter behavior and that are not learning are: (1) *fatigue*, which, since it affects all mental processes, may lower one's receptivness to learning and performance; (2) *disease*, which can affect intellect and motivation; (3) *sensory adaptation*, which

---

**Box 5-1   The Spider and the Wasp:
Instinct versus Intelligence**

This is "a classic example of what looks like intelligence pitted against instinct—a strange situation in which the victim, though fully able to defend itself, submits unwittingly to its destruction." The wasp avoids the wrong kind of tarantula, because only the "right" type will submit.

The hair of the tarantula is very sensitive and its stimulation results in immediate and swift attack if the spider is hungry. When the spider is not hungry, stimulation only causes him to shake the limb which was touched. An insect can safely walk under him. The spider's defenses, which ordinarily protect him well, fail him when he meets the digger wasp, Pepsis. The adult wasp only lives a few months and the females have only a few eggs to lay. Each egg must have its own host—a tarantula—in which to develop. The wasp must locate, sting, and paralyze one adult tarantula for each egg. The larvae does not eat or drink anything else.

When the wasp is ready to lay her eggs, she goes out looking for signs of a tarantula. Although the sex of the tarantula is not important, each type of Pepsis requires a particular type of tarantula. It won't attack a different species and is normally no match for a tarantula. In order to identify the species of spider the wasp must explore the tarantula's body with her antennae, a procedure which usually results in instant attack against insects by the hungry spider.

is our capacity to adjust to a monotonous stimulus such as the hum of an air conditioner.

Learning may now be defined as *a relatively enduring change in behavior caused by experience*. Fatigue, disease, and sensory adaptation certainly are not behavior caused by experience.

CONDITIONING

Habit is . . . the enormous fly-wheel of society, its most precious conservative agent.

William James

What James means is that the personal habits of individuals must conserve and maintain the stability of a society. Adapting to change is, of course, necessary and desirable, but it is also essential that a society endure. Among the varieties of learning are two types of conditioning which deal with habit learning. First, we must distinguish between classical and operant conditioning.

Classical Conditioning

The knee-jerk reflex is a natural, built-in response that occurs whenever the proper stimulus (a blow to the knee) is present. A conditioned reflex, by contrast, is a learned response. *Classical conditioning is the process of associating a new stimulus with an existing reflex*. That is,

---

Once the wasp is satisfied that the victim is the right kind of tarantula he withdraws—to dig the spider's grave. Later the wasp returns and once again explores the spider to make sure. Then there is a scuffle which the wasp invariably wins, stinging the spider in its only vulnerable spot, where the leg joins the body. As soon as the wasp's poison takes effect the spider falls over on its back paralyzed. It is then dragged into the hole where the wasp lays an egg on it, and covers it up, hiding all traces of the grave. Having provided for her offspring the wasp flies away.

The most remarkable thing about all of this is the complexity of the relationship these two species enjoy. The female tarantulas, which are extremely productive, lay 200–400 eggs at a time and they have been known to live up to 25 years. The wasp, in contrast, lives only a couple of months and produces only a few eggs. Petrukevitch expands on how complicated these relationships may become:

> There is a certain wasp, Pimpla inquisitor, whose larvae feed on the larvae of the tussock moth. *Pimpla* larvae in turn serve as food for the larvae of a second wasp, and the latter in their turn nourish still a third wasp. What subtle balance between fertility and mortality must exist in the case of each of these four species to prevent the extinction of all of them! An excess of mortality over fertility in a single member of the group would ultimately wipe out all four (p. 21).

Petrukevitch: 1952.

one learns to respond to a new stimulus in the same way he responded to the old. For example, a person who was involved in an auto accident shortly after buying a container of fried chicken found that, from that time on, the smell of fried chicken (the new stimulus) repelled and sickened him (the new reflex), since it always reminded him of the accident.

The conditioned reflex was first studied experimentally by an American, E. B. Twitmyer, about the turn of the century, although the importance of his work was not recognized in his own time. Instead, it was a Russian Physiologist, Ivan Pavlov, who gained scientific notice, when he demonstrated that a natural reflex could be associated to a new stimulus situation. Pavlov showed that classical conditioning begins with a natural stimulus-response reflex, such as a dog's salivating (reflex) to food powder (stimulus) placed in his mouth (See Figure 5-1).

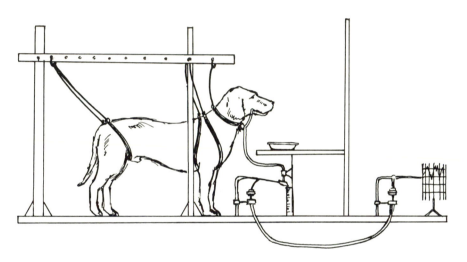

Figure 5-1. Pavlov's classical conditioning apparatus. Pavlov tied the dog in position with a harness and placed a dish of food in front of it. He used a glass tube to carry the saliva from the duct of one of the dog's salivary glands to a lever. The lever activated the stylus (far right) which recorded the rate and quantity of salivary secretion.

Without any learning, the stimulus, food powder, produces *naturally* the response of salivation. The food powder is called an *Unconditioned stimulus* (US), and the salivation is called an *unconditioned reflex or response* (UR). (Modern usage prefers "response" over "reflex.") To this stimulus-response pair Pavlov associated a new stimulus—a sound or tone—which was called a *conditioned stimulus* (CS). The term conditioning stimulus emphasized the fact that the pairing up of these two stimuli—the food and the tone—must occur a sufficient number of times before a full-strength response (salivation) is created. The repeated pairing of the two stimuli *reinforces* the learned connection, and sufficient reinforcement establishes a *conditioned* response. The idea of reinforcement is a very important one in learning. In general, it means to add to or strengthen something. In classical conditioning, reinforcement occurs when the conditioned stimulus is presented along with the unconditioned stimulus. Actually, the CS must be presented slightly *before* the US—for example, the tone must precede the giving of the food powder. A time lag of less than half a second is best, for if too much time passes, the animal is likely to fail to associate the two stimuli. Recall the person who had just bought chicken prior to an accident. Obviously, as he rode into his accident the smell of the fried chicken was very much with him. What now sickens him is not the act of buying fried chicken or seeing fried chicken, but of smelling fried chicken.

Once the conditioned response has been established, it can be tested by omitting the unconditioned stimulus (food powder) to see if the conditioned stimulus alone (the tone) will elicit the conditioned response (salivation). Consider again the fried chicken example. You can see that "everytime he smells fried chicken" is a "test trial" of conditioning that occurred. No other accident has followed the smell of fried chicken. How classical conditioning works is summarized in Figure 5-2.

The reverse of the reinforcement procedure is called *extinction. When we continuously omit reinforcement, we are extinguishing a conditioned response.* Sometimes after a response has been apparently extinguished, it makes a partial reappearance called *spontaneous recovery of a conditioned response.* During a series of extinction trials, fatigue as well as nonreinforcement occurs. At some later time, the effect of fatigue is gone, and some tendency to respond remains. The recovery was called "spontaneous" because it occurred when no further conditioning trials had followed the extinction trials. For example, Pavlov's dog salivates once again to the sound after a rest, although the response had apparently been extinguished.

It is easy to misinterpret the significance of extinction. An

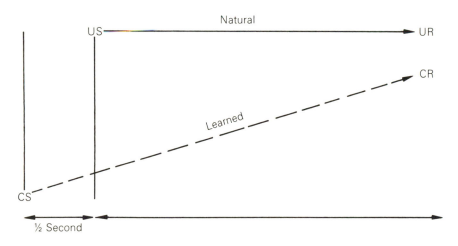

Figure 5-2.   What happens in classical conditioning. The diagram suggests (1) the time lag between Conditioned Stimulus (CS) and Unconditioned Stimulus (US), the optimum gap being a half second or less between the onset of CS and that of US; (2) that CS and US become associated together through reinforcement; and (3) that eventually the CS comes to elicit the CR because of reinforcement, just as the US elicited the UR before conditioning.

extinguished response may still be there, although the person has learned not to perform it. He may not have forgotten the learned association or the extinguished conditioned response at all, and if given the conditioned stimulus while under hypnosis, for example, may be able to again produce the conditioned response.

One more word about the student and the fried chicken. He has not lived through massed extinction trials; he probably does not often smell fried chicken, and may avoid places where he must smell it. Can you design a way for him to get over his conditioned response to the smell of fried chicken, so that he can once again enjoy it?

Sometimes the learner will make the conditioned response to a stimulus *similar* to the conditioned stimulus, a situation known as the *generalization of conditioned response*. For example, if you come to dislike someone in your childhood, in later life any person of similar appearance may evoke the same kind of dislike without his having done anything to make you feel that way. In much the same way, a person may develop a specific fear that will generalize to a class of similar objects. Watson & Raynor (1920) describe the case of "Little Albert," which has become the classic example of conditioned fear (see Figure 5-3). Initially it was found that Albert approached animals such as white rats and rabbits without fear. Using Pavlovian conditioning, the scientists paired the sight of a white rat (CS) with a loud sound (US), which frightened the subject and caused him to withdraw (UR). After repeated pairings of the two stimuli (reinforcement), the sight of the rat alone (CS) came to evoke the fear response (CR). Then generalization began

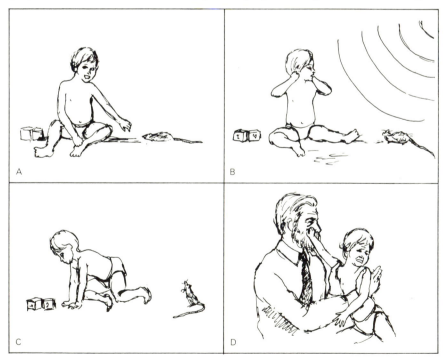

Figure 5-3.   The case of Little Albert. In this study, an unconditioned baby reached without fear toward a rat (A). Then a loud (frightening) noise was presented to the baby along with the rat (B). After the child had been conditioned, he feared not only the rat (C) but a man with a white beard which obviously reminded him of the rat (D).

to occur. Albert withdrew when he was shown a white rabbit that was not involved in the conditioning. Before the experiment he had approached the rabbit eagerly. Eventually Albert even withdrew from the experimenter's white beard. Generalization tends to occur unless the learner is specifically taught to discriminate between slightly different stimuli. Seeing such distinctions is called *stimulus discrimination*.

Generalization may account for some of the more irrational kinds of learning known to occur in human beings. Sometimes simply by accident two stimuli become associated. We can see some of the possibilities in the emotional reactions that have been conditioned to odd stimuli. Recently investigators have made discoveries that suggest that psychosomatic disorders—such as peptic ulcer, bronchial asthma, ulcerative colitis, essential hypertension, and rheumatoid arthritis—may represent unfortunate examples of classical conditioning. In a study by Sawry, Conger, & Turrell (1956) rats were exposed to a bright flash of light at the same time they were injected with insulin, which produces a drop in blood-sugar level that can lead to a state of shock and unconsciousness. After repeated pairings of the two stimuli, the shock occurred without the insulin; the light alone was sufficient. The Russian scientist Fel'beraum (1952) has conditioned the salivary response to pressure on the intestinal wall, indicating that a learner may acquire rather improbable connections between various internal body states. Such stimuli arise both from the outside stimulus world and from within the body of the learner.

Operant Conditioning

Unlike classical conditioning, which often seems irrational, our day-to-day activities appear logical and goal-directed. We learn behavior patterns that satisfy our needs, motives, and values. For example, in preparing for an occupation, the college student takes courses in order to learn what he must know to succeed in his chosen field. Likewise, in adjusting to life, a person acquires habits that he feels will serve his psychological needs.

In classical conditioning the response is caused by the stimulus. In operant conditioning, however, the response must come first—that is, no learning occurs until the response has been made. Then the learner continues to perform the response because he discovers that it serves some purpose. The learner acts on his environment, or operates on it, producing changes that affect it. Operant learning (also called *instrumental learning*) occurs because of its consequences. Most of our incidental learning, such as our initial acquisition of speech, are probably examples of operant conditioning.

The laws of learning already discussed, such as reinforcement and extinction, apply equally well to operant conditioning. *In operant conditioning, reinforcement is a stimulus that strengthens the association between the response and the stimulus that follows it.* For example, when you smile in the presence of a person of the opposite sex and the person smiles back, you feel good. Feeling good reinforces your tendency to smile again in similar circumstances.

This is in contrast to classical conditioning, where reinforcement is the association built up between two stimuli, conditioned and unconditioned. Operant conditioning involves building up a response-stimulus connection, whereas classical conditioning involves a stimulus-stimulus connection.

As in classical conditioning, extinction begins when reinforcement is omitted. In operant conditioning reinforcement is sometimes equated with reward and punishment, although some types of reinforcement are neither reward nor punishment. Psychologists prefer the term reinforcement because it covers all the conditions that *affect* the response. Sometimes mere knowledge of results, *feedback* about what is happening, is enough to reinforce behavior, although it would not seem sensible to call such feedback *rewarding*. "Punishment" is also a troublesome term because common sense tells us that punishment ought to stop the behavior. But punishment does not affect the strength of a response so long as reinforcement also occurs. For example, if a child is punished for stealing cookies, but is also reinforced because the stolen cookies taste good and he gets away with it most of the time, he will probably continue to steal cookies. Under special circumstances, punishment may even enhance the value of reinforcement, thus appearing to strengthen the response, for example, stolen fruits taste sweetest. Many common child-rearing techniques fail because they ignore this fundamental fact.

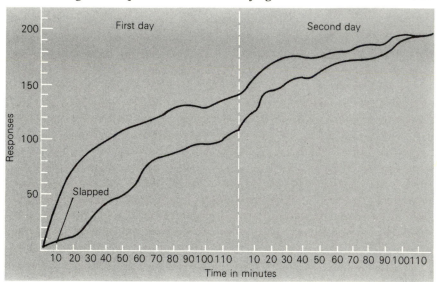

Figure 5-4.   The effect of punishment on extinction. Temporary response suppression following punishment. Initially, the rate of bar-pressing was significantly lower in the punished group, but by the end of the second day the effects of punishment had disappeared. (After B. F. Skinner, The Behavior of Organisms. Copyright 1938, D. Appleton-Century Co., Inc. Reprinted by permission of Appleton-Century-Crofts.)

If we wish a person to learn a response, we must reinforce it after it has occurred. If we wish him to stop making a response previously learned, we must stop reinforcing it, causing it to be extinguished. It is often much easier to get a person or animal to learn a habit than to unlearn one. Well-established habits continue because they are being reinforced or because the learner failed to notice extinction conditions. Punishment may not cause extinction, but it can temporarily depress the response rate. In the long run, the response is unaffected by moderate punishment; however, very severe punishment, such as electric shock, may produce quick suppression of the response. Such punishment is not recommended because the emotional reactions of the person being trained might interfere with further learning.

In child rearing the easiest way to make an undesirable habit extinct is simply to stop reinforcing it. Often this means just doing nothing—something that is easier said than done, for when a parent pays any kind of attention to annoying behavior, that attention is often reinforcing. In a practical sense, parents can best deal with a child's behavior by trying to emphasize the positive—by reinforcing good and ignoring bad behavior.

Reinforcement affects the learner because of his motivation. When a reinforcer produces natural consequences, such as the effect food has in reducing the hunger drive, we talk of *primary reinforcement*. When a learner must first learn the drive or motive before consequences have any meaning, we talk of *secondary reinforcement* and secondary reinforcers. Money, used to buy food to reduce the hunger drive, is an example of a secondary reinforcer. Human learning is made much more complex because of the variety of secondary reinforcers that affect behavior.

Intermittent Conditioning

So far our discussion has assumed that each response a person makes is reinforced. Often this is not the case. In real life a child behaves in various ways, some of which are reinforced only occasionally or intermittently. The rate at which learning takes place is affected by the type and amount of reinforcement. Intermittently reinforced responses grow in strength more slowly than continuously reinforced ones but are more difficult to extinguish. If a child were reinforced with reward each time he did the right thing, say in telling the truth, the first time he was not reinforced he might stop responding. Thus learning which is designed to produce a permanent habit might best reinforce only some correct behavior. Intermittent reinforcement occurs according to some definite *schedule*, either a ratio or an interval schedule. An example of a ratio schedule would be if we were to reward a dog every *third* time he begged at the table; an interval schedule if we were to reward him once every ten seconds.

A ratio schedule holds for much work done in agriculture or in the clothing industry; the worker gets so much for each unit he turns in. The interval schedule is not a common schedule in real life, but traffic lights regulate the *time* at which stopping or going across intersections will be "reinforced" by getting somewhere safely.

Also common in daily life, and very powerful in controlling behavioral persistence are those ratio and interval schedules that are irregular in pattern; the slot machine pays off according to the number of times you "feed" it and pull the lever, but you never know *which* lever pull will bring the payoff. Similarly, if you phone a friend and get no answer, you know you must wait *some* length of time before anyone will be home, but you seldom know *how long* it will be before the friend returns.

Many psychologists believe that the persistent kind of mal-adaptive and self-defeating behavior typical in neurosis may have been learned and maintained under an extremely irregular reinforcement schedule. The neurotic often fails to get the point that his behavior does not work well enough to satisfy his rational goals.

Shaping of behavior.   How is an animal led to make a complex response (perhaps a series of acts) that is to be reinforced? Initially, he might do something by *trial and error* that is reinforced. With a human being, however, the task is sometimes easier, because he can be instructed or shown. With an animal a procedure called *shaping* is typically used. For instance, suppose we want a pigeon to peck at a disk directly in front of him. At first, any slight movement he makes toward the disk is immediately reinforced. Next, only that behavior which is a better approximation of the final goal we want is reinforced. By small steps, then, a complex sequence of behavior can be shaped.

The pioneering work in schedules of reinforcement and operant shaping of behavior was done by B. F. Skinner and his co-workers at Harvard, but this work has since been taken up by practical men such as animal trainers and the techniques refined enough so that many species of animals have been trained to do fairly complex tricks (see Figure 5-5): a chicken plays a miniature piano, a pig runs an all-electric miniature kitchen. One investigator has even applied the same procedures to training pigeons to be industrial "quality-control" inspectors (Verhave, 1966).

Perhaps the most fascinating application of animal training techniques was made by Skinner himself during World War II, when he trained pigeons to make a different response to the shapes of friendly and unfriendly warships (Figure 5-6). A pigeon was strapped into a harness that permitted him to peck at "unfriendly" shapes, and he viewed the ships through a special transparent screen. When he pecked at shapes, he closed an electrical circuit connected to a guidance mechanism. The pigeon was trained to peck continuously, tracking the targets

until payoff—the payoff being food. The purpose of all this training was that the pigeons were to serve as "kamikaze" pilots of aircraft loaded with TNT. The planes were to be launched over the sea on autopilot in the general direction of the enemy until the pigeon "pilot" spotted an enemy ship, at which point he would start the pecking that would override the autopilot and guide the plane straight into the target, at which point the pigeon was to be rewarded with an unexpected payoff! To dispel doubts that a pigeon would be able to make the right decisions when confronted with several targets simultaneously, Skinner arranged for each plane to be guided by three pigeon pilots; the guidance mechanism would be run by committee and any dissenter would simply be outvoted.

Figure 5-5.   We have all seen results of shaping behavior. Circus animal trainers such as those seen in these two photographs use the techniques of shaping and generally reward the animals with food.

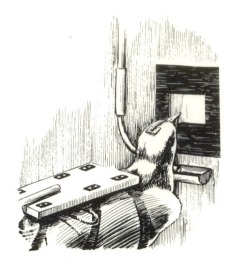

Figure 5-6.   Shaping up the Kamikaze (After Skinner, 1960). Arrangement for studying the tracking behavior of the pigeon. A gold electrode covers the tip of the pigeon's beak. Contact with the semiconducting surface of the translucent screen on which the image of the target is projected sends a signal informing the controlling mechanism of the location of the target. A few grains of food occasionally given to the pigeon maintains the tracking behavior. From Swartz, Psychology: The Study of Behavior, Van Nostrand Co., Inc., 1963. Original illustration by Russell Peterson. Reprinted by permission of Van Nostrand Co., Inc.

Frames from a simulated approach: a pigeon controls the orientation toward a ship at sea (image projected by motion picture film) as seen from an approaching airplane (After Skinner, 1960).

Although Skinner's invention appeared to be foolproof, it was never used because it was not taken seriously (Skinner, 1960).

The technique of shaping is probably an unwitting method of parents in bringing up their children: table manners, courtesies, household tasks, even imitation of parents' mannerisms are behaviors which the child shows awkwardly at first, but through praise and affection and amusement the parents gradually lead the child to more accurate or effective performance. Currently a number of psychologists and educators are discovering ways of using this technique to make educational tasks less tiresome. We will take up some of these applications in Chapter 9.

VARIETIES OF LEARNING

So far we have just discussed the types of conditioning. Another way of looking at learning is in terms of what psychological processes are being affected. In perceptual learning we establish expectations about the stimulus world. In motive learning we learn to value new kinds of activity and choice. In habit learning we acquire useful skills through feedback. Finally, in modeling we may acquire behavior that is not obviously reinforced.

Perceptual Learning

Perceptual learning involves three kinds of associations: (1) classical conditioning, (2) object learning, and (3) concept learning. Examples of classical conditioning are when an infant learns that his mother will come in response to his cries and reduce his hunger, or when an animal learns that light (conditioned stimulus) will be followed by shock (unconditioned stimulus). An example of object learning is when the same infant learns that certain stimuli belong together, such as his mother's face, hair, arms, and general appearance; it is the kind of

learning by which he discovers and identifies things, people, and events. An example of concept learning is when he learns that different objects (chairs, for instance) possess common properties, such as color, size, shape, or function; here he learns that many dissimilar objects can be used in the same way because they have the same function. In all three kinds of perceptual learning, the person builds up expectations about what goes with what in the stimulus world.

Failure of perceptual learning has not been given sufficient attention in discussions of the problems that many children have in school. Experience from compensatory education has revealed that many so-called disadvantaged children begin school with perceptual handicaps. They often lack essential information about their environment. If a child lacks the ability to identify common objects (such as the colors, sizes, and shapes), relationships (such as "over," "under," and "through"), and functions (such as "it is used for . . ."), he cannot describe his experiences so that others can understand him. Of course, he also cannot understand fully what others describe to him.

Generally, perceptual learning involves building up *if . . . then* expectancies about the stimulus world.

Motive Learning

It is not difficult to understand why an animal does something: he is always motivated by inborn drives such as hunger or thirst. A human being, however, learns to value many things, events, and activities that are not related to primary drives in any obvious way.

Achievement is an important, learned motive which has been studied extensively. A person who achieves by performing at a satisfying level experiences two kinds of consequences: *informational* and *affective feedback*. Informational feedback tells him the effect of his behavior on the environment. Affective (emotional) feedback is the pleasant feeling he gets from performing well. If he does not perform at a personally satisfying level, the emotional feedback is unpleasant.

Generally, research shows that people who achieve at a high level have been taught to value achievement in many different situations, and are likely to have had parents who reinforced good work and independent behavior. The child who is encouraged to be self-reliant and confident is likely to value achievement. High achievement produces both recognition and affective feedback, or emotional satisfaction, which is necessary for realistic feelings of self-esteem. Thus, we see how the social environment reinforces the behavior of high-achieving people.

If a boy is taught to value honor, courage, and excitement, he could grow up to be a military hero, or he could be driven into behavior that is hard for others to understand: wanton destructiveness, for example, or stealing things he does not keep or use. Perhaps the stealing and destructiveness are being reinforced, as Yablonsky (1952) has shown happens in youth gangs, where antisocial aggressiveness is often a factor in gaining status and acceptance. Again, we see how the social environment of a person reinforces certain kinds of motivation and behavior.

Habit and Skill Learning

A person driving a car demonstrates several kinds of learned skills. He steers the car, making continuous corrections as a result of visual and muscular feedback from the road. He depresses the clutch and shifts the gears upward and downward as speed requires. All this is done almost automatically. But all these individual stimulus-response habits had to be learned and chained together into a complex skill. Only later does the skill seem effortless and unconscious.

According to Gagné & Fleishman (1959): *"A motor skill is a sequence of habitual responses the order of which is partially or wholly*

determined by sensory feedback from preceding responses" (p. 38). When a person learns a motor skill, such as golf, he gradually improves his skill. A coach's instruction as well as direct experience provide feedback—both informational and affective—that helps the learner improve his performance. The kind and frequency of feedback influences directly the skill the learner displays at the end of instruction. Indeed, with some tasks where feedback is denied, no learning at all takes place.

To become a proficient golfer or musician, one needs expert instruction. Initial instruction is very important because higher levels of skill depend on previous mastery of lower level skills. If the instruction is inadequate, some components of the skill will hinder effective performance of the entire skill. For example, typists who teach themselves before receiving competent instruction may find that they can never become fast and error-free typists. Gagné & Fleishman note that "some motor skills are primarily controlled by internal feedback from the muscle sense, whereas others are primarily controlled by external feedback arriving through other senses" (p. 40).

We see feedback for one task, learning how to fire a weapon, illustrated in Figure 5-7. The level of skill attained by gunnery students who got the "buzzer"—a continuous noise which sounded when they were on target—was nearly double that of those who received no feedback. The more precise the feedback, the more useful it is. In a training situation such as the one illustrated, there is also the possibility of increasing the motivation of the learner by means of the influence of the group. Group support can be an important factor in individual

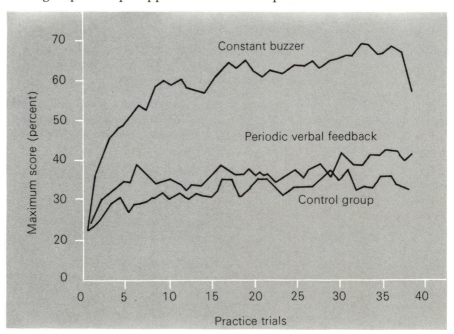

Figure 5-7.   **Feedback or knowledge of results. Subjects were given various kinds of feedback or knowledge of results, as they practiced on a gunnery trainer. The top curve represents the group given the sound of a buzzer whenever the subjects were on target. The middle curve shows the performance of the group that was given periodic verbal feedback. The bottom line represents the control group which was given no feedback at all. (Goldstein and Rittenhouse, 1954. Reprinted by permission of the American Psychological Association.)**

performance. Many an athlete is "cheered on" to his best performance only by the enthusiasm of the crowd.

Gagné & Fleishman give three rules for increasing the usefulness of feedback in motor-skill learning (pp. 248–249): (1) The training situation should be as *life-like* as possible so "wrong" stimuli will not become part of the skill. Thus, prospective skiers, for instance, should begin practice in full ski attire on real snow—not on hay. (2) The attention of the learner should be directed to *"correct"* stimuli, such as the proper knee action to get proper balance on skis. (3) The learner should be provided with *verbal rules*, such as "when skiing along the side of a slope, one's weight is distributed almost exactly the opposite of what common sense would suggest." All of these procedures help to reduce the amount of time it takes to discover "correct" stimuli, thus speeding up skill learning.

Modeling

Our discussion so far has emphasized the ideas of reinforcement and feedback to the point where the reader might conclude that without them no learning can take place. However, at least two lines of research suggest learning may occur without observable reinforcement of the usual sort: (1) the latent learning experiment, and (2) modeling research.

In the latent learning experiment, it was demonstrated that learning could take place incidentally without observable reinforcement

"Do as I say, not as I do."
Punishment of aggression sometimes has the paradoxical result of producing a more aggressive child.

(Brogden, 1939). A group of rats who were not reinforced with rewards learned a maze just as fast as another group who were reinforced. They did not demonstrate, however, *in their performance* (speed of running the maze) that they had learned until rewards were introduced. (It may be that acquiring a mental "map of reality" is intrinsically reinforcing to most higher animals.) As soon as reward was made a part of the procedure, the unreinforced rats began to equal the performance of the rats who had been reinforced all along. You have probably had the experience of going along for a ride with someone and just incidentally learning the route. If knowing the route becomes important through the introduction of reinforcement, such as a young man's interest in the possibility of a date with a girl, he will probably even be able to find his way back alone.

Acquiring a skill just by observing another is called learning by imitation, observational learning, or learning by *modeling*. A series of experiments by Bandura (Bandura, Ross & Ross, 1963) has demonstrated that children can learn to be more aggressive by watching films of models acting aggressively, even when they personally receive no reinforcement, but the model does. Like the latent learning situation, the aggression that has been learned may or may not be performed, depending on the circumstance.

In past times public floggings and executions were commonly administered to wrongdoers. Undoubtedly, those who authorized such events believed in the effectiveness of observational learning, believing that they served their purpose by creating fear of punishment among the public. People tend to identify with someone being punished and to some extent "feel with" or empathize with him, thus the punishment has some emotional impact on the onlooker too.

Much of a child's social behavior is learned through modeling of parent behavior. Nothing seems quite so irritating as when a child imitates the worst in the parent's behavior, but a parent should not be puzzled by the fact that his child is not likely to follow the advice, "Do as I say, not as I do." Psychotherapists also often observe patients who imitate the behavior of the parent they disliked the most. A boy who hated the shabby way his alcoholic father treated his mother may himself become an alcoholic father who maltreats his wife. Thus, families may unknowingly perpetuate patterns of behavior for many generations through observational learning.

There is considerable evidence that a child may learn a kind of general aggressiveness by observing his parent being aggressive. This fact may be one of the main reasons why punishment does not work very well to eliminate aggression in a child (Sears *et al.*, 1972). Parents who depend primarily on physical punishment in disciplining their children produce more delinquents than parents who use psychological means of control (Glueck & Glueck, 1950, p. 132).

MODIFYING BEHAVIOR

Let us consider again the social learning view of Bandura. Behavior is learned and maintained, states Bandura, by three different regulatory systems: (1) Some behavior is primarily controlled by *external stimuli*. Biological responses and emotional behavior can be brought under the control of classically conditioned environmental stimuli. Some operant behavior is similarly regulated. (2) Much behavior is controlled by *reinforcing* consequences. (3) Perhaps the most important way behavior is regulated is through *mental representation*, as when one anticipates getting future reinforcement if he behaves in a certain way. This system involves building up rules and strategies about behavior in different situations. For example, in modeled behavior, sometimes it is permissible for the child to be aggressive, while at other times it is not. Because one learns or builds up expectancies, he is able to develop self-reinforcing control of his own behavior. As Bandura puts it:

> In this conceptual scheme man is neither an internally impelled system nor a passive reactor to external stimulation. Rather, psychological functioning involves a reciprocal interaction between behavior and its controlling environment. The type of behavior that a person exhibits partly determines his environmental contingencies which, in turn, influence his behavior (1969, p. 63).

Figure 5-8.   The learning of aggression through modeling. Imitation as a factor in the aggressive behavior of children. The top rows of pictures are frames from a film the children saw. The other two rows show the behavior of children after seeing the film. (Bandura, Ross, and Ross, 1963, Photos courtesy of Dr. A. Bandura).

MAYA PINES

How Three-year-olds Teach Themselves to Read—and Love It

When introduced to Dr. Moore's Talking Typewriter, they think it is a glorious kind of toy—and they may never find out that it is, in fact, a remarkably effective "learning machine."

SITTING alone in a bare cubicle, a little girl of five happily pecks away at a specially designed automated typewriter and composes a poem. A two-and-a-half-year-old teaches herself to read and write by banging the jam-proof keys of a similar "talking typewriter." Along with several dozen other youngsters, they are taking part in a series of experiments which may have loud repercussions and a surprisingly humanistic effect on education as a whole. The project is the brainchild of a Yale sociologist, Dr. Omar Khayyam Moore.

He believes that the years from two to five are the most creative and intellectually active period of our lives. This is when children first acquire speech and begin to classify their environment. Normally they receive no schooling at this time. And certainly they should not be stuffed with rules and facts. But—says Dr. Moore—they are capable of extraordinary feats of inductive reasoning if left to themselves in a properly "responsive" environment. Furthermore, performing such feats may become a habit and lead to a new breed of highly individualistic, highly imaginative human be-

ings far better prepared than their parents to cope with a complex and unpredictable society.

To Professor Moore—himself highly individualistic and imaginative at forty-three—this is the significance of his "Responsive Environments Laboratory." A man of medium height, with close-cropped hair and deep-set expressive eyes, he is now on sabbatical from his associate professor's post at Yale. He spends most of his time at Hamden Hall Country Day School, a small private school near New Haven, Connecticut. In his laboratory, which is supported by the Carnegie Corporation of New York, Hamden Hall's pupils learn to read, write, type, take dictation, and compose their own stories before they enter first grade. To Dr. Moore this accomplishment is just a happy by-product of his extensive research on culture, learning theory, and "human higher-order problem solving" behavior.

The children who come to his Lab spend no more than half an hour a day there. They may stay away if they wish, or leave after only a few minutes. While the child is in the Lab he is free of all outside pressures. His parents never come in with him and are never told how he is doing. Even his regular teachers, to whom he may be emotionally attached, stay out of the picture. Staff members themselves—half-a-dozen young wives of Yale graduate students—try to be as impersonal as possible.

The "talking typewriter" consists of a standard-size typewriter keyboard with colored keys, a small speaker, an exhibitor (a frame on which printed matter can be displayed) with a red pointer, a projector which resembles a miniature TV screen, and dictation equipment. Blank paper in the typewriter stands ready to take anything the child types, in jumbo type. There is nothing in the sound-proof, air-conditioned booth to distract the child's attention from the machine. Only the keyboard is accessible to the child; all the other gadgets are enclosed in plexiglass or in a wooden cabinet behind the typewriter.

The child discovers immediately that this interesting, adult-looking typewriter is his to play with on his own initiative. The younger the child, the more joyous his response.

The game begins when he presses a key. At once a large letter, number, or punctuation mark appears on the paper, and a soft voice names it through the loudspeaker. The same things happen no matter what part of the keyboard he strikes, as rapidly and as often as he desires. (To test his new-found powers, one two-year-old gleefully struck the asterisk key seventy-five times in succession.)

JOYOUS DISCOVERIES

When the teacher who has been watching through a one-way mirror sees that the child's interest is waning, she switches a control dial. A curtain lifts over the exhibitor and a red arrow points to a single letter. At the same time the machine's voice names it. Puzzled, the child may try to depress a key, but to his surprise it doesn't work. He tries more and more keys, until he finds the right one. Then the key goes down and prints the letter while the voice names it again. As a new letter pops up on the exhibitor, the child faces an exciting puzzle, a game of "try and find me." Every time a number, letter, or punctuation mark appears on the exhibitor, he hunts for it amid the blocked keys until he hits the jackpot.

From stage to stage, the rules of the game keep being changed for the child, who must constantly adapt himself to fresh situations.

Meanwhile he is learning to touch-type without effort. Each set of keys to be struck by a particular finger has its own identifying color, and the group meant for the right hand responds to a slightly different pressure from that meant for the left. He is also learning to recognize different styles and sizes of type as they appear on the exhibitor, and handwritten letters which may be flashed on the projector's screen.

About once a week the child plays with a blackboard and chalk in a booth which has little automated equipment. (Only one "talking typewriter" is fully automated at present, and the children are assigned to booths at random.) Under ordinary circumstances, when you give a child a piece of chalk, he will scribble or draw pictures. But there are horizontal lines on this blackboard which discourage art work, and eventually the child tries to make letters. At this point, the teacher helps by putting a letter on the projector and suggesting that he draw one like it. Soon the child learns to write the letters he has begun to read and type.

The teacher's role depends on the degree of automation in the booths. Sometimes she takes over the machine's voice part, speaking as gently and patiently as the "talking typewriter." Sometimes she operates the exhibitor by hand. When using the fully automated booth, she merely watches the child through a one-way mirror and comes to his rescue if he raises his hand for help. This may happen if the machine gets stuck (until now the Lab has had only an experimental model to work with) or if the child needs a handkerchief or human company.

As the child advances he finds that the exhibitor suddenly shows him a series of letters, such as "CAT." By now he may be able to pick out a "T" right away, but when he tries this the key is blocked. "A" is blocked, too. When he strikes "C" however, the machine responds by typing it and saying, "C." The exhibitor's red arrow, which had been pointing to "C," then moves to the right over "A." As he strikes all three keys in the proper sequence, the machine prints them, names them one by one, and then says, "Cat." From now on, letters appear only in series—but to the child they are still letters, not words. Then one day, although no one has been "teaching" him, the child suddenly realizes that the letters he knows so well determine words. Overwhelmed by the revelation he is likely to run out of the booth ecstatically—a reaction the Lab has witnessed over and over again.

This joy in discovery, Professor Moore believes, is sadly lacking in most methods of early childhood education. "By the time a child is three, he has achieved what is probably the most complex and difficult task of his lifetime—he has learned to speak," he points out. "Nobody has instructed him in this skill; he has had to develop it unaided. In bilingual or multilingual communities, children pick up several languages without accent at a very early age. There's plenty of information-processing ability in a mind that can do that."

I visited his "Responsive Environments

Laboratory" a few weeks ago. It is a modest, green, prefabricated structure with a narrow corridor, five cubicles with "talking type-writers" in various stages of automation, and a few offices.

At 8:30 in the morning I watched a very small girl enter the building, trailed by a few slightly older children. After being helped to remove her coat and muffler, she walked over to a long table on which stood open jars of bright-colored paints and let a teacher paint her fingernails different colors, to match the color code on the typewriter keys. Then she went into the automated booth and sat down at a chair facing the typewriter. First she pressed the carriage-return key a couple of times, seeming satisfied with the noise it made and the voice which said, each time, "carriage return." Then she banged on "C" and listened to the machine's response, "C." For a while she hummed a tune. Next she fiddled with a side lever. Finally she began to type a few letters rapidly, glancing up at the characters she pro-duced and alert to the voice which came from the loudspeaker. After eighteen minutes in the booth, she suddenly raised her hand. A teacher came in to help her off the chair. "Bye-bye," said the little girl, and walked out.

She was exactly two years and eight months old. In less than two months she had taught herself all the letters in the alphabet, both upper and lower case, and could also write some of them on the blackboard.

Most children pay little attention to the adults in the Lab—they are too fascinated by the machine. The only exceptions are some older ones who have learned to be careful before they start work at the Lab. Thus one newcomer, a little boy of six, would go into his booth and hesitantly press a few keys, then run out to ask the teacher, "Am I doing it right?" He could not get used to the idea that *anything* he did was all right.

Watching the children in the nursery group, mostly four-year-olds, I saw that several who had been in the Lab no more than four months were writing full sentences.

"Barry is a RAT," one little boy typed in complete, silent concentration. He had ranged all over the keyboard, typed the numbers from 16 to 20 in proper sequence, played with the quotation marks, and written several nonsense words before producing his gem, to which he suddenly added, "and a cat." He was using correct fingering technique. Later on, checking his records, Professor Moore told me that while the boy was bright, he did not test in the "gifted" range, which begins above an IQ of 140. He did have one incalculable advantage however: permissive parents who laid heavy emphasis on intellectual skills, thus giving him much to relate to what he learned in the Lab.

Because of their individual differences, I found it hard to gauge the progress of the kindergarteners, the next group, who had been in the Lab for a year and four months. But the first-graders were impressive. Two of them—aged six—were busy in one of the offices editing a newspaper which they and a few classmates had dictated into the tape recorder and then typed. It contained little stories, poetry, and riddles: "Why is grass like a mouse?—Answer: because the cat'll eat it (cattle)." One poem by a girl of five was en-titled "A Duck" and read as follows:

There was a duck
Who could kick.
He had good luck,
Because he was quick.

He could run in a race,
He would win.
He would get some lace
And a magic pin.

When I met the pint-sized poet she was engrossed in her daily session with the "talking typewriter." From the projector she fluently read a story about Aladdin's lamp. Then she questioned the teacher about the plot and answered the teacher's questions about the meaning of certain words and the story. When she came out of the booth, she sat down with me in an empty office. I asked her whether she wanted to be a poet when she grew up. "No," she replied without hesitation, "I want to be a housewife." Writing poetry was fun, she said, but the really nice part was being able to work on the newspaper "with Jeff," one of the editors. Did she prefer the Lab when a teacher was there, as today? She liked it best when she was alone in it, she replied emphatically, "so I can do *exactly* what I like."

The most advanced children in the Lab are the two young editors. One is Professor Moore's gifted daughter, Venn, who started playing with the "talking typewriter" when she was two years and seven months old and could read first-grade stories before she was three. Jeffrey, who is the same age, joined her in Professor Moore's early experiments at Yale, and now both children read seventh-grade books with pleasure. To test their skill, I opened a copy of *Scientific American* at random and asked them whether they could read it. They did so exuberantly, taking turns. Al-though they stumbled over some words which they did not understand, they could clearly handle anything phonetically.

THE CRUCIAL YEARS

People have an idealized version of the playpen as happy and *mindless*, Professor Moore observes. "They say, 'Life is hard enough as it is, let's leave the early period alone.' But we're using only half-an-hour a day! And with the 102 children we've seen so far, we have yet to run into one who'll come in, explore the place, and not want to come back. Of course the children still have their sandbox and paints and so on—in fact, the Lab actually allows us to prolong some of these things.

"As traditionally handled now in the reasonably good nursery schools, at least the children are free, though they receive little intellectual stimulation. But comes the first grade, and the game is over. At the very time when he is becoming interested in the wider world around him, the child must divorce himself from such matters and confine himself to squiggles. He must learn the alphabet, learn to print, and because of his low skill, read baby stories that are not appropriate for him. All of this takes so long that many important things are dropped as frills—painting and music, for instance.

"No wonder so many children develop a hatred for intellectual work early in school. Yet intellectual things are as natural as anything else."

The human mind is extraordinarily open between the ages of two and five. The problem, Dr. Moore believes, is not to miss this critical period. Researchers have found that even rats and monkeys have an inborn curiosity which impels them to seek new territory for its own sake. Experiments have also demonstrated that the key to a rat's learning ability is what happens to it during infancy—which lasts only a few weeks. If rats are exposed to a stimulating environment during this crucial period, they

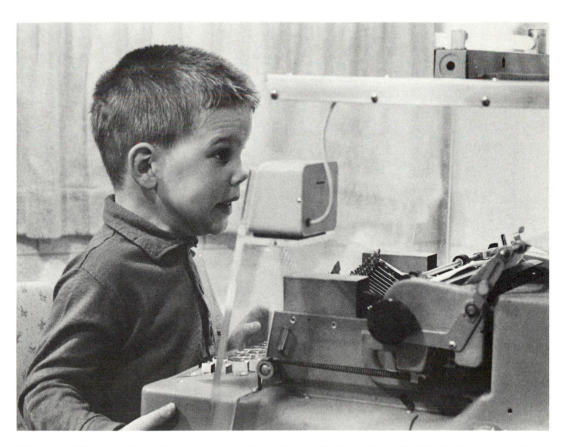

Moment of discovery! . . . He has found and typed correctly the letter called for by the recorded voice. (Photo by Paul Berg, St. Louis Post Dispatch.)

acquire skills with ease later. If not, their whole subsequent performance is impaired.

"If animals are comfortable and have free time, then they will explore," says Professor Moore. In human beings, behavioral scientists have begun to recognize this same "competence drive" as a major motivation along with the drives of hunger, thirst, and sex. But often the drive is stifled. "Every year we lose hundreds of thousands of children who have the ability to learn but who don't go on to college," Professor Moore says. "They have made a nearly irreversible decision very early in life, long before they reach the guidance people in the last year of high school."

For this reason he feels that our educational spending habits are topsy-turvy. "If I had a certain sum to spend on twenty Ph.D. candidates and twenty nursery-school children, I'd use most of it on the youngest children," he says. "They're the ones who need it most." But generally, he points out, schools provide only minimum equipment and teachers for nursery school and kindergarten.

"We're going to have to change our whole notion of how much capital investment should go into education, especially in the early years," Dr. Moore says. "If necessary, we can cut down on expense later; older students should be able to make use of more community facilities, and anyway they can do more on their own."

Dr. Moore has recently set up additional experimental centers in Boston, Massachusetts, and Freeport, New York. Another is being established in Cooperstown, New York. He wants to find out whether his methods work equally well with children in other settings and also to explore the problem of cost.

The matter of expense is possibly the major objection voiced by visitors to his Lab. And indeed it does present a problem. The first production model of his fully automated typewriter (called "A.R.E." for "Automated Responsive Environments") cost an estimated $400,000 to develop. Built by the Thomas Edison Research Laboratory of West Orange, New Jersey, it is a cross between an analogue and a digital computer, new enough to have been patented, and small enough to be portable. The computer coordinates the action of the typewriter keyboard, the voice, the dictation equipment, the exhibitor, and the projector. Even on a mass-production basis, this combination would not be cheap. An effort is now being made to develop a low-cost, only par-

tially automated device that can do many of the same things.

But even so, the Moore program cannot be a bargain. The "talking typewriter" actually increases the need for skilled teachers. There must be several monitors in the Lab, at least for young children. In addition, regular classroom teachers must be able to deal with unusually inquisitive, individualistic youngsters. This requires teachers who are not wed to routines.

MORE FUN FOR FATHER

At Hamden Hall, as the Lab produced more and more small children who could read, write, and think independently, some teachers were upset. All their past training seemed threatened when first the kindergarten, then the first grade, were reorganized to make use of the children's skills. One dogged conservative simply refused to face facts. Although nearly all her charges could read and take dictation, she insisted on the standard "reading readiness" exercises.

"That's like giving young children a 'talking readiness' test, and not letting them speak until they pass it," scoffs Professor Moore. "It would mean never saying anything in front of a child that he can't understand, when actually he bathes in speech from the time he is born, and eventually catches on to its patterns."

It was Edward I. McDowell, Jr., headmaster of Hamden Hall, who three years ago took the initiative in bringing Professor Moore and his experiment to the school, in which 340 boys and girls attend classes running from nursery through twelfth grade. Like some of the teachers, a few of the trustees have not been happy about the consequences and last year they tried to oust McDowell. With the backing of parents whose children were directly involved in the experiment he fought back and won out.

This year the first-grade class is reading fourth-grade geography books, going on field trips (to a bakery and other nearby points of childhood interest), and enjoying other extras usually called "enrichment." The children are also plodding—with considerably less enthusiasm—through penmanship practice and the standard school work-books (the latter at third- and fourth-grade level).

Mr. McDowell foresees far more drastic changes in the kind of school that might in the future evolve from these experiments. "It's going to lead to an ungraded school system all the way up the line," he says. "Educationally this is nothing new, but administratively it's quite a problem. It means the children won't stay in the same room all day long; when it's time for math, for instance, they'll have to split up. In general they'll remain with their own age groups. But in reading-writing, math, and science, they will be grouped according to achievement."

Before starting in the Moore program, each child is given a battery of intelligence and projective tests by a clinical psychologist, as well as physical and eye examinations and hearing tests. A speech expert evaluates his ability to make sounds and a sociologist takes a look at his parents and his home. The clinical psychologist checks up on the children at various stages of the program. So far, there have been no negative results, and according to the psychologist the children's Rorschach tests show "greater richness and better balance" as they advance in the program. Some of their parents report that their children become more interesting.

"Now that letters and numbers are her friends, everything has more meaning for her," commented one mother. Another child's father admitted, "I was waiting for my boy to grow up before I spent time with him. Now, I'm sorry when he goes to bed."

Many aspects of the program are specifically designed to give the child an early grasp of reality. When the child learns to read into the recording equipment and then take his own dictation, for instance, he becomes his own judge of what constitutes adequate reading. If his original reading from the projector is unclear, he realizes that he is the source of his difficulties; if he reads well, he will find that he is helping himself. Such objectivity presumably should help children to think better and develop a more adequate "social self."

"However, we keep watching for other, negative consequences," Professor Moore says. "Maybe they will show up in time."

Meanwhile, Dr. Moore hopes that the less gifted children will benefit even more than the brighter ones from their sessions with a "responsive environment." Because they are alone with the machine, those who don't understand quickly need not be embarrassed or suffer from constant comparison with the faster learners. In the standard classroom, the gifted child often supplies virtually all the central principles, interpretations, and key facts; thus slower students are deprived of exhilarating discoveries. This may be one of the reasons why slower students come to resent the gifted child, he suggests: they intuitively associate him with their loss.

A "talking typewriter" has infinite patience. It plays no favorites. It does not hold out bribes or threats, nor need the child feel anxious about losing its love. For these reasons, it seems ideally suited to teaching retarded children and others with severe handicaps.

Last year, five retarded boys and girls who had been rejected by public kindergartens because of their low IQs and behavior problems came to the Lab, tried out the gadgets, and liked them. After seven weeks of work their attitude improved enough for their schools to agree to take them back conditionally. After a year of work in the Lab, all had learned to read simple material. Their IQs ranged from 59 to 72, classifying them as "educable" retarded who, with the best of standard methods and three to four years of painstaking drills, might begin to read around the age of nine. Yet here was a six-year-old boy (IQ 64) typing away, "The goose laid a golden egg." Although it might take them five or six times as long to reach the same stage as a normal child, they made steady progress at their own pace.

Had these five children been institutionalized or simply deprived of further education, they would probably have become wards of the state for the rest of their lives. In this case the cost of the machine was clearly justified.

Professor Moore plans to concentrate his future research on the deaf, the retarded, and others with severe handicaps. The Responsive Environments Foundation, Inc., a nonprofit organization he has set up with Mr. McDowell, will open its doors to such children next fall.

These experiments with children evolved from Professor Moore's earlier work for the Office of Naval Research. For the past nine years he has dealt with the kind of "human higher-order problem solving" involved in mastering artificial symbolic languages. As his emphasis shifted from deductive to inductive processes, his research with adults became more and more difficult. What he needed was a research lab in which an entirely new order of things had to be discovered.

"Rather than create a whole new environment that was strange enough," he said, "I decided to go in for ignorant subjects."

The most ignorant subjects, of course, are

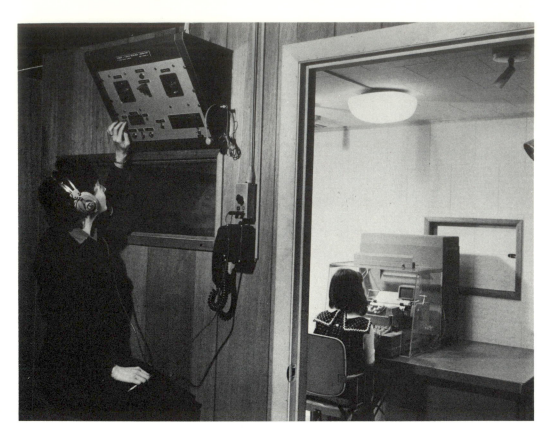

Watching behind a one-way mirror, the teacher can lend a hand as a child goes from random typing to reading and writing. (Photo by Paul Berg, St. Louis Post Dispatch.)

newborns. The most practical time to start experimenting was when these children were up and about, at two-and-a-half or three.

LEARNING MACHINES OR TEACHING MACHINES?

Unlike parrots, young children don't learn item by item, but by overall search—they absorb whole patterns, Dr. Moore believes. Instead of just repeating a word or phrase over and over, they make up their own sentences. This is the key difference between the "responsive environments" approach and usual "programed instruction" or "teaching machines." Some children explore the keyboard systematically, others scatter their efforts—they are not all sent along a pre-set path from A to B to C.

This flexibility may make it possible to program the "talking typewriter" for six languages simultaneously. The teacher can then select the language she wants by the flick of a switch. She can program the projector to show, for instance, a picture of a cat with the word "cat" in a foreign language. After the student has seen the word, typed it, and heard it pronounced, the machine may ask him to repeat it, and then play back his own and the correct pronunciation. If the dials are set correctly, anybody can insert his own program simply by typing and talking into the machine. Unlike other computers, this machine does not require a mathematician to translate commands for it.

All kinds of unfamiliar subjects can be presented in this fashion. A system for teaching basic arithmetic, using an electric calculator, has been worked out in a preliminary way. The Navy and Air Force plan to try out the "talking typewriter" with adult illiterates as soon as enough machines are available. The city of Freeport, New York, has passed a special bond issue to build a new-model "Responsive Environments Laboratory" for its kindergarten and first-grade pupils next year;

circular in design, it will consist of ten booths monitored by a yet undetermined number of teachers in the center of the Lab. And Israel—despite the problems involved in converting to a different alphabet—expects to put several machines on trailers in the near future and send them out to far-flung kibbutzes, to help new immigrants learn Hebrew.

Meanwhile the machines which already exist represent a unique "learner-tracking system," in the words of P. Kenneth Komoski, President of the nonprofit Center for Programed Instruction, Inc., which is supported by the Carnegie Corporation. Very little is known about how children actually learn; most of our theories on the subject really deal with performance, rather than the learning process. Yet here are some machines—Mr. Komoski prefers to call them "learning machines," rather than "teaching machines"—which keep records of every relevant or irrelevant path their subjects take while learning.

"Suppose we discover that children with certain kinds of background learn in a certain, restricted way," he speculates. "Eventually it may become possible to open up such closed systems and show these children other ways. Studying the tracks they leave, one might figure out some exercises which would help them break out of overly limited patterns of thought."

Even more important is the impact Professor Moore's work may have on programed instruction as a whole, according to Mr. Komoski. "Programing today takes the best we already know about teaching and puts it into a more efficient means of communication," he says. "It makes the students come up with the right answers, but it is very didactic, with all the little pieces in a preconceived sequence. And because of the tremendous commercial activity in the field, a lot of unimaginative programing is being sold—or oversold. Professor Moore's work is the only real attempt, in automated teaching, to keep alive the student's curiosity and ability to deal with new problems."

TOMORROW'S THINKERS

If future experiments prove as successful as those to date at Hamden, what passes for early-childhood education in most nursery schools may come to seem a terrible waste. Professor Moore, however, declines to be drawn into the controversy that is almost certain to result. He has wisely steered clear of an area where slogans like "Why Johnny Can't Read" can arouse the nation, where proponents of the "look-see" method of reading instruction can wage a sterile fight for years with teachers of "phonics," and where the very age at which children should be taught reading is an explosive issue.

"We've been trying very hard to develop an adequate technology and test it carefully. We do not advocate that other people use it" he says. "We don't yet have a finished program. We want to keep the atmosphere free for further experimentation." When the Department of Agriculture wished to convince farmers to shift to hybrid corn and contour farming, he points out, "they simply put up a few model farms here and there, where farmers could come and watch. They did not argue." Professor Moore hopes similarly to proceed by example.

The one issue on which this quiet man speaks with undisguised emotion is the need to develop the next generation's inductive processes. "Modern society is evolving so dynamically that we can no longer depend on child-rearing methods which were adequate before," he says. "We have no time. We can't stand pat. We have more new problems today than we can even name, and we must turn out larger and larger numbers of youngsters who can make fresh inductions about our world.

"A new kind of person is needed to handle the present rate of change. This is our chief trouble today: Technological change but intransigent behavior. It's too late for us—our generation can't make it. At best, we are just the transition group."

Summarizing Statements

1. We infer learning from changes observed in behavior. Changes produced by instinct, fatigue, disease, or sensory adaptation are excluded because they are not produced by experience.

2. Reflexes, which are less complex than instincts, are unlearned, inborn patterns of behavior elicited by stimulation. An instinct is a complex pattern that is universal to the species. Instincts often require the help of inborn "releasing stimuli" to set them off. Instincts are useful in helping an animal to adapt, but they lack the flexibility of learned, intelligent behavior. Intelligence is characteristic of the higher organisms.

3. Learning is a relatively long-lasting change in behavior caused by experience.

4. In classical conditioning a natural stimulus-response reflex becomes associated with a new stimulus. Conditioning occurs as a result of reinforcement. When sufficient reinforcement occurs a conditioned reflex or response (CR) is created. The absence of reinforcement is called extinction. Extinction is not forgetting, but rather an active withholding of the CR.

5. Sometimes the CR generalizes to other stimuli. In human learning the most important instance of generalization occurs when there is a spreading effect in emotional conditioning, such as in conditioned fear responses. There is a good possibility that psychosomatic disorders may represent unfortunate examples of classical conditioning.

6. Some very improbable connections, such as learning to salivate in response to pressure on the intestinal wall, have been classically conditioned.

7. In operant conditioning the learner learns and continues behavior because it serves some purpose: the consequences of behavior reinforce it. Classical conditioning involves stimulus-stimulus learning, while operant conditioning involves response-stimulus learning.

8. In operant learning the concept of reinforcement covers both reward and punishment, as well as other conditions which affect the response, such as feedback.

9. If we wish a person to learn a new response we must reinforce it after it has occurred. To stop a person from making a response previously learned, we must stop reinforcing it. Punishment has the effect of depressing the response rate only temporarily unless the punishment is extremely severe.

10. When a reinforcer produces natural consequences, such as the effect of food on hunger, we talk of primary reinforcement. A secondary reinforcer is one that must itself be learned. Partial reinforcement is applied only occasionally according to some schedule of reinforcement. Learning is more slowly acquired under partial reinforcement, but is also less easily extinguished. So-called neurotic behavior may be an example of behavior acquired under an extremely irregular reinforcement schedule.

11. Complex animal learning occurs through a process called shaping, which reinforces better and better approximations of the final response desired. Skinner's kamikaze pigeon is an example of what can be done in the shaping of animal behavior.

12. Perceptual learning involves classical conditioning, object learning, and concept learning. Many so-called disadvantaged children begin school with perceptual handicaps that make it difficult for them to communicate with others about their experiences.

13. Human beings learn to value many things, events, and activities that are not originally motivating. Satisfying achievement produces both informational and affective or emotional feedback. Achievement motivation is learned in a supportive family environment.

14. The social environment of a person reinforces certain kinds of valued behavior. For example, delinquent gangs may reinforce stealing, fighting, and wanton destructiveness, and reward with status those members who conform to these values.

15. A motor skill is a sequence of habitual responses, partially or wholly determined by sensory feedback from preceding responses. The kind and frequency of feedback influences the degree of skill displayed by the learner at the end of instruction. In some cases if there is no feedback, there is no learning.

16. The latent learning experiment highlights the difference between performance and learning. It demonstrates that a learner can learn a behavior but not demonstrate it in his behavior until he is rewarded for performing.

17. In learning by modeling, a learner who is not reinforced at all learns to imitate the behavior of a model. Again, the learning may not be demonstrated in behavior unless the situation is felt to be appropriate. Learning by modeling is the means by which children acquire most of their social responses. This may clarify why the advice "Do as I say, not as I do" is so useless.

18. According to Bandura, there are three different systems for behavior regulation: (1) Some behavior is primarily under external stimulus control. (2) Much behavior is controlled by reinforcing consequences. (3) The most important category of human behavior is regulated through mental representation or expectancies, such as the anticipation of future reward.

19. Man is neither driven wholly from outer nor from inner stimuli. The behavior he shows partly determines his environmental feedback, which in turn affects his behavior.

READING SELECTION

20. O. K. Moore's "talking typewriter" is a teaching or learning machine that provides tutorial attention and response to every action of a child. It is a computerized typewriter that talks, listens, presents pictures and graphs, comments and explains, presents information, and responds to the child's typing. It represents one of the most advanced applications of feedback control of human learning yet devised. Moore thinks of it as a responsive environment.

21. Moore believes that the ages of 2 to 5 years are the most creative and intellectually active period for learning. The responsive

environment concept makes use of the child's interest, curiosity, and natural motivation to learn, and his "joy in discovery" of things for himself. Because of the way the typewriter keyboard is programmed, the child cannot complete incorrect responses, which guarantees that all trials will be followed by success.

22.   Two essential features of the system are that it is user controlled, or self-paced, and that information is presented to many senses of the learner simultaneously. The machine can record the learner's voice, and play it back with a comparison model prerecorded in the machine. Thus the machine closes a perceptual circle in which the skills of reading, writing, and understanding are combined.

23.   Long, drawn-out reading programs may be ignoring the implication that learning to read well is the result of easy, early success followed by plenty of reading.

Terms and Concepts

Classical conditioning: the process of associating a new stimulus to a reflex already in existence.

Conditioned response: the response made after successful association of the conditioning stimulus and the unconditioned ʽstimulus. Achieved as a function of reinforcement.

Conditioned stimulus: the new stimulus that is associated with a natural stimulus in conditioning.

Expectancy learning: a form of perceptual and conceptual learning in which rules and strategies are built up about different situations. Expectancy learning assists in the development of self-control of behavior. For example, a child may learn that at some times it is permissible to be aggressive while at other times it is not.

Extinction: the omission of reinforcement to a previously learned association which produces a gradual end to responding. When a response is extinguished it is no longer performed. In classical conditioning it is not the same as forgetting, but roughly synonymous with unlearning.

Feedback or knowledge of results: information about performance. Informational feedback tells the learner what effect his behavior has had on the environment. Affective feedback refers to our emotional reaction—of pleasantness or unpleasantness—to the performance.

Generalization of a conditioned response: the eliciting of the conditioned response by a stimulus similar, but not identical, to the conditioned stimulus.

Instinct: inherited behavior that is unlearned, complex and universal to the species.

Intermittent reinforcement: reinforcement that is applied continuously but according to some schedule of reinforcement.

Learning: a relatively enduring change in behavior caused by experience. Not to be confused with instinct or the changes caused by fatigue, disease, or sensory adaptation.

Modeling: learning by observing the behavior of someone else, which may occur without observable reinforcement. Also called *imitation* or *observational* learning.

Motor Skill: a sequence of habitual responses partly or wholly determined by sensory feedback from preceding responses.

Operant conditioning: learning produced by its reinforcing consequences. The learner acts or operates on his environment, producing changes; goal-oriented learning. This kind of learning is instrumental to satisfying the learner's motivation.

Perceptual learning: learning what goes with what in classical conditioning; learning the identity of objects; learning the common properties of objects (concepts).

Primary reinforcement: reinforcement which affects unlearned drives (motives) of the learner.

Psychosomatic disorders: physical ailments in which psychological events or causes are known to play a role.

Punishment: inflicting a penalty on a learner for wrong behavior.

Reflex.   a simple stimulus-response connection that is inborn and automatic. Not to be confused with instinct.

Reinforcement: those events which affect the strength of the learned connection; in classical conditioning presenting the conditioning stimulus along with the unconditioned stimulus is reinforcing. In operant conditioning, reinforcement is a stimulus which when presented affects the strength of the association or connection between stimulus and response.

Secondary reinforcement: reinforcement the significance of which the learner must learn; affecting learned motivation.

Shaping: a procedure by which the learner is lead to give better and better approximations of the end response desired through systematic control of reinforcement.

Unconditioned response: the *natural* response in a preexisting stimulus-response reflex.

Unconditioned stimulus: the *natural* stimulus in a preexisting stimulus-response reflex.

Genius, in truth, means little more than the faculty of perceiving in an unhabitual way.

William James

Perception

6 MOST of us take for granted the facts delivered up to us by our senses, the fantastic array of sights, sounds, smells, tastes, and feelings. The mystery of how it all happens, however, we usually acknowledge only dimly.

Perception is a marvelously complex process. Almost everything in psychology has something to do with perception. Learning, development, personality, adjustment—all affect perception by transforming the raw information of the senses into something organized and meaningful. The common-sense belief that no two people perceive things in exactly the same way is literally true. What we are influences the way we perceive things; our motivation and experience filter the process. A man who is hungry sees more food in his world than a man who is not. Because he is sensitized to food stimuli, he may even exaggerate the size or attractiveness of food whenever he sees it.

Perception is not a one-to-one representation of the stimulus world in the mind. Rather, it is more like a free translation of poetry from one language into another. Liberties are taken, different phrasing and figures of speech are used. Sometimes the transformation goes too far. If motivation is high or the distortion of self too extreme, what is yielded up as perception may be far from objective reality. At any rate, perception is always a construing of experience, a meshing of the outer stimulus world with the realm within.

Let us now consider how sensation and the higher mental processes influence, distort, and transform the way we perceive.

SENSATION

The eyes are the windows to the soul.

What we know of the world comes through our senses. All of our sensations are created by variation in the pattern of nerve impulses that reach the brain. Such sensory "messages" sometimes contain more,

sometimes less information than we need to know the world adequately, but fortunately we have a talent for ignoring deficiencies in the message. In semi-darkness, for example, we can often guess what the visual message is and arrive at a correct visual impression. If we have reason to expect some particular person to meet us in the shadows, just an outline will suffice to identify him. When conditions cause doubt, what we know to be true from our experience influences how this "filling in" of the sensory message occurs.

Perception begins with stimulus and receptor. In vision, light, the stimulus, falling on the receptors in the eye begins the process. The eye is an extension of the brain and a part of the central nervous system. The actual receptors in the eye are biochemical analyzers. When sufficient light excites them, they generate nerve impulses, which are organized and patterned, and then conveyed along the visual nerves toward the brain. Each eye has millions of these receptors operating continuously when excited by light. Somehow, the brain is able to make sense of and interpret all this information. But this apparently simple sensory process is complicated. The following box shows that a person's pupil size, which is basically regulated by the level of illumination, can also be affected by various emotional stimuli, such as the sight of a pretty girl, or a pleasant landscape. This gives some support to the old belief that "the eyes are the windows of the soul." In hearing the process is much the same. To understand sensory psychology fully one should have considerably more background in the biological sciences than we can go into here. Let us assume instead, then, that the sensory information is already at the brain, and begin to consider perception at that point.

Box 6-1   Changes in Pupil Size in Response to Various Pictures

These changes appear to be an objective measure of subjective emotional state. Such data may be more useful than a person's verbal report

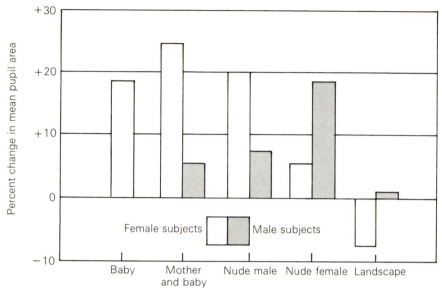

Changes in mean pupil size in terms of percentage of decrease or increase in area from size during viewing of control patterns in response to various pictures.

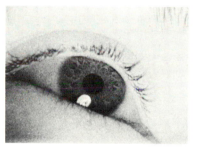 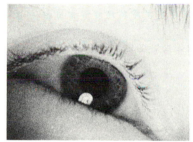

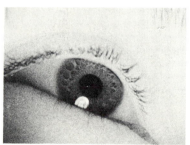 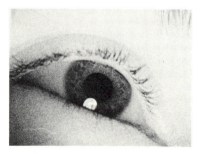

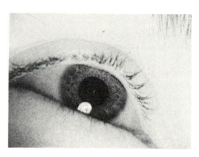

Pupil size varies with the interest value of a visual stimulus. These five frames show the eye of a male subject during the first two and a half seconds after a photograph of a pinup girl appeared on the screen of the pupil apparatus. His pupil diameter increased in size by 30 percent. (Photos courtesy Eckhard H. Hess.)

in which he might be tempted to conceal or distort his true feelings. Perhaps poker players who wear sun glasses while playing know something of this and are motivated beyond just appearing "cool."

Data from Hess and Polt, 1960, p. 350.
Photographs from Involvement in Psychology Today.

ATTENTION

Have you ever noticed how, when you're in a crowded room, you can shift your attention from one conversation to another without moving your position? If a monophonic tape recorder were placed in the same position it would produce a completely garbled taped record; a human listener, however, can easily shift his attention from one conversation to another, especially in response to a stimulus such as hearing his name mentioned. Of course, having two ears—that is, having stereo hearing—makes this possible. But this example also illustrates other aspects of attention. It shows that one can narrow the range of possible stimulation he might respond to by focusing on part of it selectively. It shows how other stimulation that is beyond conscious awareness is still attended to *at some level*. Finally, it shows that a listener pays attention relevantly—that is, to those things that are important to him.

Attention depends on (1) the nature of the stimulus itself, (2) the perceiver's mental set, and (3) the perceiver's motivational state.

Nature of the Stimulus

Dramatically *intense* stimuli, such as shouts in the library, immediately gain our attention. A stationary rock in the middle of a swiftly moving stream stands out by *contrast*, as does a sharp stab of pain in an otherwise resting arm. *Repetitious* stimuli, such as a person stuttering, gain our attention. (Note: habituation also occurs if the repetition brings no new information.) *Size* differences are also important; large objects stand out among small ones. Thus, we see that intensity, contrast, repetition, and size are all important factors that may determine attention, though only one may suffice at any given time.

Mental Set

If one is told to look for special features in a stimulus situation, he will, of course, because of his mental set, tend to focus on those features—even at the expense of other events that may be equally important. Magicians, for example, take advantage of our mental set— of what we expect to see—when they use sleight-of-hand in making something disappear.

Police officers are specially trained to attend to factors used in the identification of suspects, while most of us are not. The coffee or wine taster tastes more than we usually do; the farmer "reads" the state of crop progress by small signs others do not see; the auto mechanic "hears" an engine's needs that the owner may miss until the car quits running. The rest of us could acquire similar skills if it were important for us to do so.

A completely unexpected stimulus, a novel one, may cause a momentary or permanent shift in attention. A novel stimulus that has inherent interest is one basis for creating an effective advertising message, one that we pay attention to.

Try this experiment, which illustrates several things about set and perceptual judgment. Pretend you are walking on campus, on your way to meet your best friend. You spot someone walking toward you about 125 yards away who seems to look like your friend—about the same in height and gait, and at the right time and place. You are sure that it is he, but at 80 yards the person turns away. Would you swear— under oath, say—that your friend was at that place at that time, based on this much information? Most of us have had a similar experience.

Motivation in Attention

In general, we are more likely to attend to relevant stimuli and less likely to attend to irrelevant ones. Under conditions of semi-starvation, for instance, people become much more likely to selectively attend to "hunger-relevant" stimuli or opportunities to gratify their hunger. For most well-fed Americans, hunger stimuli are not very pressing; such stimuli are, therefore, almost always below conscious awareness. Being able to selectively focus on just part of the entire range of stimulation undoubtedly plays an important role in learning.

Box 6-2 Organizing Perception: The Case of the Man Who Couldn't Forget

The Russian psychologist A. R. Luria reported (1968) the case of S, a newspaperman, whom he studied for nearly 30 years. S had almost unlimited powers of memory, possessing total recall of visual perception. It was as if this man's mind sponged up every event. He could remember everything that had ever happened to him—in fantastic detail.

In his first encounter with Luria, S was able to reproduce a long list of unrelated words and numbers without error. Luria gave him longer and longer lists to reproduce, but S never failed. Luria was unable to carry out the simplest measurement of the capacity of S's memory because it was apparently without limit. Further, S could reproduce these lists both front-ward and backward. There was no loss with the passage of time. At times Luria tested S on various lists he had memorized 15 years earlier. After a few moments spent in recalling the setting in which the list was learned, S recited the list. Invariably he was successful.

S reduced each element in a list of items to be memorized to a graphic image—a very vivid, detailed visual image—and then "distributed" them along a "mental walk" on some imagined, familiar street. These images were distributed along the way "at houses, gates, and store windows." Luria noted that although S never reproduced memorized material inaccurately, he sometimes omitted elements altogether. It was as if he placed an image along the "mental walk" in a dark corner. In attempting recall, it seemed that S walked on without noticing the image. Luria concluded that these errors were not "defects of memory," but were, in fact, defects of perception." These defects could only be explained "by certain factors that influence perception (clarity, contrast, the ability to isolate a figure from its background, the degree of lighting available, etc.)'' (p. 35).

S's memory caused him difficulties in unexpected ways. He could not understand most poetry and when he listened to a story, if it progressed too fast, the flood of images soon swamped him and he lost its meaning. With poetry each word called up concrete images, but usually not those intended. Even simple sentences were hard to understand. ''The work got underway normally,'' for example. Could there be any difficulty with such a sentence?

> . . . I read that ''the work got under way normally.'' As for *work*, I see that work is going on . . . there's a factory . . . But there's that word *normally*. What I see is a big, ruddy-cheeked woman, a *normal* woman . . . Then the expression *get under way*. Who? What is all this? You have industry . . . that is, a factory, and this normal woman —but how does all this fit together? How much I have to get rid of just to get the simple idea of the thing! (p. 128).

S's problem was that each word produced images that distracted and confused him and blocked his ability to grasp the meaning of the sentence. Similarly he could not remember faces very well because they changed all the time, due to mood and expression, and the common element eluded him. Eventually S went on the stage as a memory expert. Once he was fooled into memorizing laboriously a mass of numbers which involved a simple progression (1, 2, 3, 4, 5, etc.), although a principle would have enabled him to reproduce the whole table without memory at all. But then, that was the point, he did not use meaning or logic to remember. Often his intelligence was completely overshadowed by the images in his memory. He found it difficult to form abstractions. He could not extract common elements from the mass of his memory. Details, yes, but generalizations, no.

All of his images were also unusual in that they involved more than one sense. A person's name, for example, not only had a characteristic sound but a taste and smell as well. (This is called synesthesia, or cross-sense perception.) A sneeze or a noise from the street was likely to be incorporated into an image being memorized. He had little power to exclude anything. S noted, ''If I read when I eat, I have a hard time understanding what I'm reading—the taste of the food drowns out the sense . . .'' (p. 82).

As S grew older he began to work on techniques by which he could forget unwanted images. Most of us don't have that problem. But after he went on the stage, he needed to find a way to erase material from previous acts, so the images would not conflict with the next act, especially since each act was rather similar in nature.

The case of S makes it clear that selecting and abstracting stimulation is absolutely necessary for the useful functioning of the mind. We simply cannot handle all of the perceptual stimulation potentially available. As S grew older he learned to abbreviate his images, to use symbols instead of the rich graphic scenes, and to cut down on what was to be remembered.

S's marvelous memory was a dubious asset. It did not permit the easy abstracting of principles and generalizations which is the hallmark of intelligent thinking, nor the use of such generalizations in his own adjustment. He had developed a very passive attitude toward life, always hoping that something great was going to happen to him, which seemed to preclude organized striving toward goals.

A. R. Luria, *The Mind of a Mnemonist: A Little Book About a Vast Memory.* Basic Books, New York, 1968.

ORGANIZATION

Patients blind from birth who have cataracts removed from their eyes—bringing them the potential of sight—are not at first able to see clearly form, color, and contour. The difference between a square and a triangle eludes them.

M. V. Senden

As we attend to stimulation, we organize it in different ways. (1) When we see figures against a background, they appear in a *figure-ground* relationship. (2) We tend to *group* various stimuli that are similar. (3) We fill in or complete incomplete figures to give us a better impression, a form of organization called *closure*. Finally, when stimulation can be organized in several different ways, the best "good figure" wins out.

Figure-Ground

If we view a blob of solid ink on a page that is otherwise blank, the blob will be seen as a *figure* against the plain *ground*. All figures or objects appear to have a kind of "thingness" or existence or unity apart from their ground. This "thingness" does not reside in the stimulus itself but rather in our organization of the stimulus information. When we look at a reversible figure-ground picture, the figure changes back and forth but nonetheless still retains its "thingness" so long as we see it as a figure. In Figure 6-1, for instance, you see alternately images of angels or devils but not both simultaneously. This aspect of a person's perceptual organizing is one of the first which a newly-sighted cataract patient achieves, indicating its primary unlearned nature (Hebb, 1949).

Figure 6-1. Reversible figure and ground. This woodcut by M. C. Escher is called "Heaven and Hell." Either the black or the white elements can easily be perceived as *the* figure. When we look at either figure, the opposite color becomes the background. (From the collection of C.V.S. Roosevelt, Washington D.C. Reprinted by permission of C.V.S. Roosevelt.)

Grouping

   We tend to group together various stimuli that are close to one another and appear to form a pattern. As Figure 6-2 shows, it is the pattern that gives the stimuli their "thingness." The space between dots is not perceived as being any *thing*. When we look at different elements (Figure 6-3), we tend to group similar ones together. Sometimes grouping isn't based either on closeness or similarity but rather on logical *continuation*. In Figure 6-4, "1" could be made up from either "2" or "3." What do you see?

•   • •   • • •   • • • •   • • • • •   • • • • • •

Figure 6-2.   Grouping according to closeness. Do you see 21 dots or 6 groups of dots?

```
•   •   •   •   •        •   •   x   •   •
•   •   •   •   •
                         •   •   x   •   •
x   x   x   x   x
                         •   •   x   •   •
•   •   •   •   •
        1                        2
```

Figure 6-3.   Grouping according to similarity. Does it make any difference which way the dots run? When they create a good figure they are seen as belonging together. Note that even when dots are closer together—running up and down in 1— they are not necessarily grouped. The x's are always grouped together, even when they are closer to the dots.

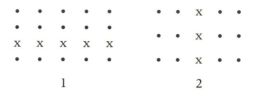

1

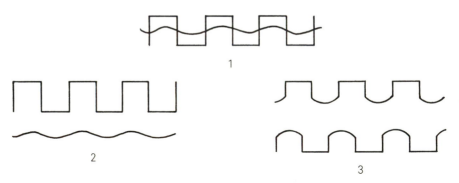

2

3

Figure 6-4. Grouping according to continuation. Is "1" made of the parts of "2" or "3"? Continuation means that wavy lines will be seen as continuing, while straight lines belong together.

Closure

   When small gaps are made in parts of a circle, the mind fills in the missing parts, achieving closure. Experiments reveal that rather large sections can be removed without affecting most people's ability to close the figure (see Figure 6-5). Perhaps the most impressive demonstration of closure is produced with a specially constructed, one-eyed view of a brick wall that has a hole in the exact place where most people cannot see it. Each eye has a so-called "blind spot" in the retina, the receptor surface, where the visual nerves exit. Because all the nerves come together at this spot, there are no receptors and therefore no visual receptivity. Yet, both in this demonstration and in everyday life, we are unaware of the "blind spot." The mind closes in the missing bricks!

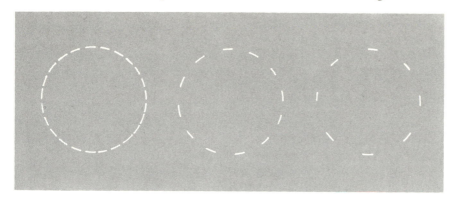

Figure 6-5. Illustration of closure. Small gaps in a circle are filled in, which is called achieving closure. The gaps can be fairly large without destroying an impression of the circle.

PERCEPTUAL LEARNING AND CONSTANCY

*To the infant the world is just a big, blooming, buzzing
confusion.*

William James

Perceptual Learning

As the infant begins to try to make some meaning of his sensory world, he organizes information in new ways. Strang (1952) points out that at first the infant is probably not aware of the boundaries between self and not-self. He is probably confused during his first year when he observes that his booties come off at night while his feet do not. As he grows older, he learns that the foot is part of his own body, part of himself. In learning about his perceptual world, the child becomes more complex. As he becomes more complex, he also becomes more able to make increasingly complex perceptual observations. In other words, his developmental maturity affects the way he perceives things. Furthermore, there is a good deal of evidence to suggest that language spurs on this process. As he develops language concepts, he is able to notice many more differences and similarities perceptually. Some perceptions would be unlikely if not for the aid of language. Talking about perception involves recall of information from memory. Storage of the information in the first place depends on having a linguistic concept for it. If different kinds of snow were relevant to our survival, as they are for Eskimos, we might provide different names for the types, as they do. Worf (1940) observes that Eskimos have different words for "falling snow, snow on the ground, snow packed hard like ice, slushy snow, wind-driven flying snow—whatever the situation might be." They "notice" differences among types of snow that we do not see. Having noticed these differences, they can then remember them. In our culture, most women can make many more correct color discriminations than most men. Apparently, when faced with half a dozen different shades of blue, they can discern the differences better because of their richer color vocabulary. Having concepts and names for the possibilities makes the difference. So it is with the child and his development. As he becomes more complex mentally, he is more able to make increasingly complex perceptual observations.

A child's developing self-image transforms the way he understands his experience. Growth of the sense of self involves both perceptual *differentiation*, or *analysis* of perceptual differences, and *integration* of perceptual information into a more complex whole. Likewise, the adult's self-image transforms his experience. A generally insecure and fearful person has a fundamentally more inhibited way of interpreting sensory information. A *paranoid* person characteristically distorts what he perceives so greatly that an objective but naïve observer can scarcely believe it.

Shape Constancy

Distortion can occur, of course, in a favorable direction also. As mentioned earlier, what we know to be true cannot be discounted under normal perceptual conditions. If we view a stimulus that forms an ellipse on the retina, as in the left panel of Figure 6-6, it will be seen as an *elliptical* figure against a plain background, until we learn that it is supposed to be an outline of a dinner plate. Then it will be seen as a *round figure*.

If you are asked to remember what you saw in (b), you are likely instead to reproduce (c), unless you noted to yourself that you saw a dinner plate *at an angle*. Shape constancy it is seen, is the *retention of a figure's identity under many different viewing conditions*.

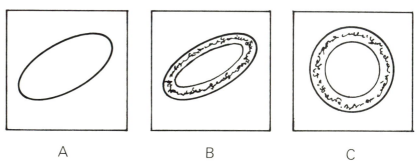

A   B   C

Figure 6-6. An illustration of shape constancy. The dinner plate is seen as round regardless of the angle of view.

Color Constancy

Once a particular color has been associated with an object, it is always seen as having that color, even under extreme conditions of illumination. A piece of white paper, for example, can be held half in bright sunlight and half in deep shade. Even though the two parts reflect vastly different proportions of the available light, the object retains its identity and both halves are judged to be the same shade of white. You will perceive your bright red car as red even at night (when there is not enough illumination to perceive color at all), for you will know that it *is* red. Actually, our night vision is only capable of yielding sensations of black and white and the intermediate shades of gray.

Size Constancy

Our judgments of the size of known objects at a distance are based both on the size of the projection on the retina and what we know to be true. If the object's size is not on the human scale, we must then estimate both distance and size (see Figure 6-7).

Obviously, we are able to read into our perceptual judgments what we know to be true most of the time. This ability is developed through experience. It serves us well, because the "distorted perceptions" that result are usually more accurate than they would have been had we relied merely on the raw sensory information.

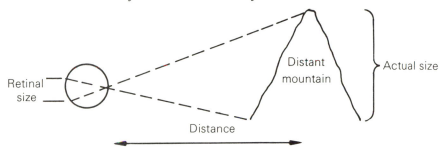

Figure 6-7. Making a size-distance judgment. Retinal size will not be the sole basis for judgment except if other factors are absent. When we know size, judging distance is easy.

Box 6-3   Differences in Perceptual Style:
Field-Dependent versus Field-Independent Perception

Witkin (1959) and his associates conducted experiments on how people perceive the upright or vertical dimension. Ordinarily there are man-made cues such as the vertical and horizontal lines of buildings, but even if they were blindfolded most people would be able to maintain their balance. They receive this perceptual information as (1) cues from the visual world and (2) cues from the sense of balance in the inner ear.

To study the operation of these two kinds of cues independently, Witkin devised a "tilting-room, tilting chair" apparatus (see figure), which

permitted a person to base his judgment of what was upright either on external cues—that is, from the room around him (which would be rotated)—or from the internal cues of his sense of balance. The subject could control the tilt of the chair in which he sat, but the experimenter controlled the rotation of the room. If the subject depended on internal cues, he would disregard the cues from the room; if he depended on external cues, he would line up his chair with the way the room was tilted.

Witkin expected people would use a combination of the two sets of cues. He was surprised, therefore, to discover that people tended to rely on one or the other set of cues, not both. The people who were dependent on the external, visual cues he called *field-dependent*; those dependent on the sense of balance were *field-independent*.

Differences between these two groups have been found in regard to sex, age, personality, intelligence, and adjustment. These nonperceptual differences seem to be explained partly by certain features in the upbringing of the two groups.

Witkin found that females are more field-dependent than males at all ages. Young persons also tend to be field-dependent but grow less so as they get older. For both sexes, maximum field-independence is reached at late adolescence, declining slightly thereafter.

In personality, the field-dependent person is more passive, less complex, and less aware of his own needs than the field-independent. The defenses and controls with which he manages his adjustment are less well-developed, and his interests tend to be narrow.

Intellectually, the field-independent person tends to get significantly higher IQ test scores, excelling especially on analytical matters, which involve isolating essential components from a context and recombining them in new arrangements. This skill is necessary for success with the embedded figures test (see figure). The embedded figures test is a simple test which measures much the same abilities as the tilting room, tilting chair experiment.

Maladjustments were found in both groups. Perceptual style does not indicate whether a child will have a "healthy" personality, although it may suggest the form that maladjustments may take, if they develop at all. Witkin notes that "personality disturbances in field-dependent children . . . tend to be of the kind that stem from relatively primitive, amorphous, chaotic personality structure." Also, "in field-independent children the personality disturbance is more likely to take such forms as over-control, over-intellectualization and isolation from reality."

Perhaps the most important investigation was that conducted to find out why people seemed to favor one or the other of these perceptual styles. The mothers of the two types, for instance, had different reactions toward their children. In Erikson's terms it might be said that they reacted in different ways to the normal growth crises of their children. Those with field-independent children tended to be "growth fostering," whereas the others tended to be "growth constricting"—to dominate their children, limit their curiosity, stress conformity, and in other ways tend to prolong their dependency period.

Sensory and Perceptual Sex Differences

It is known that some sensory differences exist between the sexes (perhaps because of different hormone systems, but this hypo-

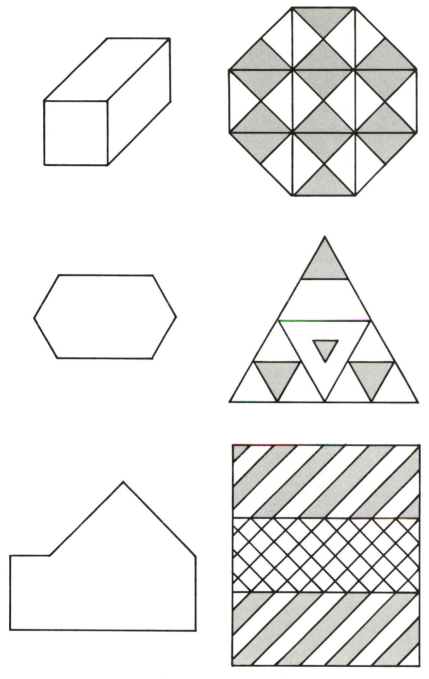

The embedded figures test challenges the subject to find the pattern at left in the more complex patterns at right, thereby testing his ability to perceive the visual field analytically. In Witkin's research, field-dependent persons were less able to perform this task than were field-independent persons.

thesis needs further investigation.) The range of sensitivity differs in hearing, smell, and in color discrimination. In hearing, there is a different range and threshold of sensitivity. In general, females have lower sensory thresholds for high-frequency sounds; they can hear them adequately at lower intensities—a piece of information that might avoid some strife between the sexes.

Many differences in sensory thresholds for smells have been traced to factors of inheritance. Some smells, such as musk, can be detected by the average woman much better than by the average man. Moreover, a woman's sensitivity may increase so greatly during ovulation that she can detect it in 1/1000ths of its normal value (Le Magnen, 1948).

The differences in visual perception probably have more to do with sex differences in language and the socialization of personality than with biology. In the study mentioned earlier, it was found that women could distinguish slight color differences much better than could men—probably because of a richer color vocabulary.

Box 6-4 Perception and Behavior: Some Behavioral Characteristics of Adequate Persons

"Adequate personalities behave more effectively and efficiently than their less adequate fellows. The great reservoir of positive perceptions and the capacity for acceptance of self and the world gives the adequate person a tremendous advantage in dealing with life. Being under no great necessity for self defense he has less need to distort his perceptions or to select them in terms of his peculiar unfulfilled goals or desires. He is able to behave more effectively and efficiently because he behaves in the light of more and better data. Being more open to experience, he has a wide phenomenal field on which to base his behavior. He is able to behave more often from choice than from necessity. . . .

"In the dynamic relationship of perception to behavior, more adequate perceptual fields must necessarily result in more adequate behavior. People who perceive more efficiently will behave more efficiently. The individual who is able to behave from a phenomenal field open to more data has a great advantage over the rest of us. He is able to play a better game because he holds more and better cards. With more data available, adequate personalities are able to penetrate more directly and sharply to the heart of problems. They often possess an uncanny ability to place their finger on the core of issues and are thus able to deal with matters more precisely and appropriately. Their perceptions are less complicated by extraneous events, personal goals and values, or the necessity for immediate self gratification.

"Because adequate persons feel fundamentally secure they are able to evaluate themselves more accurately. Their levels of aspiration are far more likely to be realistic and attainable. They are able to deal with events, and with themselves, with greater objectivity and equanimity. Feeling secure within himself, the adequate person has less need to hide from the unpleasant and can feel more comfortable with himself even when under attack. This fundamental security makes it possible to deal with events with less "personal axes to grind." It even makes it possible for the adequate person to risk himself. He is capable of placing himself in a poor or unflattering light if necessary, and this makes possible the consideration of evidence not open to the individual who is fearful and defensive of self."

DUANE M. BELCHER

Vision for the Sightless

THOSE of us who are sighted take for granted that our vision will come to us through our eyes. When sight is lost permanently, however, the person must either adjust to complete loss of sight, or be provided with sensory information in some other way. The seeing eye dog, of course, has a long and honorable record as substitute eyes for the blind. But these animals must be given an expensive education before they may be put into use, and a single blind adult might require a half dozen, or more, guide dogs in an active lifetime. Many blind people never get a guide dog at all.

The devices developed to aid the blind—such as dogs and canes—have usually settled for less than a full, point-by-point representation of the visual pattern. A cane may provide both auditory and tactile information to a blind person as he moves about. He may feel obstructions, curbs, light posts, doorways, and so on. Also by tapping his cane he may develop a kind of limited sonar, learning to tell if obstacles are in his path, how far away they are, and perhaps something of their size by reflection of sound.

The blind can obtain information from books either by being read to or by reading in Braille. Braille is a system of raised characters, a code, which the blind person can learn to read

with his finger tips. Unfortunately, people must be specifically trained to read and write Braille, and most blind people never become fully proficient at it. Also Braille books are very bulky. *The American Vest Pocket Dictionary*, for example, in Braille form takes up an entire file drawer.

Some animals, notably bats, have developed their ability to appreciate objects in the environment through the sense of hearing. Bats do not need to see in order to navigate around their nocturnal world; they are able to discriminate fairly small differences in size, shape, and movement with a kind of biological sonar (Simmons, 1968). Some proposals have been made to equip the blind with television cameras, and somehow "translate" visual information into an auditory signal that they could interpret. So far these efforts have not been particularly successful.

Any substitute for vision must include both sensors and a "route to the brain." It may be that the wrong route to the brain has been under consideration. The sense of hearing is already rather fully utilized. What is needed is an underutilized sense, capable of being trained, to carry the information to the brain.

Recently an optical reader, the Optacon, has been developed by Professor John Linvill at Stanford University. This device uses a silicon retina to sense print directly and translates it into a vibrating pattern recognizable

Professor John Linvill demonstrates the optacon reader to his daughter, Candy, who is blind.

through touch. The Optacon is small, light-weight, and portable enough so that a blind person can use it at home, at school, and wherever he goes. It is a modern, integrated-circuit device. Its pattern discrimination is very good and the blind person can read any print style or any handwriting with which he is familiar.

The sense of touch is the sense with the most useful characteristics of both vision and hearing. By touch we can discriminate between pin pricks on the surface of the skin, even when they are fairly close together. Also, most importantly, the sense of touch can discriminate duration (time) very well. These ideas have been incorporated into a system, Vibratese, developed by Professor Frank Geldard at Princeton University. It uses five different points for stimulation by electric vibrators on the chest (see figure). Signals could vary in intensity (weak, medium, and strong) and in duration (short, medium, and long), permitting 45 separate signals ($5 \times 3 \times 3$). This system

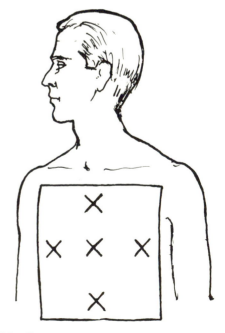

Geldard's system.

was sufficient to represent the alphabet, and Vibratese could be mastered in a few hours. One person was trained to receive at about twice the usual speed of Morse code. Now Geldard is experimenting with different body sites for placement of the vibrators. This new system uses 10 different vibrators spread out widely on the body surface. It carries a great many different signals at optimum speed, permitting easy combination of characters into words (Geldard, 1968).

These are developments in progress. The technology now exists to provide the blind with aids that are far advanced over what is available today. Nevertheless, the system that might duplicate all of the capabilities of vision is still a dream. Science fiction gives us some idea of what it should be able to accomplish. The television show "Star Trek" featured a play in which a blind woman saw by means of a "visual net," an extremely sensitive sensing system built into her dress. The visual net gave a point-by-point correspondence to vision. How the sensory information was routed to the brain, however, was not described.

Summarizing Statements

1. Many different psychological processes affect perception by transforming raw sensory information into something intelligible. The main emphasis is on the way the higher mental processes influence, distort, and transform the way we perceive.

2. Sensations are created by variation in the patterns of nerve impulses which reach the brain. We compensate for deficiencies in the message. When perceptual conditions are ambiguous, we fill in the sensory message with what we believe to be true. Light excites the visual receptors, generating nerve impulses which are conveyed to the brain, where they are interpreted.

3. The size of the pupil is affected by the emotional impact of the visual stimulus.

4. Attention allows us to selectively respond to relevant stimulation. The nature of the stimulus, the perceiver's mental set, and the perceiver's motivational state all affect how one attends to stimulation.

5. In perception, a mental set means a readiness to react to the environment in accord with expectations. A novel or unexpected stimulus may cause a shift in attention.

6. Motivation affects the likelihood of our attending to relevant stimuli.

7. A person with eidetic imagery, or total recall of visual perception, might be overwhelmed with detail.

8. As we attend to stimulation, we organize it in different ways. Figures are seen against grounds. We group various stimuli according to closeness, similarity, and continuation. When stimulation can be organized in several different ways, we achieve closure on the best "good figure."

9. As the child learns about his perceptual world, he becomes more complex. And as he becomes more complex he becomes increasingly able to make complex perceptual observations. Language makes possible noticing important differences. Noticing differences and noting them makes memory more likely. Having names for the

possibilities improves memory. The cyclical growth of the child's perceptual ability involves perceptual differentiation and integration into a more complex whole.

10. Perceptual constancy describes how objects retain their normal appearance even under extreme perceptual conditions. What we know to be true is taken into account in interpreting sensory information.

11. The Embedded Figures Test challenges a person's ability to perceive the visual field analytically. This ability is associated with the field-independent perceptual style.

12. Field-dependent persons tend to have dependent personalities, and to score lower on intelligence tests than field-independent persons. They are also more passive, dependent, and submissive. They possess lower self-esteem.

13. People have well-established, preferred ways of perceiving which correlate with personality and life history differences.

14. Young persons and women tend to be more field-dependent than older persons and men. Field-dependent personality is less complex, with less-well-developed defenses and controls. The mothers of field-dependent children tend to be growth-constricting, while the mothers of field-independent children foster growth. Growth-constricting mothers restrict, dominate, and overcontrol their children, and such behavior tends to prolong the period of natural dependency.

15. Sensory differences exist between the sexes in hearing, smell, and vision. Some of these differences are probably due to hormonal differences. The differences in visual perception probably have more to do with sex differences in language and the socialization of personality than with biology.

16. An adequate personality has less need to distort perception or to select stimuli in terms of unfulfilled goals or desires. Better perception necessarily results in more adequate behavior. An adequate person is able to evaluate himself more accurately and set realistic and attainable levels of aspiration. The adequate person is more able to risk himself. He is able to consider evidence not open to a fearful or defensive person.

Reading Selection

17. Although devices developed in the past to aid the blind have not been able to give them a point by point representation of the visual pattern, dogs and canes have permitted them to get about in the environment, and live readers and Braille have provided them with access to the written word.

18. The Optacon reader is a new device which senses print directly and translates it into a vibrating pattern which the blind can learn to recognize through touch. The sense of touch is the sense with the most useful characteristics of both vision and hearing.

19.   Vibratese is a system for presenting language to the blind in an easily mastered code. A modern version permits transmission of a much larger number of different signals at optimum speed. The ideal system, however, is still a dream.

Terms and Concepts

Attention: the selective process by which we narrow down the range of stimulation; a focusing or directing of awareness. Attention depends on: (1) the nature of the stimulus itself, (2) mental set, and (3) the perceiver's motivational state. Paying attention often involves an orienting of one's body and sense organs toward a particular source of stimulation.

Blind spot: that part of the retinal surface which has no visual receptors because the nerves come together there as they exit from the eye. We are usually unaware of its existence because (1) we have two eyes with blind spots located in different parts of their respective visual fields, and (2) we fill-in expected detail mentally, imagining that we see it.

Mental set: a readiness to react to the environment in a certain way, generally in accord with a pattern. In this chapter "set" is used to refer to a perceptual readiness to perceive in accord with expectation.

Phenomenal field: everything, including itself, experienced by an organism at any moment. Objects present but not perceived are not part of the phenomenal field, while objects not present but thought about are. Definition adapted from English & English.

Perception: the process by which sensory information is interpreted. Perception is a construing of experience involving many other psychological processes such as habit, set, motivation, and linguistic experience which may have transformed the sensory message.

Perceptual constancy: the fact that objects retain their normal appearance even under widely varying stimulus conditions. What we know to be true is taken into account in interpreting sensory information. A plate looks round regardless of the angle from which it is seen.

Perceptual differentiation: the process by which an infant is able to make a progressively better analysis of perceptual differences.

Perceptual integration: the process by which an infant incorporates perceptual knowledge into a more complex view of self and world.

Perceptual style: the fact that people have well-established, preferred ways of perceiving. These styles correlate with personality and life history differences. Witkin identified two types: field-independent and field-dependent perceivers.

Receptor: the structural unit in the sense organ which, when irritated by adequate stimulation, generates a nerve impulse.

Retina: the inner surface in the eye which contains the actual receptors for vision.

Sensation: the most basic unit of sensory knowledge; the process by which stimulation is brought to the brain for interpretation.

The real "haves" are they who can acquire freedom, self-confidence and even riches without depriving others of them. They acquire all of these by developing and applying their potentialities. On the other hand, the real "have nots" are they who cannot have aught except by depriving others of it. They can feel free only by diminishing the freedom of others, self-confident by spreading fear and dependence among others, and rich by making others poor.

—*Eric Hoffer*, The Passionate State of Mind

Motivation

7 ALL behavior is motivated or caused. You were motivated when you got up this morning, ate breakfast, and went to school. When a person acts, he acts because of some motive or motives. Motivation *arouses and directs behavior toward a goal*. If motivation is thought of as a cycle (see Figure 7-1), the first step is the arousal of the person which gets him in motion, the second step is a search among the alternatives for the kind of behavior that will attain the goal, and the third step is the attainment of the goal in satisfying the person and reducing his pressing motive.

Principles from both perception and learning can also be used to explain parts of the cycle. Step 2, the search, is like what happens during the perceptual screening process: a person attends to and interprets situations involving choice. Step 3, satisfaction, may be seen in terms of reinforcement: the acts a person continues to use are those that have led to goal attainment, which is reinforcing.

Motivation may be classified into physiological, general and social motives. The *physiological* are innate motives such as hunger and thirst. They are necessary for survival. *General* motives, which can be either learned or innate, are those such as exploration and sensory stimulation; they are not necessary for survival, although for the species they may have survival significance. *Social* motives, which are mostly learned, are those such as achievement.

PHYSIOLOGICAL MOTIVES

The physiological motives are drives that arise directly out of body need or deficit. Thirst, for example, reflects a state of dehydration in the body tissues; as a motive, it creates a state of tension, which propels the person into action to obtain relief.

Specific deficits operate in the same way, as shown by the unusual case of a 3-year-old boy with an extreme craving for salt reported by Wilkens & Richter (1940). He was admitted to a hospital

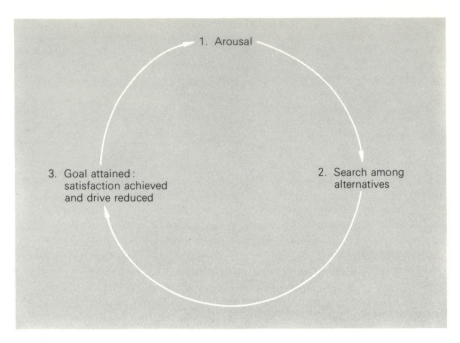

Figure 7-1. The motivational cycle. Motivation arouses and directs behavior toward a goal.

for observation because of some developmental problems and put on a hospital diet, but within a week he suddenly became sick and died. Afterward the parents revealed that he had always demanded an unusual diet with large quantities of salt. He ate by itself a spoonful of pure salt each day, raided salt shakers as some children raid cookie jars, and consumed about four times as much salt on everything he ate as would most people. The autopsy revealed that his adrenal gland was defective and had failed to prevent abnormal loss of salt from his body through his urine. Thus, he literally died of salt deficiency.

Behavior designed to restore a "balanced steady state" is called homeostatic. One of the best examples of homeostasis is the way the body regulates its temperature automatically at a constant 98.6 degrees. Many other human motives are also regulated homeostatically. The most important of the drives (as discussed on the following pages) are hunger, thirst, and sex. Others are temperature regulation, air hunger, the need for sleep, and elimination pressures.

Hunger and Thirst

Hunger is generated out of our need for food to live and maintain our vital processes. It used to be thought that hunger was produced by contractions in the stomach; however, it can occur in the absence of contractions, and even in cases where there is no stomach at all. Furthermore, contractions sometimes occur after a person has eaten a full meal. Morgan & King (1971) believe that "probably the physiological source of the hunger motive is some product of metabolism in the blood, but we have not found out what it is." It is known, however, that there are two brain centers having to do with hunger. One is an eating center that energizes a person to seek food; the other is a satiation center that, when stimulated, causes him to stop eating. This fact suggests that there is some metering device in the central nervous system that regulates the "on" and "off" of hunger. Besides this basic biological process, other things can induce you to eat also: restlessness, the sight of friends eating, the offer of a delicacy, and so forth.

Human beings have a tendency to elaborate even apparently simple drives like hunger into something more complex. We do not normally gratify our hunger in the most direct way—and indeed when someone does, we're apt to compare his behavior to an animal's: "He eats like a pig." Some languages even have different verbs for animal and human eating (for example, the German *fressen* and *essen*).

Recent research suggests that in obese people eating is controlled in a fundamentally different way than it is in normal people (Schachter, 1971). Normal people eat enough to meet their nutritional needs and then stop. Obese people, however, eat when stimulated by pleasant-looking or good-smelling food, and eat even when they are not hungry if the available food appeals to them. The obese are also much governed by the clock, and eat when they believe it is time to eat (whether they are hungry or not). Thus, whereas with most people, eating is controlled by internal need, overweight people are also controlled by *external* stimuli; many derive emotional gratification from food. To control overweight, therefore, one must (a) limit food intake and (b) learn to control response to external stimuli for eating (see Box 7-1).

Thirst is another drive that operates basically in a homeostatic way. Lack of sufficient body fluid energizes the person into searching for a means of reducing the drive by drinking something (attaining the goal). Like hunger, thirst is easily elaborated by social factors into a

---

Box 7-1   Control of Overeating

Stuart (1967) describes a way of building self-control over eating which involves, first, identifying the specific situation in which overeating occurs and, second, developing alternative responses to those situations. For instance, since most obese people lack control, the patient is instructed to interrupt each meal for a minute or so and do nothing; waiting demonstrates that he can control something. Also, since obese people tend to eat large amounts very quickly, the patient is instructed to eat very slowly, savoring each bite; he is thus taught to enjoy less food more, and the emphasis shifts from quantity to quality. During danger periods of high temptation, the patient is instructed to engage in some other activity he likes. Before treatment, it is determined what kind of things he or she likes to do. For example, if a housewife usually takes an unnecessary snack at 10:00 A.M., she is instructed to call a friend at that time instead. These "likely" acts can then be used as secondary reinforcers. The patient also is instructed to weigh herself four times a day. All of these devices, combined with medical supervision, result in steady weight loss. Although this process is not a diet, the procedures tend to result in voluntary restriction of intake. A loss of a pound or two a week for six months or a year is not an unrealistic goal. The fact that the procedures work suggests that achieving better self-control—in other behavior as well as eating—cannot be just an internal motivational matter, but must also involve an analysis of the situations in which behavior takes place.

---

complex mixture of motives. Eating and drinking become family and social occasions in which these other motives may play a dominant role.

Sex

Like hunger and thirst, sex is basically a biological drive that becomes elaborated into a more complex motive through social learning. The male and female sex hormones play a role in human sexuality. In adolescence, sex hormones stimulate the development of the body's secondary sex characteristics, including masculine and feminine body shape, distribution of hair, vocal characteristics, and mature sex organs.

In lower animals, sex hormones also determine the seasonal timing and frequency of sexual activity. If male rats are castrated, they will soon cease sexual activity altogether; among humans, however, the same operation produces various effects: some males lose their sex motivation and some are unaffected. Human sexuality is much more governed by nonhormonal motivation than is the sexuality of lower animals. For instance, monkeys and apes show their sexual activity to be far less controlled by hormones than that of the lower animals.

Among many lower animals, sexual receptivity is seasonal in the female (being "in heat"), marked by an increase in sex hormones, swelling of the sex organs, and an increase in the sex drive. The female's need and condition of receptivity apparently have a direct stimulating effect on the male's drive condition. Thus, his interest and her need are remarkably well correlated. In other words, the mating of most lower animals is governed by seasonal or cyclical changes in drive level. Although humans may have some similar cyclical hormone arrangement, they do not show marked seasonal changes in sexual interest—once again indicating the control external conditions exert over sexual arousal and behavior.

Maternal Affection

Studies of monkeys have revealed that the drive of maternal affection is essentially innate among nonhuman primates (Harlow, 1971). A mother monkey will engage in maternal care of any infant who clings to her and behaves like a proper newborn monkey. If her own infant is taken away and she is given a newborn kitten, she will attempt to mother it at first. Of course, the kitten will not clutch and cling like a newborn monkey, and so she will reject it. She will readily adopt, however, another infant monkey if it is offered to her, and after a time will seem to form a specific attachment to it and will no longer mother any infant indiscriminately. Mother monkeys seem to have considerable difficulty in forming attachments to twin infants. They cling as much to each other as to her, and in turn, elicit ambivalent mothering.

It appears that human mothers may also have an indiscriminate maternal response to any newborn, and only develop a specific attachment after some weeks' contact with a particular child. Adoption agencies try to get a mother to give up her child immediately after birth, presumably to avoid her developing a strong attachment to the child, and to permit the adoptive mother to receive the infant when it will arouse in her the strongest affection.

Harlow (1971) believes that maternal affection is unlearned and innate, that it is only the particular object of affection—for both mother and child—that must be learned (see Box 7-2).

Box 7-2 The Mystery of Love

The apparently reasonable assumption that an infant's love of his mother originates in nursing because she satisfies his basic physiological needs has been challenged by observations that some animals (including humans) form attachments to inanimate objects. A cage-raised baby monkey, for example, becomes very agitated when his diaper pad is removed for cleaning. Like the unhappiness of Linus in "Peanuts" when his security blanket is removed, this response suggests that affection toward one's kind originates in the *contact comfort* between mother and child, as when the infant is clutched close to the mother's body. Both newborn babies and their mothers find such attachment comforting.

© 1961 United Features Syndicate, Inc.

Harlow (1959, 1962, 1971) has for some years examined this issue. In one experiment, newborn monkeys were raised from birth by model mothers (see Figure 7-2) constructed out of wire, some covered with terry cloth sheaths (cloth mothers) and some not (wire mothers). Some of the models had a built-in bottle for feeding the infants. Each monkey had both a wire and a cloth mother, but half were nursed on one and half on the other.

 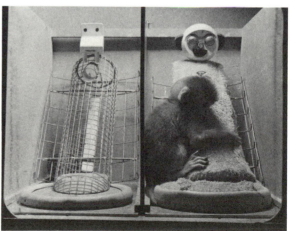

Figure 7-2. Cloth and wire mother-surrogates.

It was found that monkeys nursed on wire mothers spent most of their time on their cloth mother, taking only enough time on the wire mother to feed. Of course, the monkeys nursed on the cloth mothers spent nearly all their time on them. This experiment demonstrated that preference—one measure of love—was not based on the satisfaction of the hunger need.

So strong was the monkeys' affection for their cloth mothers that even after they were separated for as long as two years, the monkeys recognized their cloth mothers, ran to them, hugged them, and showed exaggerated emotional responses.

Other Harlow experiments studied the monkeys' reaction to threat. When young monkeys were threatened by a mechanical monster, or by being placed in a strange playroom, they ran off excitely to the source of their security, their cloth mothers—regardless of whether they were nursed on wire or cloth mothers. After clutching the cloth mother for a time, the frightened monkeys became visibly relaxed, and often turned on the monster, making threatening gestures and loud cries. It seemed that these monkeys had been emboldened by their mother's presence. When other monkeys were put in a threat situation without their cloth mothers, they acted fearful, hid in the corner, whimpered, and seemed to be paralyzed by fear. They did not recover their courage to explore and cope with the environment. The young monkey's urge to explore his environment, his curiosity, and his manipulation of objects seem to depend on feelings of security normally developed in the infant-mother relationship.

The development of the infant's love for his mother is just the first step, however, in the unfolding of this most complicated emotion. Perhaps more crucial for the mature adult is the further development of the young monkey's affection in the relationships with his peers.

In the normal course of events, the mother's love too goes through three stages. At first, the mere presence of the baby—any baby—and its clutching to her will elicit her affection. Later she forms a specific attachment to her own infant. In the second stage, the mother becomes ambivalent: she provides her baby with a base for security but also begins to punish dependent behavior, though she will protect him if he is really in trouble. In the third stage, the mother rejects infantlike behavior, a separation often made complete by the appearance of another newborn infant.

An important feature of any infant emancipation from the ties that bind him to mother is in his curiosity about and exploration of the environment. The monkey child usually develops adult behavior patterns gradually in play with his peers, and this coincides with mother's efforts to emancipate him. Much of his sexual behavior is innate but requires "environmental stimulation" at the right time in his maturation to develop. Successful courtship among mature male monkeys requires them to make an aggressive display and to give chase to the female. A monkey female will not tolerate a male who does not play the expected role. Normal young males develop "rough and tumble play" among their peers. Apparently this element of the aggressive masculine chase is a crucial part of the adult male sexual response. Likewise, grooming of the male by the female is an aspect of normal female courtship behavior. These "links in the chain" of courtship are only developed if monkeys have had an opportunity to play with their peers during crucial periods of their development. These links were absent in those of Harlow's monkeys who were deprived the opportunity to associate with their peers in infanthood. These monkeys were also deficient in several other important respects. They failed to defend themselves against attacks from others, and they were extremely antisocial in their behavior. Harlow (1962) concludes that among monkeys,

... our experiments indicate that there is a critical period somewhere between the third and sixth months of life during which social deprivation, particularly deprivation of the company of its peers, irreversibly blights the animal's capacity for social adjustment.

The long-term implications of Harlow's work suggest that all the animal's social motivation, his affiliation with others of his kind, his patterns of social aggression and dominance, and his sexual behavior all begin with biological need. But as the animal matures, behavior developed in one situation comes to play a part in another.

It becomes more and more difficult to maintain a hard and fast line between motivation that is clearly rooted in biological processes and motivation that is obviously acquired through learning.

Complexity of Physiological Motives

Even motives like hunger are often more complex than they may at first appear. Human eating is further regulated by several complex, social motives, such as custom and habit. We see this when we imagine a private dinner for two, with candlelight and wine, soft music and fine food. In this example we see three of the chief physiological drives (hunger, thirst, and sex) combined into a single motivational setting in which many other complex, learned motives may also play a part.

This elaboration or combination of physiological motives and general or social motives into a complex motivational state is very common among human beings. It may even be the usual state of affairs. Thus, the isolation and discussion of any motive of a "pure" type is always artificial and difficult.

GENERAL MOTIVES

A number of unlearned motives are not well explained by the idea of drive reduction. Such motives are (1) exploration, curiosity, and

manipulation, and (2) sensory stimulation and activity. The satisfaction of these motives does not result in obvious reduction of drive states, as does the satisfaction of hunger and thirst. These motives appear in the normal course of development—if certain basic physiological motives are routinely satisfied. In other words, these needs will probably emerge universally *unless* handicapping events occur to prevent their development.

Exploration, Curiosity, and Manipulation

When a young monkey is threatened by a novel or frightening object, he runs to his base of security, his mother. Her presence comforts him, and he seems to recover his courage and ability to cope with and explore the threat (Harlow, 1959, 1962, 1971). The development of curiosity and exploration seems to be a normal part of the young monkey's emancipation (much like Erikson's stage of autonomy). It now appears probable that the development of these motives *does not* depend on external reinforcement, but somehow creates internal reinforcement within the activity itself. Monkeys have been observed to work for long periods at solving puzzles, with no obvious reinforcement beyond being able, say, to catch a glimpse of another monkey through a window (Butler, 1953, 1954).

Among human beings these motives rarely operate alone. A scientist who might be motivated by curiosity in his work may also be motivated by a complex of social motives such as achievement, status, and power.

Sensory Stimulation and Activity

People enjoy being stimulated, and for that reason the parks of a crowded city are often very popular. The plants, trees, and flowers are fragrant and beautiful, the sounds of birds chirping and children at play are all pleasant. On the whole, people enjoy flooding their senses with pleasant stimulation, just for the sake of stimulation. The effect may be to make them either more relaxed or more excited.

Many people like to swim, cycle, or play tennis. The simple exercise of muscle systems can be pleasurable too. Activity motivated by stimulation needs, unlike the activity generated by homeostatic motives, often has the effect of stimulating further activity. A little dancing, for example, may overcome fatigue and lead to continued dancing. The behavior produced by these motives may be engaged in for its own sake.

Competence Motives

A number of writers have argued that competence is a master motive. Competence is the desire to *develop and exercise our best potentialities*. This motive is similar to self-actualization (Goldstein, 1939, and Maslow, 1954, 1971) and self-expansion (Angyal, 1941). Infants may be observed to practice endlessly the activities involved in mastery of a skill such as grasping or walking. They appear to need to exercise their potentials, and are very pleased with themselves when they finally get a skill right. White (1959) maintains that motives like curiosity and manipulation should be included in the more general concept of competence. White has made it clear that competence motivation is unlearned. We should keep that in mind in considering social motives.

SOCIAL MOTIVES

Much of the motivation of lower animals is based on unlearned drive conditions, whereas many of the goals man pursues are themselves learned, and this difference sets man apart. In the hierarchy of motivations unlearned goals are called *primary goals*; learned goals are *secondary goals*. Money is a common example of a secondary goal; its value must be learned before it acquires the power to reinforce behavior. Social motives are those such as achievement and power motives which propel us toward secondary goals.

THE ACHIEVEMENT MOTIVE

The reward of a thing well done is to have done it.

—*Ralph Waldo Emerson, "New England Reformers,"* Essays: Second Series

What is the use of running when we are not on the right road?

— *German proverb*

Industrial countries such as the United States and the Soviet Union owe much of their position in the world to the strength of the achievement motive in their working populations. Our society's most compelling value is undoubtedly the achievement motive, with success, status, and power the dominant payoffs. The achievement motive may be defined as *an internalized standard of excellence* motivating a person to do well in any achievement-oriented situation.

The achievement motive is primarily learned, although unlearned competence motivation may be a part of it. It is not universal, being deficient or absent in sizable parts of our population. Indeed, whole cultures are characterized by rather low average levels of such motivation. American society puts a good deal of emphasis on acquiring material possessions, getting ahead and being promoted, and obtaining recognition, all of which tend to reinforce the achievement motive. How strange this may appear to someone from another culture is revealed in this recollection (Hepner, 1941) of a conversation between an American Indian and a missionary bent on helping him develop new habits and ways of thinking.

MISSIONARY: Brother, why don't you go to the big city and get a job in a factory?

INDIAN: Suppose I get a job, what then?

M: If you get a job, you will get money and you can have many things.

I: What then?

M: Well, if you do your work well, you will be promoted, become a foreman, and have more money.

I: What then?

M: Oh, then you may become the superintendent of the factory if you work hard enough.

I: What then?

M: If you study all about the business and work harder, you may be the manager of the whole business.

I: Suppose I become the manager, how would that benefit me?

M: If you are an able manager, you can start a business of your own and have more money than ever.

I: What then?

M: Oh, eventually, you will have so much money that you won't need to work at all.

I: That, paleface, is what I'm doing now. Why go to so much trouble to gain what I already have? The white man has the restless sea within his bosom, but the Indian dreams with the stars and looks on (pp. 393–394).

Some people within our culture also do not seem to be much motivated to distinguish themselves by superior achievement. They do not seem to care about keeping up with the Smiths or about accumulating things. Obviously, setting one's sights high is an expected motive in most business and industrial situations. And being security conscious too openly can lead to dismissal. Most people link up the achievement motive in their thinking with the basic goals of a materialistic culture.

McClelland (1955, 1958) has studied the achievement of individuals for a number of years. He has found this motive a stable and predictable individual motive. More recently he has also done a number of studies of the achievement of entire cultures (1961). He found that by studying the achievement imagery of a culture's literature it was possible to predict the rise and fall of civilizations. Cultures on the rise had a much higher proportion of achievement-oriented themes in their literature than later as they were falling.

What High Achievers Are Like

People who score high on tests of achievement motivation do well consistently in a variety of different situations. In their work and in games designed to resemble real-life situations in which decisions must be made, they tend to be *moderate* risk takers. They do not like to gamble in games of pure chance. In games of skill they bet moderately, in relation to the odds and their own skill.

The whole process is aptly illustrated by children throwing bean bags, as shown in Figure 7-3. In these the boy is required to select a goal box from several which are all at different distances from him and throw his bean bags in it. Boys with low achievement motivation and low self-esteem are likely to select a close goal box; it is easier to hit, of course, but does not provide much satisfaction because there is

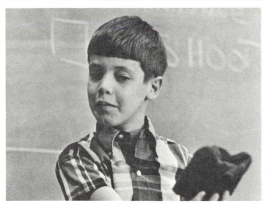

Figure 7-3. Beanbag Experiment was designed to explore the relation between a subject's level of self-esteem (as determined from other tests) and the level of the goals he sets for himself. A higher score could be won by tossing the beanbag into a more distant target.

The choice of which target he would shoot for had to be made by the boy before he proceeded to aim and toss. He could try for a safe shot but one that would win him a low score or he could aspire to achieving a high goal, although one with more risk attached to it.

The shot followed the boy's announcement of the target he had selected. All the boys who participated in the experiment agreed as to what the ideal score would be, but those with high self-esteem displayed greater assurance that they could actually achieve the ideal. (From Scientific American, February, 1968. Copyright © 1968 by Scientific American, Inc. Reprinted by permission of Scientific American.)

no feeling of accomplishment. Boys with low achievement are also equally likely to select a very distant goal box, one which they have almost no chance of hitting. Again, performance has a low chance of giving satisfaction. Boys with high achievement motivation (and high self-esteem) select intermediate goal boxes, ones that are fairly challenging but which offer good odds of success.

You get an idea of the boy's feeling after a successful bean bag toss in the last photograph of the series. In most achievement situations, success should *not* be defined in just objective terms. Each person ought to be able to experience success in relation to the standard of his own talents. Unfortunately, many people are unable to evaluate their own performance realistically and derive satisfaction from an objectively commendable performance.

Upbringing and Achievement Motivation

People who display high achievement motivation strive to do well in all situations in which they believe they are being evaluated on intellect or achievement. High-achievement motivation is fostered by the kind of upbringing that encourages and reinforces early independence. The parents of such children expect and get independent behavior much earlier in development than the parents of low achievers.

One study (Winterbottom, 1958) found, for example, that 68 percent of the mothers of high-need achieving 7-year-olds, but only 25 percent of the mothers of similarly aged low-need achievers, expected

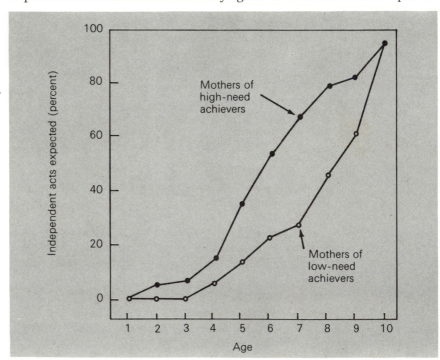

Figure 7-4. Ages at which mothers expected their children to have achieved various kinds of independent behavior. (From the Relation of need for achievement to learning experiences in independence and mastery, by M. R. Winterbottom. Taken from J. Q. Atkinson, *Motives in Fantasy, Action and Society.* Copyright © 1958 by Litton Educational Publishing Inc. Reprinted by permission of Van Nostrand Reinhold Company.)

their children to have developed various kinds of independent behavior such as obedience to traffic lights, undressing and putting themselves to bed, entertaining themselves, earning their own spending money, and choosing their own clothes (Figure 7-4). The mothers who reported giving physical affection for independent behavior had sons who scored twice as high on achievement motivation as those who did not.

Competition and Cooperation

Our society encourages people to value achieving in a competitive situation. It has long been understood in sports that a man will do much better in competing against others than in competing against the clock. But not all people respond positively to competition. In terms of sex roles many women do their best when *not* in competition. In general, we might anticipate that if a person is uncertain about himself, he might react poorly to the pressure of competition.

Among people who live less competitively, such as the Navaho Indians, cooperation and group problem solving is encouraged. Navaho children have been observed to avoid answering the questions of white teachers in school if they felt that other children might be embarrassed by not knowing the answers.

Box 7-3   Achievement and a Perfectionist Level of
          Aspiration: Playing the Game to Fail

A 40-year-old man who held advanced degrees in atomic physics and worked in top-secret research was nevertheless suffering from an acute sense of inferiority, and came to the author for treatment. His delusions had become so flagrant that he was unable to continue his work, because there was too much tension between him and his associates. He suspected everyone of attempting to "get his job." But the most striking thing about him was his attitude of *perfectionism*.

We might imagine that a desire to do the "right thing" and make "right decisions" would be an admirable goal. For this man, however, doing better than he had done before was not good enough. He had to do things *absolutely* right or else he was not satisfied. He was very careful in his work and continuously went over it, checking and rechecking it. He never handed in technical reports until the absolute deadline, because he had to make sure they were accurate down to the last decimal point. He sometimes made his typist type a page over again if he detected a single error in it.

One day he came to therapy and started right off talking about a new job that had been offered him. He had not talked long when suddenly he produced a list from his pocket. It contained, on one side, 20 reasons why he ought not to accept the new job. On the other side there were 20 reasons why he should take it. We talked all hour about the pros and cons of this issue.

When next I saw him I asked him what he had decided. He replied that he had been unable to make up his mind in time. The opportunity had been offered to and accepted by someone else. He was very depressed over the loss.

Later it became apparent that this was the typical way he handled decisions. Not making a decision turns out to be a decision after all, because the "brass ring" of opportunity slips on by. He was so concerned with making the right decision, with being absolutely right, that he could not make a decision at all.

Most of us are daily faced with situations in which we must make a decision with somewhat inadequate information. We usually do the best we can, given the information on hand, and learn to live with the consequences. When we make a mistake, it is usually not crucial. We learn to avoid making similar mistakes in the future. This patient was so afraid of being wrong that he couldn't act at all. His desire to be absolutely correct—which is an unrealistic goal—paradoxically guaranteed that he would fail. It was what we might call a "no-win" game, or perhaps "no-lose" would be better, since in a way he was really motivated to fail. Only failing would confirm his sense of inadequacy. The greatest irony was that he managed to achieve defeat in spite of high intelligence and substantial achievement.

Today in American public education the value of insisting on competition in the school is being questioned. Glaser (1969) observes that many children are currently convinced by the schools that they are failures at learning. The competitive model for grading school performance assumes that we must have losers in order to have winners. The old-time spelling bee is the worst example: every child except the winner gets defeated. How well can the second- and third-best child spell? Objectively, they may be very good spellers, but they feel defeated unless they are the only ones left standing.

It is not surprising that some children fail when under unnecessary pressures of competition. A better idea is to teach spelling and other subjects noncompetitively. After being given time to study, the child is tested, the first time, to see how much he has left to learn. He studies some more and is retested. When he learns the list, he earns 100 percent. In this way, each child gets a feeling of accomplishment. Some may take longer than others to learn, but mastery of the material is the important thing. Furthermore, the cooperative learning model encourages children to help one another master the material. Testing

Box 7-4   Can Motivation to Achieve Be Taught?

Since 1960 McClelland & Danzig have been engaged in motivational training designed to teach people the motivation to achieve. In working with businessmen in India they measured the achievement motive by analyzing a person's fantasy. McClelland reasoned that perhaps achievement could be taught by helping people to form the fantasy responses which, in a certain sense, can be considered the motive itself. The trainees in their program learned to consciously shape their fantasies, which are, of course, related to actual performance.

Games were used in which the trainees learned to set moderate goals and take responsibility for solving problems. They learned to seek out feedback with which to adjust their performance. In an interview, McClelland said:

> The Indian businessmen who took achievement-motivation training started four times as many new businesses, invested twice as much new capital and created more than twice as many new jobs as the control groups who didn't take the training. That all happened within two years after the experimental courses, which ran only 10 days each and I'm sure the long term efforts will be much greater (Harris, 1971).

Several companies have picked up on this kind of research and are teaching motivation to various groups. In Connecticut, Education Ventures, Inc. is conducting workshops in motivation for teachers. In Boston, Massachusetts a group of black businessmen has been trained by various black companies. Also, the Boston office of Economic Opportunity has contracted with Training Development Systems to train drug addicts to redirect their high achievement needs in more constructive directions. It seems clear that this motive can be fostered by special training.

can be appreciated as a guide to learning, not as a potentially humiliating evaluation of one's worth as a person.

As the reading at the end of this chapter makes clear, business and industrial leaders have also begun to question the ideas of scarcity, status, and economic power, which in the past have been the driving forces of our society.

AGGRESSION

Violence is essentially wordless, and it can begin only where thought and rational communication have broken down.

—*Thomas Merton, introduction to selected texts from Mohandas K. Gandhi's* Non-Violence in Peace and War

An animal, it has been observed, acts aggressively "when it inflicts, attempts to inflict, or threatens to inflict damage on another animal'' (Carthy & Ebling, 1964). It was once widely believed that aggressiveness was an instinctive drive; however, now we are uncertain. What we can say is that aggression is not universal and that at least in some animals it is behavior that can be modified. There are societies, human as well as animal, which display little or no aggression.

Animal Aggression

Studies have shown that animals that humans have traditionally considered hostile and dangerous are not always aggressive. The wolf, for example, in a fight with one of its own kind, is unlikely to kill or even seriously injure the other animal. Only if he is cornered and there is no escape is the fight likely to end in death. Aggression between members of the same species is more like an exhibition or a tournament, a ritual acted out to accomplish certain goals.

Animals, of course, kill other animals for food, but they do not kill for sport or amusement. Many animals, in fact, avoid aggressive contact as much as possible. Among social animals, there is usually a *dominance* hierarchy in which one animal, usually an older, stronger male, dominates the rest. There is an ordering of individuals from top to bottom. The bottom-ranked animal is dominated by all the others. These low-ranking animals usually exist at the edge of the group. Unlike the more dominant, they may not possess a territory or a mate or be able to reproduce. If the group is attacked, they are the most likely to fall victim.

Most aggressive contact among social animals does not lead to a fight to the death in combat, as we might imagine when we hear of the "struggle for survival." Instead, there is ritual fighting in which one animal threatens and challenges another's status (see Figure 7-5). The one challenged must either fight or flee. If he decides to fight, the combat is often brief. After threat and counterthreat—and a little actual fighting—one animal decides that he cannot win. He surrenders presenting an appeasement signal, such as by offering his vulnerable throat in surrender, or by running off quickly. If the challenger wins the fight, he gains in status. If he loses, he resumes his subordinate position. Paradoxically, a dominance hierarchy actually insures that there will be a minimum of aggressive conflict within the group. The threat of aggression is also used to minimize conflict between different groups. Among monkeys, loud threats are sounded when the troop hears another troop in the neighborhood. Aggressive threats serve to mark off the troop's territory and prevent actual fighting between troops. Thus, among social animals, aggressive behavior is adaptive and constructive.

Human Aggression

The situation with man is, unfortunately, different. His destructive capacity is so great that many animal species have already become extinct, and many more are threatened with the same fate. We are just now becoming aware of how efficiently man has ravaged his environment. Now even his own survival is in question. This threat comes from several sources: the wholesale destruction of the physical

Figure 7-5. Male marine Iguana of the Galapagos Islands defends his territory against intruding males. As the rival approaches (a), the territory owner struts and nods his head. Then the defender lunges at the intruder and they clash head on (b), each seeking to push the other back. When one iguana (c) realizes he cannot win, he drops to his belly in submission. (From Scientific American, December, 1961. Copyright © 1961 by Scientific American, Inc. Reprinted by permission.)

environment, the likelihood of overpopulation, and the awesome risk of nuclear warfare.

The instruments of violence in warfare have become so powerfully destructive that several nations possess the capability of destroying the entire planet. Washburn & Hamburg (1968) have analyzed the problem thus:

> The situation relative to human aggression can be briefly stated under three headings. First, man has been a predator for a long time and his nature is such that he easily learns to enjoy killing other animals. Hunting is still considered a sport, and millions of dollars are spent annually to provide birds, mammals, and fish to be killed for the amusement of sportsmen. In many cultures animals are killed for the amusement of human observers (in bullfighting, cockfighting, bear baiting, and so forth). Second, man easily learns to enjoy torturing and killing other human beings. Whether one considers the Roman arena, public tortures and executions, or the sport of boxing, it is clear that humans have developed means to enjoy the sight of others being subjected to punishment. Third, war has been regarded as glorious and, whether one considers recent data from tribes in New Guinea or the behavior of the most civilized nations, until very recently war was a normal instrument of national policy and there was no revulsion from the events of victorious warfare, no matter how destructive. Aggression between man and animals, between man and man, and between groups of men has been encouraged by custom, learned in play, and rewarded by society. Man's nature evolved under those conditions and many men still seek personal dominance and national territory through aggression.

The Socialization of Aggression

Aggression in human beings is much more complicated than in animals since man displays aggression in both physical and mental ways. Besides attacking physically, a person can insult and berate and subject others to mental cruelty. Sometimes, even, the aggression can be passive, as when a dependent person ''manipulates'' the behavior of the one he depends on. For example, if a wife is somehow unable to learn to drive a car, she may have to be driven on errands or to the doctor's office.

Man is subjected to a continuous attempt to socialize his aggression. Most children in our culture are taught that they ought to inhibit their aggression. They are taught to channel aggressive feeling into socially approved ways of coping with problems. They are told countless times, "We don't settle things with our fists; we talk things out." Most parents agree that the cultural ideal is of a person who is able to control his aggressive impulses. Unfortunately, this is not all of what the culture teaches us; and the rules for transformation of raw feeling into constructive action are vague and poorly understood.

Actually, American culture is ambivalent even about physical aggression and violence, and in many situations, encourages the use of force. In the home, the right of parents to control their children—with force, if necessary—is respected. In the school and the streets, aggressiveness has something to do with peer group acceptance. Of course, most of this cultural lesson is directed at males, and females are supposed to be protected from it. Much of our culture, not just lower-class youth gangs, idealizes an image of masculinity that prizes aggression and dominance. Males demonstrate their masculinity through physical activity, sports, fighting—or at least a show of willingness to fight—and in aggressive domination of girls and women. Finally, every nation wages war in which *its* aggression is defined as legitimate. Men have reveled in war as the supreme opportunity to glorify their manhood.

The mass media, especially television, play an important role in the socialization of—or failure to socialize—aggression. The constant barrage of violence, gunfire, and death, held up as a model of aggressive, masculine behavior, is not without influence. Bandura (1963) has shown that film exposure to aggressive models increases the likelihood that children will respond aggressively in the future (see Figure 5-8).

Control of Aggression

Before we can think about how to control aggressiveness, we must understand that there are three different conditions that are likely to stimulate aggressiveness. Aggression may be a reaction to frustration; injury, insult, or threat; and deprivation.

Box 7-5   What of International Aggression?

The threat of nuclear war is perhaps the most pressing problem of man's existence. At the international level there is a greater lack of order and useful mechanisms for solving disputes than at any other level of human affairs. We all know something about the problem posed by escalation of the arms race. It is a social-psychological fact that the possession of arms increases the likelihood that they will be used as the solution to disputes.

The techniques of cooperative bargaining are most likely to be employed in the absence of great armaments. But the pacifist solution of unilateral disarmament seems too dangerous to most people to be seriously considered. They ask, "what would inhibit an aggressor nation from ruthless invasion of weaker neighbors?"

In his book *An Alternative to War or Surrender* (1962), psychologist

Charles Osgood suggests that we might take some sort of small first step toward disarmament that would be very noticeable and that would be done without consultation with our major adversary. This would be some dramatic event like deciding *not* to build yet another air base near the Soviet Union, which seems to the Russians to threaten their national security. Taking this small first step would constitute an invitation to the adversary to take a similar first step toward reducing tensions. If he did so, we would then take a second step unilaterally and with proper safeguards for our national security. This would invite him to do likewise. This plan, which Osgood calls Graduated Reciprocation in Tension-reduction (GRIT), would, in effect, constitute deescalation of the arms race.

Frustration. Whenever ongoing motivated behavior is somehow blocked, we experience frustration, the most likely consequence of which is aggression. Some things can be done to reduce this likelihood, however. Children can and are taught as they grow up to "learn to wait." Their impulses cannot always be satisfied just when they want. They can also be taught to accept substitute gratifications. One's frustration can also be decreased by education and developing greater self-awareness. In some cases, psychotherapy may be needed to resolve conflict, make repression conscious, and develop more effective habits and realize one's best competencies.

Injury, Insult, or Threat.   Militant youth have learned that they can elicit aggressiveness from authorities, such as police, by taunts and threats. The authorities have learned that they can best control confrontations by training their men to "actively ignore" taunts and threats. Everyone has discovered belatedly that it is necessary to keep in mind one's objectives. Physical aggression is often the least constructive action we can take in our own self-interest.

Deprivation.   Animals hunt other animals because they need food. The thief traditionally steals for gain because he feels deprived. War is often waged for territorial gain. The Germans said, for example, that "territory to live in" was their major objective in their expansion before World War II. Youth gang members fight for status and "rep" (reputation), for control of their "turf" (territory), and for the favors of girls.

It would seem fairly obvious that if we wish to modify the aggressiveness produced by frustration, threat, or deprivation, we must teach children how to reach their goals through behavior that does not bring them into conflict with society. A youth gang member must have some alternative to violent aggression as a way of earning status and reputation. What are the alternatives? (a) One can earn status in a symbolically aggressive way such as in competitive sports. (b) One can learn to achieve in different, more acceptable ways, such as in school subjects or in activities. (c) One can let off steam, such as in working out or jogging. (d) One can learn to admit that frustration is sometimes unavoidable and must be accepted. And perhaps it is time to put our minds to creating some further alternatives to violence that are socially constructive. In a sense, the current youth culture's attention to crafts, skills, and music might be seen in that light.

DRUG MOTIVATION

The most powerful motives of man, some psychologists argue, permit escape from truth and reality. Every civilization has sought and found mind-distorting drugs, almost always extracted from plants . . . to achieve liberation from truth and reality.

—Jozef Cohen, "Secondary Motivation," Eyewitness series in psychology.

Drug taking is an example of behavior motivated by complex social motives, involving physiological drive conditions. Drug addiction is defined as an *uncontrolled, compulsive use of mind-distorting substances*. Addiction involves (a) psychological dependence, (b) physiological dependence, and (c) often some degree of tolerance.

In the United States the most significant drug problem—in terms of numbers of people and the cost of abuse—is alcoholism, a legal form of drug taking. The government estimated that in 1963 there were 5 million alcoholics in the United States—6 percent of the adult population. But as everyone knows, illegal drug taking, loosely called narcotics addiction, has also become a problem of growing concern. There are five main classes of drugs that may be considered addictive:

—the *opiates*, which include opium, morphine, and heroin;

—the *psychedelics*, or marijuana, peyote, and LSD;

—the *analeptics*, such as cocaine, and amphetamines;

—the *sedatives* or barbiturates;

—the *intoxicants*, or alcohol and ether. The discussion will be limited to the three types of drugs of greatest concern to the public.

Opiates

Opium, morphine, and heroin are derived from the opium poppy, which, along with other drug-producing plants, is shown in Figure 7-6. Opiate effects were understood before recorded history, and the ancient Egyptians prescribed opium for crying children. Morphine is the active ingredient in opium. Morphine, a prescription drug, is used solely as a pain killer. Heroin, a completely illegal drug, is morphine treated with acetic acid. It is about twenty-five times stronger than morphine.

Addicts report that opiates produce various kinds of sensuous delight. At first a person may be motivated to take the drug to experience a pleasant feeling or to escape pain and unhappiness. He then becomes psychologically dependent and later, as the brain becomes saturated, develops a tolerance so that increasing amounts of the drug are required to produce the same "high." Finally, he becomes completely dependent physiologically, his tolerance soars, and the cost of his habit skyrockets to the point (perhaps as much as $150 a day) where there is no way—not even through stealing—to raise the money. At that point the addict "crashes" and must undergo withdrawal, whose terrifying symptoms have been described as follows:

Withdrawal sickness, in one with a well-developed physical dependence, is a shattering experience. . . . About 12 hours after the last heroin

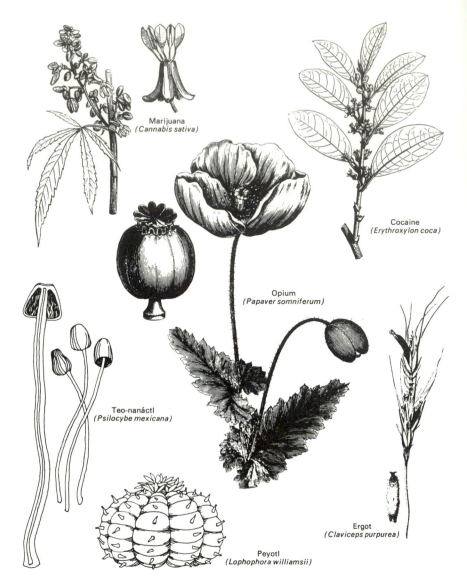

Marijuana
(Cannabis sativa)

Cocaine
(Erythroxylon coca)

Opium
(Papaver somniferum)

Teo-nanáctl
(Psilocybe mexicana)

Ergot
(Claviceps purpurea)

Peyotl
(Lophophora williamsii)

From Jozef Cohen,
*Eyewitness Series in
Psychology*, p. 24.
Copyright © by Rand
McNally and Company.
Reprinted by
permission.

Figure 7-6. Drug producing plants.

dose, the addict begins to grow uneasy. He yawns, shivers, and sweats, while watery discharge pours from inside his nose—described as "hot water running into my mouth." For a few hours, he falls into an abnormal restless stupor known among addicts as "yen sleep." On awakening 18 to 24 hours after his last drug dose, the addict enters the lower depths of his personal hell. Yawning may violently dislocate his jaw. More watery mucous pours from his eyes and nose. His pupils are dilated widely. The hair on his skin stands erect, and his skin shows that typical goose flesh called "cold turkey" in the parlance of the addict. . . . His bowels act with violence. Great waves of contraction pass over the stomach walls, causing explosive vomiting frequently stained with blood. . . . The surface of his abdomen appears corrugated and knotted, and abdominal pain is severe. Constant purging occurs and more than 60 large watery stools may be passed in a single day. . . . Thirty-six hours after his last dose, the addict presents a dreadful spectacle. In a desperate effort to gain comfort from body chills, he covers himself with blankets. His body is shaken by twitchings and his feet kick involuntarily, the origin of the addict's term "kicking the habit." . . . He obtains neither sleep nor rest. His painful muscular cramps keep him ceaselessly tossing. Profuse sweating alone keeps bedding and mattress soaked. Filthy, unshaven, disheveled, befouled with his own vomit and feces, the addict presents an execrable appearance (DeRopp, 1964).

All persons experience the negative pain-relieving effects of the opiates, but the positive, pleasurable effects are felt only by addiction-prone, emotionally unstable people—which is why so few people have become accidentally addicted as a result of medical treatment. At one time there were a great number of medically addicted people, the first wave occurring during the Civil War, a disorder called "the soldier's disease."

It was long believed that the pain-relieving and addicting properties of the opiates were inseparable, but there are now pain-relieving and nonaddicting compounds that are superior to morphine— pentazocine, for instance, has no side effects except respiratory depression. Another discovery that may help solve the addiction problem is a synthetic type of morphine called Methadone, which has been used experimentally in treating heroin addicts. Although it too is addictive, it produces much less severe withdrawal symptoms, and when combined with psychotherapy, it offers some prospect of helping more addicts remain free of drugs. At present, according to the statistics of the federal narcotics hospitals, 75 percent of narcotics addicts resume taking opiates within 5 years of treatment.

Vigorous effort by federal law enforcement agencies has reduced the rate of morphine and heroin addiction greatly during the last half century. As Figure 7-7 shows, the number of addicts per thousand persons in the U.S. population has declined radically since the high point in the 1900s.

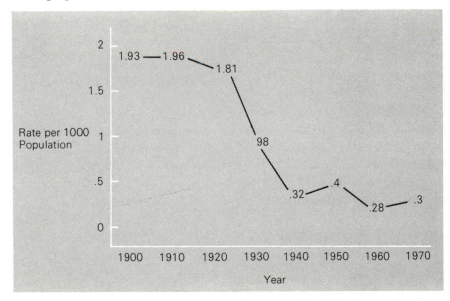

Figure 7-7. Opiate addiction in the United States, 1900–1970. (Data taken from Federal Bureau of Narcotics.)

Marijuana

Psychedelic, a term coined by novelist Aldous Huxley that means "mind-manifesting," applies to drugs such as marijuana, peyote, and LSD, which produce distorted perceptions and unusual sensual experiences. Marijuana comes from Indian Hemp, *cannabis sativa*, a weed that grows and flourishes in almost every climate. Marijuana is one of several products of the plant with psycho-active ingredients. THC (tetra-hydrocannibinol), recently synthesized, is the active ingredient in these drugs. In the Middle East and the Orient, the flowers of the female plant are used to produce a resin called hashish, which is eaten or smoked. Hashish has been used for at least 4000 years and its psychological effects (such as euphoria) were understood from the beginning.

It is probably somewhat misleading to talk of addiction to drugs in the psychedelic category. For example, people do *not* develop increased tolerance for marijuana; in fact, they develop reverse tolerance. In other words, less drug may produce the full effect with continued use. It is a fact, however, that tolerance and physiological addiction are *not* produced by continued usage. Psychological habituation, however, does occur. Continued usage leads to dependence on the drug. One long-time marijuana user explained this as follows: "I have used marijuana for 25 years without its becoming a habit."

The studies on marijuana identify at least several kinds of persons as being addiction-prone. The habitual user feels euphoric under its influence. He may be quiet or contemplative. Ultimately, since the drug is a depressive the user sinks into a state of passivity. Ausubel (1958) believes that habitual marijuana usage serves an important adjustive function for some people who have inadequate personalities or who are anxiety neurotics or depressives. These people use marijuana to cope with conflict. Marijuana, Ausubel says, "has adjustive value for these individuals because it generates a sense of well-being and adequacy and restores damaged feelings of self-confidence." Others are more casual in their use and less dependent psychologically.

Mental abilities are little affected by its use. There is no evidence that habitual use of marijuana produces any physical effects, such as the nerve cell destruction that occurs with habitual use of alcohol.

Alcohol

Alcohol, one of the class of drugs called intoxicants (others are *ether and nitrous oxide*), is America's greatest drug problem. Nearly 6 percent of the adult population are alcoholic addicts, and about 40 percent use alcohol regularly. Genuine alcoholism shows all the aspects of addiction previously mentioned: psychological and physiological dependency and increased tolerance. In the first stages of intoxication, one may feel euphoric, but later, as Figure 7-8 shows, alcohol has a stupefying effect, immediately limiting perception and judgment. Driving skills are seriously impaired; in fact, 73 percent of all drivers responsible for fatal or disabling accidents have blood alcohol levels of 0.2 percent or more—and legal intoxication is defined usually at only 0.15 percent (Cohen, 1970).

Technically, alcohol is a depressant, which means that it depresses the activity of the central nervous system. The apparent gaiety and euphoria at cocktail parties is produced by the suppression of restraint and inhibitions. Alcohol is not digested but is absorbed

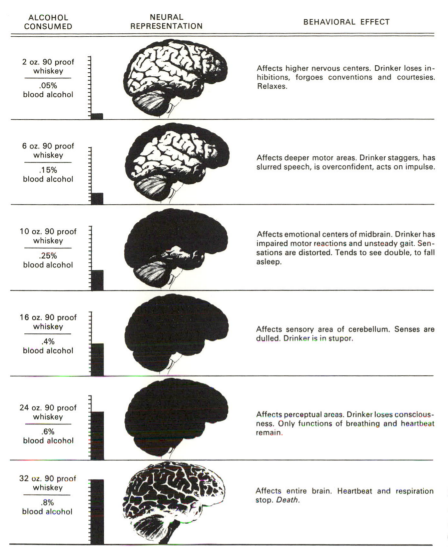

ALCOHOL CONSUMED	NEURAL REPRESENTATION	BEHAVIORAL EFFECT
2 oz. 90 proof whiskey .05% blood alcohol		Affects higher nervous centers. Drinker loses inhibitions, forgoes conventions and courtesies. Relaxes.
6 oz. 90 proof whiskey .15% blood alcohol		Affects deeper motor areas. Drinker staggers, has slurred speech, is overconfident, acts on impulse.
10 oz. 90 proof whiskey .25% blood alcohol		Affects emotional centers of midbrain. Drinker has impaired motor reactions and unsteady gait. Sensations are distorted. Tends to see double, to fall asleep.
16 oz. 90 proof whiskey .4% blood alcohol		Affects sensory area of cerebellum. Senses are dulled. Drinker is in stupor.
24 oz. 90 proof whiskey .6% blood alcohol		Affects perceptual areas. Drinker loses consciousness. Only functions of breathing and heartbeat remain.
32 oz. 90 proof whiskey .8% blood alcohol		Affects entire brain. Heartbeat and respiration stop. *Death.*

From Jozef Cohen, *Eyewitness Series in Psychology*, p. 44. Copyright © by Rand McNally and Company. Reprinted by permission.

Figure 7-8. The behavioral effects of alcohol are correlated roughly to blood-alcohol content and its corresponding suppression of higher mental functions.

directly into the blood stream, where it remains until oxidated by the liver. The rate of oxidation is near constant, which means that a person who has drunk enough alcohol to be legally intoxicated will be free from its effects after about 10 hours. Such devices as black coffee, walking around, and fresh air, incidentally, have no effect—nothing speeds up the rate of oxidation.

Again as the figure shows, continued heavy use of alcohol over a period of years can cause severe damage to body tissues, particularly the steady, irreversible destruction of the central nervous system. Moreover, addiction to this drug contributes to personality change and interpersonal conflict. As the alcoholic centers his life more and more around drinking, he may neglect his work and family life, avoid his friends, and attempt to drown his sorrow in drink and self-pity. Eventually he neglects his health and nutrition, loses interest in sex, and, in the final stages, experiences hallucinations (delerium tremens) and alcoholic psychosis.

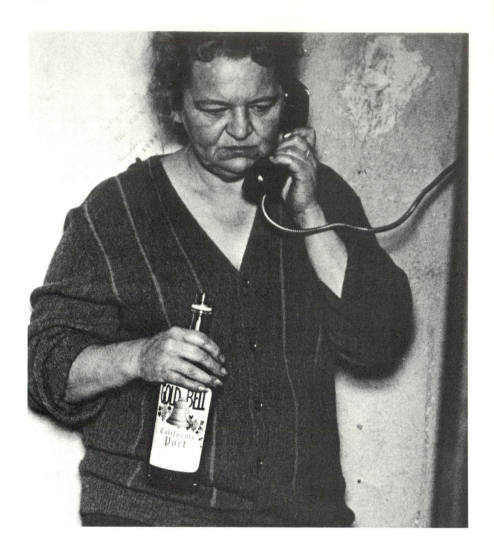

Box 7-6   Synanon: A Community of Ex-Addicts

"We don't really give a damn if your grandfather was an alcoholic, your mother hustled, and your father slugged you daily," says Charles Dederich, founder of Synanon. "None of it is an excuse for bad behavior in Synanon!" Synanon starts with the behavior to be changed.

Lefty committed several offenses of the following type: He would bully or threaten another member, usually a smaller guy. He never used any violence, because he knew that he might get kicked out for it. On about his third offense, Chuck and I were in a synanon [a special type of group session] with him, and the two of us began to work him over, with the group's help. What happened in this particular case was that he had picked up a tire iron and threatened Bill Crawford. Bill had ordered him to do something in the course of a work project. Compared to Lefty, Bill is a physical lightweight.

Well, in the synanon, we confronted Lefty with his atrocious behavior. He began to use a psychological mish-mash of terms to defend. He said that he had a psychological block, that he was displacing aggression, and a whole bunch of other rationalizations and bullshit.

Chuck and I glanced at each other and decided to really put him on. Chuck said something like "Well, let's examine the psychological implications of your behavior with Bill." Lefty brightened up, and we went at it. Chuck said, "Let's analyze it. Is there any significant figure in your earlier life or is there any situation that comes to your mind when you think about the Crawford incident?"

Lefty's eyes began to glitter, and he said, "Let me think." Chuck saw him take the bait and said, "This may explain the whole thing, think hard." Lefty pursed his lips, acted pained, wrinkled his brow, stared up at the ceiling, and went off into a reverie of deep thought.

He then said, "Gee, that makes a lot of sense. It certainly brings something to my consciousness. At one period, when I was a kid, and I use to wash dishes . . ."

"Who did you wash dishes for?"

"It was my grandmother! She had a certain way of talking to me and a nasal twang and . . ."

"That's it! Crawford sounds just like my grandmother. She use to make me wash dishes and nag at me when I wanted to go out and play. She really used to incite my hostility."

Then Chuck said, "Well, maybe we've hit on it. Crawford, with his particular approach and his voice tone, seems to trigger you, and you associate his behavior with hers." Everyone in the session joined in to confirm Lefty's exciting insight discovery.

Lefty picked up on the group's approval and went on further: "By God, that's it exactly—when Crawford comes on like he does, it's my grandmother all over again. No wonder I blow up and . . ."

At this point, Lefty was beaming—carrying on and everything—and then Chuck pushed him right off the cliff. "You lying son-of-a-bitch, you're so full of shit, it's ridiculous!" With that, everyone in the group broke up in a loud roar of laughter.

Here he was trying to rationalize away his bad behavior with this bull story he had dug out of Psychology I. Of course, he couldn't get away with it in Synanon. The Lefty story spread all over the club; and from that day on, anytime anyone tried to pull that crap to avoid personal responsibility for their behavior, someone will say, "You're a Lefty!" or, "It sounds just like Lefty's grandmother."

The United States attempted to do away with the sale and consumption of alcohol in 1919 with the passage of the Eighteenth (Prohibition) Amendment, which was so complete a failure that it was repealed 14 years later. Now the control of alcohol addiction is generally left to the helping professions—medicine, psychiatry, and psychology—which try to treat both symptoms (effects of alcohol) and the disease itself (causes of psychological and physiological dependency). Individual and group psychotherapy are recommended to deal with psychological dependency. Reports vary on the number of cures claimed in attempts to rehabilitate alcoholics. The success of professional psychiatrists and psychologists has not been impressive. Self-help groups such as Alcoholics Anonymous have done better. These groups are operated on the principle that "it takes one to help one," meaning that a former alcoholic addict is in the best position to inspire confidence in the addict in his ability to shake the habit. Not the least of the advantages of such groups is that they are usually on call 24 hours a day, seven days a week, for help in crisis situations—compared to the one to five hours a week usually available under "professional" conditions. The nonprofessional group, since it is composed entirely of addicts or former addicts, is in the best position to point out various kinds of self-deceptions and evasions. Such groups may seem relentless at times in getting at truth, but the individual comes to feel that the others do care what happens to him. The cruelty of truth is leavened with love. But they do insist that he cut out lies and evasions and stop making excuses and deceiving himself. The message seems to be, "A new life must be based on truth-seeking."

CONFORMITY, COMPLIANCE, AND FREEDOM

What do you think and feel about the following person? After each statement, add something to the total impression. This man was:

1. a good family man, a responsible husband and father.
2. a conscientious and efficient worker.
3. highly respected by his superiors.
4. a loyal citizen, patriotic.
5. a member of a political party, concerned about politics.
6. a German who lived through the Second World War.
7. a Nazi, an S.S. Lt. Colonel.
8. the chief administrator of Hitler's "final solution" to the Jewish problem.
9. the man most directly responsible for the murder of 6 million Jews.

This man was Adolph Eichmann. How are we to understand such a mentality? Like many Germans, Eichmann claimed he was just carrying out orders, merely doing his job as efficiently as possible. His job, unfortunately, was to arrange to have people killed. Yet by most standards of conventional society, he was a model citizen, a good family man, respected and hard working. Half a dozen psychiatrists pronounced him sane at his trial. One psychiatrist who examined him, obviously perplexed, said that Eichmann was a normal person, "more normal, at any rate, than I am after having examined him" (Arendt, 1963). He was a normal man, not a fanatic anti-Semite, who even professed to have "private reasons" not to be a Jew-hater. He claimed that he had been enthusiastic in helping Jews emigrate out of Austria before the war. He was even a Zionist during the time when his job called for facilitating the emigration of Jews out of Austria and Germany.

Surely, either Eichmann or the culture he lived in was sick. Eichmann's crimes are horrible precisely because he was so normal—

an ordinary petty bureaucrat, a simple organization man. He was not so different from many other so-called "normal men." He had middle-class values, was something of an idealist, bragged too much, and was guilty of rather too much self-deception.

Most of us would like to believe that we are different from Eichmann. Given the same circumstances, we imagine, *we* would behave differently. A most disturbing line of research casts doubt on this belief.

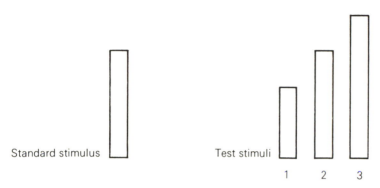

Standard stimulus   Test stimuli

1   2   3

Figure 7-9. The Asch experiment.

Suppose you are asked to match the stimulus on the left in Figure 7-9 with one on the right. Over 99 percent of subjects make this judgment without error, matching it to number two. However, suppose you are asked to perform this task in a group composed of people who, unknown to you, are paid assistants to the experimenter. Imagine that you are the next to the last person to make his judgments. All the other subjects have said, "Number three is the right one." What will you say?

Solomon Asch has performed this experiment hundreds of times. He found that about one-third of naïve subjects conformed to the wrong judgments of the group. The actual effect varies somewhat with the size of the group supplying the false information. When conforming subjects were interviewed afterward, many of them unconsciously "forgot"—that is, repressed—the tension, the profuse sweating, and feelings of anxiety generated in the experiment. After being informed of the real purpose of this experiment, most subjects expressed appreciation for having been allowed to take part in it. Often the opinion is volunteered that the experiment taught them something important about tolerance (Asch, 1955).

You might object that the judgments required in Asch's experiment are not important. What difference does it make if so many people conform to the giving of such false perceptual judgments? Almost everyone believes that if "the chips were down and it were important, he would resist." An experiment by Milgram (1965) is directed to this issue. Milgram asked subjects to assist him in what they supposed was a learning task. They were instructed to administer electric shock to other subjects as part of an experimental procedure supposedly designed to study the effects of punishment on memory. The intensity of the shock was to be increased progressively up to a maximum of 450 volts. The "shocked" subjects, however, were not actually getting shocked; they were paid confederates of the experimenter.

Most people administered the shock as directed even when the supposed level of the shock went past the level that was clearly labeled as dangerous on the shock box. The confederates put on a good show and complained. Milgram describes what happens next:

> The responses of the victim are standardized on tape, and each protest is coordinated to a particular voltage level on the shock generator. Starting with 75 volts, the learner begins to grunt and moan. At 150 volts he demands to be let out of the experiment. At 180 volts he cries out that he can no longer stand the pain. At 300 volts he refuses to provide any more answers to the memory test, insisting that he is no longer a participant in the experiment and must be freed. In response to this last tactic, the experimenter instructs the naïve subject to treat the absence of an answer as equivalent to a wrong answer, and to follow the usual procedure.

Depending on the exact circumstances of the experiment, one-third to two-thirds of the subjects in this experiment complied with unreasonable requests to continue administering shock because of the authority of the experimenter and because of the apparent validity of the situation— a scientific study. Even when they felt distress at administering shock they usually continued to do so. The apparent cries of the victim were to no avail. As Milgram puts it:

> With numbing regularity, good people were seen to knuckle under the demands of authority and perform actions that were callous and severe. Men who are in everyday life responsible and decent were seduced by the trappings of authority, by the control of their perceptions, and by the uncritical acceptance of the experimenter's definition of the situation. . . .

Erich Fromm has been in the forefront of psychologists who have considered man's need to avoid freedom and independence. In his pioneer work *Escape from Freedom* (1941), Fromm traces the rise of the Nazi state to certain authoritarian character trends among the Germans. He could just as well be talking of America today: "Modern society affects man in two ways simultaneously: he becomes more independent, self-reliant, and critical, and he becomes more isolated, alone, and afraid." In his avoidance of alienation man may rush headlong into submission to some figure who seems to offer psychological security.

Box 7-7   Escape from Freedom

It has been the thesis of this book [Fromm's *Escape from Freedom*] that freedom has a twofold meaning for modern man: that he has been freed from traditional authorities and has become an "individual," but that at the same time he has become isolated, powerless, and an instrument of purposes outside of himself, alienated from himself and others; furthermore, that this state undermines his self, weakens and frightens him, and makes him ready for submission to new kinds of bondage. Positive freedom on the other hand is identical with the full realization of the individual's potentialities, together with his ability to live actively and spontaneously. Freedom has reached a critical point where, driven by the logic of its own dynamism, it threatens to change into its opposite. The future of democracy depends on the realization of that individualism that has been the ideological aim of modern thought since the Renaissance. The cultural and political crisis of our days is not due to the fact that there is too much individualism but that what we believe to be individualism has become an empty shell. The victory of freedom is possible only if democracy develops into a society in which the individual, his growth and happiness, is the aim and purpose of culture, in which life does not need any justification in success or anything else, and in which the individual is not subordinated to or manipulated by any power outside of himself, be it in the State or the economic machine; finally a society in which his conscience and ideals are not the internalization of external demands, but are really *his* and express the aims that result from the peculiarity of his *self*. These aims could not be fully realized in any previous period of modern history; they had to remain largely ideological aims, because the material basis for the development of genuine individualism was lacking. Capitalism has created this premise. The problem we are confronted with today is that all of the organizations of social and economic forces must be arranged, so that man—as a member of organized society—may become the master of these forces and cease to be their slave.

DON FABUN

Reward and Punishment: The Carrot and the Stick

Most human motivational systems are based on the belief that, through the offer of rewards and the threat of punishment, individuals can be led to expend their energy in a desired direction. All of our institutions—business, government, education, military, religious—are based on that premise.

Historically, these institutions were forged in a tough furnace; they were created in a world-economy of scarcity—a largely agrarian society where rewards were meager, hard to come by, and therefore treasured, and where punishment was apt to be sudden and severe, and for that reason, all the more feared.

This may still be true in many parts of the world, but in the highly developed Western technological societies, neither economic reward nor punishment appear to have the motivational force they once had. Nevertheless, most of our institutions continue to operate their motivational systems *as if* they were still in the pre-technological age. There is nothing intrinsically wrong with this approach, except that it fails to take into account the infinite multiplicity of responses of which human beings are capable, nor does it provide the environmental "cues" that would enable the individual to develop his own personality

while still expending his energies in the interests of the institution.

It is possible that much of the growing alienation and non-involvement of some members of our society is due to the narrow and doctrinaire interpretation of rewards and punishments preserved by the "establishment" of each type of institution.

The apparent disinclination of top college students to desire positions in business may be one reflection of a business attitude that conceives of rewards primarily in terms of money.

The disinclination of many people to enter the government bureaucracy may well be the result of a policy that interprets rewards largely in terms of security and gradual promotion within a rigid hierarchy.

Perhaps one reason more young people do not become active in church organizations is that the promise of salvation in a hereafter does not seem as challenging to them as an opportunity to be of service to others in the here and now.

In an increasingly affluent society, the power of money rewards as a motivator decreases, because beyond a certain point the difference in living styles becomes marginal and for this reason less motivating.

B. J. Hoffman, Jr. (in "Behavioral Aspects of Motivation") says: "It is easy to understand why managerial practices become antiquated or to see how the environment of most working people has changed. . . . Environment in its larger sense takes in not only the physical confines of a person. Consider the general upgrading in education of almost everyone. Think about the demand for the worker that makes him more independent. Realize that most workers are paid adequately so that they require more satisfaction than the mere providing of desirable food and general living conditions. . . . Motivational methods which worked quite well until recent times are increasingly ineffective today."

It is not only that rewards in the economic sense are not as motivating as they once were. In an increasingly socialized society, punishment is less of a motivator because the loss of a job is not as disastrous as it used to be. Workmen's compensation, social security, medical aid programs, retirement plans, savings plans and welfare programs tend to decrease the importance of punishment as a motivator.

With both monetary rewards and the threat of punishment decreasing as effective motivators, institutional management may have to search for other means to enlist and direct men's energy. These probably will involve providing environmental "cues" for the elaboration of the "secondary" drives—curiosity, exploration, greater personal identification with the over-all goals of the institution, opportunities for the individual to extend his education, new opportunities for social contacts within the working environment (seminars, workshops, group projects), and increased opportunities for social service in the community with appropriate recognition by top management.

The basic concepts of the "new" motivational theory are (1) to make the job itself so challenging that it becomes its own reward and (2) to create an institutional environment in which the employee finds opportunity for personal growth and the development of his own personality and self-fulfillment.

Many business organizations, taking their cue from an earlier era when most employees had little formal education, have broken down the production process into relatively simple, repetitive tasks. The employee who has such a job is playing a child-like role. Like any child, he resents being placed in this inferior position and takes frustration out against the "parental authority" (management) by restricting his productivity, thus "punishing" his "parents." When his job is redesigned to give him a more mature role, he may respond by trying harder to prove he is worthy of it. If the challenge is not too great, most men rise to meet it; but if

they feel their job is beneath their dignity, they may not try at all.

The changing value of the "reward-punishment" concept also applies to our educational system. Like the business application, it developed out of an era of scarcity, when money was short and jobs hard to get. The concept does not work as well in an "economy of abundance." Under the still-prevailing concept, getting "good grades" leads to the reward of getting a "good job," which in turn leads to making "good money."

Such a scheme no longer motivates many of today's students and they find it irrelevant to the concept they have of themselves in today's society, which is that they are agents for social and economic change in an era of transition. Awareness of the irrelevancy of an educational system that fits them for a now-mythological world of economic scarcity underlies much of the unrest on university campuses today. For these students, at least, the old motivators no longer work.

The same thing, in reverse, would appear to happen at the junior high and high school level for students from the "disadvantaged" ethnic and economic groups. They find little or no motivation in educating themselves for jobs that, within the realities of our contemporary society, they are unlikely to get or, worse yet, may not exist at all by the time they graduate, because mechanization and cybernation will have eliminated them. Nor does punishment act as a motivator; one cannot fear the loss of a job that he isn't going to get.

If the education system were based on a reward program for the development of the individual human personality in all its manifestations, perhaps there would be fewer "drop-outs" (and this includes those who may be physically in attendance but have *mentally* "dropped out"). Failure to develop a sense of personal value is its own punishment and needs no reinforcement from "the system."

Because it so permeates most conventional applications of motivation, it may be worthwhile going a little deeper into the idea of why monetary reward is considered so important by one generation and is not considered so by the next.

Earlier we discussed "imprinting" and said that it occurs during the very early years of life, that it is largely non-verbal, that it consists in part of the emotional aura around an event, and that it is virtually ineradicable in later years.

Reward and Punishment Systems in our Society

REWARD	PUNISHMENT

If you expend your energy the way we want you to,

you'll get . . .	if you don't you'll get . . .

Business

A job	Fired
Advancement	No promotion
Salary increases	No raises
Prestige	Non-recognition
Security	Insecurity

Religious Order

Acceptance	Non-acceptance
Participation	Excommunication
Salvation	Damnation
Heaven	Hell

Educational Institutions

Acceptance	Non-acceptance
Advancement	Non-advancement
Graduation	Expelled
Higher degrees	No degrees
Chance for a better job	Poorer job

Political Institutions

Participation	Ineligibility
Appointment	Passed over
Elected	Defeated
Diefication	Obscurity

Military

Accepted	Not accepted
Promotion	Passed over
Permanent rank	Temporary rank
Medals and honors	Court martialed
Retirement at rank	Dishon. discharge

Social and Fraternal

Acceptance	Blackballed
Exposure to others	Excluded
Committee work	Not appointed
Officer position	Not elected
Retirement banquet	Expulsion

Consider, then, that most people who today have children old enough to attend high school and college were small children during the early 1930's. This was an era in which money and jobs were extremely pressing problems for most families.

Consider, further, that imprinting involves the exposure of a young child to the emotional aura surrounding an event. The principal emotional event in most households at that time was the lack of a job and thus lack of income. Fear and anxiety were predominant. The imprint on the young child was clear and indelible. It could be paraphrased something like this: "Lack of money is painful, it 'hurts'; it makes mama cry and daddy get angry. Whenever there is some money coming in, things are better. When I grow up, I'll make sure I always have plenty of money, so that I won't hurt."

And so the present "older" generation (now "the power structure," now "the Establishment") grew up with that thing inside it. Nearly all of our subsequent experience was strained through the mesh of that imprinted screen: "Will it make money?"

The offer of money for the older generation has been—and is—a most important motivator. We measured other people by "how much he makes," rather than the kind of person he is. We measured our own place in society by how much "we made" and accumulated as compared to others of our generation. And, for the most part, we still do.

But the present young generation, who are in high school and college now, were "imprinted" in the early 1950's—the post-war boom and pre-Korean war boom eras. Jobs were relatively easy to get; wages and salaries were good; the economy was expanding. The family was still concerned about money, but the concern no longer had the powerful emotional aura about it that it had in the households of the early 1930's.

And so the older generation (ours!) imprinted with the desire for money (because having it reduced deeply rooted anxieties), reinforced over the years because the more we had, the more secure we felt, had become involved in a compulsion, an acting out in our adult lives of a childhood fantasy, "If I have money, I won't hurt."

When, today, we try to motivate young people with promises of "good jobs" and "good money" we are trying to motivate *our-*

selves as we were at the age of 18 or 20. It's not working very well, and so perhaps new systems of motivation may be necessary.

Again, it appears that there may lie in the direction of the elaboration of "secondary drives."

What existing institutions produce, for the most part, is boredom—particularly the big, bureaucratic institutions that more and more dominate our society. To see what *might* be done in the motivation field, consider the extraordinary transformation that takes place among secretaries after five o'clock; of nearly everyone as quitting time approaches on Friday afternoons; on the ebullience of people who are suddenly "freed" to go on vacation. This outpouring of energy, this exuberance, is seldom manifested within the confines of a routine job, in the same old office or factory, day after day.

Yet, it is possible that this energy *can* be harnessed. This is exactly what is done with executives in business firms and officials in government: a rather constant switching around of job responsibilities, with the new challenges they create; frequent trips for changes of environment, with all the releases of energy that these bring; private offices that they can decorate to suit their own mood and taste; occasional leaves of absence to perform socially valuable services or to further personal education—all these things work to release energy through secondary drives—challenge, curiosity, exploration and self-expression.

It could be argued that all these things "cost money," and that therefore they still represent "monetary reward." And this may be true. But for the individual the motivation does not appear to be money, but excitement through new experience.

It may well be that increasingly the motivators in our society will be more and more directed toward creating excitement as means for releasing energies that are no longer called forth by traditional reward and punishment systems.

Summarizing Statements

1. Motivation deals with the *why* of behavior; it arouses and directs behavior toward a goal. Motivation may be classified into physiological motives, general motives, and social motives. Physiological motives are unlearned and necessary for survival. General motives may be either learned or innate but their satisfaction does lead to drive reduction. Social motives are not necessary for survival, but are important to the general well-being of the organism.

2. Drives are motives rooted in biological need. Most drives operate homeostatically, which means that they are automatically kept in a balanced steady state.

3. Hunger is regulated by several factors. (a) It is probable that one regulator is a product of metabolism in the blood. Also, (b) there are two brain centers that produce eating and satisfaction.

4. Obese people seem to be stimulated to overeat by external stimulation, like good smells. Normal people eat and stop eating according to their internal needs. Control of obesity involves an analysis of the situation in which overeating takes place.

5. Physiological motivation is often elaborated by complex general and social motives through custom and habit.

6. Basically, human sexuality is a physiological drive, elaborated complexly by social motives. Animal sexuality is much more regulated by hormones than is the case with humans.

7. Some general motives such as activity, curiosity, sensory stimulation and manipulation of objects are unlearned. Most social motives are learned. Competence, which may be the master motive, is unlearned.

8. The infant's love for his mother arises out of contact comfort and not in the nursing relationship, as previously thought. Monkey infants demonstrate their affection in preferring to be with mother, in going to her when threatened, and in being able to explore and manipulate their environment when assured of her protection. Besides adequate mothering, monkey infants need the stimulation of their peers to develop normal defensive, sexual, and social behavior. There is a critical period during which social deprivation spoils the monkey's capacity for social adjustment.

9. The achievement motive, basically a social motive with elements of competence, is our society's most compelling value. High achievement is rewarded both by (a) increased self-esteem and by (b) success, status, and power. Individuals and cultures vary tremendously in the amount of achievement motivation present.

10. High achievers tend to be moderate risk takers, to make careful decisions, and to possess confidence in themselves. They are not gamblers. Their parents tend to expect and get early independent behavior from them. The need to achieve is part of the emphasis of our materialistic culture.

11. Achievement in various areas such as school and sports has long been spurred on by competition between individuals. Not all people react well to competition. Some people perform better under noncompetitive standards of performance. The author argues that school performance should not be competitive.

12. A noncompetitive learning system encourages the person to learn or master an agreed-on body of essential information. He is free to learn at his own pace. He is tested only to determine if he has mastered the minimum amount necessary to proceed on to the next unit. A cooperative system also encourages children to help one another.

13. Achievement motivation can be and has been taught deliberately. In India, businessmen were trained motivationally and as a result achieved at about double the rates of their untrained counterparts.

14. Adopting a perfectionist level of aspiration guarantees that the person will fall short of his goal in his performance. Perfectionism ensures failure and produces feelings of inferiority.

15. Aggression is a common motive among animals and men. Aggressive display often serves a constructive purpose among animals, (a) to spread out competitors on the available territory, (b) to minimize destructive hostility by establishing a status system, a *dominance hierarchy*, or pecking order, and (c) to ensure survival of the species by providing for the mating of the strongest and most vigorous members.

16. Aggression in man is a different matter, because man has developed such efficient and destructive means of aggression that his own survival is in question. Man has been a predator and has learned to enjoy killing other animals for sport. Man has also enjoyed torturing and killing other human beings (Roman arena, public executions, boxing). Man has reveled in warfare as the supreme opportunity to glorify his manhood.

17. The mass media, especially television, play an important role in the effort to socialize—or failure to socialize—aggression. Viewing filmed aggression increases the likelihood that children will respond aggressively.

18. Control of aggression depends on the cause. Frustration-produced aggression can be lessened by reducing frustration, especially by teaching children *how* and *when* their wants may be satisfied. They can learn to postpone satisfaction or accept substitute gratification. *Threat*-produced aggression can be lessened by (a) understanding the nature of threat and (b) keeping in mind one's own objectives. *Deprivation*-produced aggression can be lessened by teaching children how to reach their goals through behavior that does not bring them into conflict with society.

19. Among the most powerful human motives is drug taking, which permits escape from truth and reality. Drug addiction is an uncontrolled, compulsive use of mind-distorting substances. Addiction involves psychological and physiological dependencies and often tolerance. There are five main classes of drugs that may be considered addicting.

20. Opiate (opium, morphine, and heroin) addicts are motivated to take the drug either to produce a pleasant feeling or to avoid pain and unhappiness. Because of increasing tolerance, it takes more drug to produce a satisfactory "high." Eventually the addict cannot raise the excessive and constantly increasing cost of his habit, even through stealing, and must suffer withdrawal. Some people are addiction-prone. Most opiate addicts are unable to remain off drugs on their own initiative. The rates of opiate addiction have declined greatly since 1920.

21. The psychedelic drugs such as marijuana, peyote, and LSD produce distorted perceptions and unusual sensual experiences. The psychedelic drugs do not produce addiction in the full sense. One may become psychologically dependent on marijuana, for example, but there is no physical dependency or conventional tolerance. In fact, reverse tolerance seems to occur.

22. Excessive use of alcohol is our greatest drug problem. Alcohol is a factor in most serious auto accidents. Excessive use of alcohol can cause damage to body tissue, personality change, and interpersonal conflict.

23. Nonprofessional groups such as Alcoholics Anonymous and Synanon have been more successful than the helping professions

in assisting alcohol and narcotic addicts in becoming drug-free. Former addicts seem to be in the best position to inspire confidence in the addict's ability to change.

24. Many people can be induced to conform to false perceptual judgments if faced with group consensus that contradicts their own view. Interviewed afterward, many of them had repressed the tension, sweating, and anxiety that accompanied the experience.

25. People can also be induced to deliver large amounts of harmful electric shock when directed by the authority of a scientific experimenter. It seems clear that for many people there is a motive to submit and comply with the direction of controlling authority.

26. The conditions of modern life may well generate a condition of alienation that leads men into new dependencies. Some men appear motivated to "escape from freedom."

READING SELECTION

27. Business and industry are beginning to realize that the "old" motivation theory, based on scarcity, does not work for today's younger generation. Neither do the rewards or punishments function as expected.

28. The new motivation theory believes that jobs should be made challenging and should provide opportunity for personal growth.

Terms and Concepts

Achievement motive: an internalized standard of excellence motivating a person to do well in any achievement-oriented situation.

Aggressive motive: inflicting or attempting to inflict damage on another animal; promoted by frustration; injury, insult or threat; and deprivation.

Alcohol: a depressant drug that produces, in its early stages, a mild euphoria and loosening of inhibitions.

Competence motive: the desire to develop and exercise our best potentialities, based on general motives such as curiosity, exploration, manipulation, sensory stimulation, and activity. Syn.: self-actualization.

Conformity motive: a motive to conform and submit to the direction of others, probably based on personality and adjustment.

Dominance hierarchy: the pecking order among a group of animals which indicates status and privilege; established through ritual fighting. Serves to minimize conflict and aggression.

Drug addiction: an uncontrolled, compulsive use of mind-distorting substances. Addiction involves psychological dependence, physiological dependence, and usually tolerance.

General motives: motives not dependent on drive reduction, which may be either inborn or learned.

Homeostasis: a condition in which the body system is in a balanced, steady state.

Motivation: the arousing and directing of behavior toward a goal.

Opiates: a class of narcotics drugs, including opium, morphine, and heroin, which produces a euphoria and a profound addiction.

Perfectionism: the setting of impossibly high levels of aspiration in achievement situations, which results in "failure" and lowered self-esteem.

Physiological drive: inborn motives necessary for survival and arising directly out of body need. Includes hunger and thirst and sex.

Psychedelic drugs: a class of drugs producing distorted perceptions and unusual sensual experiences. Includes marijuana, peyote, and LSD.

Repression: motivated forgetting in which threatening and anxiety-provoking information is forced out of the mind and cannot be ordinarily remembered.

Social motives: learned motives.

Among blacks in our country as compared to whites

- *Tuberculosis is 3 times as common*

- *Death during child-birth is twice as common*

- *Early childhood death rates are more than double*

- *Life expectancy is 6.7 years less*

- *Most are employed in low-status, poor-paying jobs*

- *Housing is less adequate and the average cost per square foot is greater*

- *Most are poorly educated and thus ill-prepared to catch up with the main-stream of our society*

—Time magazine, April 6, 1970.

Prejudice and Racism

8 THERE are many different kinds of prejudice. Racism is only one form. Others are class hatred, snobbism, religious antagonism, and anti-intellectualism. All reflect a relative inability to deal with reality in a sensitive and flexible fashion. Prejudice affects every aspect of the life of the person: his relationships with people are tense, and he perceives the world in a fearful and hostile way. His abrasive personality reflects itself in a lack of contentment and anxiety. He is apt to use his antagonisms toward certain groups as rationalizations of his own plight.

STEREOTYPING

According to Allport, prejudice is *"a feeling, favorable or unfavorable, toward a person or thing, prior to, or not based on, actual experience"* (1958, p. 7) (emphasis added). Often it involves an avoidance of persons simply because they belong, or appear to belong, to a certain group. For instance, some people dislike persons with long hair because they assume that long-haired people are anti-establishment, smoke marijuana, and have loose morals. In fact, however, if one attempts to predict attitudes or political orientation from hair length among students, he is going to be just as often wrong as right (see Figure 8-1). Knowing or not knowing such individuals doesn't seem to make a difference: one can hate someone he has never met, as evident from the expression, "They all look alike."

This tendency to improperly classify a person as being just like all others in a class or category is called *stereotyping*. By assuming the truth of the stereotype, one is supposed to be able to predict what individuals will do. Although stereotyped predictions are unlikely to be correct, *selective perception* and *selective forgetting* are employed to confirm what we need to believe. If we meet a person with long hair who is pro-establishment, anti-drugs, and politically conservative, what do we do? Amend the stereotype? Or define the person as an exception that leaves the rule intact?

Figure 8-1.   Bregenzer's study of stereotyping demonstrates that just looking at a student one can predict his politics only slightly better than chance (54 percent). (Photographs by Ralph Morse. From *Life,* March 13, 1970.)

An essential fact about stereotypes, according to Allport, is that they are not based on factual evidence. They are not logical, but psychological, serving certain emotional needs. Just how they develop in the first place is not altogether clear, but they may develop as rationalizations (irrational justification) of our conduct or from projected fear and guilt. If, for example, a moral person wrongs another, he generally must either justify that wrong or else feel guilt and want to atone for his behavior.

The fact that white men exploited black women sexually during and since slavery gave white men, in the racist system of race relations, sexual gains or advantage (Dollard, 1937, pp. 134–172). Consequently, black men were oppressed and thus felt humiliated and devalued in their own eyes. Is it so strange, then, that part of the modern stereotype about the Negro male is the projected fear that he is oversexed and that he lusts after the white woman?

The same projected fears and guilt may prompt aggressive action, too—a process that may be encouraged by the use of derogatory language (for instance, calling a Negro a "nigger," a woman a "cow," or a policeman a "pig") which helps to prepare one to move aggressively—perhaps violently—against another. Sometimes people attack the object of their fear because they believe that will ward off the threat. In the most extreme example, a paranoid person, a person with a projected irrational fear of persecution, attacks all those people he believes are conspiring against him—before they have an opportunity to attack him.

DISCRIMINATION

Stereotypes are not necessarily true or false, although sometimes there is a remote basis for the belief (Allport, p. 120). For example, a common anti-Semitic assertion is that Jews tend to monopolize banking and high finance. This belief goes back to the Middle Ages, when Christians in Europe were prohibited by their religion from being money lenders (Allport, p. 121). Since there was a need for money lenders, an occupational vacuum was created into which the Jews moved. Today in America, however, the situation is quite different. Although many Jews are businessmen, very few work either in banking or on Wall Street. As Allport notes, "while the Jews constitute 3.5 percent of the American population, only six-tenths of one percent of the bankers are Jewish" (1958, p. 120). Thus, Jews meet active discrimination when they try to enter these occupations.

Discrimination arises out of prejudice when we apply different, unfair standards in evaluating one person or group as compared to others. When an employer will not consider Jews (or blacks, women, longhairs) for employment or hires them for an inferior job, regardless of qualifications, that is discrimination. A person may discriminate either because of his individual belief or because the situation encourages it and he feels it is expected of him.

When a person projects from a stereotype, he may often

contradict himself, making statements that are not necessarily consistent. If Jews believe in mutual self-help, they may be called "clannish," but if they try to gain admission to a discriminatory country club, they may be thought "pushy." Group traits are not really the issue. Dislike seems to come first, then reasons to justify it. For instance, in one experiment (Hartley, 1946), students were asked to rank their preferences of a list of nationalities. The list contained three nationalities that simply did not exist. How did the students rate these fictitious nationalities? At the bottom of the list!

Box 8-1   The Stereotype of the Chinese

Stereotypes of ethnic groups may be based on exaggerated and distorted group traits that actually exist, on projections of the stereotypers, or on both, although some stereotypes have no factual support at all. Rarely mentioned as explanations of stereotyping are the effects of economic and historical events.

The American stereotype of the Chinese has done several rather abrupt historical turnabouts. Initially, during the early 1800s the stereotype was favorable, since Chinese immigrant labor was needed, but it became negative in the 1860s, probably because these immigrants competed with white labor for jobs. It became more positive again after 1937 and during World War II, when China was at war with Japan.

Schrieke has collected many of the descriptive phrases applied to the Chinese during their residence in California. The stereotype is summarized by Klineberg (1954) thus:

In the beginning, the Chinese were among "the most worthy of our newly adopted citizens," "our most orderly and industrious citizens,"

The stereotype of the Chinese has changed.

"the best immigrants in California"; they were spoken of as thrifty, sober, tractable, inoffensive, law-abiding. They showed an "all-round ability" and an "adaptability beyond praise." This was at a time when the Chinese were needed in California. Most of the White immigrants from other parts of the United States were anxious to make money quickly; they had no patience with domestic labor or with working in cigar factories or making boots and shoes. The Chinese were welcomed into these occupations, particularly during the hectic gold-rush period. Then came competition in the fields which the Chinese were occupying. In the elections of 1867 both both political parties pledged themselves to enact legislation protecting Californians against Mongolian competition. The following phrases were now applied to the Chinese—"a distinct people," "unassimilable," "keeping to their own customs and laws," "they did not settle in America," "they carried back gold to their homes," "their presence lowered the plane of living," "they shut out White labor." They were spoken of as clannish, dangerous because of their secret societies, criminal, secretive in their actions, debased and servile, deceitful and vicious, inferior from a mental and moral point of view. They smuggled opium and spread the use of it, and China-towns were full of prostitution and gambling. They were "filthy and loathsome in their habits." They were "undesirable as workers and as residents of the country" (pp. 10–12). Here is an instance of a diametrical change in the alleged characteristics of a group without any actual change in the nature of the population. There was no increase in native aggressiveness on the part of the White group. There was no heightening of an instinctive consciousness of kind. There was, however, a change in the economic conditions in California which made it to the advantage of the Whites to eliminate the Chinese as a factor in competition, and the attitude toward them was an effect of this situation (pp. 528–529).

Organized labor waged an unrelenting war against Orientals during that era and successfully lobbied through Congress the 1882 Asian Exclusion Act. The Chinese reacted to such white hostility by withdrawing into safe ethnic enclaves, "Chinatowns." Between 1870 and 1920, the occupations of miner and common laborer suffered a 99.5 percent decrease of Chinese, while domestic service workers increased 280 percent, and traders and dealers increased 960 percent, all reflecting the better opportunities of an urban ghetto compared to those of a rural environment. Occupational discrimination began to decline noticeably during World War II, when the Chinese entered war industries formerly closed to them and did well. Housing segregation also began to crumble about that time, so that today in New York, for instance, only about a quarter of the Chinese live in China-town (Yuan, 1963).

The stereotype also changed considerably: a 1967 study by Karlins *et al.* found Princeton students showed a rather pronounced shift toward a more favorable view of the Chinese, compared to students surveyed in 1933 by Katz & Braly. In 1933 the five most frequently chosen terms (from a list of 84 terms) to describe Chinese were: "superstitious," "sly," "conservative," "tradition loving," and "loyal to family ties." In 1967 they were: "loyal to family ties," "tradition loving," "industrious," "quiet," and "meditative."

Today, according to Weyl (1969), the Chinese are the most successful ethnic group in America, with, in proportion to their numbers, the highest rates of people in high-status occupations. Their experience parallels that of the Jews in America: Both groups withdrew into ghettos and have had a conservative, closeknit family life. Both established an economic base—according to Glazer & Moynihan, "it has been estimated that the income of Chinese from Chinese-owned business is, in proportion to their numbers, *forty-five* times as great as the income of Negroes from Negro-owned business" (1963, p. 37). Finally, both have promoted extensive educational institutions to maintain their cultural identity.

Material from Klineberg reprinted by permission from O. Klineberg, *Social Psychology* (New York: Holt, Rinehart and Winston, 1954).

The process would be funny if it were not so cruel in its short-term effects and so potentially dangerous in its long-term consequences. When people act on their prejudiced assumptions, great injustices occur. German fear and distrust of Jews led a civilized people to attempt *genocide*—the systematic destruction of an ethnic group—in which 6 million Jews were determinedly murdered. Similar prejudices guided religious wars against "infidels" in the Holy Land for several centuries, creating personal and environmental havoc in many countries of Europe and the Near East.

SEGREGATION

Segregation is a refinement of prejudice and discrimination. In *segregation the informal and sporadic discrimination of some people becomes formalized into rules, codes, or laws affecting everyone.* Segregation may be *de facto*, which means practiced in fact but without legal support, or *de jure*, which means supported by law. In the United States, all *de jure* segregation has been declared invalid by the courts, but it is practiced in some countries such as South Africa.

Once established, segregation makes discrimination a great deal easier and almost self-enforcing. It becomes more difficult for nonprejudiced people of the controlling group to resist discriminating.

The path of least resistance is to go along with these practices and accept them. The mistaken belief that "you can't legislate morality, you must change the mind and heart of man" flies in the face of recent law in this field, which has been properly directed against segregation and discrimination, not against prejudice itself. One's individual prejudices are a psychological concern mainly of interest to the person himself. However, when prejudice is institutionalized through segregation, it becomes a grave social and political problem.

Victims of prejudice often feel they lack control over the essentials in life—and objectively this may be true. They feel *alienated* or powerless to control their own destiny. In a very real way they have to live and adjust to a much less rational world.

RACISM

The concept of racism helps us to understand better how the forms of prejudice work. *Racism* is commonly defined as *an attitude justifying privilege for a supposedly superior group at the expense of another group.* An example is the attitude taken by European colonial powers in justifying their exploitation of other nations as the duties and obligations of "the white man's burden." Commerce, civilization, and religion were the supposed benefits of colonialism, while generations of "self-sacrificing" Europeans just incidentally became enriched—obviously an intellectual rationalization that permitted men who thought themselves ethical to behave unethically.

A more subtle example of racism is when a white person refuses to sell a Negro his house but will sell him his car. What, after all, is the difference between the two types of sales? Such a person may not himself be prejudiced, but he is discriminating and helping to maintain segregated housing patterns and is also affirming a racist system. One need not be an outright bigot, or even greatly intolerant, to be a racist. One is a racist who by his actions or beliefs helps to maintain racist institutional practices.

Perhaps the most significant way racism operates is in our thinking about ourselves and others, in particular, the way we use language. Consider the expression "the forces of light and darkness," the phrases "pure as the driven snow" and "white is the color of innocence" versus "black sheep," "blackguard," "black lie," and "black hearted." The English language itself reinforces white and black stereotypes about people.

A study of Roget's *Thesaurus* shows that "white" terms are used in a clearly negative fashion less than 20 percent of the time, whereas "black" terms are so used over 66 percent of the time. In other words, "white" words are five times as often good as bad, while "black" words are twice as often bad as good. According to *The Dictionary of American Slang,* when "white" is used as an adjective, it means *ethical, honest, fair; faithful, dependable, decent, friendly,* and *regular.* Used as an adverb, it means *fairly.* Roget adds that it means *respectable, above board, guileless,* and *virtuous.* As you might imagine, most of the meanings of "black" are negative, such as *dark, evil,* and *wicked.*

The assertion that Columbus (or Leif Ericson) "discovered"

America implies certain things about how whites feel about the people who were already in the New World when Columbus arrived. It implies that the white, Western European culture is the standard for evaluating everything else. But, of course, many of the Indians (especially the Mayans, Aztecs, and Incas) had developed complex civilizations, which the Europeans didn't realize until they had destroyed them. It is not difficult to see why Mexican-American children, who may be descendants of these high cultures, might not be motivated to learn history, since the ''Anglos'' have unconsciously made their position clear about superior and inferior people by claiming to have discovered them.

TWO KINDS OF PREJUDICE: PERSONALITY AND SITUATIONAL

Let us consider some distinctions having to do with causes of prejudice to sharpen our understanding. There are several distinct types of prejudiced people, but in general a distinction can be made between personality-determined prejudice and situational prejudice.

Personality-Determined Prejudice

Nothing is so firmly believed as what we least know.

—*Michel de Montaigne,*
Of Divine Ordinances

There is a great deal of evidence that certain closely connected beliefs, attitudes, and kinds of behavior go together enough to make up what has been called ''a prejudiced personality type,'' the *authoritarian personality* (see box 8-2). *The authoritarian personality possesses stereotyped attitudes toward others,* such as ethnic groups, women, and

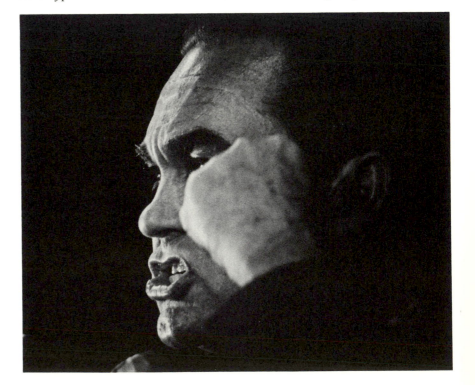

people of other religious faiths. He *is also rigid and inflexible, tends to project blame and hostility, and appears relatively unwilling to consider a psychologically insightful view of men and their behavior.* Further, he is usually *ethnocentric,* which means that *he imagines that his own in-group standards are right and superior.*

Box 8-2   Prejudice and Personality

The authors of *The Authoritarian Personality* discovered a number of personality characteristics that distinguish highly prejudiced from un-prejudiced persons. These characteristics cluster together well enough in the case of the prejudiced to be called the authoritarian personalty type.

High Prejudice (Authoritarian)	*Low Prejudice (Nonauthoritarian)*
Distrusts human nature, sees man as bad and in need of strong external control.	Sees man as perfectable, able to develop self-control.
Not psychologically minded, opposed to looking inward, lacking integration of conscious and unconscious impulse.	Psychologically minded, conscious and unconscious impulse better integrated.
Conformist to conventional, traditional values, uncritical admiration of parents and other authority.	Individualistic, considered values, critical but realistic attitude toward parents and other authority.
Extreme masculinity or femininity, rejects any suggestion of opposite sexed traits.	Willing to accept some traits of opposite sex, less threatened by deviation.
Highly ethnocentric, aggressive and punitive toward outgroups, identifies uncritically with ingroups.	Tolerant toward outgroups, more critical of ingroups (even family and nation).
Accepts easily common stereotypes of outgroups, over generalizes, relies on black-white thinking.	Rejects stereotyped thinking, can accept more ambiguity.
Authoritarian: dominates inferiors, submits to superiors, power oriented in relationships with people.	Values democratic, equalitarian relationships with family and groups, values people for their intrinsic worth.
Defensive, tending to project own fears and hostilities on others, rigid and moralistic, basically threat-oriented.	Not so defensive, more accepting of own impulses, more objective in evaluating information, flexible and tolerant.
Manipulative, sexist attitude toward opposite sex, selects friends because of their status or utility.	Values opposite sex due to true respect, selects friends because he likes them.

Adorno, T. W., Frenkel-Brunswik, L., Levinson, D. J., and Sanford, R. N. *The Authoritarian Personality* (New York: Harper, 1950).

There may be other personality types in which prejudice also plays a central role. We know that prejudice may serve needs and motives of more normal persons in a variety of ways. As Krech (1962) points out:

> Prejudice may serve the functions of justifying pathological hostility, rationalizing culturally unacceptable wants and behavior in the service of culturally acceptable aspirations, managing repressed wants, enhancing feelings of self-regard, protecting the self against threats to self-esteem, helping a person to become wealthy, providing a "reasonable" explanation of why one remains poor. In the service of these varied functions, prejudice can be many things to many men (p. 182).

Table 8-1 illustrates how prejudice can justify varying degrees of political and economic dissatisfaction toward Jews, providing a rationalization for one's own condition. For example, if a person is not successful in his occupation he might blame or use someone else as a scapegoat such as the Jews.

Table 8-1: Relationship Between Economic and Political Satisfaction and Percentages Expressing Different Attitudes Toward Jews (Campbell, 1947).

Attitude toward Jews	Economic and political satisfaction					
	Satisfied in both	Satisfied in one; inter-mediate in other	Inter-mediate in both	Satisfied in one; dissat-isfied in other	Dissatisfied in one; inter-mediate in other	Dissatisfied in both
Express liking for Jews	12	12	9	20	2	8
Show no dislike of Jews	73	61	48	26	38	25
Express mild dislike	8	21	34	13	19	30
Dislike Jews, avoid them	7	5	6	32	25	13
Show active hostility	0	1	3	9	16	24
	100	100	100	100	100	100
Proportion of total sample	20	31	14	9	18	8

*Reprinted by permission of Holt, Rinehart & Winston.

Situational Prejudice

Although the general levels of prejudiced attitudes are higher in the southern parts of the United States, the *percentage* of authoritarian people is the same as in all other parts of the country. Similarly, although persons who are anti-Negro also tend to be anti-Semitic, in the southern U.S. this effect is not as great as elsewhere. In the same vein, a racist country such as South Africa has high levels of general prejudice toward nonwhites but not higher levels of authoritarianism than elsewhere (Pettigrew, 1958, pp. 29–42).

What these and several other lines of evidence suggest is that *many* people behave indistinguishably from authoritarian personalities but must be acting out their feelings for different reasons: they are conforming, acting out roles expected of them, and merely reflecting the norms of indoctrination about race common to their culture.

In growing up, every person adopts a series of *social roles* which in part comprise his distinct *identity*. These roles, which are related, depend on the various levels of status he occupies in the social structure, such as his occupation, age, parenthood, and leadership positions. Many of the common social roles contain specific prescriptions as to how one should behave toward others in a complimentary or inferior position. Thus, children pick up prejudiced talk quickly but only gradually learn the full implications of these prejudiced beliefs. Young children may be aware of prejudice and talk as if they accept it but show no evidence of discrimination or hostility. By adolescence they learn that prejudiced action goes along with the talk, and they show general avoidance of contact with the victim. Groups, says Newcomb (1965), are a major conveyor of prejudice:

> . . . Most prejudices against other groups are shared within one's own group. . . . Group norms stipulate that members shall maintain relationships of avoidance, or even outright hostility, toward members of the outgroup, and shall express to one another attitudes consistent with such out-group relationships (p. 437).

People usually assume that prejudice develops solely out of personal contact and experience. Of course, that is sometimes true, but often we develop prejudices in spite of relatively pleasant experience with the group as a whole. And, surprisingly, it is also true that many people develop prejudiced beliefs even with no direct experience with the objects of their dislike. Both of these findings have been explained by Newcomb in discussing anti-Negro sentiment: ". . . It seems fair to conclude that emerging attitudes toward Negroes are now chiefly determined not by contact with Negroes, but by contact with the prevalent attitudes toward Negroes" (p. 439). In other words, if a white person grows up observing blacks always playing subservient roles and deferring to whites, that fact will be more important in determining how he treats blacks than his actual experience with them. He will then assimilate other parts of the stereotype into his thinking to justify the supposedly natural superior-inferior relationship.

Such expectations about how people are supposed to behave lead whites to demand deference—with its implication of superiority—from blacks as a condition of interaction. When such deference is forthcoming, the interaction between black and white proceeds without conflict. If there is conflict, it is usually about form rather than substance, about the way the black has approached interaction, rather than about the content of the conversation. Obviously, this whole demeaning process damages the black's self-respect, and current strife must be understood in the light of this. Evidence abounds that Negroes are increasingly refusing to submit to psychological humiliation. Riots often find their start in attempts by whites, such as policemen, to force deference of the older sort from people no longer able to give it (Conot, 1967).

Another way in which situational factors affect prejudice and racism is when people behave in a discriminatory fashion because they think not to do so would threaten their status or social acceptance. If the perceived community standard demands adherence to discriminatory practices for acceptance, then most people will conform to these pressures. If the community standard demands adherence to the doctrine of equality, tolerance, and nonprejudiced attitudes and behavior, then most people will conform to that. It is even possible for people to adhere to one set of standards in one situation and the other set in another situation, as some men do at an integrated Army base in a segregated southern town.

CONTACT

There is evidence that contact between races can lessen prejudice. In 1948, President Harry S. Truman, with little preparation or fanfare, ordered immediate, full desegregation of the armed forces. The result was startling, because there was a complete lack of resistance and almost no conflict or difficulty. No one attempted to reeducate those servicemen who were racially prejudiced. In many cases, verbal orders alone were sufficient to effect integration. Men of all kinds were thrown together. In a 1945 War Department study of white attitudes before and after integration of combat infantry units, it was shown that initial resistance was overcome as a result of experience. Before their units were integrated, nearly two-thirds (64 percent) of both officers and noncommissioned officers rated the prospects of desegregation unfavorably. After two months of living and working together with black platoons integrated into their units, attitudes shifted dramatically, with over three-fourths (77 per cent) of both groups rating the experience favorably. A similar study is illustrated in Figure 8-2, which shows that among white merchant seamen, prejudice declined with increasing experience living and working with Negro shipmates. Thus, there is good evidence that enforced contact of living and working together actually lessened the prejudice of the servicemen in these studies. Clearly, what happened in these cases proves that the relationship between prejudiced attitudes and discriminatory behavior is complex. People whose behavior is changed—for whatever reason—often experience a corresponding change in their attitude. The sig-

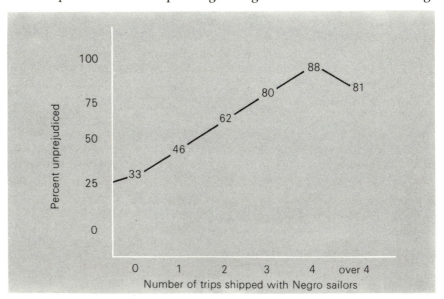

Figure 8-2.   Prejudice among white merchant seamen lessens with experience at working and living with Negro seaman. (After Brophy, 1946, p. 462.)

nificant point is that attitudes do not necessarily have to change first. Soldiers adjusted to the behavior expected of them; if they did not necessarily like it, they accepted new behavioral standards because it was "the Army way" (Raab & Lipset, 1962, pp. 140–141).

In contrast, school integration has been more turbulent. One reason is that it is not contact itself, or experience with another race itself, but rather the *conditions* of contact which determine whether contact reduces or increases attitudes of prejudice. To produce change for the better, contact must involve (a) people of approximately equal status, (b) working toward common goals, (c) support by changing cultural norms. In the case of school integration, we can expect contact to reduce prejudice *if* the status of minority youngsters is approximately equal or superior to that of the majority youngsters, *if* the two groups are working together toward common goals, and *if* the norms, or behavioral expectations, of both groups are changing in the direction of greater tolerance and acceptance of the other group.

Apart from simple bigotry, the opposition of white parents to school integration is based partly on fear and apprehension about what *might* happen. They fear that their children will suffer academically when integrated with blacks, and they worry too about their children's safety. When neither of these fears is sustained by events, as is usually the case, their opposition diminishes.

The evidence to date suggests that the academic performance of whites attending integrated schools does not suffer. The performance of blacks, however, improves and excels that of blacks in nonintegrated schools, even when those schools get sizeable compensatory education grants. As described in Chapter 3, blacks in integrated schools significantly out-perform blacks who are segregated. The main effect was attributed to the influence that peers have on a student's achievement motivation and sense of fate-control.

White parents' fear for the safety of their children is usually groundless. Usually the incidence of aggressive incidents actually declines after integration. The young people involved often seem to make it work in spite of parent attitudes.

Box 8-3   Resolving Group Conflict

Usually prejudice is studied in people who already display intolerant attitudes in their dealings with others. However, Sherif *et al.* (1956) were able to create these attitudes experimentally.

Carefully selected 11- and 12-year-old boys at a summer camp were divided into different groups with antagonistic goals—that is, one group could not achieve its goal if the other achieved its goal. The groups were pitted against one another in a tournament of games. The groups spontaneously developed leadership, *esprit de corps*, structure, and behavioral norms, and eventually each group came to stereotype the other group in hostile terms and to prescribe in its norms hostile treatment for the out group. Casual contact between members of different groups, such as in the meal line, usually created friction which often produced shouting matches and fights.

In the second part of the experiment, the groups were given problems that could be solved only if they worked together cooperatively. For example, they were told that the camp's water supply had been interrupted. Both groups volunteered to look for the trouble. After a day's search, they located and corrected the difficulty.

This joint effort did not produce immediate reduction in the negative attitudes that the boys had about one another, but eventually little signs indicated that change was taking place. Boys began to form friendships among the boys in the other group, something they did not do in the first phase of the experiment. Also they began to arrange joint activities and to share treats.

The experimenters found that during the conflict phase the majority of the boys in both groups (53 percent in group A and 78 percent in group B) were willing to say that they thought *all* the boys in the other group were cheaters, sneaks, and so on. During the cooperative phase these figures declined greatly (averaging more than 50 percent), and many boys said they welcomed the opportunity to revise their previous ratings of the boys in the other group, since they had changed their minds.

The experiment illustrates that contact between groups can reduce hostility and prejudice against outgroups if the contact takes place among equals, involves both groups in working toward mutual goals, and is supported by changing norms of behavior.

In a 1958 study of white high school youth, just before and six months after school integration, Campbell found a general change toward more favorable attitudes toward Negroes as a result of having class contact and friendship with Negroes. However, some youngsters changed by becoming more prejudiced. Several studies of black youngsters' reaction to integration show attitudes toward whites becoming more favorable for the majority of black youth, but that *some* blacks change in the direction of being even less favorable than before contact.

THE MEANING OF PREJUDICE

Practical politics consist in ignoring facts.

—*Henry Adams,* The Education of Henry Adams

What does poor health, poor schooling, job discrimination, and inferior housing mean in terms of life and human suffering? What does 6 years' difference in life expectancy mean? It means for 22 million blacks in this country—132 million lost years of life! It means that more blacks will die at birth, that more will suffer from major diseases. To be victimized by prejudice is to have to live one's life in a dream world, in a less rational way, with less ability to control one's own fate.

Aside from conformity to racist standards, there is the matter of concrete gains and losses in the economic, political, social, and psychological areas. The subordination of one group often profits another in the short run, but ultimately everyone must pay higher costs.

For example, in the ghettos, the *de facto* segregation in housing that exists everywhere in the United States, people must buy and rent in a smaller housing market. Hence there is usually much greater demand for the housing available, resulting in greater cost per square foot—which translates into higher rent for less "home." Ghetto housing is inadequate in every way: the houses are smaller, older, and have fewer conveniences. Ghetto inhabitants don't like their neighborhood, but they have nowhere else to go. Since many cannot afford to own property, there is a high percentage of absentee landlords, slumlords whose profits are astronomically higher than profits in other kinds of business. We can learn much about economic justifications for prejudice

by looking at housing in New York slums. And the process is the same, essentially, elsewhere.

New York slumlords are continually being cited for being in violation of the law, chiefly the health and safety codes. Usually, the tenants are unable to get landlords to fix broken pipes, provide enough heat in winter, collect the garbage, and make elevators work. Tenants have rights protected by law, but enforcement is difficult. First, the authorities must identify the owners—who often take elaborate precautions to conceal their identities. Second, someone must complain to the rental agent, and when nothing is done, the authorities. Third, city inspectors must ascertain that needed repairs are not being made, and must cite the owner. Fourth, time passes during which repairs are supposed to be made. Then there are extensions of time, periods of grace during which the state still does not move against the slumlord. Finally, the last deadline comes—and the slumlord has just sold the property, probably to another slumlord who may have only traded a similar property for it. Then the process must begin all over again. Is it hard to understand the frustration of the tenant in this situation?

Most slum buildings are sold often, with each owner milking it for what he can get in rent money without putting anything into it. The income is great compared to the capital investment involved. Many slumlords need only a couple of years to double their money. The typical slum dweller is powerless to do anything about his inadequate housing.

Bad housing contributes importantly to the defeated atmosphere of the ghetto, characterized by crime, disease, mental illness, and family disorganization. Thus, we see in the case of housing how institutional racism works. Some people gain *economically* by the subordination of others. This exploitation is supported unwittingly by those citizens who do nothing to see that justice for the slum tenant is attained. Surely the state bears some responsibility too, since the evasions of law could be dealt with much more severely, and more importantly, quickly.

Americans commonly believe that the U.S. is the best example of democracy in the world. But democratic ideals are on a collision course with the facts of racism. As the 1968 National Advisory (Kerner) Commission on Civil Disorders has stated (pp. 407–408):

> The Nation is rapidly moving toward two increasingly separate Americas. Within two decades, this division could be so deep that it would be almost impossible to unite. . . . Permanent division threatens us with two perils. The first is the danger of sustained violence in our cities. The timing, scale, nature, and repercussions of such violence cannot be foreseen. But if it occurred, it would further destroy our ability to achieve the basic American promises of liberty, justice, and equality. The second is the danger of a conclusive repudiation of the traditional American ideals of individual dignity, freedom, and equality of opportunity. We will not be able to espouse these ideals meaningfully to the rest of the world, to ourselves, to our children. They may still recite the Pledge of Allegiance and say "One nation . . . indivisible." But they will be learning cynicism, not patriotism. . . . We must choose.

BELIEF PREJUDICE

We select friends and spouses primarily on the basis of shared beliefs.

—*Paraphrase of Milton Rokeach, in* The Open and Closed Mind

People are usually unwilling to form close friendships with other persons who are perceived as having values too different from their own.

—*Paraphrase of Rokeach*

Racial prejudice is such a dominant force in American life that it obscures the equally important fact that there are *many* kinds of prejudice. We have difficulty in dealing with reality in a sensitive and flexible manner in the face of many conflicting sources of information.

A person who attempts to bolster his self-image or social status by being snobbish often uses many of the racist's tricks, such as stereotyping and discrimination. Often he deceives himself about why he does the harm he does. Snobbism is a type of class prejudice. The old-fashioned class prejudice evident in novels of 50 years ago appears to be declining rapidly in our society, but a disguised form of the same prejudice is found in common attitudes toward the poor, especially those on welfare. The general attitude is that "the poor get what they deserve." The welfare poor are used as handy scapegoats by the rest of the society. An elaborate myth has been created that fills the classic stereotype—that is, that the welfare poor are immoral, lazy, dishonest, and unmotivated to help themselves. The stereotype is usually combined with hostility and vague beliefs in harsh remedies.

Perhaps one basis for such hostility is a *perceived* difference in life styles, centering around an alleged freer sex life. Evaluate this belief against the fact, according to the Department of Health, Education and Welfare, that only approximately 13 percent of illegitimate children wind up on welfare (Anonymous, 1960, pp. 35–36). When actual facts do not correspond to the stereotyped belief, something has to give; unfortunately, it is often the facts. Many people have an investment in the myth. For example, it is clear that some politicians who know the truth about the welfare poor are willing to play hypocritical games in which they make blatant appeals to this kind of prejudice. It is a very ancient game, a tried-and-true propaganda technique; curiously, though many agree it is reprehensible, those who use it get power—for a while, at least. It seems easier to exploit prejudice and hatred than to attempt to deal with a complex political reality.

If the average man believes the welfare myth, he has adopted a belief that then influences his attitudes about many other issues, reflecting a need for consistency among one's beliefs. As Rokeach says, "facts suggest that each person is somehow motivated to arrange the world of ideas, of people, and of authority in harmonious relations with each other" (1960, p. 400).

Nonethnic types of intolerance and prejudice seem poorly explained by present theories. Rokeach has extended the thinking behind the authoritarian personality studies mentioned earlier to cover authoritarianism of all political hues. The original research was criticized because it suggested that authoritarianism was a monopoly of the political right. But Rokeach has shown that authoritarians are found on the right and the left and even in the center. He points out that it has more to do with process than content. For example, a person may espouse his belief in democracy intolerantly.

What kind of people do we like? Rokeach says we tend to like others who we perceive share important values with us. We like people "who are right"—that is, who think as we do. Thus, our own beliefs are the essential basis for prejudice.

If Rokeach is right, perhaps we can explain some troublesome observations. For example, why is it that under certain circumstances a bigot may like a member of a normally despised group—for instance, a white bigot who hates Negroes will like an Uncle Tom? On the other hand, why is the renegade so detested? Is he not a member of the in-group? Perhaps Uncle Tom thinks right, but the renegade does not.

Rokeach's theory enables us to understand the perplexing photograph of George Lincoln Rockwell, late commander of the American Nazi Party, embracing Elijah Muhammed, spiritual leader of the Black Muslims in America. These two men, both avowed racists and both segregationists and separatists, seemed to be able to make common cause when it suited them. Similarly, members of the John Birch Society can take great pride in the one or two Negroes they parade around their speakers' circuit, although many blacks feel the main emphasis of their present program is anti-Negro and opposed to the whole civil rights movement.

What can be done? Man often behaves as if he is a frightened, vicious animal, but he is also capable of rising to the heights of courage and dignity. If we are capable of distorting what we see, we also seem to distort no more than is absolutely necessary—in order to maintain a consistent view of ourselves.

Beyond all else, intolerance in thinking represents a fear of the unknown. People seem to be afraid to be other than they think they are. Enjoyment of new and diverse events and people seems to be a cultivated taste. A man whose mind is bound by the excess baggage of prejudice is not able to travel far. Psychotherapists talk of *openness to new experience* as being a central characteristic of those personalities that seem most capable of achieving maturity (Rogers, 1964).

Although racism probably will not disappear until the very language we use to define ourselves and others is changed, some things can and are being done now. We can challenge irrational stereotypes by communicating sound knowledge. We can lessen the effects of discrimination by legal and political action. And when we realize we are part of racist institutions we can attempt to change them from inside, becoming part of the solution instead of remaining part of the problem.

DUANE BELCHER

Welfare—Myth and Reality

WE all have attitudes toward public welfare. I believe there is a welfare myth which, like other myths, is a response to psychological need rather than to reality. This welfare myth is the embodiment of the affluent majority's prejudice, hostility, and ignorance about the poor. According to George Gallup, of Gallup Poll fame, no other issue divides so well people of a liberal persuasion from those who are more conservative.

1. The myth has large numbers of able-bodied men sponging off the public. The fact is that of all welfare cases, only 0.8 percent (about 125,000) are able-bodied males. Nearly 70 percent of adults on welfare are blind, aged, or disabled. Parents of dependent children make up 16 percent. Almost all other cases are children. The Hineman Report (1969) noted, "in 1960 there were 2.6 million poor families headed by non-aged able-bodied men. These men and their 10 million dependents, were excluded from Federally assisted Public Assistance. . . ."

2. Myth has it that large numbers of people are on welfare permanently, as a way of life. But only 7 percent of AFDC (Aid to Families with Dependent Children) cases are on welfare for 10 years or longer. The average case receives welfare for 23 months. A third of the cases are on and off welfare within a year's time. Most of these cases are not seen again.

3. Myth has it that large numbers of people "cheat" and draw welfare illegally. Most abuse is simply clerical error. Welfare fraud in California has been estimated at less than 2 percent. According to the statistics of the State Department of Social Welfare "an average of 3 tenths of 1% of the total caseload in both programs [AFDC and Unemployed Parent Families with Fathers] is convicted of fraud. This was true in 1965, and it is true today."

4. Myth has it that a large part of our local property-tax dollar goes to welfare. The fact is that over 80 percent of the costs are borne by the state and federal governments.

5. Myth has it that our welfare grants are so high people are not interested in work. However, nationwide two people are eligible—but *not* getting welfare—for every one who is. The Hineman Report (1969) states that less than two-fifths of the poor get aid from any kind of public assistance program. Moreover, the average grants are less than two-thirds of the minimum poverty level (64 percent).

6. Myth has large numbers of women with countless children getting large grants. The fact is the nationwide average AFDC grant in 1969 was only $176. In California it would take a busload of children (77) to get a grant up to $800 per month. A family with 10 children (maximum grant $392) would only get $6 more for each additional child. Understandably there are few grants of $800!

7. Myth has welfare mothers wasting part of their children's grants on luxuries such as hair preparations for themselves. Here we have a revealing bit of prejudice.

If *welfare is a right* for those who qualify, who is to say how the money is to be spent? The object is to provide for those who cannot provide for themselves through no fault of their own. But if welfare is seen as a privilege, *granted* (welfare grants!) to those who qualify (that is, are morally acceptable) then society has a right to demand certain things in return

223

for its charity: subservience, obedience, and gratitude. The poor are begrudged what little they get.

Need I go on citing myth and reality, or has the point been made? Common beliefs about welfare and welfare recipients are not factual. They bear little or no relationship to reality.

What then is the *meaning* of the welfare myth? Are the myth holders immoral people? I don't think so. Let us give people credit for being essentially moral. How is it then that we can't get most of them interested in taking action on our significant social problems, such as poverty?

The welfare myth is probably related to a psychological fact: people tend to evade uncomfortable truth. *The welfare myth represents an inspired ignorance of the true plight of the poor.* Morally, one does not have to do anything about a problem which one does not recognize. When outright denial of truth is difficult, one transforms it, distorts it. A distorted view of reality may suggest a different solution from a realistic view. In this case, outright denial is difficult and one's assessment is most easily changed by minimizing the legitimacy of the welfare recipient's claim on society. By distorting and minimizing the numbers of cases which are too old, too young, or too sick (84 percent) it is possible to evade or distort the legitimacy of their claim. The scapegoats become the supposedly vast numbers of able-bodied men and immoral welfare mothers. We ignore the fact that of all illegitimate children born only about 13 percent wind up on welfare. Ignoring the numbers should no longer surprise us. It permits psychological evasion of the truth and our own responsibility to those who are unfortunately not able to provide for themselves.

Making the recipient out as a morally reprehensible person makes him seem unworthy of our charity. And the recipient is not seen as a human being with rights. By condemning him, we can evade "feeling" his real suffering. We condemn him as a pariah and a pariah has no real claim on our benevolence.

Furthermore, the public is not generally receptive to welfare as a right. All this makes discrimination against the recipient—especially the welfare mother—inevitable. The size of her average grant has not increased much during the last twelve years in spite of an estimated 31 percent inflation. According to a report made to the California State Assembly in 1969 (*Malnutrition: Our Key to the Poverty Cycle*), "in the last twelve years the purchasing power of the maximum AFDC grant allowable under California law has declined 29 percent." The grants of other types of recipients have been increased somewhat to offset inflation: Aid to Blind was increased from $110 to $193; Aid to Aged from $89 to $188; Aid to Disabled from $88 to $159. Is this not discrimination, pure and simple? But who defends the scapegoat? The value of the scapegoat—for explaining things—is that he is defenseless.

In closing, let us compare public attitudes toward another kind of welfare, agricultural subsidies. The amounts of federal money are comparable. In 1969 the total federal outlay for farm subsidies was $4.2 billion and $6.3 billion for welfare in all categories. Read the companion article on the attitudes of those getting subsidies and those getting welfare.

Do we begrudge the farmers their welfare? How do you feel about one farmer in California getting a grant of $3.5 million? Or a couple of hundred farmers in one county getting $20 million? What kind of double-think makes acceptance of this inequity possible?

The Puritan ethic says that those who work have value as people. Work is good, *per se*. Not to work is immoral. Agricultural welfare grants are good because farmers are viewed as productive members of society. Ironically the subsidy was originally designed to help the small family farm. This policy has failed completely and this program has helped it along. By enriching the big industrial farmers, it has hastened the end of the small farm. This reality too is unpleasant, and not likely to lead to votes against subsidies by the established political forces in the nation. For some reason we do not phase out government programs just because they have failed.

So you see, attitudes have something to do with perception of reality.

FRESNO BEE

Farm Subsidies Yes, Welfare for Poor No

IT is more blessed to give than to receive?

A devastating survey of attitudes of federally subsidized growers in Madera County seems to indicate it might not be.

The study, conducted by a Stanford University law student, Robin Yeamans, under auspices of California Rural Legal Assistance, Inc., shows "federally subsidized growers were found to be hostile toward most forms of federal assistance to the poor. The more closely the federal assistance paralleled the assistance [growers] received through agricultural subsidies, the greater their hostilities."

In 1966, the federal government paid 185 Madera County growers $5,000 to $133,555 to encourage them to restrict production or to raise the price of crops basic to needs of the United States.

COMPILES RESULTS

More than $3 million was granted to Madera County. During the week ending November 3, a random sample—a fourth of the subsidized growers—was taken by Miss Yeamans. Results of her study were compiled by CRLA's deputy director, Robert L. Onaizda in San Francisco.

Miss Yeamans asked five basic questions, including:

Are you opposed to welfare assistance?

Do you favor the food stamp program?

Should welfare assistance be raised to meet the minimum needs of poor persons?

Do you oppose a guaranteed annual income?

Do you favor providing a family of five with as much as $4,000 a year not to work when there are too few jobs, too many potential workers and it would be advantageous to pay certain workers not to work to keep wages of other workers high?

DESCRIBES PROCEDURE

Miss Yeamans, a 23-year-old, soft-spoken Stanford coed, said the study took her about two days by telephone.

"I was surprised at the growers' attitudes—they were so willing to talk," she said. "I think it was a good sample. The survey speaks for itself, more or less, and I felt like the results were valid. I didn't feel they were tricky questions."

She said she simply obtained a government publication listing the amounts paid to each subsidized grower, made up a statistical sample from all income levels and began dialing the telephone.

CRLA Deputy Director Onaizda said he varied all amounts the growers had obtained from the federal government to protect the farmers from persons who might get a copy of the same publication and check amounts against names.

PARALLELS PROGRAM

The final question was the closest Miss Yeamans could come to duplicating the grower subsidy program.

With the exception of the question on the food stamp program, more than 50 percent of farmers answered "no" to all questions.

The final question, which paralleled the assistance growers received, was opposed by 94 percent of all growers.

"Virtually every subsidized grower is opposed to providing assistance to poor persons comparable in nature and effect to what he received from the federal government," the study stated.

Further, 8 of every 10 subsidized growers opposed a guaranteed annual income to the poor. Some 57 percent were opposed to welfare assistance in general. Only one-fourth of the growers supported raising welfare payments, with 55 percent opposed and 19 percent undecided.

The food stamp program won approval from 85 percent of the subsidized growers surveyed, however.

GROWER REACTIONS

Miss Yeamans reported some answers to her questions:

A grower who received $30,000 in farm subsidies, who was opposed to all programs except the food stamp program, said:

"I'm worried about abuses. Work's good for everybody."

Another, who received $27,000 and was opposed to all programs except the food stamp program, answered:

"Anyone healthy shouldn't get more than what they can earn."

A grower opposed to all but the food stamp program, who received $9,000 in federal subsidies, answered:

"We don't want to create generations of idle people."

A grower who received $12,000 in subsidies and was opposed to all but the food stamp program, was quoted as saying:

"They [poor people] make more than anyone today."

AGAINST HANDOUTS

Another, who received $17,000 and was opposed to all but the food stamp program, stated:

"I can't understand having things handed to you."

The wife of a Madera County grower who received $29,000 from the agricultural subsidy program explained her opposition to federal assistance to the poor by saying:

"Giving causes loss of pride."

Of the 185 growers who received subsidies, 45 were included in Miss Yeamans' random sampling. Madera County is the 37th wealthiest agricultural county in the nation—ranking in the top 2 percent. At the same time it has the highest concentration of poor families—29.8 percent—in California, and it has one of the highest infant mortality rates in California with an infant death rate of 10.1 per 1,000.

Summarizing Statements

1. Racism is only one type of prejudice. All forms reflect a problem in dealing with reality in a sensitive and discriminating fashion.

2. An essential feature of prejudice is the tendency to stereotype, or improperly classify individuals into oversimple and probably misleading categories or groups. They may arise as rationalizations of our conduct, or from projected fear or guilt.

3. Discrimination arises out of prejudice when we apply different, unfair standards of evaluating one person or group as compared to others. Sometimes the situation encourages a person to discriminate.

4. Segregation involves making informal discrimination and containment more regular, based on custom, rules, codes or laws affecting everyone. Segregation makes discrimination easier.

5. Racism is an attitude justifying privilege for a supposedly superior group. One is a racist who by his actions or beliefs helps to maintain racist institutional practices. Racism forces the victim to

adjust to a basically irrational world and logic. Objectively he has less ability to control his own fate.

6. The failure to come to grips with racism could lead to a conclusive repudiation of the traditional American goals of individual dignity, freedom, and equality of opportunity. Our democratic ideas are on a collision course with the facts of racism.

7. An example of personality-determined prejudice is the authoritarian personality, who tends to be anti-Semitic, anti-Negro, and ethnocentric.

8. Many prejudiced people are not authoritarian, and their prejudice can be best explained in terms of the cultural situation, social roles, and the norms prescribing appropriate conduct for people occupying different statuses. It was concluded that prejudiced attitudes are learned chiefly not by contact with victims, but by contact with the prevalent attitude toward them.

9. Failure to realize that racial definitions of attitude and conduct are changing has led to serious conflict and violence.

10. Nonprejudiced conduct can be engineered in prejudiced people. People whose behavior is changed—for whatever reason—often experience a corresponding change in their attitude.

11. Contact between minority and majority can reduce prejudice when it takes place among people of approximately the same status, who are working together toward common goals, and when contact is supported by more tolerant norms among both groups.

12. Some people are prejudiced and discriminate because there is concrete economic gain to do so—for example, there are big profits in slum housing.

13. The prejudice against the poor, especially the welfare poor, is a kind of class prejudice. There is a myth about the welfare poor which is not supported by the facts.

14. We have a need for consistency among the beliefs which we accept.

15. Authoritarianism exists on the political right, the left, and in the middle. Even supposedly tolerant people may espouse their beliefs intolerantly.

16. We tend to like people who, we believe, think similarly to ourselves. We tend to dislike the renegade because, as a member of the ingroup, we imagine he ought to think as we do.

17. Although we distort our views to make them more consistent, we apparently distort them no more than is absolutely necessary.

18. Intolerance in thinking represents a fear of the unknown. Openness to new experience is a characteristic of growth-oriented personalities.

19. Racism will probably not disappear until the very language we use to define ourselves and others is altered.

20. If we want to do something about prejudice now, we can challenge irrational stereotypes by communicating sound knowledge; we can lessen discrimination by supporting legal and political action;

and we can attempt to change racist practices in those institutions of which we are a part. Prejudice and racism are deeply ingrained, and probably none of us living is completely free of them as yet.

Reading Selections

21. The welfare myth represents an inspired ignorance of the true plight of the poor which enables us to believe that the welfare recipient is unworthy of our assistance. This belief makes discrimination against him inevitable.

22. Agricultural subsidies are a kind of welfare about which the public is fairly positive. Growers receiving subsidies seem hostile toward giving the poor comparable assistance during times when they are seasonally unable to work. Growers are not able to see readily the similarities in the two programs.

Terms and Concepts

Alienation: a mental condition in which one is greatly at odds with himself or his culture.

Authoritarian personality: a type of person characterized by stereotyped attitudes and a rigid and inflexible personality, tending to project blame and hostility and being relatively unwilling to consider a psychologically insightful view of man and behavior.

De facto segregation: informal arrangements in which discrimination is imposed on everyone.

De jure segregation: legally sanctioned containment of a minority group with definite rules and codes imposing discriminatory behavior on everyone in the group.

Discrimination: a process of unfairly using standards in evaluating one person or group different from those used to evaluate others; prejudicial action based on stereotypes.

Economic gains in prejudice: profiting from the exploitations of an oppressed group.

Ethnocentrism: a habit of mind in which a person imagines that his own in-group's standards are right and proper, superior to those of others; judging outsiders by the standards of one's own group.

Genocide: annihilation of an entire race.

Identity: the unique individuality of the person, based at least partly on competence in playing the social roles to which the person is assigned.

Institutional racism: impersonal policies, precedents, and practices that are not intended deliberately to maintain racism but that nevertheless perpetuate it. For example, a college admission policy based on test scores which, though not intended to admit whites only, excludes almost all black, ghetto-educated students.

Norms: the standards of conduct expected when playing a social role.

Openness to experience: an attitude of being able to examine new ideas, people, and events openmindedly; the major characteristic of personalities that are able to grow and become more fully actualized.

Paranoid person: a person with a severe mental disorder in which projection of guilt and hostility play a major part in distorting reality.

Political gains in prejudice: being a successful politician by exploiting the popular prejudices of the voters; playing up false issues for political profit.

Psychological gains in prejudice: feeling more adequate unrealistically because of an alleged superiority over others. For example, poor whites sometimes feel that any white is better than any black.

Prejudice: a feeling, favorable or unfavorable, toward a person or thing, prior to or not based on actual experience.—Allport.

Projection: a defense mechanism in which a person unconsciously disowns his own motives and misperceives them operating in the behavior of others. For example, if one is angry or hostile, he may perceive angry feelings as motivating others.

Racism: (1) an attitude justifying privilege for a supposedly superior group at the expense of another group (example: "the white man's burden"); (2) aiding directly or refusing to take action against known racist institutional practices.

Rationalization: a defense mechanism in which we unconsciously give "good" reasons rather than the real reason for our behavior.

Segregation: a separation of groups and a structuring of relationships on some basis such as race or belief.

Selective forgettings: an unconscious disowning of those memories that are least consistent with present belief.

Selective perception: attending to stimulation on the basis of need rather than reality.

Sexual gains from prejudice: sexual privilege is taken by a "superior" person by reason of the powerlessness of an oppressed group.

Situational prejudice: a kind of prejudice based on conformity and expectation rather than on personality factors.

Social role: a typical pattern of behavior based on the status a person occupies in the social structure—for example, fatherhood.

Stereotype: a package of beliefs, usually without foundation, about a particular group which forms the basis for predicting their behavior, and functions to justify (rationalize) our conduct toward them.

Language is, without a doubt, the most momentous and at the same time the most mysterious product of the human mind. Between the clearest animal call of love or warning or anger, and a man's least, trivial word, *there lies a whole day of Creation—or in modern phrase, a whole chapter of evolution.*

—*Susanne Langer,* Philosophy in a New Key, *"Importance of Invention of Language"*

Modification of Behavior Through Learning

WHAT are the ways of changing problem behavior? Here we shall consider some of the underlying theories and new explorations in the field. Let us first consider imitation and identification and how they affect language development. Then let us discuss the social situation in which language and other behavior is developed—in man and in chimpanzee. Finally, let us consider child-management techniques, first with normal children, then with delinquents, and then with severely abnormal and retarded children.

IMITATION, IDENTIFICATION, AND LANGUAGE LEARNING

We tend to take language too much for granted, yet, if one thinks about it, it is amazing that almost all children learn to speak, most without difficulty. Our understanding of how language is acquired is limited, but we can learn something about the process by asking why, in rare cases, children do *not* learn to speak. Here strained emotional relationships between parent and child are often important; both interact with one another and both control some aspects of the other's responding.

The child's learning of language depends on the consequences or usefulness of the language to him, but, in general, he will learn that which increases his ability to control his own environment and to satisfy his wants and pleasures.

Imitation

Why do so-called "talking birds" imitate sounds so unlike their natural sounds as those of human speech? Mowrer (1950) tells us that not all of the birds of these species learn to talk. By the time we see a bird who says, "Polly wants a cracker," we are observing the end product of training. The bird, of course, does not understand what he is saying; he does not have a complex enough brain to comprehend or to

"Watch how easy it is to get my trainer to feed me. All I have to do is to say, 'Polly wants a cracker'—and he really jumps."

use language meaningfully, although he can repeat the sounds in the proper order. However, once he has begun to imitate human sounds, he can use them to summon his trainer, who will present him with a cracker, thus demonstrating to Polly that he can control a human being. The trainer, of course, has a different idea of what is happening.

The bird and a child may have more in common than we might at first suspect. Consider the child's spontaneous babblings. Child psychologists have found that infants are capable of spontaneously making all of the sounds in all of the languages known to men during their first half year. Eventually, many sounds disappear and only the sounds in the child's native tongue are retained. Probably, the sounds that disappear are those that have not been reinforced. During the time of spontaneous babbling, many opportunities for reinforcement occur. One of the earliest sounds is usually something like "ma-ma" or "da-da" which presumably has no meaning for the infant but which, once he makes it, begins to change the behavior of the parent: When Daddy, for instance, hears "da-da," his face lights up, he smiles, talks, and becomes excited. The child will most certainly notice this attention and respond to it. Thus, the father's reaction will have reinforced the sounds the child made, and the child will learn that repeating these sounds will tend to elicit similar reactions in the future.

Mowrer points out something interesting about talking birds— namely, that they lose interest in their own kind and no longer mate and reproduce. Instead, they form an affectionate bond with the trainer. Such a relationship, Mowrer believes, may be essential if the birds are to imitate sounds. So it may be also with the tragically withdrawn or *autistic* child. *Autism is* childhood schizophrenia, *a withdrawn condition in which a child does not relate meaningfully to others.*

Autistic children usually speak defectively or not at all.

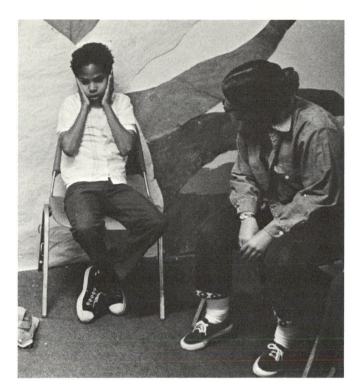

Figure 9-1.   An autistic child.

Their learning is retarded and they usually remain relatively un-socialized. Frequently, there is a lack of affection between parent (usually mother) and child, a "frosted" mother-child relationship. Ordinarily, a child imitates the sound his parent makes, but in autism this may not happen: failure to imitate, in fact, may be one of the prime causes of autistic development. Typically the parent also imitates the child: a mother will coo to her infant and a father will play peek-a-boo games. But in cases of autism the opposite often prevails, in which the child imitates exactly what has been said to him but with no apparent comprehension. He imitates but fails to use sounds to indicate his wants, increase his satisfactions, and control his environment. This is not to say that no communication occurs; often an autistic infant can get his wants satisfied by nonverbal means, such as by pointing, stomping, crying out, and so on. Unfortunately, in this case those who respond have been reinforcing nonverbal rather than verbal communication. What works for the autistic child in the home will not work with other people who don't understand the cues.

Identification and Self-Actualization

Identification is similar but not identical to imitation. *Identification* means to *accept as one's own the purposes and values of another person or group.* A child, for instance, comes to feel like his parents, incorporates their values into his own conscience, and learns to model his behavior after their example. That is, of course, just another way of saying that he comes to accept and live by the major values and beliefs of those who are entrusted with his upbringing.

Children gain increased confidence through success. As we

discussed in Chapter 7, we all have a drive for mastery or competence —what Maslow (1954, 1971) has called the need for *self-actualization*. When children are successful in communicating, they increase their satisfactions and reduce their frustrations. In a real sense, when their language development is successful, they increase their control over their environment and become more independent.

TEACHING APES TO SPEAK

Until very recently, it was thought that man was the only animal capable of using language. Talking birds mimic human speech, but they cannot be said to use language meaningfully. Apes raised in a human environment, were almost completely unable to profit from language development (Kellog, 1933; Hayes, 1951), although their motor development was more rapid than that of a human child—in fact, an ape reared with a human infant outperformed him in motor skills and intellectual development up until the age of three years, when the child began to surpass him intellectually.

These experiments shed interesting light on human language development, because they force us to consider more of the details of the process, and the ways it can go wrong.

Recently, however, the psychologist Premack (1970) began to teach a chimpanzee language, using operant conditioning principles and techniques. Because the ape's ability to vocalize is very limited, Premack substituted plastic chips to stand for various words and grammatical categories. Earlier methods (such as Hayes') had taught a primate to speak only four words, but Premack's chimpanzee, Sarah, though she does not actually talk, knows and understands more than 130 words and has been able to master four important functions of language: word, sentence, question, and "the use of language to teach language." For example, in training Sarah, "blue triangle" was the name for "apple." Sarah can organize her thoughts into sentences by arranging plastic chips to express them. She can repeat simple directions in her language, and she understands negatives. She can imagine *the possible* as expressed in the "as if" relationship. The pioneering work of Premack (and the Gardiners—see Box 9-1) represents a momentous breakthrough. Now we know that the chimpanzee's inability to speak is not because of his lack of intellect or brain but because his vocal cords, larynx, tongue, and lips cannot readily form speech sounds; intellectually he is capable of understanding and using language. One of the most important practical consequences of teaching chimpanzees how to communicate may be in discovering better methods of teaching psychotically withdrawn children to speak. Before we can consider this it will be necessary to consider methods of child training in general.

METHODS OF MANAGING CHILDREN

The formal training a child gets is called education, the informal training—chiefly that of the home—is called *socialization*. A well-socialized child has a firm sense of right and wrong—that is, an internalized conscience. Children are not born with such knowledge

Box 9-1   The Planet of the Apes: Teaching a Chimpanzee
Sign Language (Gardner & Gardner, 1969).

The Gardiners, of the University of Nevada, have been engaged for several years in teaching a young, female infant chimpanzee, Washoe, the American Sign Language (ASL), which is used by the deaf in North America. Use of ASL seemed like an excellent way of overcoming the ape's inability to vocalize the way humans do. ASL involves hand gestures that are well within the chimpanzee's ability to mimic—an important consideration in animal training. This sign language is composed partly of iconic gestures—gestures that represent concepts directly—and partly of arbitrary gestures. The sign for "flower" is an example of an iconic gesture, indicated by closing all five fingers together and touching them in turn to both nostrils. The sign for "always" is an obviously arbitrary gesture, made by closing the hand in a fist with index finger extended, and rotating the arm. The fact that ASL is neither completely iconic nor completely arbitrary makes it well suited as a research tool.

All the experimenters' communications with Washoe were limited as far as possible to ASL. They rejected the idea of combining ASL with spoken English because if she learned speech sooner or more easily, the development of two-way ASL might be retarded.

Chimpanzees are good subjects for this training because they are very intelligent, highly social animals who easily form attachments to human beings. Their social nature makes it possible to use events of an everyday nature to promote language learning. Washoe "converses" with the experimenters in the course of meals, during play, and when engaged in practical activities, such as brushing her teeth. She can ask and answer questions, and form simple sentences with combinations of signs. She makes demands, such as asking for rides in the car, and many of these sign combinations are ones that she has invented herself. She readily transfers signs from one situation to another. Current testing of her ability to use language indicates that she uses what she knows with about 85 percent accuracy. Occasionally she makes a mistake, such as confusing the sign for cat with dog or with animals in general.

The Gardiners used random hand movements similar to signs they wanted Washoe to learn, analogous to the vocal babblings of a human infant, in "shaping up" signs in ASL. An example of this babbling was a gesture Washoe made similar to the sign for "hurry." She spontaneously shook her open hands vigorously at the wrist. The investigators began to mimic Washoe, thus reinforcing the gesture and shaping it in appropriate situations.

At the end of the twenty-second month of the project, when Washoe was 30 to 36 months old, she could use 30 to 34 signs accurately. By the end of the next year she had mastered 87 signs. This is somewhat less than the average human vocabulary at that age, but better than any other ape so far. The Gardiners believe that many mistakes were made in the training of Washoe and that the rate of growth in sign vocabulary will be much faster in the next animal trained. Still, Washoe's vocabulary continues to grow at an increasing rate, and it is anyone's guess what it will be when she is fully-grown at about 13 years of age.

The Gardiners' research has obvious practical usefulness in understanding the deaf, and their language learning problems, which are considerable. It is likely that their experience in teaching ASL to primates will benefit the education of the deaf generally. It is also fascinating to contemplate the next round of research, after several animals have grown up using ASL: they will be the first apes able to communicate with *each other* in ASL! Perhaps a "culture of the apes" will be born.

but are taught continuously in the family what they need to know as they need to know it.

The Development of Conscience

In our culture the parent roles are specialized, and we tend to expect different kinds of things from fathers and mothers (Fromm, 1956). The mother-child relationship is usually of first importance in molding the unsocialized human infant into a full human being. We expect mothers to socialize the emotions of their children. Ideally, mother love is a selfless kind of love in which the mother gives affection and security to the child, who cannot at first reciprocate. A child's ability to reciprocate love is drawn out slowly, but eventually he comes to return the affection his mother has lavished on him. With fathers, however, our culture prescribes a more authoritarian role; a father expects and reinforces culturally approved behavior. Many fathers commonly expect "good behavior" as the price of their love and approval.

The psychoanalytic explanation of personality development reflects this cultural expectation. Freud (1923) credits the development of a child's *ego ideal* (self ideal) to his identification with his mother, while the *conscience*, with all its prohibitions, arises out of his identification with his father, who is both loved and feared. The child reflects this conflict by being ambivalent toward his father—that is, by having both positive and negative feelings about him simultaneously.

A conscience is a well-developed, internalized system of moral values which provides the basis for evaluating one's own behavior. The conscience sets the standards for behavior. When a person fails to live up to his conscience, he feels guilt. According to psychoanalytic thinking, a child's conscience will develop best if he is emotionally secure. The father will have an easier time in playing out his authority role if it is clear to the child that his father has real affection for him.

The establishment of the conscience begins in the emotional relationship between mother and child, which is essential to building confidence and security. It then proceeds to the father-child relationship, in which greater opportunities for conscience training occur. It should be noted that the distinct separation of parental roles required for this theory to hold appears to be declining radically in modern society.

In contrast to psychoanalytic thinking, other writers (Mussen, Conger & Kagan, 1969) conclude that "a parental discipline which is based on a close, affectionate relationship with a child is likely to foster the development of internalized reactions to transgressions (feelings of guilt, self-responsibility, confession)" (p. 364). They agree with Sears, Maccoby, & Levin (1957), who found that a boy with an accepting father had a better developed conscience than one with a rejecting father. Contrary to psychoanalytic expectation, they found that when both parents, not just the father, made love and approval contingent on good behavior the conscience was most fully developed.

Reinforcement and Discipline

Systems of training and discipline must take into account the child's age, as there is an appropriate age for most kinds of learning. Child training in the home is accomplished by the use of various kinds of guidance, technically known as *reinforcers*. When we want a child to learn something new, the best way to get him to do it is to elicit the behavior desired and then follow it immediately with positive reinforcement or reward. Positive reinforcement can be shown to produce quick and reliable learning. The number of reinforcements and the way in which they are delivered can be systematically varied to produce desired results.

Sometimes, however, the child has acquired behavior that continues without apparently identifiable reinforcement by the parents; that is, the child has learned a bad habit the parent would like to get

rid of and it is maintained by reinforcement the parent cannot understand. Clearly, the parent and child then face an unlearning task. The typical parental response is to administer punishment, but punishment is often ineffective in causing a child to stop doing something he has learned to do. One reason is the effect of emotion on the learning process; anger, hostility, and resentment may interfere with or block learning. If the child feels that the punishment is unjust, he may conclude that the parent has no right to administer it, thus rejecting the legitimacy of the parent's right to interfere in his affairs. Thus, we may see why punishment sometimes provokes a child's rebellion, although it was certainly not what the parent anticipated when he administered it. On the other hand, sometimes the reinforcer that maintains so-called "bad" behavior is merely the attention a parent pays to it.

Nonreinforcement and Temper Tantrums

If a child throws a temper tantrum—a dramatic display of loss of control in which he shouts, bellows, and cries—after a parent has told him he is not allowed to do something, it may be a manipulative attempt to get the parent to change his mind. And if the parent does indeed change his mind, the child learns that temper tantrums pay off; his tantrum behavior is being positively reinforced. Because tantrums are usually attempts at manipulation or attention getting, the way to eliminate them is *not* to reinforce them, either positively or negatively. The best strategy for the parent is to pay no attention to the temper tantrum. This refusal to respond to the child's unreasonable behavior will usually show rapid results, for one law of learning is that *nonreinforced behavior diminishes and eventually disappears*. Sometimes punishment of a very mild sort, such as a frown or a verbal reminder, may help suppress an undesirable response, but that punishment must not be so forceful as to produce the strong negative emotions that incapacitate the learner's ability to learn. The new and desired response that we want to replace the undesirable behavior must be reinforced positively and quickly.

Continuing Behavior Is Motivated and Reinforced

Behavior is not maintained in a vacuum; regularly occurring behavior is maintained by reinforcement of some kind, even though it may not be obvious. That a parent cannot immediately tell what reinforcers are maintaining behavior does not mean there are none; sometimes ingenuity is needed to discover them. Effective systems of discipline are based on respect for the child and his wants and needs. Parents should never deprecate the child's motivation, for without it he probably will not learn. Fortunately, most children have motivation in great abundance. A parent can get some idea of his child's motivation by simply observing the child's behavior and keeping a record of it during regular time samples. One can also keep track of what the child asks for and infer other wants from his behavioral preferences. Then the trick is to use this motivation to teach constructive lessons by tying in his wants with the tasks parents select. Parents should be careful not to establish so many rules as to frustrate the child unnecessarily. Unavoidable frustration causes enough trouble. Some rules, however, are necessary in order to create a healthy environment. Arbitrary and unnecessary rules, however, should be avoided.

Unavoidable Frustration

When the child's wants must be frustrated, as they often are when he wants to do something at a time it cannot be done, then the task of discipline is to teach the child to wait for a better time. If the child wants a cookie just before dinner, it is reasonable to deny it to him then, but he needs to be taught that at a later time his want may be legitimately gratified. Such frustration is endurable and the child learns to delay without much difficulty. When the child is told "No, no, never," instead of "You must wait," the frustration is much more difficult for him to accept. Later, when the child is older, the parent may involve him in deciding how the rules are to be formed, what the rewards are for obeying them, and the punishments for disobeying them. If the rules are clear, the rewards specific, and the consequences of misbehavior certain, the child is much less likely to misbehave, especially if he has had his say in formulating the standards.

"Timing-Out" and Withdrawing Privileges

Two specific child-management techniques are "timing-out" and withdrawal of privileges. *Timing-out*, a common technique used in school, believed by teachers to be the most effective means of controlling misbehaving youngsters, consists of *removing the child from the environment in which he has just misbehaved*. This technique of discipline is not punishment but rather an example of nonreinforcement. If a child is about to throw a temper tantrum in the kitchen and is sent to his room, the timing-out *non*reinforces the tantrum behavior. In school, the misbehaving youngster is denied his reinforcements—his audience—and thus the misbehavior diminishes. Of course, if the child likes the timing-out place better than the classroom, the technique will not succeed. One psychologist tells the story of how he defeated a teacher's attempt to discipline him through "timing-out" when he was a child. When he was bad he was sent to the cloakroom—where he made a habit of eating the teacher's lunch. The teacher soon discontinued the practice.

Withdrawing privileges is another good technique. Many activities the child likes and engages in are commonly allowed him free, without strings. By making such activities a reward for good behavior, a system of discipline can be created in which the duties and obligations of a child are related clearly to his rights and privileges. The child will learn that privileges must be earned, and that misbehavior leads to their withdrawal. If the rules are clearly specified and the consequences of misbehavior certain, the child makes his own decision and takes the consequences, good or bad. A failure to live up to a certain obligation is met merely by the withdrawal of a certain privilege. There need be no great argument about the infraction of the rule.

The Ideal Discipline System

As noted, systems of training and discipline must take into account the child's age and maturity. Still, we may state that an ideal system of discipline for the older child has four characteristics:

(1). *It must be created by mutual agreement between parent and child.* The child is consulted about the decision to draw up the rules, and about the specific ground covered by them. He agrees on what the consequences are to be—both in terms of rewards for good behavior and punishments for bad behavior. For example, a child is apt to inconvenience the entire family if he continually gets home so late as to delay dinner. He must realize there is some *consequence* of coming home late as he himself is likely to agree, if consulted. If it is to be punishment, it is the *certainty* rather than the severity of it that determines its effectiveness. Much of the same thinking is behind the expansion of the U.S. criminal court system to provide speedier trials—namely, that it is the certainty rather than the severity of the punishment that will deter crime.

2. *The consequences must be appropriate to the behavior in question.* If a child misbehaves in some minor way, the consequence should also be minor, such as withdrawal of privilege. For failing to get home by dinner time, the child might be denied the opportunity to play outside the next day. To keep a child in his room for two weeks after school as punishment for telling a small lie, however, is punishment inappropriate to the importance of the misbehavior. Two weeks gives a child a lot of time to feel unjustly treated; a lesser punishment such as a day or two would be educational and might serve to alter behavior. Effective discipline molds approved behavior in a child through "consent of the governed." When the child accepts the legitimacy of the parent's authority and the consequences of the mutually-agreed-on rules, everything goes more smoothly.

3. *The discipline must respect the integrity of the human personality.* It must not be destructive or humiliating for parent or child. Sometimes a child attempts through rebellion to preserve his own sense of worth and individuality. This is clearly apparent in those tragic cases in which a cruel parent demands unquestioned obedience to his every whim. It may be a moot point which is worse for the child—

to be crushed by cruel and irrational discipline or to rebel against the parental authority, and perhaps later against all authority. At least in the latter event, the child is attempting to preserve his developing sense of integrity. If he is fortunate, the job of socialization can be finished later. An important idea about promoting the integrity of the child is that the discipline system ought to be formulated for the good of the disciplined. Parents should not lose sight of their obligation to help a child grow away from dependence. The rules should always be concerned with the best welfare of the child. Rules should be, in other words, "child centered," although they should not, of course, ignore the rights and privileges of the parents.

4. *The discipline must reduce and manage conflict.* When rules are definite and consequences certain, there need be little cause for conflict. In the example of the child who makes a habit of coming home late for dinner, the *consequence* or penalty has been decided in advance by mutual agreement. Lateness *always* produces the penalty, and there need be no discussion. With an effective system of discipline, the child is encouraged to make his own choices, for good or ill, and observe their consequences. In this way, he is taught responsibility and independence as well as parentally approved behavior.

Every system of discipline ought to be designed so as to promote an effective development of conscience in the child. Through establishing self-control, the child learns to assume more independent roles and equips himself better to take his place in adult society. Systems of discipline that do not promote independence or self-control must be labeled faulty, even when they appear to be effective in other ways.

MANAGING DELINQUENT CHILDREN

Many delinquents and criminals are in poor mental health, and their adjustment problems constitute an important cause of their misbehavior. The neurotic delinquent often does not understand his own motivation for misbehaving. The antisocial delinquent is aware of the rules but is resentful and rebellious, often because he has been a victim of excessively punitive or brutal discipline. Delinquents are more likely to come from homes employing harsh physical punishment than those using more psychological means of control (Glueck & Glueck, 1950). Advocates of harsher laws and penalties should take note of the lesson that punishment has not worked for these youngsters in the past and therefore cannot be expected to produce better or more socialized consequences in the future.

According to Glasser (1969), nearly all delinquents have a history of school failure, combined with damaged feelings of worth and lack of confidence. Schaffer & Polk (1967) observe that teachers go to extremes to exclude delinquents rather than attempting to educate them. Boys doubting themselves develop a hyper-aggressive masculinity as a way of drawing attention to themselves, and compensating for lack of success in other areas. Unfortunately, when strong aggressive patterns are reinforced, the child is brought into conflict with authority in school and on the streets. Usually, the parents of delinquents have been unable to develop an effective system of discipline. Perhaps what they attempted was too one-sided, too harsh, lacking in consistency, or overpermissive.

Resocializing Delinquents: "Achievement Place"

Montrose Wolf, a psychologist, has devised a unique environment for the resocialization of delinquents which is like a half-way house or a foster home for delinquents. Called "Achievement Place" (Phillips, 1968), it is a *token-economy* (or token-exchange) reinforcement system in which the preadolescent and adolescent boys may earn credits for performing desired behavior.

The tokens are symbols of real and tangible reinforcers, which enable the learner to bridge the gap between the act being reinforced and a time when tangible reinforcement can be delivered. All privileges cost tokens. The boys keep their own records, and they keep them accurately, because cheating is fined heavily. However, the earning of points is made quite easy.

The first priority is school achievement. Points are given for doing homework, keeping up with the daily news, and being informed. The boys also have numerous chores for which they are paid points. Privileges that are taken for granted in most homes must be earned. Verbal aggression is discouraged by a system of fines. After dinner each night, points may be exchanged for privileges of all sorts.

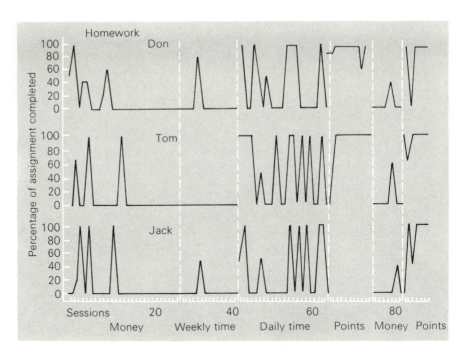

Figure 9-2.   The percent of homework assignments completed by three boys under various conditions: (1) being paid 25¢ for completing homework with less than 25 percent errors; (2) being allowed 1 hour of stay up "late-time" for completing homework, which could be spent on the weekend; (3) "late-time" which could be spent the day it was earned; (4) earning 500 points per assignment; (5) money again—same as condition 1; (6) points again—same as condition 4. (From Philips, W. L., Achievement Place: Token procedures in home-style setting for "pre-delinquent" boys. *Journal of Applied Behavior Analysis*, Vol. 1, 1968. Reprinted by permission.

Most of the rules of the home are flexible and have been set democratically by the boys themselves. They agree on rules and standards and on the consequences for obeying them (rewards) and disobeying them (punishments). The boys govern themselves and auction off leadership positions daily. The house manager's job is bid on each day, and the house manager earns his points according to the performance of the rest of the boys. Apparently, being manager raises a boy's status, because the job is much sought after; yet as manager a a boy must be fair and just or else the other boys will not do their part and he will earn nothing or even take a loss. It is truly government "with the consent of the governed." Since the boys decide most of the content of the rules, the system constitutes a system of living in which the various members of the family exchange reinforcers.

The whole environment is engineered to promote academic achievement, responsible leadership, independent behavior, and reliance on controls from within. Since the boys themselves decide on the features of the system, several have been kept which the supervising psychologist had reservations about, such as the use of punishment in the form of fines. However, it was felt that it was much more important for the boys to decide democratically on a system of rules than to try to implement some theoretical system.

Figure 9-2 illustrates various kinds of reinforcers used in trying to get the boys to do their homework. In condition 1 the boys are paid 25 cents for doing their homework. As you can see, this did not work most of the time. In the second condition, the boys were allowed 1 hour of stay-up "late time," which could be spent on the weekend. That did not work at all. In the third condition, late time could be spent on the day earned. That worked much better than the other conditions, but still failed more often than not. In the fourth condition, the boys were paid 500 points per assignment, which produced steady study— almost all of the time. The other two conditions were repeats of prior conditions, with the same results. Figure 9-3 illustrates the same experimental approach to suppressing aggressive statements among the boys. Fines of 20 and 50 points suppressed aggression better than the other conditions tried.

After controls are established through the token-exchange system, other more abstract systems of discipline are introduced. The boys can move up to the higher status *merit system*, in which all of one's privileges are given free. With the *honor system*, the most abstract system of discipline used at Achievement Place, a well-disciplined boy gets all his privileges free and performs his duties because he feels he ought to do so. This kind of progression—from token to honor system—weens the boy from being overly dependent on controls by others. At the completion of this last phase of discipline, the boy is returned either to his own home or to a foster home.

In most cases, the discipline of the original home was not completely absent but merely inept. Most parents, although wanting to create constructive discipline, had been unable to implement their intentions. It is fairly obvious that if such a boy is returned to his own home, there is need for work with the parents if the gains achieved in Achievement Place are to be maintained.

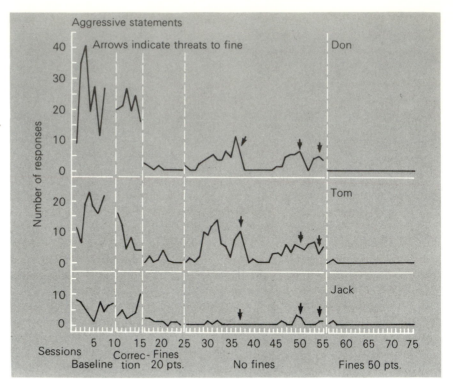

Figure 9-3.   The number of aggressive statements per 3-hour session for three boys under various conditions: (1) the regular "base-line" level of the behavior; (2) parents correct the behavior verbally, e.g., "Stop that"; (3) boys were fined 20 points for each aggressive statement; (4) no fine but occasional threat of correction for aggressive talk; (5) fines of 50 points for every infraction. The arrows indicate threats to reinstate the fines condition. (From Philips, W. L., Achievement Place: Token procedures in a home-style setting for "pre-delinquent" boys. *Journal of Applied Behavior Analysis,* **Vol. 1, 1968. Reprinted by permission.**

Resocializing Delinquents: "Behavioral Contracting"

Another line of work with delinquents which seems promising is called *"behavioral contracting."* Social work professor Richard Stuart (1970) has been applying contracting systems to the total environment of delinquent children, working with the delinquents and their parents in their own homes. Like Wolf, Stuart sees the problem of discipline as being its essentially exchange nature: both parent and child have rights, privileges, duties, and obligations, but in many delinquent families, rules and consequences for behavior are ill-defined.

To deal with this problem Stuart gets each party to the contract to make up a list of the other person's annoying behavior, which is then discussed and refined and made the substance of the contract. Eventually, a contract is worked out in which the delinquent child's rights are completely specified in writing, as are his privileges, duties, and obligations. The rewards and punishments, the consequences, are also specified in considerable detail. When everyone is satisfied that the contract is reasonable, they all put their signatures to it. The last provision of the contract is the procedure by which the contract can be amended.

The contract should take all major aspects of the relationship out of the area of argumentation. A good contract has the following characteristics: (1) It specifies the privileges of both parties. (2) It specifies the responsibilities and duties that both must observe, and these must involve a genuine exchange. (3) It specifies the consequences for any violations of the contract. (4) It specifies what each party may expect of the other. (5) Finally, there is a general statement indicating the limitation of discussion of contract items, and all who sign agree to keep the contract in effect until it is modified in writing.

The major gain from the use of a written contract is that it reduces conflict in the situation. If the child misbehaves, consequences flow inevitably without discussion or dispute. If one must withdraw some privilege, there is no need to have an argument about it. When discipline is approached in this fashion, it is often found that the parent as well as the child has a good deal of changing to do. Much of the balkiness of delinquent children is produced by the stress and emotionality of the almost continual conflict between them and their parents. The contract appears to provide an opportunity for parents to be friendly but firm, and an opportunity for the children to behave reasonably without sacrifice of integrity.

In a study of interaction patterns among delinquent and nondelinquent youth and the mothers of both, Stuart (1969) found that the nondelinquents and their mothers were much more likely to have positively reinforcing interactions than were the delinquents and their mothers. In fact, nondelinquents and their parents had four times as many positive interactions as negative ones, whereas delinquents and their parents had an equal number of positive and negative interactions. The nondelinquents got four times as many positive reinforcements as the delinquents and overall twice as many reinforcements of all types (both positive and negative), indicating that the parents of nondelinquents pay much more attention to them in absolute terms.

The work of both Wolf and Stuart appears to have many applications for typical child-rearing situations. There can be no doubt that harsh and threatening systems of child discipline are unsuccessful and unlikely to produce incorporation of the values of the parent and the kind of self-control we expect of responsible adults.

MANAGING RETARDED AND PSYCHOTIC CHILDREN

The special education given retarded children has varied depending on the degree of their retardation. With those who are moderately bright, a slower classroom pace is indicated so that academic material can be covered slowly but surely. More time is spent on repetition and questioning to insure understanding. Children with moderately low IQs spend a good deal of their time in school just being socialized and trying to develop a constructive adjustment. With children having very low IQs, the task of education is simply the most basic kind of socialization.

Educators working with retarded children find it difficult to hold the child's attention for long and difficult to motivate him. However, some studies indicate that the learning ability of most retarded children is unimpaired; the problem is to gain and hold their attention.

The work of Trabasso (1968), for example, indicates that once their attention is gained they learn as quickly as normal children. (See Figure 9-4.)

Figure 9-4.   Attention in learning. (From Trabasso, T. ''Pay Attention,'' *Psychology Today Magazine,* October, 1968. Copyright © 1968, Communications/Research Machines/Inc. Reprinted by permission.

A. Discrimination Learning usually is shown by means of group learning curve that represents an average performance. The typical learning curve forms a smooth arc, implying that learning is a continuous, gradual process. Graph A is the average learning curve for a group of mentally retarded children who learned to solve a form discrimination problem over several days.

B. When the same children are divided into fast, moderate, and slow learning groups, curves are produced that are more sensitive to the individual learning process. Graph B includes learning curves for three groups. Note the difference in shape between these segregated group curves and the single curve in Graph A.

C. When backward learning curves are constructed for the same three groups, each curve shows two distinct portions, a flat attentional phase and a climbing associational phase. The main difference between fast and slow learners is in the length of the initial flat phase. Note that in Graphs B and C the shape of all curves tend to be about the same.

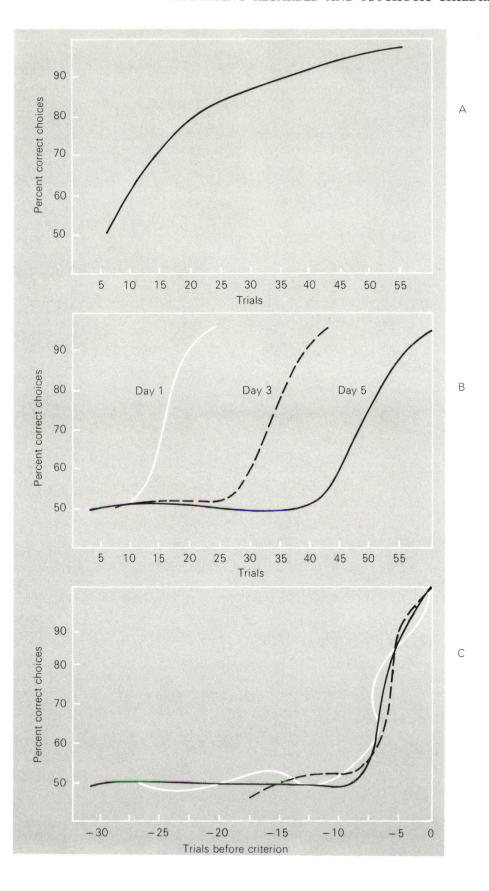

Token economy systems, used with success in managing delinquents, have also been used in institutions attempting to educate the retarded. A dramatic result is the ease with which token systems sustain the attention of retarded children over long periods of time. It now seems possible to devise school environments using many more reinforcers for learning than used to be the case. Thus, the time retarded children spend in school can be made much more profitable to them, and they can learn much more than before. An important practical limitation to applying token systems generally is that it is much easier to set them up and administer them in institutional environments than elsewhere.

MANAGING AUTISTIC CHILDREN

Some very exciting work is currently being done with autistic children, those withdrawn children with severe problems of communication. With adult psychotics, normal speech may be suppressed and the goal of therapy is to reinstate it. An autistic child, however, may have withdrawn from human contact and influence before he began to master speech; consequently, there are very limited ways of getting through to him.

Box 9-2   Token Economy Plan

Fourteen months ago, this girl used her hands to eat food from the floor. She now lives in Pomona, California, and works 8 hours a day in a community-sheltered workshop, earning a regular wage. Her dramatic development can be attributed in part to the hospital's Token Economy Plan.

When each of the daily duties on
her job card has been completed,
the girls are given plastic tokens,
which are used as money.

Something for something. The
girls learn to manage their
"income," as they must pay for
meals, off-ward trips, clothing,
and toothpaste from the ward's
"pink elephant" store. And what
could be more like the outside
community than being able to buy
on credit from the store?

California Mental Health Progress, October 1969, pp. 13–14. Published by the Office of Public Information, Department of Mental Hygiene, 744 P Street, Sacramento, California, 95814.

The causes of autism are not definitely known. Some believe
that biological causes may be responsible, and there is some evidence
to support this conclusion. But many clinical psychologists and psychiatrists believe it develops from defective parent-child relationships;
some speak of a "frosted" mother-child relationship. This view is
supported by the apparent importance of emotional factors in primitive
imitative behavior. Talking birds, for example, talk only if they have
developed an affectionate relationship with their trainer. Thus, the
processes of imitation and identification seem to be very important in
stimulating early speech.

Just as delinquents, according to Stuart, come from an environment in which positive acts are not adequately reinforced, so the same
may be true of autistic children. The spontaneous babbling of an infant
appears to be a necessary part of the process required to imitate speech.
Through parental neglect or failure to recognize the importance of reinforcing sounds resembling words, a child might be led to cease

babbling, and thus lose the opportunity to take the first steps toward speech.

In the last few years there has been great progress. Using modern behavior modification techniques, therapists are beginning to teach autistic children to speak. It is, however, a very laborious and time-consuming process. With normal children, there are literally thousands of reinforcers available. An autistic child may not respond to more than a handful of these, so the task of teaching him anything at all is staggering. Lovaas (1965) described one girl, Pamela, who could not be trained because she never paid any attention. She had learned to "tune out" the attempts of other human beings to communicate with her. It was necessary to electrify the floor in her training room so a mild shock could be delivered whenever her attention lapsed. Later she was taught sounds and words by the administration of conventional rewards such as candy, so that ultimately she began to speak—unlike most autistic children.

Box 9-3   A Token from the Teacher

1. At first he thinks the whole procedure a joke.

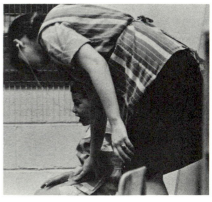

2. She becomes more insistent.

Teacher "timing out" a child by seating him away from the others for a while.

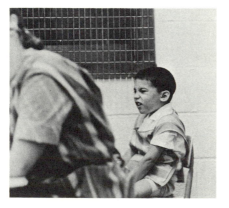

3. He discovers it is no joke.

The "token-exchange" system of learning reinforcement calls, in essence, for the quick and frequent reward and encouragement of desirable behavior, and non-punitive "timing-out"—usually by removing the child—to discourage undesirable behavior. By this means 2-year-old children have learned to read, violent ones to sit calmly and study, and the autistic to speak and to have hope.

Jimmy, an almost mute autistic child, is rewarded with a corn chip for learning to say "nose."

1. "Say 'Nose,' Jimmy."

2. "'Nose,' Jimmy, *'nose'*"

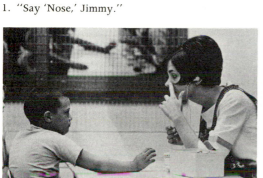

3. Jimmy says, "nose."

4. "Good boy, Jimmy!"

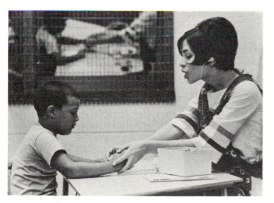

5. "*Good* boy!"

6. Triumph and reward.

The work reported here was done by the Central Midwestern Regional Educational Laboratory, a nonprofit corporation supported in part as a Regional Educational Laboratory by funds from The U.S. Office of Education, Department of Health, Education and Welfare. The opinions expressed here do not necessarily reflect the position or policy of the Office of Education, and no official endorsement by the Office of Education should be inferred.

Hamblin, R. I., Buckholdt, D., Bushell, D., Ellis, D., & Ferritor, D. Changing the game from "get the teacher" to "learn" *Trans-action*, January 1969, pp. 20–31. Photographed by Daniel T. Magdison. Reprinted by permission.

DON MOSER

The Nightmare of Life with Billy

WHEN his father's car pulled out of the driveway, I'd bolt the doors, lock the windows and the nightmare would begin." Thus Billy's mother, Pat, describes a terrifying existence in which she was at the mercy of a small boy so cunning and so violent that he almost propelled her into a nervous breakdown.

Pat's story is significant in two respects. First, it indicates that it is virtually impossible for an intelligent, well-intentioned parent to cope with an autistic youngster. Second, it shows why Pat and her husband, along with the parents of the other children, so eagerly embraced Lovaas' program even though it involved shock and other forms of punishment.

The causes of autism are no clearer with Billy than with the other children. He had suffered a traumatic birth, one that places great strain on the infant. Pat was 17 hours in labor, and when doctors had finally delivered him by Caesarean section, it was 90 seconds before he breathed, another 90 before he cried. Nor was his early environment always pleasant. His parents' marriage was going through a difficult period. His father, a doctor, was serving his internship; every other night he was at the hospital, and when he came home he had no energy left to do anything but fall into bed. Later, called into the Navy, he was separated from Billy and Pat for long periods.

Whatever the causes—organic, environmental or both—it was clear by the time Billy was 2 years old that something was very wrong

with him. He had not started to speak. He threw uncontrollable tantrums. He never seemed to sleep. Pat and her husband took the child from one psychiatrist or neurologist to another. All gave the same analysis: Billy was retarded.

Before long, however, Pat realized that Billy was diabolically clever and hell-bent on destroying her. Whenever her husband was home, Billy was a model youngster. He knew that his father would punish him quickly and dispassionately for misbehaving. But when his father left the house, Billy would go to the window and watch until the car pulled out. As soon as it did, he was suddenly transformed. "It was like living with the devil," Pat remembers. "He'd go into my closet and tear up my evening dresses and urinate on my clothes. He'd smash furniture and run around biting the walls until the house was destruction from one end to the other. He knew that I liked to dress him in nice clothes, so he used to rip the buttons off his shirts and used to go in his pants." When he got violent Pat punished him. But she got terribly distraught, and for Billy the pleasure of seeing her upset made any punishment worthwhile. Sometimes he attacked her with all the fury in his small body, once going for her throat with his teeth. Anything that wasn't nailed down or locked up— soap powder, breakfast food—he strewed all over the floors. Then, laughing wildly, he dragged Pat to come see it.

She had to face her problems alone. It was impossible for her to keep any household help. Once Billy tripped a maid at the head of the stairs, then lay on the floor doubled up with laughter as she tumbled down. And Billy was so cunning that his father didn't know what was going on. "Pat would tell me about the

Reprinted from Moser, D. The nightmare of life with Billy. *Life* magazine, May 7, 1965. © 1965 Time Inc.

things he did while I was away, but I couldn't believe her,'' he says.

As time went on, even his father realized that they had a monster on their hands. Enrolled at a school for retarded children, Billy threw the whole institution into an uproar. Obsessed with a certain record, he insisted on playing it over and over for hours. He sent the children in his class into fits of screaming misbehavior. ''He was just like a stallion in a herd of horses,'' his mother says. Billy ruled his teacher with his tantrums until, a nervous wreck herself, she could no longer stand to have him in the class. ''He became a school dropout at the age of 5,'' says Pat.

At home things were taking a macabre twist. Billy had a baby brother now, and at any opportunity he tried to stuff the infant into the toy box and shut the lid on him. His parents had bought him a doll which resembled the baby, and which they called by the baby's name, Patrick. Every morning Pat found the Patrick doll head down in the toilet bowl. Terrified of what might happen, she never left the two children alone together.

As he grew older Billy's machinations seemed far too clever for a retarded child, and

so his parents took him to see another expert. There, given a puzzle to test his intelligence, Billy simply threw the pieces against the wall. The expert delivered the same old verdict: Billy was retarded.

At the retarded children's school, the youngsters occasionally got hamburgers for lunch from a drive-in chain. Inexplicably, Billy became hooked on them—hooked to the point that he would starve himself rather than eat anything else. Within a few weeks Pat and her husband became slaves to Billy's hamburger habit. Every morning and every night Billy's father stood in line at the drive-in and bought cheap hamburgers by the sack. Eventually he became so embarrassed—he is a small, thin man, and the waitresses had begun to look at him curiously—that he cruised the city looking for drive-ins where he wasn't known. Billy ate three cold, greasy hamburgers for breakfast, more for lunch, more for dinner. ''He was like Ray Milland in 'The Lost Weekend','' Pat shudders. ''To make sure he wouldn't eat them all at once I'd hide them all over the house—in the oven and up on shelves. In the middle of the night he'd be up prowling around, looking for them. A month later I'd find ossified hamburgers in hiding places I'd forgotten.''

When they were out driving with Billy, they had to detour around any drive-ins. Billy flew into such a frenzy at the sight of one that he frothed at the mouth and tried to jump out of the moving car.

Pat knew that the boy could not survive on a diet of cheap hamburgers. She took him to places where they served hamburgers of better quality; Billy refused to eat them. Frantic, she contrived an elaborate ruse. Buying relish and buns from the drive-in, she bought good meat and made the patties herself. She put them into sacks from the drive-in, even inserting the little menu cards that came with the drive-in's orders. When she presented this carefully recreated drive-in hamburger to Billy, he took one sniff and threw it on the floor.

Then there was Billy's Winnie-the-Pooh period. Billy had become obsessed with a particular kind of Teddy bear, marketed under the trade name of Winnie the Pooh. Without it, he'd go berserk. The family was moving about a good deal then, and Pat was terrified that she would have no replacement when Billy lost his bear or tore it up. "Just to make sure I'd never run out, I found where to buy a Winnie wherever we might be going. I knew a place in San Diego and a place in La Jolla and a place in San Francisco. I even knew where to buy a Winnie in Las Vegas. I always kept some in reserve just so we wouldn't run short in a hotel. Our whole life became one long Winnie trip. Once, when we were moving, Winnie got put into the van by mistake, and we had to have the movers take everything out so we could find it. We were afraid to make the trip with Billy without a Winnie bear—we were starting to go nutty ourselves.''

Pat became so desperate that when she found something that frightened the boy, she used it as a weapon of self-defense. The one thing that did the trick, appropriately enough, was Alfred Hitchcock. For some reason, when Hitchcock came on television Billy took off like a rocket and hid under the bed. When Pat learned that photographs of Hitchcock had the same effect, she started cutting them out of TV magazines. When Hitchcock appeared on *Life's* cover, she bought a whole stack of magazines and stuck the covers up all over the house—on the icebox to keep Billy from opening it, on the fireplace to keep him from crawling around in it. When she took a bath she put Hitchcock pictures outside the bathroom door so Billy would leave her in peace.

"It was crazy," Pat remembers. She was at bay in a house with the doors bolted and the windows locked, the baby stuffed in the toy box and the Patrick doll with its head in the toilet, hamburgers hidden on shelves and a closet full of cast-off Pooh bears and the breakfast food strewn all over the floor, and little Billy raging around like an animal, attacking pictures of Alfred Hitchcock with a long stick.

By now Billy was getting so big and strong that Pat could hardly control him physically, and she and her husband were thinking of building a fence around their house to keep him from endangering others. But before doing so, they took him to one more psychiatrist. "You can't build a fence high enough," the psychiatrist said flatly. "He'll be a Frankenstein monster. Put him away."

Miserable though they were, Pat and her husband couldn't stand the thought of abandoning the boy to an institution. "We were supposed to put him away and throw away the home movies and tear up the scrapbook pictures," she said. "We just couldn't do it."

A few weeks later a psychiatrist connected with the retarded children's school told Pat and her husband that Billy might not be retarded but autistic. He suggested they take him to the Neuropsychiatric Institute at UCLA where Dr. Lovaas and his colleague, Dr. James Simmons, a psychiatrist, were choosing autistic children for a new experimental program. Pat and her husband were enthusiastic, even though they knew about the punishment that Billy would be subjected to.

Their one fear was that Billy, erratic child that he was, would flunk his audition in front of Lovaas. But they knew that one of the criteria was that the children accepted must like to eat, and must be willing to expend a lot of energy to obtain food. So Pat and her husband talked things over, and they had an idea.

When they took Billy to see Dr. Lovaas, they made a stop on the way at the drive-in. Billy, given the hamburgers during the interview, passed the entrance exam with flying colors.

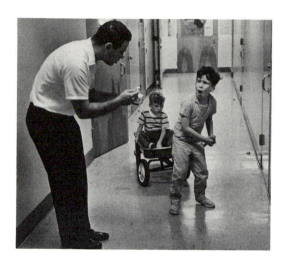

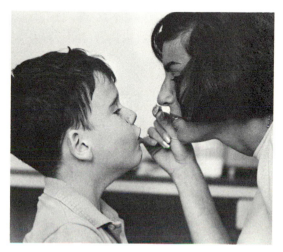

The taming and teaching of Billy takes place in the corridors and rooms of the UCLA Neuropsychiatric Institute where the children live during the experiment. Billy is being taught to play and is about to get a spoonful of sherbet for pulling Chuck in a wagon. In a speech session, a researcher holds a bit of food between her fingers to urge a right answer. A game is made of imitating adults, a normal response that autistics lack, but which is all-important in teaching them. (Photos by Allan Grant.)

Summarizing Statements

1. Language learning is sometimes impaired by a defective emotional relationship between parent and child. It is usually accomplished with a minimum of difficulty in normal children. Language learning depends on both utility and control. In general, a child will learn that which increases his ability to control his environment and to satisfy his wants and pleasures.

2. The babbling sounds of an infant are reinforced selectively, and this reinforcement tends to shape imitative behavior. So-called "talking birds" learn to imitate human sounds only if they form an affectionate relationship with their trainer. Among human infants, language failure is part of a seriously withdrawn condition called *autism* or childhood schizophrenia.

3. With the process of *identification*, a child comes to incorporate his parents' attitudes and values into himself as a *conscience*. The conscience guides behavior and provides a basis for making decisions about right and wrong.

4. We all have what may be called a drive for mastery, competence, or *self-actualization*. When children are successful in communicating, they increase their satisfactions and reduce their frustrations; they become more independent and self-actualized.

5. Apes do not speak, apparently because of structural limitations in the vocal cords, larynx, tongue, and lips. Chimpanzees have been taught language, proving that the animal is capable *intellectually* of learning and using language.

6. Informal training in the home is called *socialization*. An important goal of socialization is to develop an internalized conscience. Research indicates that parents who are warm and accepting but who use threat of loss of love to discipline their children are most successful in producing children with well-developed consciences.

7. Child training is dependent on reinforcers that strengthen behavior or discourage it. Positive reinforcement or reward is used to shape new behavior. Punishment does not have the consequences one might expect. It often arouses intense emotional behavior, which interferes with learning. Nonreinforcement is recommended as an active way of discouraging unwanted behavior. Punishment often causes a balky child to become more resistant or rebellious, perhaps even mentally rejecting the parent's right to discipline him. Punishment sometimes, paradoxically, strengthens the very behavior it is supposed to eliminate.

8. So-called "bad" behavior is often positively reinforced just by paying serious attention to it. Temper tantrums are usually attempts at manipulation or attention getting. If temper tantrums are nonreinforced, they will go away. Behavior is not maintained in a vacuum. Regularly occurring behavior is established and maintained by reinforcement of some kind.

9. A motivated child learns easily. Parents should not deprecate the child's motivation. The child's natural motivation may be used in the socialization process.

10. A system of discipline contains rules. Parents should be careful not to establish so many rules as to frustrate the child unnecessarily. If a child helps decide the rules and consequences of good and bad behavior, it is easier for him to live up to them.

11. Among school teachers, "timing out" is a popular way of eliminating bad behavior. Basically the idea is to deprive the child of his audience. Withdrawal of privileges is another effective technique for coping with undesirable behavior. Failure to live up to certain obligations simply leads to an *automatic* withdrawal of privileges.

12. An ideal system of discipline has certain characteristics. It should be mutually agreed on by parent and child. The consequences—rewards and punishments—should be appropriate to the behavior in question. Effective discipline molds behavior through the "consent of the governed." The discipline must respect the integrity of the human personality and must avoid being destructive or humiliating to either parent or child. The system of discipline must reduce and manage conflict. It must teach responsibility and independence. Most important, it must be designed so as to promote an effective conscience development in the child.

13. Delinquents are more likely to come from homes employing harsh physical punishment than those using psychological means of control. Almost all delinquents have a history of school failure in their backgrounds, combined with impaired feelings of worth and lack of confidence. With boys, hyper-aggressive masculinity is a way of compensating that unfortunately brings them into conflict with authority in school and on the streets.

14. "Achievement Place" is a special environment designed to retrain delinquent boys with the help of a token-economy or exchange reinforcement system. The boys are paid points for desired behavior. For things they want, for activity time, for privileges of all sorts they must pay or exchange points previously earned. This therapeutic environment is designed to reward school achievement, develop a child's conscience, and promote independence and initiative. A boy also learns how to function in a group, both as leader and follower. At the completion of the program, the boy is weened away from dependence on the token system, having developed his own internal controls.

15. "Behavioral contracting" is a technique being used with delinquents in which rights and privileges and duties and obligations are all worked out in a written contract. Both parent and child agree on the provisions of the contract. A major gain from the use of a behavioral contract is to reduce conflict in the situation. Its essential feature is that it sets forth the conditions for the reciprocal exchange of rewards and punishments.

16. Coercive systems of child discipline are unsuccessful and counter-productive.

17. Educators working with retarded children find it difficult to hold their attention for very long, and difficult to motivate them. But it has been found that once their attention can be gained, their learning ability is unimpaired. Token systems have been used successfully to maintain the motivation of retarded children to learn. Even their attention can be sustained with tokens.

18. Many clinical psychologists and psychiatrists believe grossly defective parent-child relationships produce autistic children. Emotional factors are apparently important in stimulating the most primitive kind of imitative behavior. Imitation may be stymied by a failure to develop the affectionate bond. Just as the parents of delinquents apparently dispensed much less positive reinforcement overall than do parents of nondelinquents, so perhaps autistic children also come from environments in which there is insufficient positive reinforcement.

19. Using modern behavior modification techniques, therapists are teaching some autistic children to speak.

READING SELECTION

20. Billy's case, says Moser, illustrates how nearly impossible it is for a well-intentioned parent to cope with an autistic child. Although he had been diagnosed as retarded, he seemed diabolically clever and hell-bent on destroying his mother. Whenever his father was at home, Billy was a model youngster, for the father punished him quickly and dispassionately for misbehaving. When the father left, Billy went on a rampage and was violently uncontrollable.

21. Billy was difficult in school. He ruled his teacher with tantrums until finally she could no longer stand to have him in the class. He dropped out of school at age 5.

22. Because Billy was untestable, most experts thought he was retarded.

23. As Billy grew and became stronger and more violently aggressive, his family was encouraged to institutionalize him. A final expert suggested that perhaps he might be autistic instead of retarded, which lead to their seeking help at UCLA.

Terms and Concepts

Autism: a withdrawn condition in which a child does not relate meaningfully to parents and others. Synonymous with childhood schizophrenia. Most autistic children do not learn to speak or speak defectively, do not learn much, and thus appear unsocialized.

Behavioral contract: an agreement between two or more persons setting forth the conditions for the reciprocal exchange of reinforcement.

Conscience: a well-developed, internalized system of moral values that provides the basis for evaluating one's own behavior.

Identification: accepting as one's own the purposes and values of another person or group. The following processes are all included in this meaning: imitation, sympathy, empathy, and introjection.

Self-actualization: a high-level motive in which a person is driven toward mastery or realization of his best potentials.

Socialization: the process by which a person becomes a social being as he grows up and learns about the pressures and obligations of group life; child training in the home concerned with values and morals. A well-socialized child has a firm sense of right and wrong and an internalized conscience.

Token economy (or token exchange) system: a reinforcement scheme in which tokens or symbolic reinforcers are delivered instead of tangible or real reinforcement, and later exchanged. The purpose of such a system is to provide the learner with a bridge between the unavoidable delay between the act and a time when real reinforcement can be delivered.

*All men should strive
to learn before they die
what they are running
from, and to, and why.*

—James Thurber, "The Shore and
the Sea"

*When one is a stranger
to oneself then one is
estranged from others
too.*

—Anne Morrow Lindberg,
"Moon Shell"

*The questions which
one asks oneself begin,
at last, to illuminate
the world, and become
one's key to the
experience of others.*

—James Baldwin, Nobody Knows
My Name

Adjustment

10

MANY people imagine that the word "adjustment" means a kind of unpleasant conformity, a loss of authenticity, or a sacrifice of self for social approval. Although adjustment may indeed be these things, it is also a neutral term that simply describes what happens when a person faces the necessity for choice. *Adjustment is a process whereby one changes himself or his environment in order to satisfy most of his needs and most of the physical and social demands of reality.* It does not necessarily imply either good or bad choice—merely that choice is taking place. When a new college graduate looks for a job, for example, his motivation, the objective situation, and his behavioral efforts to secure a job may be called *the adjustment situation*.

TASK-ORIENTED AND DEFENSIVE ADJUSTMENT

A job applicant may go to a company, fill out an application, and be interviewed; such things advance him toward his goal and are, therefore, task-oriented. However, in the interview he may act nervous, bite his fingernails, and toy with the paperweight on the interviewer's desk; such symptoms of anxiety about getting the job and fear of not getting it are defensive. Anxiety is often a part of the adjustment situation for all of us, especially when the situation is a novel or important one. But it is not the anxiety itself that creates faulty adaptive behavior; it is our reaction to it. Behavior is task-oriented when one is able to cope effectively with the situation in spite of his anxiety. Defensive behavior is also an attempt at coping, but it is often the wrong behavior directed at the wrong target; it is aimed at reducing the anxiety rather than at dealing with the objective situation.

It is sometimes difficult to understand how defensive behavior —which obviously doesn't work—gets established, but it is learned just like goal-directed behavior. Anxiety is unpleasant; thus, behavior that occurs simultaneously with the reduction of anxiety is likely to be repeated in similar situations, for the reduction of anxiety is reinforcing.

FRUSTRATION AND CONFLICT

Frustration, of course, is what a person suffers when he is prevented by an outside force from moving toward his goal. *Conflict*, however, is what he experiences when he is stopped from within himself because he finds it hard to choose between two different goals or motives. Or, as Figure 10-1 shows, when the job applicant is prevented from submitting his employment application by a clerk who does not like him, he feels frustration; when he is prevented because of his own fear of rejection, he feels conflict. Conflict is likely to be much more difficult for a person to overcome, especially if he is torn between several different courses of action.

When frustrated there are a number of things one can do: he may (1) redouble his efforts, for he may have been blocked because of insufficient effort; (2) seek a new route to the goal which circumvents the block; (3) redefine the situation, decide on another goal, or accept a compromise.

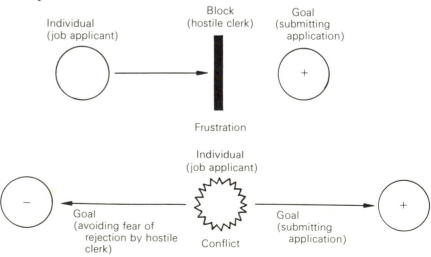

Figure 10-1.   The difference between frustration and conflict.

Conflict is more complicated. On the one hand the job applicant wants to submit his application and get the job; on the other hand he he wants to avoid the possibility of rejection and failure. What he does depends a lot on his learning history: if he has successfully reduced anxiety in the past by withdrawing, he may withdraw again. Anxiety reduction learning helps to account for neurotic (self-defeating) behavior being learned in the first place.

DEFENSES

Defeat is a school in which truth always grows strong.

—*Henry Ward Beecher*, Proverbs from Plymouth Pulpit

The only defense
that is more than pretense
is to act on the fact
that there is no defense.

—*Piet Hein, "The True Defense"*

A person who reacts defensively instead of task orientedly fools himself. *A defense mechanism is an unconscious device for self deception by which a person preserves his established self-image when dealing with an unpleasant or anxiety provoking reality.* For instance, if the job applicant withdrew rather than submitted his employment application and then we met him on the street and asked him how it went, he would not really know why he ran away. Perhaps he would offer excuses—"You know, that job had no future"—typical of the defense mechanism called *rationalization*; that is, the giving of "good," plausible, but untrue reasons for behavior. A rationalization is not

© 1962 United Feature Syndicate, Inc.

really a lie, because the person is not consciously aware of the whole truth.

Of course, all of us react defensively at times, but usually a line can be drawn—at least theoretically—between adjustive and maladjustive defensiveness.

What is *constructive* or adjustive defensiveness? If a student were to miscalculate on a particular examination and fail it, a little rationalization at that time might be healthy and help tide him over to a time when he could see the situation more realistically. This example illustrates the protective nature of defenses: a basically healthy person is protected in temporary failure against loss of self-esteem. But it also works in a similar way with people suffering from maladaptive, neurotic feelings of inferiority. Such a person expects to fail in most achievement situations. Only failure confirms the established self-image—which in this case is negative. If he were unaccountably successful, it would be success that would have to be rationalized away. He might dismiss an unexpected high score on an examination as a fluke or a mistake. Thus, defenses protect the existing self-image—whether healthy or unhealthy—through self-deception.

Most healthy persons, however, make little use of defenses for there is little need. According to authorities such as Maslow, Rogers, and Jourard, lack of defensiveness is one of the defining attributes of psychological health. Any use of defenses leads to some impairment of one's ability to perceive reality. High levels of defensiveness lead to profound impairment of a person's ability to judge reality, and are characteristic of the most disturbed personalities such as psychotics and severe neurotics.

Box 10-1   Major Defense Mechanisms

There are several kinds of defense mechanisms, unconscious devices designed to protect the established self-image—whether healthy or unhealthy—by some kind of self-deception. Foremost is *repression*, since without it none of the others would be possible. Repression is the process of "motivated forgetting" whereby anxiety-provoking information is forced out of mind and cannot be ordinarily remembered. Thirteen of the other most common defense mechanisms are as follows, which may be used singly or in combination.

Projection—disowning one's own unacceptable motivation and wrongly perceiving it in someone else's behavior; blaming someone else for own failures. May be used to rationalize failure.

Rationalization—giving of "good," plausible, but untrue reasons for behavior; justifying behavior with logically possible reasons.

Reaction-formation—repression of unacceptable attitudes and motives and developing of conscious attitudes and motives that are exact opposites.

Introjection—the internalization of attitudes, motives, and values with which the individual may not agree but which seem necessary for survival or status.

Displacement—a shift of hostility, fear, or some other feeling from one person or object to a substitute.

Regression—a return to less mature behavior that brought satisfaction at an earlier age; retreat to past security. May involve a lowering of level of aspiration.

Denial—refusal to face the significance of unpleasant events. May consist of falsifying reality.

Sublimation—acceptance of socially accepted substitute goals for sexual or other motives that are blocked.

Compensation—substitution of behavior leading to reward and success for that leading to punishment and failure; involves downgrading weak points and strengthening strong points.

Fantasy—use of imaginary accomplishments to compensate for reality.

Emotional insulation—a blunting of emotional responsiveness in situations which might prove harmful.

Intellectualization—an overly intellectualized approach to coping, often accompanying emotional insulation, in which the "emotional charge" that belongs with events is prevented by rational explanation.

Identification—a feeling of increased worth or adequacy based on the accomplishments of someone else with whom we feel great empathy. We identify with our loved ones, with powerful persons whom we admire, and with the organizations and groups to which we belong.

MALADJUSTMENT

> *We poison our lives with fear of burglary and shipwreck and, ask anyone, the house is never burgled and the ship never goes down.*
>
> —*Jean Anouilh,* The Rehearsal

> *Anxiety and conscience are a powerful pair of dynamos. Between them, they have ensured that I shall work hard, but they cannot ensure that one shall work at anything worthwhile.*
>
> —*Arnold J. Toynbee,* "Why and How I Work"

This book will not delve much into abnormal psychology, which is a big field, but it will outline the major types of maladjustments. The three main classes of disorders to be discussed are neurosis, psychosis, and sociopathic personality.

Neurosis

A neurosis is a learned pattern of essentially self-defeating behavior characterized by feelings of inferiority and various physical and psychological symptoms. A neurosis is learned in the same way as other behavior—through reinforcement—though anxiety is most commonly

Box 10-2   Conflict Learning

In conflict, a person in an adjustment situation is caught between two different sets of motives. For instance, consider this illustration of how a child's learning may become part of a conflict: Imagine that an infant has a normal urge to explore and manipulate his environment. Long before he can really understand his mother, he learns that when he is crawling around and poking into things mother sometimes gets angry at him: When he pulls the table cloth and plates off the table, she may shout and get very agitated. Thus, he finds, his desire to explore and manipulate sometimes gets him into trouble, for it seems she has motives too, one of them being to maintain order in her environment. When his motive is blocked, as it sometimes is by his mother, he learns her desires ought to be taken into account—if her love and approval are to be forthcoming most of the time.

The situation becomes more complicated if the mother decides to speed up the learning process by coupling deliberate withdrawal of love and approval to her demands that he not get into certain things. She may in effect pit her love and approval against the exploratory and manipulative motives. This situation then involves bittersweet choices for the child. No matter what he does, he suffers some unpleasant consequences. Exploring and manipulating $(+)$ are accompanied by loss of love $(-)$. Conformity to mother's need, which maintains love and approval $(+)$, is accompanied by blocking of exploration and manipulation $(-)$.

The solution of most people, probably, would be to choose love and proper, expected behavior demanded by mother and to give up any desire to decide for oneself—although this extreme conformity to convention can be a profound denial of a person's most creative urges.

The most tragic thing about such cases is that the conflict could have usually been avoided. Mother could find ways to engineer the environment so the child can explore and manipulate freely. His needs and her needs are not incompatible. Sometimes the solution is as simple as putting valuables out of the child's reach.

involved. The satisfaction a neurotic gets from reduction of anxiety accounts partly for the acquisition of the neurotic behavior, although it may be completely ineffective in the long run—that is, in actually making the external situation more satisfying. In neurosis, the learned self-defeating behavior, although not task-oriented, has been useful in coping with anxiety.

Neurosis is usually characterized by various patterns of physical and psychological symptoms. Physical illness, real or imagined, plays an important role in many kinds of maladjustments. The forms, from least to most severe, include the following: imagined ailments (asthenia), overconcern about health (hypochondria), simulated ailments (conversion reactions), and genuine but emotionally caused physical illness (psychosomatic ailments). All but the last are considered neurotic types. Neurotic symptoms ought to be seen as attempted adjustments

that are ineffective. They are generally regarded as exaggerated forms of defense mechanisms.

Let us consider in detail one type of neurosis, phobia.

Phobia.   Fear may be realistic—if you are afraid of a large, snarling, aggressive dog—but it is a neurotic, phobic fear if you are afraid of a small, friendly dog. A phobia *is a morbid or unreasonable fear.* Such fear may be concerned with almost anything. We used to give each phobia a long name, such as *claustrophobia* (fear of confined space) or *agoraphobia* (fear of open space), but now the custom is simply to modify or add to the term, as in *travel phobia.*

What happens when a phobic actually goes to the boundary of his safe territory? One phobic patient described the state of absolute panic. He was so terrified that he thought he was going to die. He developed intense internal turmoil, and claimed to experience a "dimming out" of his vision. These physical symptoms of the panic state did not pass completely for several days. Naturally, this is a very unpleasant experience. From that time on, when the phobic approaches the boundary of his safe territory he knows what is in store for him.

The rising anxiety is a signal of what is yet to come if he continues. Every time he starts out, experiences anxiety, and turns around, he is further reinforcing withdrawl as a general means of coping with his adjustment problems.

A phobic job-seeker might never get to the office where he could have applied for a job. The defense mechanisms serve to cover up the inevitable adjustment failure produced by giving in to the fear (or any neurotic device, for that matter). He might *rationalize* his behavior by saying, "That job was too far away from home for me. It would involve too much commute time. I'll look for something more convenient." He might *repress* the feelings he experienced as he approached the boundary of his safe territory. He might refuse to understand (deny) that he was becoming a prisoner of his unreasonable fear.

The phobic often accepts these restrictions on his behavior as "a small price to pay for peace of mind"—the defense mechanism of *intellectualization*. But the price can be enormous. A phobic, in fact, may not be able to go anywhere. Wolpe (1958) reports a tragic case of a travel and space phobia in a 23-year-old South African woman. One of the interesting things about the case is that her "safe territory" kept shrinking progressively.

> Three years previously she had had two fairly violent falls in the street within a few weeks and thereafter had been apprehensive of walking outside unaccompanied lest she should fall. As is apt to happen in such cases, her range of activity had then gradually become more and more circumscribed. At one stage she would walk in the street only if her mother held her arm; later she entirely refused to leave the house, and by the time I first saw her, she was practically bedridden, apart from very tense wall-hugging journeys between her bed and a couch in the drawing room, where she would sit with her legs up. If she tried to sit with her legs down, she became dizzy and nauseous, and reading even a few lines had the same effect. Sitting on the couch tired her, so that she always returned to bed by 4:00 P.M. (p. 174).

Sadly, the phobic often finds that no price is too high to pay. He becomes a total slave to his fear.

Intellectually the phobic appears baffled by his fear. He "knows" that his fear is unreasonable, but he still has it. Knowing that others are not afraid usually makes it worse, because then he is forced to doubt his own rationality. In many cases of travel phobia, the neurotic behavior provides excuse for adjustment failure. The person is unable to fulfill his ambitions because of conditions beyond his control. In a way, he is able to dissociate himself from responsibility for success and failure in his own life. He fails but is protected from devaluation because the cause is a condition beyond his control.

Physical Illness in Neurosis. Conversion reaction, better known as *hysteria*, is a neurotic reaction in which a person develops a *simulated* or imitation ailment. Common forms are hysterical paralysis of a limb, hysterical blindness or deafness, and hysterical anesthesia. A hysterically blind person reports that he cannot see, yet his eyes show normal pupilary responses, the nerves function normally, the impulses produce measurable reactions in the visual part of the brain—all the components of the visual sense are in working order, yet he has no conscious aware-

Box 10-3   Illness in Hypochondria

A hypochondriac is a type of neurotic who has an obsessive over-concern about his health. He often imagines that he is suffering from various ailments. His symptoms are vague and constantly shifting from one complaint to another. Usually a physician's examination reveals little or no organic basis for these complaints. The symptoms serve an adjustment purpose, protecting the person from feelings of failure. Of course, we can't hold a "sick" person to the same standards of achievement as a well person. The hypochondriac often gets a lot of sympathy from others. By skillfully exploiting their concern, he is often able to regulate or control things to his own advantage. If others plan something he does not want to do, he may become ill, forcing them to cancel their plans and do what he wants to do. This enjoyment of sympathy and attention, which tends to reinforce illness as a coping device, is called *secondary gain*. The following case, reported by Menninger (1945), illustrates the shifting pattern of complaints (pp. 139–140).

Dear Mother and Husband:

I have suffered terrible today with drawing in throat. My nerves are terrible. My head feels queer. But my stomach hasn't cramped quite so hard. I've been on the verge of a nervious chill all day, but I have been fighting it hard. It's night and bedtime, but, Oh, how I hate to go to bed. Nobody knows or realizes how badly I feel because I fight to stay up and outdoors if possible.

I haven't had my cot up for two days, they don't want me to use it.

These long afternoons and nights are awful. There are plenty of patients well enough to visit with but I'm in too much pain.

The nurses ignore any complaining. They just laugh or scold.

Eating has been awful hard. They expect me to eat like a harvest hand. Every bite of solid food is agony to get down, for my throat aches so and feels so closed up. . . .

With supper so early, and evening so long, I am so nervous I can't sleep until so late. I haven't slept well since I've been here. My heart pains as much as when I was at home. More so at night. I put hot water bottle on it. I don't know if I should or not. I've been wanting to ask some Dr.

I had headache so badly in the back of my head last night and put hot water bottle there. My nurse said not to.

They don't give much medicine here. Mostly Christian Science it seems! Well I must close or I never will get to sleep. My nurse gets off at 8:15 so she makes me go to bed by then.

My eyes are bothering me more.

Come up as soon as you can. My nose runs terribly every time I eat.

The trains and ducks and water pipes are noisy at night.

Annie

Reprinted from Menninger, K. A., *The human mind* (New York: Knopf, 1945). Copyright 1945 Alfred A. Knopf. Reprinted by permission.

ness of being able to see. A case has been reported of a hysterically blind person ducking in reflex action when a baseball was thrown at his head, yet he did not remember doing this.

Coon & Raymond (1940, pp. 224–225) described a young woman with a mediocre singing talent who trained to be an opera singer. As long as she was just training, her talent was not put to the test and was used as a social tool to impress friends and relatives. But one day she went to an audition. She did poorly, and in the midst of it her voice cracked and she was unable to complete the test; hysterically she lost her voice. Later it returned, but from that time on she rationalized her inability to create a great singing career by saying that her ambition led her to a premature test of her talent and the strain caused permanent loss of her singing voice. She was thus able to transfer the promise of her great talent from the future to the past. She explained that her failure had nothing to do with herself and her talent and blamed the situation and the music teacher. Furthermore, she said, she should have waited before attempting an audition. What did all this accomplish? She had bolstered her shaky self-esteem by belief in a great singing talent. Whether it was to be realized in the future or had already been realized in the past made little difference.

Conflict plays an essential role in stimulating the growth of neurotic mechanisms. The conflict may be centered around the person's failure to live up to aspirations, or around dangerous desires which threaten to break through his defenses into behavior, or around unpleasant and frustrating life situations. According to Coleman (1964), "most often, neurotic reactions seem to be exaggerations of . . . defense techniques we all learn for coping with threatening situations." Also, "it would appear that neurotic reactions reflect immaturities and faulty assumptions and evaluations and stem primarily from desperate attempts to deal with seemingly insurmountable problems" (p. 232).

Illness is unwittingly encouraged by society in several ways. A child may learn that saying he is ill provides reason enough to be allowed to stay out of school. People beg off social obligations they wish to avoid by saying that they are ill. These excuses are accepted as if they were true. Society fosters and encourages reliance on illness as an excuse in coping with situations, thus increasing the occurrences in which attention to symptoms will be reinforced.

Psychosis

A psychosis is a severe mental illness that involves loss of contact with reality, personality disorganization, and extreme deviation from normal patterns of thinking, feeling, and acting. Psychoses may be *organic*—that is, caused by physiological malfunctioning or damage to the body—or *functional*, which means they arise out of experience. Functional psychoses are primarily learned, although some people seem to be constitutionally predisposed to develop psychoses; that is, they inherit an inclination to react to stress in this way rather than in a less disabling way.

The most important feature is the break with reality: psychotics are sometimes so disoriented in time and place that they are unaware of even the most basic facts, such as what year it is or who the President is. They are often so incapacitated that they cannot hold jobs, go to school, fulfill family or social obligations, or otherwise manage their own affairs. While neurotics rarely require hospitalization, psychotics often must be hospitalized for their own protection. Psychotics often have symptoms that are rarely or never found in neurotics—for example, *hallucinations*, perceptions of voices or visions that do not exist, and *delusions*, distortions of thought that misinterpret perceptions.

An important aspect of psychosis is the disintegration or fragmenting of personality. A psychotic shows disorder both in thought, as revealed by irrelevant or incoherent speech, and in feeling, as in emotional impoverishment or blunting. Typically, he is extremely withdrawn emotionally, sometimes almost nonreactive. Personality disorganization also often involves a change in defensiveness. Although neurotic and normal persons use defenses extensively, the psychotic often displays a kind of sublime indifference to defending himself and seems to be simply overrun with his adjustment problems.

Sociopathic Personality

A sociopath is a person who relates to others in an egocentric, callous, and manipulative way, often bringing him into conflict with society. Usually the sociopath (also known as psychopath) is incapable of normal love and affection. The cause is uncertain, although it is probably a result of deprivation of love in infancy. Certainly, prolonged periods of being deprived of mother love in infancy *can* produce sociopathic adult personalities. But in some cases there may be organic causes also, since sociopaths often have abnormal brain-wave patterns. The sociopath behaves as if he does not understand human emotionality; lacking love and affection himself, he is incapable of forming ties of loyalty and tends to treat other people as things, manipulating them crassly.

He is prone to illegal and criminal behavior because he has no real conscience, no sense of right and wrong. He may con people and become a swindler because he enjoys the thrill of winning and then violating people's trust. Swindler and bank robber Willie Sutton may have expressed this attitude when, after a life of crime, he claimed his mission in life was to educate the public in how foolish it was to trust anyone. The sociopath's lack of respect for people may make him dangerous if he is highly aggressive. Since he lacks conscience, he may be able to kill other people without guilt or remorse. Therefore, he may not require much provocation to kill. Even criminals are said to fear a sociopathic killer because of the sociopath's well-known lack of loyalty. The sociopath also appears somewhat more prone than others to becoming a homosexual or drug addict.

Not all sociopaths turn to crime. The fringes of the business world provide similar opportunities. Some of them attempt to obey the law, not because they respect it or other people, but because they want to avoid trouble. The penalties for breaking the law may inhibit them.

The sociopathic person is particularly dangerous as a politician. Several authorities believe the leadership of the Nazi movement was dominated by sociopathic types. Revolutionary movements also frequently attract sociopaths and provide an alternative career to criminality.

Box 10-4   Schizophrenic Speech

Schizophrenia, which means a *split away from reality*, is the name given to the largest class of psychoses. Nearly one-fourth of all first admissions to mental hospitals are diagnosed as schizophrenics. Usually they are characterized by thinking and emotional disorder and by fragmentation of personality. The most extreme symptom of thinking disorder is so-called "word salad" speech. Coleman (1956) cites this sample: "What Master of arts under the canopy of heaven has got broad enough shoulders to let the chips remain where they fall?" (p. 271). Sometimes the schizophrenic begins a sentence and then is diverted by a "clang association," which is similar in sound; for instance, the word "hat" will remind him of "cat," and he will switch his thoughts to cats.

Careful scientific analysis has disentangled the word salad in some cases. Ostwald (1965) reports that one 8-year-old boy's speech was analyzed into three distinct kinds of messages: nonsense, slogans (songs, rhymes, jingles), and meaningful messages. Careful study of how he spoke revealed that he had three different vocal styles: chanting, normal voice, and high-pitched screech. As the accompanying chart shows, the boy was easiest to understand precisely when he was screeching at the top of his voice. But when he spoke in a normal tone, the message content was drowned out by an equal amount of slogan and nonsense material. The chanting voice was almost entirely nonmeaningful slogans. In terms of social impact, ironically, people would probably pay the least attention when he was trying the hardest to communicate. One learning expert, Staats (1968), offers this insight: ". . . for the schizophrenic, communication with others which is understandable probably introduces touchy subjects which arouse anxiety. Reversed verbal behavior and other confused speech may reduce anxiety when it produces breakdown of the communication and cessation of the anxiety-producing subject matter or of the bothersome conversation itself" (p. 354).

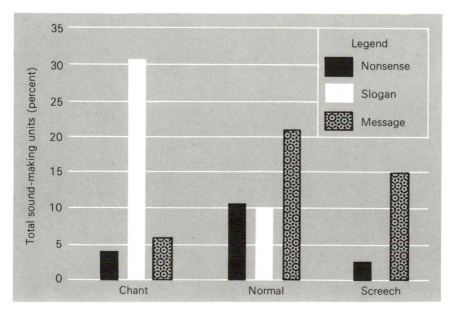

PSYCHOTHERAPY

The various types of maladjustments discussed so far all represent attempted adjustments. They may well be ineffective, but, except for psychotics, they usually belong to relatively stable personalities. One's established self-image is unlikely to change spontaneously very much. It is not incapable of changing, but usually the self develops a kind of dynamic homeostasis that resists being changed. The defenses, of course, play a major role in resisting change. How, then, does psychological growth happen in cases where the person has learned ineffective adjustive techniques?

Growth results either from accidental events or from planned intervention. Occasionally we experience events so vivid and powerful that they transform us. Such events teach us profound lessons about ourselves, and in recognizing new truth, we are induced to grow. More frequently new meanings emerge from repeated experiences. Planned intervention may be *psychotherapy, a talking out treatment for emotional disorders.* It is conducted by a trained professional therapist who is usually a clinical psychologist, psychiatrist, or psychiatric social worker. Many states certify such professionals by issuing licenses which attest to minimal professional competence.

In psychoteraphy, the patient's goal is to develop greater insight into and control over his own behavior. Individual psychotherapy involves one psychotherapist and one patient; group therapy involves one or more therapists with several patients simultaneously. The philosophical background and framework of the therapist determines his usual techniques. Therapies differ chiefly in their goals and in length and depth of treatment.

Coleman (1964) offers a typical list of goals, observing that psychotherapy involves achieving one or more of the following:

(a) increased insight into one's problems and behavior, (b) a better delineation of one's self-identity, (c) resolution of handicapping or disabling conflicts, (d) changing of undesirable habits or reaction patterns, (e) improved interpersonal or other competencies, (f) the modification of inaccurate assumptions about one's self and one's world, and (g) the opening of a pathway to a more meaningful and fulfilling existence (p. 564).

The length of therapy varies considerably from one or a few sessions to prolonged treatment lasting several years. In *behavior therapy*, derived from the psychology of learning, the goal in most cases is merely to remove symptoms—hence, treatment tends to be quite brief. In *client-centered therapy*, which follows the ideas of Carl Rogers, the goals are also modest and the therapy brief, with ten to twenty sessions being counted as successful. In *psychoanalytic therapy*, which is based on Freud and his disciples, treatment is usually extended over a period of years and the therapeutic goal is basic personality reorganization. There are also many other kinds of therapy, but these three are typical and have a large following among professional therapists. Most clinical psychologists today are not strict followers of any particular school but rather borrow techniques and theories from all of them.

Box 10-5   Behavior Therapy

Behavior therapy tries to modify behavior through the application of conditioning principles. It is usually directed at removing symptoms directly, such as in desensitizing a phobia. For instance, the woman shown in the photographs below suffered from *anorexia nervosa*, a chronic failure to eat, and was in danger of death. When she began therapy she weighed only 47 pounds (picture A) and had the appearance "of a poorly preserved mummy suddenly struck with the breath of life" (Backrach *et al.*, 1965).

Reinforcers present in her environment which she seemed to enjoy had to be identified—and removed. Thus, she was taken from her attractive room with pictures, flowers, and a pleasant view and moved to a barren room. She was also denied visitors, radio, and television so all of these could be used as reinforcers of changed behavior. The therapists enlisted hospital personnel in making the treatment a success by making clear to them that the alternative for this woman to these extreme procedures was death.

The therapists had found that social reinforcement had served to reinforce her *non*eating behavior. They therefore reinforced her by *talking to her* when she picked up a fork, brought it to her mouth, or ate. As she began to gain weight other reinforcers were introduced.

Picture B shows her after eight weeks of therapy and just before discharge as an outpatient. C shows her after 10 months as an outpatient prior to readmission to the hospital for a month of further therapy during which she gained an additional 7 pounds. D shows her 3 months after final discharge, shortly before she completed a home-study course in practical nursing and received her cap and uniform. When she left the hospital the patient's family was trained to provide social reinforcers for continued eating and other social behavior. Three- and five-year follow-ups have revealed that the patient is working, is apparently happy and successful, and is maintaining her weight at between 78 and 80 pounds.

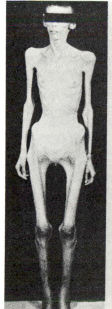   

A 47 lb.   B 64 lb.   C 74.5 lb.   D 88 lb.

From Bachrach, A. J., Erwin, W. J., and Mohr, J. P. "The Control of Eating Behavior in an Anorexic by Operant Conditioning Techniques." In L. Ullman and L. P. Krasner (Eds.), *Case Studies in Behavior Modification.* New York: Holt, Rinehart, and Winston, 1965, pp. 153–163.

Group therapy is a fairly new development which was originally introduced as an economy measure during World War II when therapists were in short supply. If a therapist could relate to many patients at the same time, it was reasoned, obviously the cost of therapy could also be drastically reduced. Now, however, it is recognized that group therapy has many advantages in its own right. In most groups, the members actually serve as co-therapists when relating to another member. With some problems, such as alcoholism and drug addiction, it is much more effective for a patient who has "been there" to point out what someone is doing. Individual and group therapy are usefully combined in some cases. As with individual therapy, there are many different kinds of group therapy. Family group therapy, for instance, takes recognition of the fact that a maladjusted patient rarely lives in a perfectly healthy environment. The patient and his family often make up a "sick" environment. In therapy with children, family therapy is the usual procedure.

All of the different kinds of psychotherapy so briefly described here are ways of increasing the probability that a patient's problem behavior will change, thereby changing the feedback he gets from people in his social environment and eventually even his notions about himself.

Psychotherapy is effective in many cases. When combined with other procedures such as drug therapy, it produces improvement in approximately three-fourths of all patients, both neurotics and psychotics. When psychotherapy works, it has been successful in creating a growth-promoting atmosphere. The goal is to enable the patient to feel free to be himself without defensiveness and to examine and learn from those conditions that have produced poor adjustment in the past. The patient's freedom to grow is facilitated because the therapist accepts him as he is, making defensiveness unnecessary. Often the therapist's role is to ask somewhat painful questions in order to bring the patient up short and force him to develop insight into why he has deceived himself. Ultimately, success and failure depend on the patient. He must be highly motivated to change and to put up with the discomfort of therapy.

SIDNEY M. JOURARD

Healthy Personality and Self-Disclosure

OR a long time, health and well-being have been taken for granted as "givens," and disease has been viewed as the problem for man to solve. Today, however, increasing numbers of scientists have begun to adopt a reverse point of view, regarding disease and trouble as the givens, with specification of positive health and its conditions as the problem to solve. Physical, mental and social health are values representing restrictions on the total variance of being. The scientific problem here consists in arriving at a definition of health, determining its relevant dimensions and then identifying the independent variables of which these are a function.

Scientists, however, are supposed to be hard-boiled, and they insist that phenomena, to be counted "real," must be public. Hence, many behavioral scientists ignore man's self, or soul, since it is essentially a private phenomenon. Others, however, are not so quick to allocate man's self to the limbo of the unimportant, and they insist that we cannot understand man and his lot until we take his self into account.

I probably fall into the camp of those investigators who want to explore health as a positive problem in its own right, and who, further, take man's self seriously—as a reality to be explained and as a variable which produces consequences for weal or woe. This paper gives me an opportunity to explore the connection between positive health and the disclosure of self. Let me commence with some sociological truisms.

Reprinted from Jourard, S. M., Healthy personality and self-disclosure, *Mental Hygiene*, 1959, **32**, 499–507. Footnotes cited in the original have been deleted.

Social systems require their members to play certain roles. Unless the roles are adequately played, the social systems will not produce the results for which they have been organized. This flat statement applies to social systems as simple as that provided by an engaged couple and to those as complex as a total nation among nations. Societies have socialization "factories" and "mills"—families and schools—which serve the function of training people to play the age, sex and occupational roles which they shall be obliged to play throughout their life in the social system. Broadly speaking, if a person plays his roles suitably, he can be regarded as a more or less normal personality. Normal personalities, however, are not healthy personalities (Jourard 1958, 16–18).

Healthy personalities are people who play their roles satisfactorily, and at the same time derive personal satisfaction from role enactment; more, they keep growing and they maintain high-level physical wellness (Dunn 1958). It is probably enough, speaking from the standpoint of a stable social system, for people to be normal personalities. But it is possible to be a normal personality and be absolutely miserable. We would count such a normal personality unhealthy. In fact, normality in some social systems—successful acculturation to them—reliably produces ulcers, paranoia, piles or compulsiveness. We also have to regard as unhealthy personalities those people who have never been able to enact the roles that legitimately can be expected from them.

Counselors, guidance workers and psychotherapists are obliged to treat with both patterns of unhealthy personality—those people who have been unable to learn their roles and those who play their roles quite well but suffer the agonies of boredom, frustration, anxiety or stultification. If our clients are to be helped they must change, and change in valued directions. A change in a valued direction may arbitrarily be called growth. We have yet to give explicit statement to these valued directions for growth, though a beginning has been made (Fromm 1947, Jahoda 1958, Jourard 1958, Maslow 1954, Robers 1954). We who are professionally concerned with the happiness, growth and well-being of our clients may be regarded as professional lovers, not unlike the Cyprian sisterhood. It would be fascinating to pursue this parallel further, but let it suffice for us to be reminded that we do in fact share membership in the oldest profession in the world. Our branches of this oldest profession probably began at the same time that our sisters' branch began, and all branches will continue to flourish so long as they meet the needs of society. We are all concerned with promoting personality health in the people who consult with us.

Now what has all this to do with self-disclosure?

To answer this question, let's tune in on an imaginary interview between a client and his counselor. The client says, "I have never told this to a soul, doctor, but I can't stand my wife, my mother is a nag, my father is a bore, and my boss is an absolutely hateful and despicable tyrant. I have been carrying on an affair for the last ten years with the lady next door and at the same time I am a deacon in the church." The counselor says, showing great understanding and empathy, "Mm-humm!"

If we listened for a long enough period of time we would find that the client talks and talks about himself to this highly sympathetic and empathic listener. At some later time the client may eventually say, "Gosh, you have helped me a lot. I see what I must do and I will go ahead and do it."

Now this talking about oneself to another person is what I call self-disclosure. It would appear, without assuming anything, that self-disclosure is a factor in the process of effective counseling or psychotherapy. Would it be too arbitrary an assumption to propose that people become clients because they have not disclosed themselves in some optimum degree to the people in their life?

An historical digression: Toward the end of the 19th century Joseph Breuer, a Viennese physician, discovered (probably accidentally) that when his hysterical patients talked about themselves, disclosing not only the verbal content of their memories but also the feelings that they had suppressed at the time of assorted "traumatic" experiences, their hysterical symptoms disappeared. Somewhere along the line Breuer withdrew from a situation which would have made his name identical with that of Freud in history's hall of fame. When Breuer permitted his patients "to be," it scared him, one gathers, because some of his female patients disclosed themselves to be quite sexy, and what was probably worse, they felt quite sexy towards him.

Freud, however, did not flinch. He made the momentous discovery that the neurotic people of his time were struggling like mad to avoid "being," to avoid being known, and in Allport's (1955) terms, to avoid "becoming." He learned that his patients, when they were given the opportunity to "be"—which free association on a couch is nicely designed to do—they would disclose that they had all manner of horrendous thoughts and feelings which they did not even dare disclose to themselves, much less express in the presence of another person. Freud learned to permit his patients to be, through permitting them to disclose themselves utterly to another human. He evidently didn't trust anyone enough to be willing to disclose *himself vis à vis*, so he disclosed himself to himself on paper (Freud 1955) and learned the extent to which he himself was self-alienated.

Roles for people in Victorian days were even more restrictive than they are today, and Freud discovered that when people struggled to avoid being and knowing themselves they got sick. They could only become well, and stay relatively well, when they came to know themselves through self-disclosure to another person. This makes me think of George Groddeck's magnificent *Book of the It (Id)* in which, in the guise of letters to a naive young woman, Groddeck shows the contrast between the public self—pretentious role-playing—and the warded off but highly dynamic *id*—which I here very loosely translate as "real self."

Let me at this point draw a distinction between role relationships and interpersonal relationships—a distinction which is often overlooked in the current spate of literature that has to do with human relations. Roles are inescapable. They must be played or else the social system will not work. A role by definition is a repertoire of behavior patterns which must be rattled off in appropriate contexts, and all behavior which is irrelevant to the role must be suppressed. But what we often forget is the fact that it is a person who is playing the role. This person has a self—or, I should say he *is* a self. All too often the roles that a person plays do not do justice to all of his self. In fact, there may be nowhere that he may just *be* himself. Even more, the person may not *know* his self. He may, in Horney's (1950) terms, be self-alienated.

This fascinating term "self-alienation" means that an individual is estranged from his real self. His real self becomes a stranger, a feared and distrusted stranger. Estrangement—alienation from one's real self—is at the root of the "neurotic personality of our time" so eloquently described by Horney (1936). Fromm (1957) referred to the same phenomenon as a socially patterned defect.

Self-alienation is a sickness which is so widely shared that no one recognizes it. We may take it for granted that all the clients we encounter are self-alienated to a greater or lesser extent. If you ask anyone—a client, a patient, or one of the people here—to answer the question, "Who are you?" the answer will generally be, "I am a psychologist, a guidance worker, teacher or what have you." The respondent will probably tell you the name of the role with which he feels most closely identified. As a matter of fact, the respondent spends a greater part of his life trying to discover who he is, and once he has made some such discovery, he spends the rest of his life trying to play the part. Of course, some of the roles—age, sex, family or occupational roles—may be so restrictive that they fit a person in a manner not too different from the girdle of a 200-pound lady who is struggling to look like Brigitte Bardot. There is Faustian drama all about us in this world of role-playing. Everywhere we see people who have sold their souls —their real self, if you wish—in order to be a psychologist, a guidance worker, a nurse, a physician, a this or a that.

Now, I have suggested that no social system can exist unless the members play their roles and play them with precision and elegance. But here is an odd observation, and yet one which you can all corroborate just by thinking back over your own experience. It's possible to be involved in a social group, such as a family or a work setting, for years and years, playing one's roles nicely with the other members—and never getting to know the persons who are playing the other roles. Roles can be played personally and impersonally, as we are beginning to discover in nursing. A husband can be married to his wife for fifteen years and never come to know her. He knows her as "the wife." This is the paradox of the "lonely crowd" (Riesman 1950). It is the loneliness which people try to counter with "togetherness." But much of today's "togetherness" is like the "parallel play" of 2-year-old children, or like the professors in Stringfellow Barr's novel (1958) who, when together socially, lecture past one another alternately and sometimes simultaneously. There is no real self-to-self or person-to-person meeting in such transactions.

Now what does it mean to know a person, or, more accurately, a person's self? I don't mean anything mysterious by "self." All I mean is the person's subjective side—what he thinks, feels, believes, wants, worries about, his past and so forth—the kind of thing one could never know unless one were told. We get to know the other person's self when he discloses it to us.

Self-disclosure, letting another person know what you think, feel or want, is the most direct means (though not the only means) by which an individual can make himself known to another person. Personality hygienists place great emphasis upon the importance for mental health of what they call "real self being," "self-realization," "discovering oneself" and so on. An operational analysis of what goes on in counseling and therapy shows that the patients and clients discover themselves through self-disclosure to the counselor. They talk, and to their shock and amazement the counselor listens.

I venture to say that there is probably no experience more horrifying and terrifying than that of self-disclosure to "significant others" whose probable reactions are assumed but not known. Hence the phenomenon of "resistance." This is what makes psychotherapy so difficult to take and so difficult to administer. If there is any skill to be learned in the art of counseling and psychotherapy, it is the art of coping with the terrors which attend self-disclosure, and the art of decoding the language —verbal and non-verbal—in which a person speaks about his inner experience.

Now, what is the connection between self-disclosure and healthy personality? Self-disclosure, or should I say "real" self-disclosure, is both a symptom of personality health (Jourard 1958, 218–21) and at the same time a means of ultimately achieving healthy personality. The discloser of self is an animated "real self be-er." This, of course, takes courage—the "courage to be" (Tillich 1954). I have known people who would rather die than become known, and in fact some did die when it appeared that the chances were great that they would become known. When I say that self-disclosure is a symptom of personality health, what I mean really is that a person who displays many of the other characteristics that betoken healthy personality (Jourard 1958, Maslow 1954) will also display the ability to make himself fully known to at least one other significant human being. When I say that self-disclosure is a means by which one achieves personality health, I mean something like the following: It is not until I *am* my real self and I *act* my real self that my real self is in a position to grow. One's self grows from the consequence of being. People's selves stop growing when they repress them. This growth-arrest in the self is what helps to account for the surprising paradox of finding an infant inside the skin of someone who is playing the role of an adult.

In a fascinating analysis of mental distress, Jurgen Ruesch (1957) describes assorted neurotics, psychotics and psychosomatic patients as persons with selective atrophy and over-specialization in the aspects of communication. I have come to believe that it is not communication *per se* which is fouled up in the mentally ill. Rather, it is a foul-up in the processes of knowing others and of becoming known to others. Neurotic and psychotic symptoms might be viewed as smokescreens interposed between the patient's real self and the gaze of the onlooker. We might call the symptoms devices to avoid becoming known. A new theory of schizophrenia has been proposed by an anonymous former patient (1958) who "was there" and he makes such a point.

Alienation from one's real self not only arrests one's growth as a person; it also tends to make a farce out of one's relationships with people. As the ex-patient mentioned above observed, the crucial break in schizophrenia is with sincerity, not reality (Anonymous 1958). A self-alienated person—one who does not disclose himself truthfully and fully—can never love another person nor can he be loved by the other person. Effective loving calls for knowledge of the object (Fromm 1957, Jourard 1958). How can I love a person whom I do not know? How can the other person love me if he does not know me?

Hans Selye (1946) proposed and documented the hypothesis that illness as we know it arises in consequence of stress applied to the organism. Now I rather think that unhealthy personality has a similar root cause, and one which

is related to Selye's concept of stress. It is this: Every maladjusted person is a person who has not made himself known to another human being, and in consequence does not know himself. Nor can he find himself. More than that, he struggles actively to avoid becoming known by another human being. He works at it ceaselessly, 24 hours daily, and it is work! The fact that resisting becoming known is work offers us a research opening, incidentally (Dittes 1958, Davis and Malmo 1951). I believe that in the effort to avoid becoming known a person provides for himself a cancerous kind of stress which is subtle and unrecognized but nonetheless effective in producing not only the assorted patterns of unhealthy personality that psychiatry talks about but also the wide array of physical ills that have come to be recognized as the stock in trade of psychosomatic medicine. Stated another way, I believe that other people come to be stressors to an individual in direct proportion to his degree of self-alienation.

If I am struggling to avoid becoming known by other persons then of course I must construct a false public self (Jourard 1958, 301–302). The greater the discrepancy between my unexpurgated real self and the version of myself that I present to others, the more dangerous will other people be for me. If becoming known by another person is a source of danger, then it follows that merely the presence of the other person can serve as a stimulus to evoke anxiety, heightened muscle tension and all the assorted visceral changes which occur when a person is under stress. A beginning already has been made in demonstrating the tension-evoking powers of the other person through the use of such instruments as are employed in the lie detector, the measurement of muscle tensions with electromyographic apparatus and so on (Davis and Malmo 1958, Dittes 1958).

Students of psychosomatic medicine have been intimating something of what I have just finished saying explicitly. They say (Alexander 1950) that ulcer patients, asthmatic patients, patients suffering from colitis, migraine and the like, are chronic repressors of certain needs and emotions, especially hostility and dependency. Now when you repress something, you are not only withholding awareness of this something from yourself; you are also withholding it from the scrutiny of the other person. In fact, the means by which repressions are overcome in the therapeutic situation is through relentless disclosure of self to the therapist. When a patient is finally able to follow the fundamental rule in psychoanalysis and disclose everything which passes through his mind, he is generally shocked and dismayed to observe the breadth, depth, range and diversity of thoughts, memories and emotions which pass out of his "unconscious" into overt disclosure. Incidentally, by the time a person is that free to disclose in the presence of another human being, he has doubtless completed much of his therapeutic sequence.

Self-disclosure, then, appears to be one of the means by which a person engages in that elegant activity that we call real-self-being. But is real-self-being synonymous with healthy personality? Not in and of itself. I would say that real-self-being is a necessary but not a sufficient condition for healthy personality. It is in fact possible for a person to be much "nicer" socially when he is not being his real self than when he is his real self. But an individual's obnoxious and immoral real self can never grow in the direction of greater maturity until the person has become acquainted with it and begins to be it. Real-self-being produces consequences, which in accordance with well-known principles of behavior (Skinner 1953) produce changes in the real self. Thus, there can be no real growth of the self without real-self-being. Full disclosure of the self to at least one other significant human being appears to be one means by which a person discovers not only the breadth and depth of his needs and feelings but also the nature of his own self-affirmed values. There is no conflict between real-self-being and being an ethical or nice person, because for the average member of our society self-owned ethics are generally acquired during the process of growing up. All too often, however, the self-owned ethics are buried under authoritarian morals (Fromm 1947).

If self-disclosure is one of the means by which healthy personality is both achieved and maintained, we can also note that such activities as loving, psychotherapy, counseling, teaching and nursing all are impossible of achievement without the disclosure of the client. It is through self-disclosure that an individual reveals to himself and to the other party just exactly who, what and where he is. Just as thermometers, sphygmomanometers, etc. disclose information about the real state of the body, self-disclosure reveals the real nature of the soul or self. Such information is vital in order to conduct intelligent evaluations. All I mean by evaluation is comparing how a person is with some concept of optimum. You never really discover how truly sick your psychotherapy patient is until he discloses himself utterly to you. You cannot help your client in vocational guidance until he has disclosed to you something of the impasse in which he finds himself. You cannot love your spouse or your child or your friend unless he has permitted you to know him and to know what he needs to move toward greater health and well-being. Nurses cannot nurse patients in any meaningful way unless they have permitted the patients to disclose their needs, wants, worries, anxieties and doubts. Teachers cannot be very helpful to their students until they have permitted the students to disclose how utterly ignorant and misinformed they are. Teachers cannot even provide helpful information to the students until they have permitted the students to disclose exactly what they are interested in.

I believe we should reserve the term interpersonal relationships to refer to transactions between "I and thou," (Buber 1937), between person and person, not role and role. A truly personal relationship between two people involves disclosure of self, one to the other, in full and spontaneous honesty. The data that we have collected up to the present time (using very primitive data-collecting methods) have showed us some rather interesting phenomena. We found (Jourard and Lasakow 1958), for example, that women consistently are higher self-disclosers than men; they seem to have a greater capacity for establishing person-to-person relationships—interpersonal relationships—than men. This characteristic of women seems to be a socially-patterned phenomenon, which sociologists (Parsons and Bales 1955) refer to as the expressive role of women, in contradistinction to the instrumental role which men universally are obliged to adopt.

Men seem to be much more skilled at impersonal, instrumental role-playing. But public health officials, very concerned about the sex differential in mortality rates, have been wondering what it is about being a man, which makes males die younger than females. Here in Florida, Dr. Sowder, chief of the state health department, has been carrying on a long-term, multifaceted research program which he has termed "Project Fragile Male." Do you suppose that there is any connection whatsoever between the disclosure patterns of men and women and their differential death rates? I have already intimated that withholding self-disclosure seems to impose a certain stress on people. Maybe "being manly," whatever that means, is slow suicide!

I think there is a very general way of stating the relationship between self-disclosure and assorted values such as healthy personality, physical health, group effectiveness, successful marriage, effective teaching, effective nursing, etc. It is this: A person's self is known to be the immediate determiner of his overt behavior. This is a paraphrase of the phenomenological point of view in psychology (Snygg and Combs 1949). Now if we want to understand anything, explain it, control it or predict it, it is helpful if we have available as much pertinent information as we possibly can. Self-disclosure provides a source of information which is relevant. This information has often been overlooked. Where it has not been overlooked it has often been misinterpreted by observers and practitioners through such devices as projection or attribution. It seems to be difficult for people to accept the fact that they do not know the very person whom they are confronting at any given moment. We all seem to assume that we are expert psychologists and that we know the other person, when in fact we have only constructed a more or less autistic concept of him in our mind.

If we are to learn more about man's self, then we must learn more about self-disclosure—its conditions, dimensions and consequences. Beginning evidence (Rogers 1958) shows that actively accepting, empathic, loving, nonpunitive responses—in short, love, provides the optimum conditions under which man will disclose, or expose, his naked, quivering self to our gaze. It follows that if we would be helpful (or should I say human?) that we must grow to loving stature and learn, in Buber's terms, to confirm our fellow man in his very being. Probably this presumes that we must first confirm our own being.

Summarizing Statements

1. Adjustment refers to what happens when a person faces the necessity for choice. The adjustment situation is comprised of the situation itself, a person's motivation, and his adjustive efforts. Anxiety is a usual part of the adjustive situation and it is how we cope with it that determines how constructive our adjustment is. Adjustment behavior is either task-oriented (constructive, realistic, and effective) or defense-oriented (directed at reducing anxiety).

2. When a person in an adjustive situation is blocked, it is called frustration. When he is caught between opposing motives, it is conflict. Conflict is more difficult to resolve than frustration.

3. The defenses are devices for protecting the self-image from information that would be devaluating. They are unconscious and irrational. Excessive defensiveness retards psychological growth and creates a distorted impression of reality.

4. Neurotic behavior is essentially self-defeating. The neurotic feels inferior and complains of various ailments. Often neurotic behavior reduces the anxiety present in the adjustment situation, although the behavior is self-defeating in the long run. However, it does represent, an attempted, although ineffective, adjustment. The defense mechanisms—for example, repression, rationalization, and denial—are used to cover up the inevitable adjustment failure by continued neurotic behavior.

5. Real or imagined physical illness is a prominent feature of much neurotic behavior. Illness can be exploited to regulate or control

the behavior of others, an example of secondary gain. Neurotic illness can be used as an unconscious excuse for failure. Sick people are not held to the same standards as everyone else. Neurotic use of illness, as an attempted adjustment, is probably encouraged unwittingly by society in various ways.

6. Psychoses are much more severe maladjustments than are neuroses, although probably the difference is just a matter of degree and not of kind. There is usually a complete break with reality in psychosis, noticeable impairment of both thinking and feeling, and a disorganization of the personality. Psychotics usually require hospitalization, but that is rarely necessary with neurotics. Psychotic behavior may reduce anxiety by producing alienation and withdrawal from adjustment situations that arouse anxiety.

7. A sociopathic personality lacks a conscience and the full range of emotions that most people possess. He may be produced by lack of love in infancy. He tends to get into trouble with society because he lacks a feeling of right and wrong. He may enjoy confidence games in which he sets out to win someone's trust and then deliberately violates it. A large proportion of prison inmates fit into one or another sociopathic category. The sociopathic personality makes a particularly dangerous politician.

8. Psychotherapy is a kind of planned intervention in a person's adjustive behavior. Most individual and group therapies are designed to generate insight into the causes of maladjustive behavior and change specific attitudes and habits, often involving an altered self-image and a discovery of one's true values. Behavior therapy is directed toward symptom removal and a manipulation of the reinforcers which sustain behavior.

READING SELECTION

9. If a person plays his roles adequately he can be regarded as having a more or less normal personality. But normal personality is not necessarily healthy. Healthy personalities not only play their roles adequately but also get satisfaction from them and manage to keep growing. A normal personality may fill the needs of society but still be absolutely miserable. People who have never been able to enact roles which can be rightfully expected of them must also be regarded as unhealthy.

10. Change of personality in a valued direction may be called growth. Self-disclosure to a therapist (or friend) often accompanies psychological growth. Some people may become "clients" in therapy because they have not disclosed themselves sufficiently to the people in their lives. Freud discovered that when patients disclosed their most secret and intimate thoughts to a therapist they got well.

11. In the playing of public roles a person sometimes becomes alienated from his real self. The alienated person identifies too much with public roles. Roles are inescapable and must be played competently or the social system will not work, but not at the exclusion of self. There must also be a chance for the person to be

himself and to know himself. Self-alienation is at the root of the "neurotic personality of our time."

12. Self-disclosure to a significant other is the means by which an alienated person can rediscover his real self. Maladjustive symptoms are seen as smoke screens between the patient's real self and the onlooker, devices to avoid becoming known to others and to self. In struggling to avoid being known by others, the person constructs a false public self.

13. Real-self-being is a necessary condition for healthy personality, making continued growth possible. "Full disclosure of the self to at least one other significant human being appears to be one means by which a person discovers not only the breadth and depth of his needs and feelings but also the nature of his own self-affirmed values."

14. The so-called expressive role of women seems more conducive to self-disclosure than the instrumental role of men. Jourard speculates that the differences in the tendency to disclosure between males and females has something to do with the higher death rates of males at all ages.

15. "Beginning evidence . . . shows that actively accepting, empathic, loving, non-punitive responses—in short, love—provides the optimum conditions under which man will disclose, or expose, his naked, quivering self to our gaze." We must learn to confirm our fellow man in his very being. To do that we must first confirm our own being.

Terms and Concepts

Adjustment: a process of change in oneself—or the environment—to obtain satisfaction for one's needs and to meet fairly well the physical and social demands of reality.

Behavior therapy: a type of psychoterapy characterized by its use of learning principles.

Client-centered therapy: a type of therapy derived from the thinking of Carl Rogers, characterized by its nondirective approach.

Compensation: a defense mechanism in which behavior leading to reward and success is substituted for that leading to punishment and failure; downgrading one's weak points and strengthening strong points.

Conflict: being caught between two antagonistic sets of motivation; retards or prevents goal attainment.

Conversion reactions: a type of neurosis, commonly called hysteria, characterized by the development of various simulated ailments, such as hysterical blindness, hysterical deafness, hysterical paralysis, or hysterical anesthesia.

Defense mechanism: an unconscious device which is designed to protect the established self-image—whether healthy or unhealthy—by some kind of self-deception.

Delusion: a serious misinterpretation of perceptual information, usually feelings of persecution.

Denial: a defense mechanism in which a person refuses to face the significance of unpleasant events; may consist of falsifying reality.

Displacement: a defense mechanism in which there is a shift of hostility, fear, or some other feeling from one person or object to a substitute.

Emotional insulation: a defense mechanism in which there is a blunting of emotional responsiveness in situations that might prove hurtful.

Fantasy: a defense mechanism in which imaginary accomplishments are used to compensate for reality.

Frustration: a feeling one gets when blocked and prevented from reaching a goal.

Functional psychosis: a psychosis arising out of experiences, primarily learned.

Hallucination: an imagined perception, usually found only among psychotics.

Healthy personality: according to Jourard, a person who plays the roles expected of him adequately, deriving satisfaction from them, and yet being capable of further growth. Distinguished from normal personality, which is merely playing roles adequately.

Hypochondria: a type of neurosis characterized by an exaggerated overconern about one's health.

Identification: a defense mechanism in which a person gets a feeling of increased worth or adequacy based on the accomplishments of someone else with whom he has empathy.

Intellectualization: a defense mechanism in which there is an overly intellectualized approach to coping, often accompanying emotional insulation, involving a cutting off of the ''emotional charge'' belonging to events.

Introjection: a defense mechanism in which attitudes, motives, and values are internalized with which the individual may not agree but which seem necessary for survival or status.

Neurosis: a learned pattern of self-defeating behavior, characterized by feelings of inferiority and various physical and psychological symptoms; developed as a means of coping with anxiety.

Organic psychosis: a psychosis caused by physiological malfunctioning or damage to the body.

Phobia: a type of neurosis characterized by a morbid fear.

Projection: a defense mechanism in which one's own unacceptable motivation is disowned and wrongly perceived in someone else's behavior.

Psychoanalysis: a type of psychotherapy developed by Sigmund Freud and practiced exclusively by M.D.s in the United States.

Psychosis: a severe mental illness that involves loss of contact with reality, personality disorganization, and extreme deviation from normal patterns of thinking, feeling, and acting.

Psychosomatic disorders: real physical ailments in which psychological events or causes are known to play a role.

Psychotherapy: a talking-out treatment for emotional disorders, conducted by a trained professional therapist; the patient's goal is to develop greater insight into and control over his own behavior.

Rationalization: a defense mechanism in which "good," plausible, but untrue reasons are offered for behavior; justifying behavior with logically possible reasons.

Reaction formation: a defense mechanism in which unacceptable attitudes and motives are repressed and on the conscious level attitudes and motives developed which are the exact opposite.

Regression: a defense mechanism in which there is a return to less mature behavior which brought satisfaction at an earlier age. A retreat to past security.

Repression: a defense mechanism in which threatening and anxiety-provoking information is forced out of mind and cannot be ordinarily remembered. Synonym: motivated forgetting.

Schizophrenia: a type of psychosis characterized by withdrawal, emotional blunting, disorganization of personality, hallucinations or delusions or both, and various physical symptoms.

Secondary gain: in illness the enjoyment of sympathy and attention. Tends to reinforce illness as a coping device.

Sociopathic personality: a type of maladjustment in which a person relates to others in an egocentric, callous, and manipulative fashion, often bringing him into conflict with society. He is usually incapable of normal love and affection and has no real loyalties. Because of his lack of commitment to people and society the sociopath often becomes a law breaker. This disorder is usually considered a defect of conscience development. Defective socialization.

Sublimation: a defense mechanism in which socially accepted substitute goals are accepted for sexual or other motives that are blocked.

Task-oriented adjustment: realistic and constructive adjustment.

Society itself is an accident to the spirit, and if society in any of its forms is to be justified morally it must be justified at the bar of individual conscience.

—*George Santayana,* Dialogues in Limbo

The final test of a leader is that he leaves behind him in other men the conviction and the will to carry on.

—*Walter Lippmann, "Roosevelt Has Gone"*

We do not really feel grateful toward those who make our dreams come true; they ruin our dreams.

—*Eric Hoffer,* The Passionate State of Mind

Groups, Leadership, and Movements

11

A WELL-ADJUSTED person is a person who is effective in coping with the life tasks he confronts. However, the individual lives in a social world, and effective coping often cannot be divorced from that. We function as individuals within social groups and organizations.

GROUPS

A group is a number of people acting together who have a common identity, a feeling of unity, common goals, and shared norms. Sherif & Sherif (1956) believe that people join groups for the whole range of individual motivations, from satisfaction of basic needs to achievement of prestige, distinction and power. Also, they note, by being a member of a group one can satisfy some motives that he could not satisfy otherwise. Belonging to a group may give a person a sense of belongingness he would otherwise lack, provide him with attitudes and values, social contacts, and activity, all of which may become part of his conception of himself (pp. 153–156).

Also, as we noted in Chapter 7, all of man's social motives, including his need to affiliate with others in groups, are probably rooted in biological need. In other words, participation in groups and movements satisfies very basic needs, which may be further enhanced by being associated with important group values.

Others suggest that two main classes of needs are satisfied by contact within groups: (1) needs such as approval, status, and recognition, which require the individual to be singled out and rewarded; and (2) needs that require the individual to be submerged in the group, giving up temporarily his individuality (Festinger, Pepitone, & Newcomb, 1952). In this case, the group may make it possible to satisfy some needs anonymously, through lessening inner restraints previously preventing certain kinds of behavior.

Cartwright & Zander (1968) make a distinction between motives that are *person-oriented*, such as the individual achieving prestige, distinction, and power through group activity, and motives that are *group-oriented*, such as those involved in loyalty to a political party, athletic team, or business firm. We may take pleasure in the satisfaction of group-oriented motives, even though individual motives are not involved. Indeed, sometimes our individual satisfactions may decline because of group involvement. The treasurer of a church, for example, may neglect his own business in volunteering to head up the church fund drive.

An individual often feels powerless to direct events toward his own advantage. Objectively, he often is powerless, because some achievements are beyond the efforts of individuals, but are possible with a group. The family is a good example. It is a miniature society with roles, role obligations or expectations, and norms. It also has leadership needs, goals, and a history of its own. As a group, the family is certainly more than just the sum of its parts. Some of man's most

basic needs, such as belongingness, relatedness, sex and companionship, seem to be most easily satisfied in a family situation.

In employment situations, organization creates different kinds of leverage. Belonging to a labor union gives one power he would otherwise lack; the group can bargain from a position of strength the individual rarely achieves. How effective is an unorganized worker's threat to withhold his services? Unorganized workers are almost always lower paid and less secure in their jobs than unionized workers.

Informal and Formal Groups

A social crowd, a delinquent gang, or a group of neighborhood boys are informal groups, organized around purposes or goals. The group of boys, for example, may come together with only play in mind but, as a result of their interaction, may develop *group-oriented* motivation affecting subsequent activity. Because one boy has access to a set of tools, someone may suggest that they build a club house. Although probably none of the boys would have built the club house alone, the combined group does.

Formal groups can be distinguished from informal ones by the extent to which group activities are structured. Many problems cannot be solved by groups possessing little organization. If you are concerned about the environment, for example, what can you do about it? There are, of course, some individual courses of action open to you. You can write to politicians letters complaining about specific abuses or encouraging various kinds of constructive legislation. You can point out to business people that you are aware of their part in the problem (the use of one-way bottles, indestructible plastic packaging, etc.). There are limits, however, to individual action; an organized group of

Groups can share (and usually do) grief and joy. Injury to one member can be a matter of personal concern to the other members.

An informal group.

ten people is far stronger than ten individuals. Like the family, a group is more than its parts. A small group of ecology-minded people, once organized, can talk up a problem, put it into proper perspective, lobby for better pollution standards, and share experiences with like-minded groups. A group can be a potent vehicle of "raising individual consciousness" about the problem. If the group can find a national umbrella for its activities by affiliating with similar groups, its combined influence can be multiplied.

Primary and Secondary Groups

A *primary group*, such as the family, is a group in which relationships are long-lasting and relatively permanent, and in which the members have a broad range of mutual rights and duties. You belong to a primary group because of *who you are*; the group is interested in you as a person. For most people, the primary group is the center of their psychological security and sense of identity. We are maximally involved emotionally in primary groups. A *secondary group*, such as a work group, is goal oriented, and the members play impersonal roles and can be replaced by one another. Such groups are interested in doing something and thus are interested in the individual only as a means to that end. Most organized groups are secondary groups, although primary relationships may become established, as in deep friendships. A group is organized when (a) its goals have been articulated or spelled out and (b) it has learned how to exercise influence on its members and its public.

Characteristics of Groups

Goals and norms.   Social norms are the rules or standards of behavior expected within the group. A person's role obligations are defined by the group's norms. A person playing the role of the leader, for instance, is expected to represent the group publicly, provide structure for it, and set and communicate its priorities. If group goals are satisfied during his period of leadership, he will probably be considered an effective leader.

In an ecology group, the goals might be (a) to promote recognition of the environmental crisis; (b) to organize the work of the group, and perhaps (c) to create a formal, secondary group with defined leadership roles, structure for communication and membership, and structured activities such as programs to promote changed behavior on the part of the public, including polluters.

The scope of appropriate activities for such a group depends on its norms. People tend to adhere to the group norms as described by the J-curve of conformity. Most members of groups (especially voluntary associations) conform to the agreed-on, shared norms. As Figure 11-1 shows, the majority of people stop at stoplights or conform to certain norms of driving behavior, and only a minority fail to stop. Similarly, the same example might be used to illustrate cheating among college students. Most students will be honest; some will take a slight dishonest advantage; a few will cheat flagrantly.

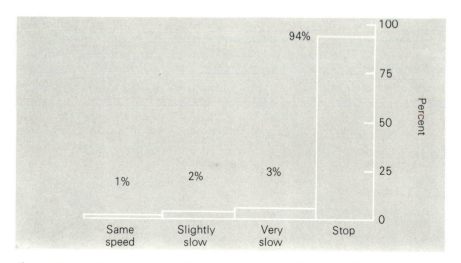

Figure 11-1.   Motorists' behavior at a stop sign. (Source: After M. Dickens' study, reported in Allport, F.H., The J-curve hypothesis of conforming behavior. Journal of Social Psychology, 1935, 5, 141–183.)

Communication.   An important aspect of group leadership is communication. The group's goals cannot be achieved (if they require sustained effort over time) unless the group has an adequate system of communication. In small groups most communication may be verbal and face to face, although there are often good reasons for keeping records such as minutes of meetings. Most larger groups find it useful to communicate by a published bulletin in order to convey the shared norms, values, and goals of the group, provide the leadership an avenue of structure, give dates and times of meetings and information about activities, and provide continuity, keeping before the members the names of leaders and candidates for leaders.

Communication is mediated by the group leadership. The chairman conducts the meetings, sets the agenda for discussion and debate, recognizes speakers, mediates disputes, and provides follow-through on any action the organization may undertake.

Unity.   A group's effectiveness depends on its cohesiveness or unity. If the membership is too diffuse while the group is being formed, it may not agree on goals and programs. To some extent, this problem can be offset by skillful leadership. Some people may make poor members of the group. It may be just as important to discourage disruptive and destructive people from joining as it is to recruit the membership as a whole. After a group is formed and its goals and norms established, selection of members becomes less of a problem. A highly unified group has a strong hold over its members and is thus likely to be successful in its work.

Morale.   The morale of a group is related to its unity. A highly unified group is likely to be task-oriented and successful, though increase in group unity is not always associated with increases in constructive results and work output. Sometimes a group unifies itself defensively around maintaining itself and is not task-oriented at all, much like an individual who adjusts defensively to personal problems. A highly unified group with high morale may turn inward, defending itself against real or imagined attack, and lose sight of its task-oriented goals. Some scholars believe that the morale of a working group is determined chiefly by conditions within the work situations itself, opportunity for promotion, conditions of work, quality of supervision, and the rewards for work accomplished (Katz & Hyman, 1947). Others believe morale comes from each person's feeling that he has made a real contribution to the group's achievement (Hoffman, Burke, & Maier, 1965). These remarks would apply mainly to formal, secondary groups; informal and primary groups, of course, would depend largely on the satisfaction of needs in close interpersonal relationships.

LEADERSHIP

He was a born leader; there is no other kind.

—*Thomas Heggen,* Mister Roberts

Every French soldier carries a marshal's baton in his knapsack.

—*Attributed to Napoleon Bonaparte*

Was Abraham Lincoln a great national leader because he was a great man, or because he was a man who rose to the challenge of his times? This question illustrates the main controversy in leadership research, the "great man" theory versus the situational or "man for the time" theory. Actually, some evidence supports each theory.

Great Man versus Situational Leadership

The great man theory generated a good deal of the early research into the traits of leadership, but the results were disappointing. Few traits have been found which generalize across different kinds of leadership situations. In some limited situations we might be able to produce lists of traits of leadership. For example, it might be possible to specify the leadership traits of the ideal combat infantry platoon leader, but these traits might differ from the traits characteristic of an effective garrison officer. The situation itself has come to be recognized as having important demands. Leading men into battle is very different from leading a voluntary organization whose members can depart if they are dissatisfied. Management leadership in a company run by a successful founder is likely to be very different from that found in a large, modern corporation stressing teamwork.

Situational theory, which provides the main stream of leadership research today, is concerned less with the leader as a man than with leadership as a functional relationship between people. A successful group, for example, may be one in which essential leadership functions are handled by *someone*, not necessarily always the same person. Bales (1952) has observed that every group has two main kinds of problems: (a) achieving a particular goal and (b) strengthening the group itself. People who come together in leaderless groups often tend to assign these two functions to two people. Thus, most groups have *task-oriented* leadership functions and *process-oriented* (or social) leadership functions. Often these two functions become specialized as separate roles (Fiedler, 1958).

Task-Oriented versus Process-Oriented Leadership

Task-oriented leaders are concerned with the work of the group, asking questions, giving information, getting things done, and implementing the goals of the group. They tend to be no-nonsense people, offering advice, making plans, and being generally instrumental in "getting on with things." Equally important, especially for morale, are the mediating or process-oriented leaders, who intervene in arguments, smooth ruffled feathers, and are tactful and concerned about people's feelings. In some ways, these two roles are like the male instrumental and the female social roles. It is rare for both of these functions to be filled by the same person. In forming a group, members might do well to try to find a pair of leaders who complement each other and who meet both functions.

Functions of Leadership

Leadership involves an exchange between the leader and his followers: the leader gives something—his skills, knowledge, and efforts—and gets something—prestige, status, and recognition. This exchange occurs in return for helping the group to achieve its goals and to become stronger.

If we are concerned with forming more effective groups to further our ends, we should ask how the leadership functions of these groups can be achieved. Such a question implies that leadership is not some mysterious quality possessed by only a few. Thibaut & Kelley (1959) put it thus: "any (and every) member of the group can be considered as exhibiting leadership insofar as he exercises power effectively, performs various functions, promotes organization along functional lines, or has symbolic value" (p. 289). An example of one performing various functions is one who performs needed work. One who promotes organization along functional lines is one who promotes organizational cohesiveness or is task oriented (both leader types fit here). An example of symbolic value would be the effect a person of high status might have on a group; for instance, if a United States Senator were a member of your church, perhaps you and other members would feel buoyed up and stronger as a result. In other words, some people might fill leadership functions just by consenting to be ordinary members. Cartwright & Zander (1968) echo a similar conclusion to that of Thibaut & Kelley in saying that "certain minimal abilities required of all leaders are widely distributed among non-leaders as well. Furthermore, the traits of the leader that are necessary and effective in one group or situation may

be quite different from those of another leader in a different setting''
(p. 303).

Can anyone be a leader? Perhaps not, but most people can learn
to play leadership roles. Consider the example of a young naval ensign,
just out of officer training, who was put in charge of shore patrol. On
his first night out, his unit encountered a large group of belligerent
sailors outside a bar. Fearful he would fail his first real test of leadership,
he suddenly asked himself, ''What would John Wayne do in a role
like this?'' He imagined Wayne as a cowboy sheriff climbing onto a
wagon, shouting authoritatively for order, picking out men he knew by
name, and asking them if they knew what they were doing. Being
singled out by name had a decidedly calming effect on the men. So he
did what he imagined an actor playing the role would do, and was
successful in averting a riot. This example also proves that every situation calls for slightly different kinds of leadership behavior.

A *leader*, then, *is one who assists a group in achieving its goals
by playing any one of several leadership roles.* Such roles or main functions
of leadership are (a) initiating organization and structure, (b) setting
group goals and priorities, (c) defining roles within the structure,
(d) mediating internal disputes, (e) acting as group spokesman, (f) facilitating decision making, (g) evaluating the progress of the group and
individual members, and (h) reinforcing successful role performance of
group members.

Power

  Power may be defined as the ability to achieve one's ends even against opposition. For a leader, power is the capacity to influence his group's members and the group's larger public. Group goals cannot be achieved unless people are successfully influenced. In the case of ecology, for instance, it is necessary to influence both the public and public officials to effect change.

  Recent research on leadership has focused on the subject of power. A leader of a voluntary group is in a different position from a dictator. To lead he must establish a mutually satisfactory exchange with the rank and file of his organization and fulfill their needs and expectations. One is not a leader because he *attempts* to influence people; his attempts must be accepted before he actually has any power. This is true even in some unlikely roles, such as leading men into battle; a combat officer must have the trust of his men to be effective, otherwise he may lead but not be followed.

Box 11-1   Training Leadership

  Can leadership be trained? Havron & McGrath (1961) reported success in training combat infantry squad members to assume leadership functions when the groups were deprived of their natural leaders.

> . . . Part of our effort was directed toward the development of a concept of leadership and a feeling of the need for good leadership in all members of the unit. Consequently, we set out early to impress trainers that the success and the very lives of combat-unit members are interdependent, that teamwork is required, that the careless mistake of one man can lead to disaster for the whole group. By both direct and indirect means we showed trainees that leadership was necessary, and that whatever the personality or capabilities of the leader, the leadership *function* must be properly performed (pp. 173–174).

  The observers found that the leadership frequently broke down in crisis situations when events occurred too quickly for the leader to assimilate them. Members were trained to offer suggestions for orders if they perceived situations the leader was not responding to, but the leader had to add his sanction to the order and know what was going on.

> Perhaps the most remarkable aspect of this training program was that it generated in the groups in question a concept of leadership that was appreciated, irrespective of who held that particular leader position. We have excellent validation of this statement. At the conclusion of the training program one test was administered which involved a mission in which the leader and his assistant were both "killed." The problem of the unit was to complete its mission. We tested 24 squads we had trained and another 24 Army-trained squads in this "leaderless" mission. We encountered a finding that is rare in sociopsychological data. There was no overlap in performance scores between the two groups. All of the squads trained by methods we had developed scored higher than any of the 24 Army-trained squads. . . . It was obvious to those who umpired both groups that in the Army-trained squads the members depended entirely upon the

leader to take initiative. As a result, once the formal leadership was withdrawn, the unit did a very poor job. On the other hand, in the squads trained by experimental methods, although both leader and assistant leader were removed and no one had been specifically designated as third leader, someone inevitably took over and the unit's performance on the mission was almost as good as the performance of those same squads when the leaders were present (pp. 174–175).

From Havron, M. D., and McGrath, J. E. The contribution of the leader to the effectiveness of small military groups. In L. Petrullo & B. M. Bass (Eds.), *Leadership and interpersonal behavior* (New York: Holt, Rinehart and Winston, 1961).

SOCIAL MOVEMENTS

Social movements are at once the symptoms and the instruments of progress. Ignore them and statesmanship is irrelevant; fail to use them and it is weak.

— Walter Lippmann, "Revolution and Culture"

A mass movement attracts and holds a following not because it can satisfy the desire for self-advancement, but because it can satisfy the passion for self-renunciation.

—Eric Hoffer, The True Believer

A social movement is, in the words of Theodorson & Theodorson (1969), "*a form of collective behavior in which large numbers of people are organized or alerted to support and bring about or to resist social change.*" Some aspects of social movements which distinguish them from other groups are as follows: (a) Their aim is to promote or resist change in society at large. (b) They are large-scale, persistent, but informal group efforts to effect or prevent change; many supporters do not join any organized segment of the movement but participate in various ways and constitute its public. (c) They are often effective in using the mass media to communicate with their loosely organized membership and public.

Some social movements of the last decade, according to this definition, are the civil rights and black power movements; the peace movement; the student, youth, hippie, and commune movements; the women's movement; and the ecology movement. All are examples of progressive movements, in that their adherents propose new goals and directions. Conservative movements, oriented toward maintaining things as they are, often develop in opposition to progressive movements. Reactionary movements advocate the restoration of a way of life already gone or a vision of past times which perhaps never really existed. The adherents to all three kinds of movements may base their ideologies on their interpretation of "fundamental American values." Not all movements are of this type. Expressive movements often simply ritually reaffirm common values; this is often the case with revivalistic religious movements.

A movement is less well structured than a group, and its leadership is more diverse. A movement may have many leaders, each representing various factions and approaches to action—in effect many groups having in common some few values. A modern mass movement relies on the press (often especially television) for its effect. Events publicized by the mass media may have an important impact, for to some extent the leaders of a large movement may be partly created by events, the response to those events, and subsequently the mobilization of the public. The press is not part of the movement, of course, but experience has taught movements how to dramatize their cases and how to create and use newsworthy events to advantage. For instance, the public response to the image of police dogs attacking peaceful, nonviolent demonstrators in the South during the early days of the civil rights movement was one of widespread sympathy and support.

Box 11-2 Nonviolence as a Goal

The late Rev. Martin Luther King, Jr., based his thinking about nonviolence on the thinking of Mahandas K. Gandhi, who in turn had been influenced by the American Henry Thoreau's theory of passive resistance. Before he successfully applied nonviolence in winning India's independence from Great Britain in 1947, Gandhi had formulated his nonviolent philosophy in an earlier struggle in South Africa. A key idea was that "in a well-regulated state, recourse to arms every now and then in order to secure popular rights would defeat its own purpose" (p. 38).

Nonviolence, or *Satyagraha*, as Gandhi called it, should be understood to mean truth (satya) born of love and firmness (agraha). Nonviolence is "the Force which is born of Truth and Love." Gandhi also described it as "soul force" because force of a physical sort was prohibited in all circumstances (p. 36). As Gandhi stated, "in *Satyagraha* there is not the remotest idea of injuring the opponent. Satyagraha postulates the conquest of the adversary by suffering in one's own person" (p. 39).

Many people find it difficult to understand that one's own suffering can cause change in his adversary and leave him more open to reconciliation and conversion. But these ideas have deep roots. Jesus said, "Whosoever shall smite thee on thy right cheek, turn to him the other also," and "Love your enemies, bless them that hate you, and pray for them which despitefully use you, and persecute you." Even if religious nonviolent action does not change the opponent's thinking, it contributes to undermining his supporters. As Sibley (1963) points out:

> In the theory of non-violence, particularly as expressed in the doctrine of non-violent resistance, it is emphasized that structures of power (governments, social organizations) always depend upon the voluntary cooperation of great numbers of individuals even when the structures seem to rely on physical force. The chief wielders of power, in other words, must have the assistance and cooperation of hundreds or even thousands of persons for the administration of physical force. The task of those who oppose a structure having physical force at its command is, therefore, to persuade hundreds of men to refuse any longer to cooperate with the tyrant or other administrator of violence. (p. 9).

After the 1955–56 bus boycott in Montgomery, Alabama, the Rev. King visited India and was impressed with how little bitterness was left over from the independence struggle. A few years after independence India became part of the Commonwealth, and the Indians and the remaining British got along with little conflict. Compare this situation to the long and bitter Algerian struggle for independence from France. The legacy of violence could affect Algerian-French relations for generations.

The goals of a movement are much more diverse too. Although the civil rights movement was rooted in the nonviolent philosophy of Gandhi and King, many people within the movement did not understand this religious philosophy of nonviolence. Even so, they accepted it as a tactic to be used as long as it worked.

For movements such as the Negro civil rights movement it is not enough for widespread frustration and hardship to exist; there must also be belief in the possibility of doing something about those conditions. As Hoffer (1951) notes, faith in the future and hope for change are necessary for movements to flourish. The leadership of a movement based on a need for greater social justice is most likely to come from those who are themselves relatively successful. For example, the modern-day leaders of Chicano youth groups are those who are most assimilated, best educated, and successful among their people. Similarly, leaders of the student movements represent the brightest and most successful among the student population.

Robert Censoni cartoon. Copyright © 1968 by *Saturday Review, Inc.* Reprinted by permission.

The Civil Rights Movement

The modern civil rights movement might be said to have started in 1960, when student Ezell Blair and his friends originated the sit-down demonstration. Or the movement might be traced back to the 1961 "freedom rides," the 1955 Montgomery bus boycott, to the 1954 U.S. Supreme Court ruling on school desegregation, or perhaps to Jamestown in 1619 when the first slave was brought to America. It is less important when it started than that it grew from a long history of oppression.

The 1955 Montgomery, Alabama, bus boycott started when a tired Mrs. Rosa Parks refused to yield her seat to a white person and move to the back of the bus. Her arrest prompted the Negro community to begin a walking boycott of the busses to demand Negro bus drivers, courteous treatment, and a first-come, first-served seating policy. Later, when the boycotters returned to riding the busses, it was under the instructions: "If cursed, do not curse back. If pushed, do not push back. If struck, do not strike back, but evidence love and goodwill at all times. . . ." The demands of the bus boycotters or "freedom walkers" soon changed to cover more ambitious goals as the blacks realized the power of their numbers. What started out as a protest against inconvenience soon grew into a national civil rights movement— a clear example of the relationship between issues and individual "consciousness of the problem." Many potential supporters of a movement start out with a low-level consciousness of the problem. But by participating in events, even if that participation is only psychological identification with the actors, they become increasingly conscious of the seriousness of the problem. The movement grows because of the effect of involvement, and its goals may become more general. As Toch (1965) puts it about the civil rights movement, "as the movement expanded, *the problem that inspired it had kept pace*" (p. 201).

Soon the movement became fragmented as various factions emerged stressing different goals, tactics, and leadership. What emerged as tactics of the movement were what actions seemed necessary to start change, then to continue it, then to speed it up. The modern activist movement, as represented by the Congress of Racial Equality, the Student Non-Violent Coordinating Committee, and The Rev. King's Southern Christian Leadership Conference, had grown up in reaction to an earlier movement that stressed the "gradualist" approach, as best represented by the National Association for the Advancement of Colored People. The NAACP had won several legal victories, the most important being the 1954 Supreme Court school desegregation decision, but in the early 1960s this approach seemed out of touch with the times.

The NAACP was an outgrowth of the Niagra movement, founded in 1905 by W. E. B. du Bois as a reaction to the earlier movement of Booker T. Washington, who, they believed, "had put economic progress before politics, had accepted the separate-but-equal theory, and opposed agitation and protest." As the Kerner Commission (1968) put it, "Du Bois and his followers stressed political activity as the basis of the Negro's future, insisted on the inequality of Jim Crow laws, and advocated agitation and protest" (p. 216). Each of these movements was a product of its time and each produced successor movements based on a revised consciousness of the problem and on new methods and tactics.

The modern civil rights movement began to fragment under the frustrations of the nonviolent philosophy. Many thought not enough was being accomplished, that racist attitudes prevented any real change in institutions. Thus emerged the black power movement, which cast aside the philosophy of nonviolence and advocated redress of grievances "by any means necessary." Black power groups, along with nationalist and separatist groups, also repudiated the chief goal of the civil rights movement of "full integration into American society" and talked of separate development of black and white races. The Black Muslims, a group stressing self-help, black pride, separatism, and nationalism, have said that they want partition of the United States, with blacks being given some states, and reparations for past injustices. Other separatists want a kind of Marshall Plan for economic development of the black ghettos. Some black power groups such as the Black Panthers have stressed the political development of the ghetto, as well as building alliances with other minority groups and sympathetic whites.

There is a kind of cyclic development of movement goals. The black power movement has "found again" many of the goals which guided Booker T. Washington. A mass movement has many philosophies and many leaders. In the long run, the civil rights struggle has room for the ideas of Washington, du Bois, King, Malcolm X, and Cleaver. They all have played a role.

The Women's Liberation Movement

The nineteenth-century feminist movement, founded in 1848 by Susan B. Anthony in Seneca, New York, was a campaign for "Votes for Women." Ironically, Seneca was not far from the place where approximately 250 years earlier, the first successful women's movement in the New World was established by Indian women at the *Iroquois Conference of Nations*.

> It was the women of the Iroquois tribes who fought what may have been the first successful feminist rebellion in the New World. The year was 1600, or thereabouts, when these tribal feminists decided that they had had enough of unregulated warfare by their men. Lysistratas among the Indian women proclaimed a boycott on love-making and childbearing. Until the men conceded to them the power to decide upon war and peace, there would be no more warriors. Since the Iroquois men believed that women alone knew the secret of birth, the feminist rebellion was instantly successful (Steiner, 1968).

The power of Indian women to decide such matters was undermined by the U.S. Government's failure to recognize these facts in dealing with the Indian nations. The government made all its treaties with the men, who, they thought, had the power. It was surprised when the treaties were not carried out. Eventually the power of the women declined.

The growth of the nineteenth-century feminist movement was spurred on greatly before the Civil War by its close association with the movement to abolish slavery, many of whose most prominent leaders

were women. The movement smoldered after the Civil War until the early twentieth century, when it became active again as a campaign for women suffrage, culminating June 1919 with the passage of the Nineteenth Amendment to the Constitution. With the right to vote won, the movement declined during the period between the World Wars, although the flapper era was a time of great emancipation of women from Victorian constraints and the sexual revolution can probably be dated from that time.

The women's movement in the United States has always been tied to the great issues and conflicts of history. It has flourished in times of war and at times when blacks were making greatest progress.

The resurgence of the modern women's movement began in the 1960s during the civil rights movement, which included numbers of women (such as Mrs. Rosa Parks). Soon, however, many women grew disenchanted with the Negro rights movement and its successors such as the black power movement. Some of the male civil rights workers, although attuned to one kind of injustice, were completely blind to another. Movement women complained that the men took them too much for granted, that women were allowed to make coffee and run mimeograph machines, but the important decisions were made without consulting them.

It was also becoming apparent that all women encountered dis-

Women earn less than men in all kinds of jobs

| Median annual earnings, full-time workers | | | Most women workers are in lower-paying jobs | | |
Occupation	Women	Men	People Employed as	Percent of all Women Workers	Percent of all Male Workers
Scientists	$10,000	$13,200	Proprietors, managers	4%	14%
Professional, technical	6,691	10,151	Professional, technical	15	14
Proprietors, managers	5,635	10,340	Craftsmen	1	20
Clerical workers	4,789	7,351	Factory workers	15	20
Sales workers	3,461	8,549	Clerks, sales workers	42	13
Craftsmen	4,625	7,978			
Factory workers	3,991	6,738	Service workers	16	7
Service workers	3,332	6,058	Household workers	6	Less than 1%

Source: United States Department of Labor, National Science Foundation data for 1968.

Source: United States Department of Labor.

crimination in employment and training. As the table shows, they average only two-thirds as much as men in comparable jobs and a higher percentage of women are in lower-paying jobs. They are also the most likely to be laid off in hard times. The widespread masculine prejudice, they discovered, was manifested in flagrant stereotyping by the mass media ("You've come a long way, baby!") and treatment by society in ways designed to infantilize them and make them content in dependent relationships. They also discovered a kind of cultural conditioning that systematically taught women to feel inferior and to doubt their intellect and competence.

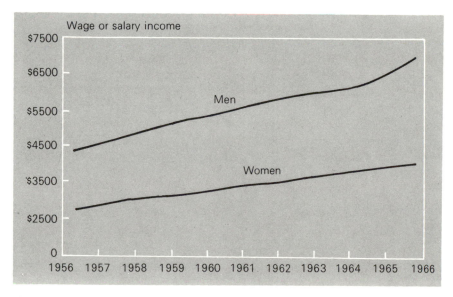

Figure 11-2. The earnings gap between women and men is widening—median wage or salary income of year-round full-time workers, by sex, 1956–1966. (Source: U.S. Department of Commerce, Bureau of the Census.)

There are at least four important goals of the women's movement:

(a) Women want an end to discrimination against them in employment, and equal pay for equal work.

(b) Middle-class women sense that work would provide them with greater meaning in life and they resent having to accept a homebound life-style because of the lack of child care centers, which would permit them to work more easily. Thus, they call for a nationwide system of such child-care centers and full tax credit for child-care costs involved in working.

(c) They want an end to the paternalistic system of cultural conditioning that teaches them to feel inferior and dependent. Like other minorities, they want to achieve a sense of control over their own fates and destinies.

(d) Many women are also demanding "control over their own bodies." They want to put an end to the double standard of sexuality, they want liberalized abortion laws, and they want a reexamination of the marriage and divorce laws and the customs that support them.

Like most other movements, the women's movement is composed of various factions, ranging from ultra-respectable business and professional women's groups, to middle-class groups like the National Organization for Women, to fringe groups such as "gay liberation." It is likely that the most conventional goals of the movement, such as the demand for equal opportunity in employment, will be accepted, or at least resisted less than the more radical goals. Some of the movement goals would, if implemented, require fundamental change in the social institution of the family and a radical reorganization of its power.

The Ecology Movement

Our survival as a race on this planet depends on our working out soon solutions to the most urgent problems of nuclear war, overpopulation, and environmental pollution. Paul Ehrlich, in the article to follow, makes it clear that these triple specters are actually related, in that failure to solve the ecological and population crises increases greatly the possibility of nuclear war.

There has seldom been a social movement in our country with fewer partisan overtones than that spawned by the present ecological crisis. Almost everyone who understands anything about it realizes that we must act immediately to end air and water pollution while we have something left to save. Ehrlich argues persuasively that it is population growth with which we must ultimately come to terms. As you read the article keep in mind that it was written in 1969.

DR. PAUL EHRLICH

Eco-Catastrophe!

[I]

THE end of the ocean came late in the summer of 1979, and it came even more rapidly than the biologists had expected. There had been signs for more than a decade, commencing with the discovery in 1968 that DDT slows down photosynthesis in marine plant life. It was announced in a short paper in the technical journal, Science, but to ecologists it smacked of doomsday. They knew that all life in the sea depends on photosynthesis, the chemical process by which green plants bind the sun's energy and make it available to living things. And they knew that DDT and similar chlorinated hydrocarbons had polluted the entire surface of the earth, including the sea.

But that was only the first of many signs. There had been the final gasp of the whaling industry in 1973, and the end of the Peruvian anchovy fishery in 1975. Indeed, a score of other fisheries had disappeared quietly from over-exploitation and various eco-catastrophes by 1977. The term "eco-catastrophe" was coined by a California ecologist in 1969 to describe the most spectacular of man's attacks on the systems which sustain his life. He drew his inspiration from the Santa Barbara offshore oil disaster of that year, and from the news which spread among naturalists that virtually all of the Golden State's seashore bird life was doomed because of chlorinated hydrocarbon interference with its reproduction. Eco-catastrophes in the sea became increasingly common in the early 1970's. Mysterious "blooms" of

previously rare microorganisms began to appear in offshore waters. Red tides—killer outbreaks of a minute single-celled plant—returned to the Florida Gulf coast and were sometimes accompanied by tides of other exotic hues.

It was clear by 1975 that the entire ecology of the ocean was changing. A few types of phytoplankton were becoming resistant to chlorinated hydrocarbons and were gaining the upper hand. Changes in the phytoplankton community led inevitably to changes in the community of zooplankton, the tiny animals which eat the phytoplankton. These changes were passed on up the chains of life in the ocean to the herring, plaice, cod and tuna. As the diversity of life in the ocean diminished, its stability also decreased.

Other changes had taken place by 1975. Most ocean fishes that returned to fresh water to breed, like the salmon, had become extinct, their breeding streams so dammed up and polluted that their powerful homing instinct only resulted in suicide. Many fishes and shellfishes that bred in restricted areas along the coasts followed them as onshore pollution escalated.

By 1977 the annual yield of fish from the sea was down to 30 million metric tons, less than one-half the per capita catch of a decade earlier. This helped malnutrition to escalate sharply in a world where an estimated 50 million people per year were already dying of starvation. The United Nations attempted to get all chlorinated hydrocarbon insecticides banned on a worldwide basis, but the move was defeated by the United States. This opposition was generated primarily by the American petrochemical industry, operating hand in glove with its

Reprinted from Ehrlich, P. Eco-catastrophe! *Ramparts*, September 1969, 24–28. © Ramparts Magazine, Inc., 1969.

subsidiary, the United States Department of Agriculture. Together they persuaded the government to oppose the U.N. move—which was not difficult since most Americans believed that Russia and China were more in need of fish products than was the United States. The United Nations also attempted to get fishing nations to adopt strict and enforced catch limits to preserve dwindling stocks. This move was blocked by Russia, who, with the most modern electronic equipment, was in the best position to glean what was left in the sea. It was, curiously, on the very day in 1977 when the Soviet Union announced its refusal that another ominous article appeared in Science. It announced that incident solar radiation had been so reduced by worldwide air pollution that serious effects on the world's vegetation could be expected.

[II]

Apparently it was a combination of eco-system destabilization, sunlight reduction, and a rapid escalation in chlorinated hydrocarbon pollution from massive Thanodrin applications which triggered the ultimate catastrophe. Seventeen huge Soviet-financed Thanodrin plants were operating in underdeveloped countries by 1978. They had been part of a massive Russian "aid offensive" designed to fill the gap caused by the collapse of America's bally-hooed "Green Revolution."

It became apparent in the early '70s that the "Green Revolution" was more talk than substance. Distribution of high yield "miracle" grain seeds had caused temporary local spurts in agricultural production. Simultaneously, excellent weather had produced record harvests. The combination permitted bureaucrats, especially in the United States Department of Agriculture and the Agency for International Development (AID), to reverse their previous pessimism and indulge in an outburst of optimistic propaganda about staving off famine. They raved about the approaching transformation of agriculture in the underdeveloped countries (UDCs). The reason for the propaganda reversal was never made clear. Most historians agree that a combination of utter ignorance of ecology, a desire to justify past errors, and pressure from agro-industry (which was eager to sell pesticides, fertilizers, and farm machinery to the UDCs and agencies helping the UDCs) was behind the campaign. Whatever the motivation, the results were clear. Many concerned people, lacking the expertise to see through the Green Revolution drivel, relaxed. The population-food crisis was "solved."

But reality was not long in showing itself. Local famine persisted in northern India even after good weather brought an end to the ghastly Bihar famine of the mid-'60s. East Pakistan was next, followed by a resurgence of general famine in northern India. Other foci of famine rapidly developed in Indonesia, the Philippines, Malawi, the Congo, Egypt, Colombia, Ecuador, Honduras, the Dominican Republic, and Mexico.

Everywhere hard realities destroyed the illusion of the Green Revolution. Yields dropped as the progressive farmers who had first accepted the new seeds found that their higher yields brought lower prices—effective demand (hunger plus cash) was not sufficient in poor countries to keep prices up. Less progressive farmers, observing this, refused to make the extra effort required to cultivate the "miracle" grains. Transport systems proved inadequate to bring the necessary fertilizer to the fields where the new and extremely fertilizer-sensitive grains were being grown. The same systems were also inadequate to move produce to markets. Fertilizer plants were not built fast enough, and most of the underdeveloped countries could not scrape together funds to purchase supplies, even on concessional terms. Finally, the inevitable happened, and pests began to reduce yields in even the most carefully cultivated fields. Among the first were the famous "miracle rats" which invaded Philippine "miracle rice" fields early in 1969. They were quickly followed by many insects and viruses, thriving on the relatively pest-susceptible new grains, encouraged by the vast and dense plantings, and rapidly acquiring resistance to the chemicals used against them. As chaos spread until even the most obtuse agriculturists and economists realized that the Green Revolution had turned brown, the Russians stepped in.

In retrospect it seems incredible that the Russians, with the American mistakes known to them, could launch an even more incompetent program of aid to the underdeveloped world. Indeed, in the early 1970's there were cynics in the United States who claimed that outdoing the stupidity of American foreign aid would be physically impossible. Those critics were, however, obviously unaware that the Russians had been busily destroying their own environment for many years. The virtual disappearance of sturgeon from Russian rivers caused a great shortage of caviar by 1970. A standard joke among Russian scientists at that time was that they had created an artificial caviar which was indistinguishable from the real thing—except by taste. At any rate the Soviet Union, observing with interest the progressive deterioration of relations between the UDCs and the United States, came up with a solution. It had recently developed what it claimed was the ideal insecticide, a highly lethal chlorinated hydrocarbon complexed with a special agent for penetrating the external skeletal armor of insects. Announcing that the new pesticide, called Thanodrin, would truly produce a Green Revolution, the Soviets entered into negotiations with various UDCs for the construction of massive Thanodrin factories. The USSR would bear all the costs; all it wanted in return were certain trade and military concessions.

It is interesting now, with the perspective of years, to examine in some detail the reasons why the UDCs welcomed the Thanodrin plan with such open arms. Government officials in these countries ignored the protests of their own scientists that Thanodrin would not solve the problems which plagued them. The governments now knew that the basic cause of their problems was overpopulation, and that these problems had been exacerbated by the dullness, daydreaming, and cupidity endemic to all governments. They knew that only population control and limited development aimed primarily at agriculture could have spared them the horrors they now faced. They knew it, but they were not about to admit it. How much easier it was simply to accuse the Americans of failing to give them proper aid; how much simpler to accept the Russian panacea.

And then there was the general worsening of relations between the United States and the UDCs. Many things had contributed to this. The situation in America in the first half of the 1970's deserves our close scrutiny. Being more dependent on imports for raw materials than the Soviet Union, the United States had, in the early 1970's, adopted more and more heavy-handed policies in order to insure continuing supplies. Military adventures in Asia and Latin America had further lessened the international credibility of the United States as a great defender of freedom—an image which had begun to deteriorate rapidly during the pointless and fruitless Viet-Nam conflict. At home, acceptance of the carefully manufactured image lessened dramatically, as even the more romantic and chauvinistic citizens began to understand the role of the military and the industrial system in what John Kenneth Galbraith had aptly named "The New Industrial State."

At home in the USA the early '70s were traumatic times. Racial violence grew and the habitability of the cities diminished, as nothing substantial was done to ameliorate either racial inequities or urban blight. Welfare rolls grew as automation and general technological progress forced more and more people into the category of "unemployable." Simultaneously a taxpayers' revolt occurred. Although there was not enough money to build the schools, roads, water systems, sewage systems, jails, hospitals, urban transit lines, and all the other amenities needed to support a burgeoning population, Americans refused to tax themselves more heavily. Starting in Youngstown, Ohio in 1969 and followed closely by Richmond, California, community after community was forced to close its schools or curtail educational operations for lack of funds. Water supplies, already marginal in quality and quantity in many places by 1970, deteriorated quickly. Water rationing occurred in 1723 municipalities in the summer of 1974, and hepatitis and epidemic dysentery rates climbed about 500 per cent between 1970–1974.

[III]

Air pollution continued to be the most obvious manifestation of environmental deterioration. It was, by 1972, quite literally in the eyes of all Americans. The year 1973 saw not only the New York and Los Angeles smog disasters, but also the publication of the Surgeon General's massive report on air pollution and health. The public had been partially prepared for the worst by the publicity given to the U.N. pollution conference held in 1972. Deaths in the late '60s caused by smog were well known to scientists, but the public had ignored them because they mostly involved the early demise of the old and sick rather than people dropping dead on the freeways. But suddenly our citizens were faced with nearly 200,000 corpses and massive documentation that they could be the next to die from respiratory disease. They were not ready for that scale of disaster. After all, the U.N. conference had not predicted that accumulated air pollution would make the planet uninhabitable until almost 1990. The population was terrorized as TV screens became filled with scenes of horror from the disaster areas. Especially vivid was NBC's coverage of hundreds of unattended people choking out their lives outside of New York's hospitals. Terms like nitrogen oxide, acute bronchitis and cardiac arrest began to have real meaning for most Americans.

The ultimate horror was the announcement that chlorinated hydrocarbons were now a major constituent of air pollution in all American cities. Autopsies of smog disaster victims revealed an average chlorinated hydrocarbon load in fatty tissue equivalent to 26 parts per million of DDT. In October, 1973, the Department of Health, Education and Welfare announced studies which showed unequivocally that increasing death rates from hypertension, cirrhosis of the liver, liver cancer and a series of other diseases had resulted from the chlorinated hydrocarbon load. They estimated that Americans born since 1946 (when DDT usage began) now had a life expectancy of only 49 years, and predicted that if current patterns continued, this expectancy would reach 42 years by 1980, when it might level out. Plunging insurance stocks triggered a stock market panic. The president of Velsicol, Inc., a major pesticide producer, went on television to "publicly eat a teaspoonful of DDT" (it was really powdered milk) and announce that HEW had been infiltrated by Communists. Other giants of the petro-chemical industry, attempting to dispute the indisputable evidence, launched a massive pressure campaign on Congress to force HEW to "get out of agriculture's business." They were aided by the agro-chemical journals, which had decades of experience in misleading the public about the benefits and dangers of pesticides. But by now the public realized that it had been duped. The Nobel Prize for medicine and physiology was given to Drs. J. L. Radomski and W. B. Deichmann, who in the late 1960s had pioneered in the documentation of the long-term lethal effects of chlorinated hydrocarbons. A Presidential Commission with unimpeachable credentials directly accused the agro-chemical complex of "condemning many millions of Americans to an early death." The year 1973 was the year in which Americans finally came to understand the direct threat to their existence posed by environmental deterioration.

And 1973 was also the year in which most people finally comprehended the indirect threat. Even the president of Union Oil Company and several other industrialists publicly stated their concern over the reduction of bird populations which had resulted from pollution by DDT and other chlorinated hydrocarbons. Insect populations boomed because they were resistant to most pesticides and had been freed, by the incompetent use of those pesticides, from most of their natural enemies. Rodents swarmed over crops, multiplying rapidly in the absence of predatory birds. The effect of pests on the wheat crop was especially disastrous in the summer of 1973, since that was also the year of the great drought. Most of us can remember the shock which greeted the announcement by atmospheric physicists that the shift of the jet stream which had caused the drought was probably permanent. It signalled the birth of the Midwestern desert. Man's air-polluting activities had by then caused gross changes in climatic patterns. The news, of course, played hell with commodity and stock markets. Food prices skyrocketed, as savings were poured into hoarded canned goods. Official assurances that food supplies would remain ample fell on deaf ears, and even the government showed signs of nervousness when California migrant field workers went out on strike again in protest against the continued use of pesticides by growers. The strike burgeoned into farm burning and riots. The workers, calling themselves "The Walking Dead," demanded immediate compensation for their shortened lives, and crash research programs to attempt to lengthen them.

It was in the same speech in which President Edward Kennedy, after much delay, finally declared a national emergency and called out the National Guard to harvest California's crops, that the first mention of population control was made. Kennedy pointed out that the United States would no longer be able to offer any food aid to other nations and was likely to suffer food shortages herself. He suggested that, in view of the manifest failure of the Green Revolution, the only hope of the UDCs lay in population control. His statement, you will recall, created an uproar in the underdeveloped countries. Newspaper editorials accused the United States of wishing to prevent small countries from becoming large nations and thus threatening American hegemony. Politicians asserted that President Kennedy was a "creature of the giant drug combine" that wished to shove its pills down every woman's throat.

Among Americans, religious opposition to population control was very slight. Industry in general also backed the idea. Increasing poverty in the UDCs was both destroying markets and threatening supplies of raw materials.

The seriousness of the raw material situation had been brought home during the Congressional Hard Resources hearings in 1971. The exposure of the ignorance of the cornucopian economists had been quite a spectacle—a spectacle brought into virtually every American's home in living color. Few would forget the distinguished geologist from the University of California who suggested that economists be legally required to learn at least the most elementary facts of geology. Fewer still would forget that an equally distinguished Harvard economist added that they might be required to learn some economics, too. The overall message was clear: America's resource situation was bad and bound to get worse. The hearings had led to a bill requiring the Departments of State, Interior, and Commerce to set up a joint resource procurement council with the express purpose of "insuring that proper consideration of American resource needs be an integral part of American foreign policy."

Suddenly the United States discovered that it had a national consensus: population control was the only possible salvation of the underdeveloped world. But that same consensus led to heated debate. How could the UDCs be persuaded to limit their populations, and should not the United States lead the way by limiting its own? Members of the intellectual community wanted America to set an example. They pointed out that the United States was in the midst of a new baby boom: her birth rate, well over 20 per thousand per year, and her growth rate of over one per cent per annum were among the very highest of the developed countries. They detailed the deterioration of the American physical and psychic environments, the growing health threats, the impending food shortages, and the insufficiency of funds for desperately needed public works. They contended that the nation was clearly unable or unwilling to properly care for the people it already had. What possible reason could there be, they queried, for adding any more? Besides, who would listen to requests by the United States for population control when that nation did not control her own profligate reproduction?

Those who opposed population controls for the U.S. were equally vociferous. The military-industrial complex, with its all-too-human mixture of ignorance and avarice, still saw strength and prosperity in numbers. Baby food magnates, already worried by the growing nitrate pollution of their products, saw their market disappearing. Steel manufacturers saw a decrease in aggregate demand and slippage for that holy of holies, the Gross National Product. And military men saw, in the growing population-food-environment crisis, a serious threat to their carefully nurtured Cold War. In the end, of course, economic arguments held sway, and the "inalienable right of every American couple to determine the size of its family," a freedom invented for the occasion in the early '70s, was not compromised.

The population control bill, which was passed by Congress early in 1974, was quite a document, nevertheless. On the domestic front, it authorized an increase from 100 to 150 million dollars in funds for "family planning" activites. This was made possible by a general feeling in the country that the growing army on welfare needed family planning. But the gist of the bill was a series of measures designed to impress the need for population control on the UDCs. All American aid to countries with over-population problems was required by law to consist in part of population control assistance. In order to receive any assistance each nation was required not only to accept the population control aid, but also to match it according to a complex formula. "Overpopulation" itself was defined by a formula based on U.N. statistics, and the UDCs were required not only to accept aid, but also to show progress in reducing birth rates. Every five years the status of the aid program for each nation was to be re-evaluated.

The reaction to the announcement of this program dwarfed the response to President Kennedy's speech. A coalition of UDCs attempted to get the U.N. General Assembly to condemn the United States as a "genetic aggressor." Most damaging of all to the American cause was the famous "25 Indians and a dog" speech by Mr. Shankarnarayan, Indian Ambassador to the U.N. Shankarnarayan pointed out that for several decades the United States, with less than six per cent of the people of the world had consumed roughly 50 per cent of the raw materials used every year. He described vividly America's contribution to worldwide environmental deterioration, and he scathingly denounced the miserly record of United States foreign aid as "unworthy of a fourth-rate power, let alone the most powerful nation on earth."

It was the climax of his speech, however, which most historians claim once and for all destroyed the image of the United States. Shankarnarayan informed the assembly that the average American family dog was fed more animal protein per week than the average Indian got in a month. "How do you justify taking fish from protein-starved Peruvians and feeding them to your animals?" he asked. "I contend," he concluded, "that the birth of an American baby is a greater disaster for the world than that of 25 Indian babies." When the applause had died away, Mr. Sorensen, the American representative, made a speech which said essentially that "other countries look after their own self-interest, too." When the vote came, the United States was condemned.

[IV]

This condemnation set the tone of U.S.-UDC relations at the time the Russian Thanodrin proposal was made. The proposal seemed to offer the masses in the UDCs an opportunity to save themselves and humiliate the United States at the same time; and in human affairs, as we all know, biological realities could never interfere with such an opportunity. The scientists were silenced, the politicians said yes, the Thanodrin plants were built, and the results were what any beginning ecology student could have predicted. At first Thanodrin seemed to offer excellent control of many pests. True, there was a rash of human fatalities from improper use of the lethal chemical, but, as Russian technical advisors were prone to note, these were more than compensated for by increased yields. Thanodrin use skyrocketed throughout the underdeveloped world. The Mikoyan design group developed a dependable, cheap agricultural aircraft which the Soviets donated to the effort in large numbers. MIG sprayers became even more common in UDCs than MIG interceptors.

Then the troubles began. Insect strains with cuticles resistant to Thanodrin penetration began to appear. And as streams, rivers, fish culture ponds and onshore waters became rich in Thanodrin, more fisheries began to disappear. Bird populations were decimated. The sequence of events was standard for broadcast use of a synthetic pesticide: great success at first, followed by removal of natural enemies and development of resistance by the pest. Populations of crop-eating insects in areas treated with Thanodrin made steady comebacks and soon became more abundant than ever. Yields plunged, while farmers in their desperation increased the Thanodrin dose and shortened the time between treatments. Death from Thanodrin poisoning became common. The first violent incident occurred in the Canete Valley of Peru, where farmers had suffered a similar chlorinated hydrocarbon disaster in the mid-'50s. A Russian advisor serving as an agricultural pilot was assaulted and killed by a mob of enraged farmers in January, 1978. Trouble spread rapidly during 1978, especially after the word got out that two years earlier Russia herself had banned the use of Thanodrin at home because of its serious effects on ecological systems. Suddenly Russia, and not the United States, was the *bête noir* in the UDCs. "Thanodrin parties" became epidemic, with farmers, in their ignorance, dumping carloads of Thanodrin concentrate into the sea. Russian advisors fled, and four of the Thanodrin plants were leveled to the ground. Destruction of the plants in Rio and Calcutta led to hundreds of thousands of gallons of Thanodrin concentrate being dumped directly into the sea.

Mr. Shankarnarayan again rose to address the U.N., but this time it was Mr. Potemkin, representative of the Soviet Union, who was on the hot seat. Mr. Potemkin heard his nation described as the greatest mass killer of all time as Shankarnarayan predicted at least 30 million deaths from crop failures due to overdependence on Thanodrin. Russia was accused of "chemical aggression," and the General Assembly, after a weak reply by Potemkin, passed a vote of censure.

It was in January, 1979, that huge blooms of a previously unknown variety of diatom were reported off the coast of Peru. The blooms were accompanied by a massive die-off of sea life and of the pathetic remainder of the birds which had once feasted on the anchovies of the area. Almost immediately another huge bloom was reported in the Indian ocean, centering around the Seychelles, and then a third in the South Atlantic off the African coast. Both of these were accompanied by spectacular die-offs of marine animals. Even more ominous were growing reports of fish and bird kills at oceanic points where there were no spectacular blooms. Biologists were soon able to explain the phenomena: the diatom had evolved an enzyme which broke down Thanodrin; that enzyme also produced a breakdown product which interfered with the transmission of nerve impulses, and was therefore lethal to animals. Unfortunately, the biologists could suggest no way of repressing the poisonous diatom bloom in time. By September, 1979, all important animal life in the sea was extinct. Large areas of coastline had to be evacuated, as windrows of dead fish created a monumental stench.

But stench was the least of man's problems. Japan and China were faced with almost instant starvation from a total loss of the seafood on which they were so dependent. Both blamed Russia for their situation and demanded immediate mass shipments of food. Russia had none to send. On October 13, Chinese armies attacked Russia on a broad front. . . .

[V]

A pretty grim scenario. Unfortunately, we're a long way into it already. Everything mentioned as happening before 1970 has actually occurred; much of the rest is based on projections of trends already appearing [*Ed. note: Remember this article was written in 1969*]. Evidence that pesticides have long-term lethal effects on human beings has started to accumulate, and recently [1969] Robert Finch [*former*] Secretary of the Department of Health, Education and Welfare expressed his extreme apprehension about the pesticide situation. Simultaneously the petrochemical industry continues its unconscionable poison-peddling. For instance, Shell Chemical has been carrying on a high-pressure campaign to sell the insecticide Azodrin to farmers as a killer of cotton pests. They continue their program even though they know that Azodrin is not only ineffective, but often *increases* the pest density. They've covered themselves nicely in an advertisement which states, "Even if an overpowering migration [sic] develops, the flexibility of Azodrin lets you regain control fast. Just increase the dosage according to label recommendations." It's a great game—get people to apply the poison and kill the natural enemies of the pests. Then blame the increased pests on "migration" and sell even more pesticide!

Right now fisheries are being wiped out by over-exploitation, made easy by modern electronic equipment. The companies producing the equipment know this. They even boast in advertising that only their equipment will keep fishermen in business until the final kill. Profits must obviously be maximized in the short run. Indeed, Western society is in the process of completing the rape and murder of the planet for economic gain. And, sadly, most of the rest of the world is eager for the opportunity to emulate our behavior. But the underdeveloped peoples will be denied that opportunity—the days of plunder are drawing inexorably to a close.

Most of the people who are going to die in the greatest cataclysm in the history of man have already been born. More than three and a half billion people already populate our moribund globe, and about half of them are hungry. Some 10 to 20 million will starve to death *this year*. In spite of this, the population of the earth will increase by 70 million souls in 1969. For mankind has artificially lowered the death rate of the human population, while in general birth rates have remained high. With the input side of the population system in high gear and the output side slowed down, our fragile planet has filled with people at an incredible rate. It took several million years for the population to reach a total of two billion people in 1930, while a *second two billion will have been added by 1975!* By that time some experts feel that food shortages will have escalated the present level of world hunger and starvation into famines of unbelievable proportions. Other experts, more optimistic, think the ultimate food-population collision will not occur until the decade of the 1980's. Of course more massive famine may be avoided if other events cause a prior rise in the human death rate.

Both worldwide plague and thermonuclear war are made more probable as population growth continues. These, along with famine, make up the trio of potential "death rate solutions" to the population problem—solutions in which the birth rate-death rate imbalance is redressed by a rise in the death rate rather than by a lowering of the birth rate. Make no mistake about it, *the imbalance will be redressed.* The shape of the population growth curve is one familiar to the biologist. It is the outbreak part of an outbreak-crash sequence. A population grows rapidly in the presence of abundant resources, finally runs out of food or some other necessity, and crashes to a low level or extinction. Man is not only running out of food, he is also destroying the life support systems of the Spaceship Earth. The situation was recently summarized very succinctly: "It is the top of the ninth inning. Man, always a threat at the plate, has been hitting Nature hard. It is important to remember, however, that NATURE BATS LAST."

Summarizing Statements

1. Men form groups because of the whole range of individual motivations and because in joint action many goals can be achieved that are beyond individual men. Group-oriented motives arise out of the interaction within the group. Groups may be highly structured, like voluntary organizations, or barely structured at all, like a group of neighbors engaged in a common task. A distinction was made between formal and informal groups, and between primary and secondary groups. Groups require leadership to accomplish their goals. Group activity may be necessary to "raise individual consciousness about a problem."

2. Organized groups develop ideology or social norms in which role obligations are set out, goals articulated, and tactics agreed on. Most members of groups (especially voluntary associations) conform to the agreed-on, shared norms.

3. All but the smallest groups need lines of communication between the group's leadership and its membership. A published bulletin may be the best way of communicating the shared norms, values, and goals of the group.

4. A group's morale is related to its sense of unity. If the group is highly task-oriented and the members have a sense of successful accomplishment, morale is likely to be high. To some extent, unity depends on the group's ability to agree on its goals, values, and tactics.

5. The "great man" theory of leadership postulates that "personality traits" distinguish leaders from non-leaders. Few traits have been found that generalize across different kinds of leadership situations. The "situational leadership" theory postulates that the situation itself has important demands on those who play leadership roles. Situational theory has led research into uncovering the functions of leadership.

6. Every group has two main types of problems: (a) achieving particular goals and (b) mediating the group process itself. Most groups require both task-oriented leadership, which is primarily instrumental in achieving its goals, and process-oriented leadership, which is concerned with people interacting in a group setting. These roles are very much like the male instrumental role and the female social role found in the traditional family.

7. Leadership is not some mysterious quality only possessed by a few. Any group member exhibits leadership when he exercises power effectively, performs leadership functions, promotes the organization along functional lines, or has symbolic value to the group. Often the functions of leadership are organized into well-defined leadership roles.

8. The main functions of leadership that need to be satisfied, but not necessarily by one leader, are: (a) initiating organization and structure, (b) setting group goals and priorities, (c) defining roles within the structure, (d) mediating internal disputes, (e) acting as group spokesman, (f) mediating the social-emotional processes of the group, (g) evaluating the progress of the group and individual members, and (h) reinforcing successful role performance of group members.

9. A group's leadership must learn to exercise power, both in influencing members of the group and the group's larger public. Group goals depend on influencing people successfully. Leadership involves a transaction. The membership must accept the leader's attempts to influence before he gains the power to carry out his role.

10. It is possible to train members to recognize the functions of leadership in their group and to assume that leadership in the absence of the group's regular leaders.

11. Social movements are informal, loosely organized groups aimed at promoting or resisting change in society. Supporters may or may not be members of organized groups. The need for communication between mass movements and their public is largely met by the mass media.

12. Movements are less structured than groups and have many more leaders. Movements are partly coalitions of more formally organized groups, plus unattached supporters. A mass movement may include many partially conflicting ideologies and tactics.

13. During the late 1950s, the civil rights movement followed the philosophy and tactic of nonviolent direct action. Movement goals enlarged from requesting minor adjustments in the pattern of segregation to demanding an end to the entire racist system of race relations, as individuals became more and more aware of the depth and severity of the problem. This change in understanding may be called "consciousness raising."

14. The leaders of progressive movements tend to come from the brightest, least-disadvantaged elements of the movement. Movements feed on the belief that change not only is necessary, but also is a real possibility. Those who feel hopelessly downtrodden seldom revolt.

15.   The goals and leadership issues of the modern civil rights move-
      ment were traced backward in time to predecessor movements and
      forward to the emergence of the black power movement.

16.   The civil rights movement's history can be traced backward in
      terms of goals, issues, and tactics to several previous movements:
      the NAACP, the Niagra movement, and the movement of Booker
      T. Washington. The black power movement emerged as the civil
      rights movement began to fragment under the frustrations of its
      nonviolent philosophy.

17.   The modern women's movement is aimed at: (a) ending job
      discrimination against women, (b) changing attitudes of both
      masculine superiority and feminine inferiority, and (c) altering the
      relationship between man and woman so as to promote genuine
      equality between the sexes.

18.   Women, like other minorities, are striving to achieve a sense of
      control of their own destinies and to end their passive and depen-
      dent status.

READING SELECTION

19.   Paul Ehrlich discusses what the world will be like in a few years
      if present trends in environmental destruction continue. The
      agricultural "food chain" depends on a proper ecological balance
      between birds, animals, rodents, insects, fish, and plants. Destruc-
      tion of any element in a food chain may cause a catastrophic im-
      balance that destroys many others. "Eco-catastrophe" describes
      the most spectacular of man's attacks on the systems which sustain
      his life.

20.   Use of pesticides has polluted the entire planet, including the sea.
      Along the California seashore, bird life is dying out because of the
      use of chlorinated hydrocarbon pesticides, which interfere with
      the birds' reproduction. Red tides are destroying fish life. Other
      mysterious "blooms" of previously rare microorganisms are in-
      creasing. Many species of animals and fish are facing extinction
      directly at the hands of man.

21.   The bird predators that control rodents are being destroyed by
      pesticides made to control insects. Meanwhile, the insects are
      developing immunity. Eventually the rodents will multiply un-
      checked. The "pesticide treadmill" can only end in widespread
      crop failure and starvation.

22.   Pesticides are also involved in the problem of air pollution. In the
      future chlorinated hydrocarbons will become a major constituent
      of air pollution in all American cities, causing huge increases in
      death from hypertension, cirrhosis of the liver, liver cancer, and
      many other diseases.

23.   The world population, which took several million years to reach
      2 billion in 1930, will have doubled by 1975. The population curve
      is rising so steeply that it is only a matter of time before worldwide
      starvation is commonplace. Today half the world is hungry, and
      10 to 20 million will die of starvation this year. Meanwhile, the
      average American family dog consumes more protein in a week
      than the average Indian does in a month.

24. Three inevitable "death rate solutions" to the population imbalance—plague, thermonuclear war, and famine—all become more likely as population growth continues. The imbalance of birth over death rates will be redressed.

Terms and Concepts

Consciousness raising: a sense of increasing understanding about a social problem by the individual as a result usually of being involved in the activities of a social movement.

Group: a group is a number of people acting together, who have a common identity, a feeling of unity, common goals, and shared norms.

Ideology: "a set of related beliefs held by a group of persons." "The ideology of a social movement is a statement of what the members are trying to achieve together, and what they wish to affirm jointly." The movement is defined by its ideology.—Toch (1965, p. 21)

J-curve of conformity: a curve shaped like a "J" which states that most members of groups conform to the agreed on, shared norms of the group.

Leader: one who assists a group in achieving its goals by playing any one of several leadership roles. The two main types are task-oriented and process-oriented. Main function of leadership: (a) initiating structure in group, (b) setting group goals and priorities, (c) defining roles within the structure, (d) mediating internal disputes, (e) acting as group spokesman, (f) facilitating decision making, (g) evaluating group progress, and (h) reinforcing successful role performance of group members.

Power: the ability to secure one's own way or achieve one's ends even against opposition; power implies the capacity to influence others successfully.

Primary group: a group in which relationships are long lasting and relatively permanent and in which the members have a broad range of mutual rights and duties.

Process-oriented leader: a leader who deals with the social and emotional problems of the group.

Satyagraha: an Indian word for nonviolent resistance, meaning the truth (*satya*) that is born of love and firmness (*agraha*); also "soul force."

Secondary group: a group that is goal oriented, in which members play impersonal roles and can be replaced by one another.

Social movement: a form of collective behavior in which large numbers of people are organized or alerted to support and bring about or resist social change.—Theodorson & Theodorson (1969)

Social norms: rules or standards of behavior expected within the group. The role obligations of members are defined by its norms. The scope of appropriate activities depend also on the group's norms.

Social role: "an organized pattern of behaviors expected of the individuals who perform certain functions in the group. All groups define roles and, through expectancies, see that roles are performed." —Sanford (1970, p. 537)

Task-oriented leader: a leader who is primarily work oriented and instrumental in helping the group achieve its goals.

No man can reveal to
you aught but that
which already lies half
asleep in the dawning
of your knowledge.

—Kahlil Gibran, "On Teaching"

The machine does not
isolate man from the
great problems of
nature but plunges him
more deeply into them.

—Saint Exupéry, Wind, Sand,
and Stars

The only way to predict
the future is to have the
power to shape the
future.

—Eric Hoffer, The Passionate
State of Mind

Today and Tomorrow

12 THIS final chapter describes some developments on the frontiers of psychology. First we will be concerned with the relatively new field of environmental psychology. The term "environment" has traditionally referred to influences on the individual arising outside himself— usually social factors. Only recently has interest turned to the physical environment—for example, how space, design, and architecture may influence the social development of a person. Territoriality, crowding, and spatial factors all influence social behavior. Next we shall consider the psychology of the immediate future, which, with computers, teaching machines and educational technology, and the exciting new field of bio-feedback, offers the prospect of strikingly new styles of individuality. Finally, the inspired science fiction of George Leonard's *Education and Ecstasy* reveals prospects for a more humanistic education of our children just beyond the immediate future.

THE PSYCHOLOGY OF TODAY

> *As crowds increase we build our forts of inattention, and the more we talk the easier it is to mean little and listen not at all.*

—*Frank Moore Colby, "Simple Simon"*

Territoriality and Crowding

Earlier we noted that ritual fighting among lower animals served constructive purposes, such as ordering relationships—that is, establishing a social dominance hierarchy, a pecking order—and lessening conflict. Ritual fighting is often a feature of *territorial behavior*. The need to establish territorial control is a near-universal feature of all animal life. Among animals, aggression tends to be limited, except when they are hunting for prey, to a few situations. Ritualized aggres-

sion serves to spread out individual animals (or groups of social animals) of the same species on the available territory, thus permitting control of the food supply to best advantage of all. Submission to aggression also provides protection to weaker members of the species who tend to be either very young or old.

Among some animals, territorial aggression varies according to how near or far they are to the center of their territory. Lorenz (1966) describes how among some species of fish the winner of a ritual fight can be predicted by the distance each is from the center of his territory.

> If we know the territorial centers of two conflicting animals, such as two garden redstarts or two aquarium sticklebacks, all other things being equal, we can predict from the place of encounter, which one will win: the one that is nearer home.
>
> When the loser flees, the inertia of reaction of both animals leads to that phenomenon which always occurs when a time lag enters into a self-regulating process—to an oscillation. The courage of the fugitive returns as he nears his own headquarters, while that of the pursuer sinks in proportion to the distance covered in enemy territory. Finally the fugitive turns and attacks the former pursuer vigorously and unexpectedly and, as was predictable, he in his turn is beaten and driven away. The whole performance is repeated several times till both fighters come to a standstill at a certain point of balance where they threaten each other without fighting.
>
> The position, the territorial "border," is in no way marked on the ground but is determined exclusively by a balance of power . . . (p. 33).

When an animal stakes out a territory he is insuring an adequate supply of food, opportunity for sex and reproduction, and security in which to raise his young. If the number of animals or groups of animals becomes excessive for the resources of the territory, many aspects of life may become disrupted. Crowding does not affect behavior directly but produces effects that do. To some extent feeling crowded depends on what has been customary in the past.

The main effect of crowding among animals in a natural environment is, for low-ranking animals, to cause them to die off. They do not get enough food or reproduce successfully. Crowding produces stress that affects all animals' biological functioning. When animals respond adversely to stress they seem to age prematurely and to suffer deterioration of many important internal organs. Under stress an early death from exhaustion of the adrenal gland is common. Also, reproductive behavior is severely inhibited.

Calhoun (1962) observed that severe overcrowding in a population of rats in an experimental environment resulted in a spectacular drop in population, even when there was adequate food. Normal social relationships became disrupted, and grossly abnormal behavior patterns emerged. Females were unable to carry pregnancies to full term or to provide adequate maternal care of the young if birth occurred. Infant mortality rates soared. Disturbed behavior among males ranged from homosexuality to cannibalism, from frantic overactivity to extreme passivity. Disturbed males sometimes became active only when most of the rats were asleep.

Calhoun concluded that these effects were produced both as a result of overcrowding, which created a *behavioral sink*, and territorial behavior, which caused overcrowding in the first place. As Figure 12-1

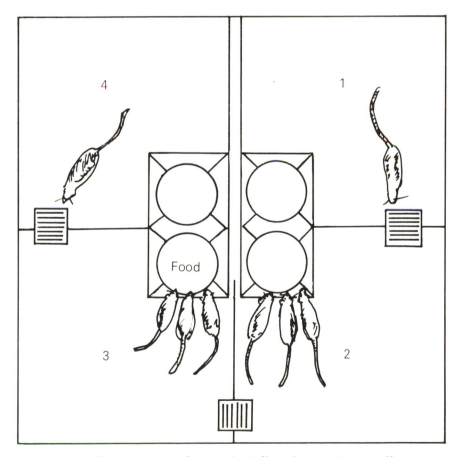

Figure 12-1. **Living quarters for rats in Calhoun's experiment. All pens are interconnected except pens 1 and 4. The crowding and group arrangements tend to promote the development of a behavioral sink in pens 2 and 3. Crowding does not occur in the end pens (1 and 4) because dominant males have established territorial control. The behavioral sink results in widespread development of abnormal behavior and extremely high mortality rates. (After Calhoun, 1962).**

shows, in pens 1 and 2, where the behavioral sink developed, individual rats would not eat—and there was starvation amid plenty—unless other animals were present. (They had been conditioned to eat socially, although this was not a deliberate feature of the experiment.) This behavioral sink might be seen as a kind of unhealthy togetherness that tended to disrupt other essential activities such as courting, nest building, nursing, and the care of the young. When a behavioral sink developed, infant mortality ran as high as 96 percent.

In Calhoun's experiment, some dominant males were able to establish control over certain territory (pens 1 and 4 in the figure), creating a harem of many females and excluding all other males except those in abject submission to them. The females who lived in these territories displayed normal behavior, and infant mortality rates were also normal. In the behavioral sink, there was an excess of males who had left the end pens and been prevented from returning by the dominant males. Calhoun explained that the behavioral sink developed in the middle pens because of the spatial arrangements of the eating troughs. Since these pens were overcrowded the rats were reinforced (classical conditioning) when they ate in the presence of other rats. They became

accustomed to social eating and would not eat alone at other places. Near the end of the experiments, most animals were sleeping as well as eating in the sink area. More and more crowding required more and more extreme adjustments. In some cases, animals were unable to get to the food while others were feeding. After a while, these animals often gave up and starved. When the other animals retired to rest, they did likewise, even though they easily could have eaten. Calhoun's study illustrates the basic importance of the spatial environment in promoting or disrupting normal social behavior.

There is evidence that overcrowding affects human behavior comparable to the way it affects rats. It is well known that the rates of most major diseases are much higher in the slums than elsewhere. Crowding affects both the physical and mental health of slum residents. It affects some diseases directly, especially the communicable ones. However, the strictly psychological effects of crowding on humans have not yet been studied much.

A study of students in an experimental environment (Skolnick et al., 1971) compared a highly crowded "urban" environment (8 square feet per person) to an uncrowded "nonurban" environment (16 square feet per person). In the crowded environment, social behavior broke down, people were selfish, territorial aggression developed, hoarding and theft occurred, and the members of the group would not organize to further their common interests. In the uncrowded condition, social organization occurred at the outset of the experiment. The group engaged in joint activities throughout, and there was no aggressive territorial behavior, stealing, or hoarding. The uncrowded people amused themselves in talk and games—mostly absent in the crowded condition. The crowded group accumulated a great amount of trash and became oblivious to it; in fact, they astonished observers with their ability to adapt to pollution. The uncrowded group organized a detail to pick up and dispose of trash. Interestingly, although the people in the crowded experiment were free to leave at any time, only one subject out of 87 did. None of the 14 subjects in the uncrowded environment left.

Davis (1971) points out that there are several ways to reduce the ill effects of crowding among humans. "The information about the social organization of animals," Davis says, "indicates the importance of stability; indivduals must be fully aware of their position in an organization." Well-defined social organization, in other words, can lessen the disorganizing effects of crowding. Studies of the behavior of prisoners of war have shown that well-organized prisoner groups were much more resistant to institutional reactions such as apathy and psychological withdrawal (Biderman, 1963).

Another important factor is the size of the group: large groups produce less social behavior than small groups. It is commonplace to observe that people in large cities have fewer strong social attachments than residents of smaller towns. Perhaps in cities there is less possibility for stable organization to develop, and most people remain strangers to one another. Just as human organization started with small bands, where everyone was appreciated for his individuality, perhaps people still function best this way. As group size increases, people tend to deal with others in more formal and ritualized ways. Thus, we become more impersonal. Clearly, we face a big discrepancy between placing a *value* on each person's individuality and being able to *behave* in a personally responsive way.

Sivadon (1965) observes that certain vistas are anxiety-producing. In discussing the Palace of Nations in Geneva, he notes that "it had become clear to us that a corridor longer than 40 meters, even if well lit, was anxiety producing if it had no shelter or better yet, side exits." Personnel working at the palace reported an abnormally high frequency of depression. The usual response by architects is to say that one simply has to get used to his environment; however, Sivadon concludes that people can hardly be expected to learn to overcome suffering caused by space and design that induce insecurity. Environmental psychology is turning to the study of the relationship of function to design and architecture.

Sociofugal and Sociopetal Space

Osmond, a physician, (1957) observed that most hospitals, like railway stations, seemed designed to keep people apart. Osmond called such arrangements of space *sociofugal*. Other space, like the arrangements of tables in French cafes, seemed designed to bring people together. He called this space *sociopetal*.

Osmond noticed that the arrangement of dayroom furniture in his hospital was an example of a sociofugal seating pattern: the chairs were put directly up against the wall, making social interaction among the patients difficult. He also noticed that a newly constructed women's ward seemed to make patients withdrawn and depressed. A study revealed that the patients had no space to call their own, no private *territory*, except their beds. Osmond equipped recreation rooms with small, square tables with chairs arranged intimately around them, thus facilitating social communication. Patients were also given small bedside tables, and dayroom seating was no longer lined up against the wall. At first, the patients resisted attempts to convert sociofugal into sociopetal space, but eventually spatial arrangements were instituted which promoted interaction. A count then revealed that the number of conversations had doubled and the amount of reading had tripled.

**Box 12-1   Should Library Space Promote Privacy
or Social Interaction?**

Osmond's work (1957) illustrates the importance for a hospital of using space to bring people together. Not all design should be sociopetal, however. The *function* of the space should always be considered.

Sommer (1966) studied the use of space at a university library. He found that the library patrons who arrived first tended to stake out places at one or the other end of long tables (seating 12). Generally, the patrons would all sit at end spots at separate tables until every table had at least one occupant. Seats occupied by the next round of arrivals tended to be at the other ends of the tables. The seat directly alongside the first occupant and those opposite him were rarely occupied at all unless the number of library users became very large.

Library patrons displayed various kinds of territorial behavior to protect their privacy.

... Physical objects, such as coats, handbags, books, personal belongings ... are used to mark out individual territories. A table space can be defended by position, posture, territorial markers, or some combination of the three. These are more than academic considerations as indicated by librarians' complaints about room capacity lowered by empty chairs, "staked out" by students occupied elsewhere.

Sommer concludes that:

The ideal library would not be one with all individual study rooms or all open areas but, instead, would contain a diversity of spaces that would meet the needs of introverts and extroverts, lone students and group studiers, browsers and day-long researchers. It is a serious mistake to assume that all people have the same spatial needs. . . .

Gregariousness as well as privacy has a place in a library serving as a community resource.

Institutionalized Reactions

Goffman (1961) has analyzed the way "total institutions" like mental hospitals train their inmates to play institutional roles that are incompatible with the prime goals of recovery and release. For example, giving patients institutional haircuts, issuing them coarse hospital uniforms, or denying them most personal possessions all make staff work easier but make recovery less likely. In time, patients become demoralized, dependent, and depressed. These procedures are assaults on the patient's individual dignity. A patient's long-term residence in such an institution tends to produce apathy or untraining "which renders him temporarily incapable of managing certain features of daily life on the outside, if and when he gets back to it" (p. 13).

Observers such as Maxwell Jones (1953) have commented on the nontherapeutic effect of the medical status system on patient recovery. The most prestigious are psychiatrists, psychologists, psychiatric nurses, and social workers, who have spent the most time in being educated to work with patients. Less prestige is accorded to staff such as regular nurses, physical therapists, and technicians, and still less to the attendants, aides, practical nurses, and food service and custodial personnel. But the irony of modern hospital practice is that it is precisely those with the least training who spend the most time interacting with patients. Psychiatrists, psychiatric nurses, and psychologists often find themselves saddled with administrative responsibilities. Because of high patient-doctor ratios, for every hour a psychiatrist spends with patients, attendants will chalk up thousands of hours.

The professionalism of most staff positions creates increasing barriers to communication between patients and staff. Most professionals are middle class and bring middle-class biases and expectations to their work. A prime aspect of professionalism implies an ability to control one's working conditions and relationships with others. Professionals usually do not punch time clocks, and they have considerable freedom of action to define their duties and responsibilities. They are often more concerned with their status among their colleagues than with the institutional goals. An untrained aide may be more prepared in his attitude to carry out certain service functions for mental patients than a nurse, whose definition of her professional role may prevent her doing work not clearly related to medical matters.

Box 12-2   The Medical Status System as Revealed in the Doctor-Nurse Game

Stein (1967) has written about a status game that doctors and nurses play out with one another that poses a serious obstacle to meaningful communication. The game involves a kind of mutual deception in regard to information and recommendations about the condition of patients and what is needed to assist their recovery. A doctor has the ultimate responsibility for *all* treatment recommendations, but often he is not in the same position to know needed information, compared to his nurse, on which treatment should be based. The nurse's game involves communication of treatment recommendations to doctors without seeming (a) to undermine medical authority, which is reserved to doctors, or (b) to ruffle masculine dignity by being overly assertive (most doctors are men and most nurses are women, so the game is also made necessary by sexist prejudice).

The object of the game is as follows: the nurse is to be bold, have initiative, and be responsible for making significant recommendations, while at the same time she must appear passive. This must be done in such a manner as to make her recommendations appear to be initiated by the physician. . . .

The cardinal rule of the game is that open disagreement between the players must be avoided at all costs. Thus the nurse must communicate her recommendations without appearing to be making a recommendation statement. The physician, in requesting a recommendation from a nurse, must do so without appearing to be asking for it. Utilization of this technique keeps both from committing themselves to a position before a sub rosa agreement on that position has already been established. In that way open disagreement is avoided. The greater the significance of the recommendation the more subtly the game must be played.

Why is the game played? Stein says medical school training builds up an unreasonable attitude in most students about making mistakes; in fact, it is an outright phobia. The way any person manages a phobia is to avoid the source of the fear. Here the result is that "the physician develops the belief that he is omnipotent and omniscient, and therefore incapable of making mistakes." Stein notes that physicians have an extraordinarily high fatal-accident rate as private plane pilots. Their rate is four times as high as the average of other private pilots. He cites a Federal Aviation Agency official who attributes the high death rates of doctors to flying with "the feeling that they are omnipotent." Apparently they take too many unnecessary risks. Thus, as Stein points out, "the extremes to which the physician may go in preserving his self-concept of omnipotence may threaten his own life."

Nurses are trained all along to respect the doctor, to do his bidding as if he were infallible, and to avoid making any remark that would reflect on his competence. Nurses learn early that making direct recommendations to a doctor may be seen as insulting or belittling.

The rewards for game players are considerable. Each defines the other as good. To the doctor, a "good" nurse is one who can carry off the game without damage to the doctor's ego. To the nurse, a "good" doctor is one who picks up the subtle communications about what is to be done *and* orders that it be done.

Stein believes that the game is stifling, anti-intellectual, and neurotic and that game players are not likely to be able to function effectively in a mental health setting, especially in a truly therapeutic community.

The Therapeutic Community

According to the concept of the therapeutic community, formulated in England by Maxwell Jones (1953, 1968), every detail of the total environment in a mental hospital should be organized into a continuous program of treatment. Some part of every patient is well and, as Kraft (1966) points out, all institutional resources should be focused on that part to promote recovery. The total environment as a therapeutic community should become a school for living.

When patients are institutionalized for long periods, they often become withdrawn, uninterested in social activities, careless of their appearance, and childishly quarrelsome. However, many of the symptoms of chronic mental illness are produced not by illness but by reactions to prolonged institutionalization itself. These symptoms are referred to as *institutional apathy*. Proponents of therapeutic community have argued that these symptoms would disappear if patients were treated humanely within each aspect of the total environment. The growth of the community mental health movement is also largely a

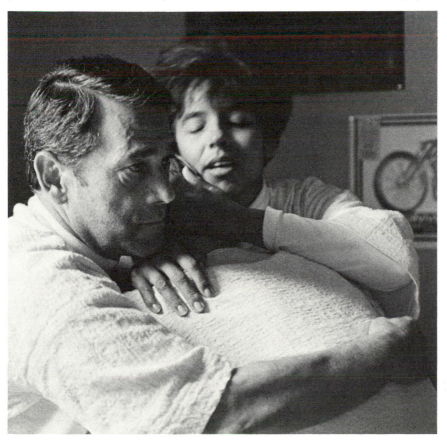

Therapeutic communities can involve heated encounters between members.

response to widespread recognition of the difficulty in treating patients therapeutically in mental institutions.

The main goals of the therapeutic community are to promote the patient's recovery and to prevent institutional reactions. All kinds of supportive therapy commonly used in most mental hospitals are employed: work therapy, recreation, physical therapy, and group and individual psychotherapy. In a therapeutic community, however, patients are involved as a matter of principle in the planning of hospital activities. Such planning and decision making is often just as therapeutic as the activities themselves. A functioning therapeutic community restructures staff and patient roles. Patients assist less well-integrated patients and promote their own recovery by being involved in meaningful activities. The therapeutic community encourages self-government in order to promote the patients' responsibility for their own welfare.

Both patients and staff members make decisions that would ordinarily be made by medical authorities. The patient is given maximum opportunity to participate in decision making. Even the medical status system itself may come into question. The traditional authority relationships in medicine have encouraged the patient to rely on others rather than on himself. In therapeutic communities, authority is vested in the group.

A therapuetic community is usually composed of at least an entire ward of patients and its staff. In its daily meetings the group sets rules of conduct for the ward. It evaluates the progress of patients, perhaps suggesting that a patient is well enough to take a furlough or make a visit to his home. It may discuss another patient's reaction to medication, suggesting modification of his dosage.

In the main, the therapeutic community idea has produced an enthusiastic response where it has been possible to really implement it. It does make people anxious who resist questioning their professional roles, but it focuses our attention on neglected aspects of treating the mentally ill.

PSYCHOLOGY OF THE FUTURE

We have the power to make this the best generation of mankind in the history of the world—or to make it the last.

—John F. Kennedy, address, United Nations General Assembly, September 20, 1963.

The danger of the past was that men became slaves. The danger of the future is that men may become robots.

—Erich Fromm, The Sane Society

Computers

The age we live in might well be known to the future as the age of computers. The high-speed computer is already revolutionizing human society in the developed world, and today man is on the threshold of developing new computers with unprecedented capacities. It is likely that computers of the future will be able *to learn* to do things they were never programmed to do. Kahn & Wiener (1967) predict that:

> By the year 2000, computers are likely to match, simulate, or surpass some of man's most "human like" intellectual abilities, including perhaps some of his aesthetic and creative capacities, in addition to having some new kinds of capabilities that human beings do not have (p. 84).

The speed of computer development has been astounding. Computer capabilities have increased tenfold every several years since their introduction. It is likely that computers of the future will be radically different from those of today. They will undoubtedly have improved sensory facilities or inputs, so that human communication with them, both oral and written, can occur in ordinary language. It is likely too that they will be equipped not only with visual capabilities of the human sort but also telescopic and microscopic vision and receptors for many other kinds of sensing. Computers will probably display "artificial intelligence" of the highest sort. These developments are happening very quickly. Even today computers have been programmed to recognize analogies (considered a high-level intellectual skill), use information gained in learning to solve new problems, and ask pertinent questions of its human operators when more information is needed to solve a problem (Kahn & Wiener, p. 89). Computers are already linked up with sensors and outputs at remote locations. In the future, it is likely that private homes will be connected in various ways in vast computer complexes.

Most business operations will be controlled by computer, including credit and banking, trading, inventory control, market analysis, and analysis of consumer tastes. Medical diagnosis will be computerized, with automatic laboratory analysis and recordkeeping. Central storage of a patient's medical record will facilitate treatment, as each physician will have access to the entire medical file of each patient. Weather prediction and control will be done by computer.

Box 12-3   Teaching Machines, Programmed Instruction,
and Computer-Assisted Instruction.

A teaching (or learning) machine is a device for presenting carefully programmed instruction in the most individualized way for each learner. Programmed instruction differs from ordinary instruction in a number of ways: (a) *Individualized instruction* offers the student the opportunity to interact with the instructor (the program) in a one-to-one relationship. Unlike the conventional class lecture, it seeks to use "feedback" from the student to govern the course of instruction. (b) *Knowledge of results* provides the student with feedback at each step in the learning process. Errors are quickly corrected by this process and only correct responses are learned. (c) *Student-paced instruction* permits the student to determine the rate of instruction, and the program only advances when the student has demonstrated understanding of previously presented material by answering questions successfully. (d) *Branching* is a flexible process that permits adept students who master the material to progress quickly. It is also appropriate for students who need extra review or remedial instruction; they are "branched" off into special material designed to ensure their mastery of the material.

O. K. Moore's learning machine, discussed in Chapter 5, is a computerized electric typewriter used to teach reading and writing by the "discovery" method. The child, in playing with the machine, "discovers" that spoken words and sounds are composed of letters and that letters can be represented by marks on paper. This "talking typewriter" has a number of remarkable capacities: it talks, listens, presents pictures and graphs, comments and explains, presents information, and responds to the child's typed inputs. It represents one of the most advanced applications of feedback control of human learning yet devised. The talking typewriter, however, only does what its human programmer has programmed it to do. Its adaptiveness is limited.

Computerized teaching machines of the future will be both more adaptive and more flexible. They will be able to learn from experience, something they cannot now do. As a result, they will be able to reprogram themselves to do things not anticipated by their builders. Like a live tutor, they will be able to think. If a student makes an error, the machine will diagnose the difficulty and branch him off into remedial material, which will correct that deficiency. A totally flexible program, approaching the one-to-one ideal of a teacher on one end of a log and the student on the other, becomes possible. Every student will get a tailor-made course of instruction. Failure will become obsolete, mistakes will be corrected immediately, and everyone will learn. The lower ability students, who today fail, will be educated to fairly high levels of subject matter comprehension. In a sense, the effective intelligence of the entire population will be raised dramatically. Even people with severe mental deficiencies will be given enough training so that most of them will be able to manage their own lives instead of being institutionalized, as they are at present. It is difficult to imagine what these developments will mean for the gifted. The saying, "training always increases individual differences" will probably continue to apply. High IQ performance, however, may be obscured by the superior performance of ordinary people who have been well trained by machines.

Educational Technology

The most probable application of computer development to psychology is in education and communication. The accumulated knowledge of mankind will all be stored in vast computer-connected libraries. A person will be able to select any printed book ever published from his own home-computer work station. The material may be displayed on a screen or printed out electronically. Teaching will probably be affected greatly because much of the routine imparting of knowledge will be presented by computer-controlled teaching machines right in the home. Unlike the "Model T" teaching machines of today, these sophisticated machines will be able to present courses tailor-made to each individual's capacities and curiosities. This will effectively guarantee that every student will master almost all the relevant information he needs or wants. These machines will truly converse with each student. The kind of failure in learning that today results in a student's becoming a dropout will be unknown in the future. Formal education as we know it is likely to be transformed; lifetime learning will be fully accepted as a necessity by much of the population. Indeed, in many occupations even today, trained people discover that they need frequent refresher courses just to keep up with the knowledge in their fields.

Communications will be revolutionized. As people become able, via computer and television screen, to draw on knowledge located at distant sources, many of the reasons for concentration of the population in huge cities may disappear. People will be able to live almost anywhere, yet still feel involved in the activities of city life. Wired television will probably replace broadcast television because of the tremendous increase in channel capacity and picture quality it offers. Cable TV is the first step in this direction. Perhaps the most important capacity of wired television is that it is not limited to one-way transmission. Wired television can carry "audience feedback" back to the program source. Public opinion polling could be combined with many public affairs programs. Advertisers and politicians will be able to find out quickly whether their appeals have succeeded. Wired television could offer an almost limitless number of channels simultaneously. Special programming for very small audiences will be possible. Wired television also makes selective blanketing possible: Programs might be directed to a particular area, or just to a particular occupation or interest group. Public meetings could be directed just to the sets in the areas within the political boundaries concerned. Indeed, the feedback possibilities could make possible audience participation in many events such as lectures and public meetings. The distinction between the wired television set and the telephone has already begun to disappear. Some meetings, conferences, and conventions are transmitted both in picture and sound. Group psychotherapy could be conducted in the same way. Coding devices could be employed for such programming to prevent nonmembers from eavesdropping.

Self-Control of Behavior Through Bio-Feedback

Research is being conducted with biological feedback (biofeedback) systems offering the prospect of controlling many of the body's physiological systems. Previously it was an article of faith that these systems were completely under involuntary control. It has long been known that special patterns of brain waves (measured by the electroencephlograph) were characteristic of people asleep, others of people in the normal waking state, and still others of people in intense concentration. But it was not known until recently that if these patterns were fed back through vision or hearing to the person generating them, he could sometimes control them. It did not take long to make the added discovery that most people could learn to control many of the so-called involuntary systems—if the feedback was efficient enough. Soon there were reports of alpha training (a type of brain wave associated with tranquility), learning to "drive your own heart," cooling or warming feet and hands, lowering blood pressure, and so on. At present, it is an open question how many of the supposedly involuntary functions can be brought under control of the conscious mind. Attempts are in progress to control spastic colon, epileptic seizures, anxiety symptoms, muscle tension, and the rate of urine formation by bio-feedback training.

Bio-feedback explains some things that have long puzzled mankind. The great magician Harry Houdini astounded people by his ability to escape from locked chains while enclosed in a sealed coffin immersed in water. Houdini always submitted to search before hand to

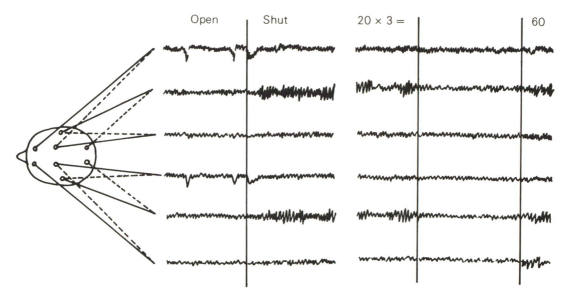

Figure 12-2. Typical record showing alpha brain waves produced by electroencephalographic measurement. Electrodes are placed on the head at the places indicated. The brain waves characteristic of light sleep and the normal waking state—varying from 8 to 13 cycles per second—are called *alpha* waves. *Theta* waves, not shown here, are characteristic of deep sleep and vary from 4 to 8 cycles per second. Bio-feedback devices are currently being used to establish conscious self-control of both alpha and theta waves. Typically, an auditory device delivers a changing tone which deepens as the mind generates more and more waves of the alpha frequency. Many people seem to be able to learn how to induce alpha and the calm state associated with it. The phases illustrated in the drawing: alpha with eyes open; alpha with eyes shut; alpha suppression during a math problem; alpha subsequent to giving the answer.

assure his audience that he did not have a key. Actually, the locks could not be unlocked without a key. Houdini concealed a key by swallowing it and keeping it suspended in his throat. Normally a person could not prevent the gagging reflex that would expel the object. But somehow Houdini had learned control over this supposedly involuntary reflex. As soon as the coffin was sealed, he recovered the key and began his escape.

Indian mystics have long baffled us with their apparent ability to achieve a state of suspended animation. Some of them have been able to survive being buried alive for long periods of time. Normal oxygen requirements would seem to make survival under such conditions impossible. Recently, however, this ability has been demonstrated under conditions of strict scientific control. In one carefully documented demonstration shown on television, a mystic was sealed in a special chamber where most of his important physiological systems could be monitored. His consumption of oxygen dropped after he went into the trance to about one-fourth of what scientific experts had claimed was the absolute minimum to sustain human life. Apparently, the mystic had learned to control heart rate, respiration, and many other biological functions.

The possibilities are staggering. It is likely that in the future physicians will teach patients with heart trouble to lower their blood pressure, thereby controlling or averting heart attack. Psychotherapists will be able to teach overanxious patients to control their alpha rhythms to achieve the calm state correlated with alpha. People who wish

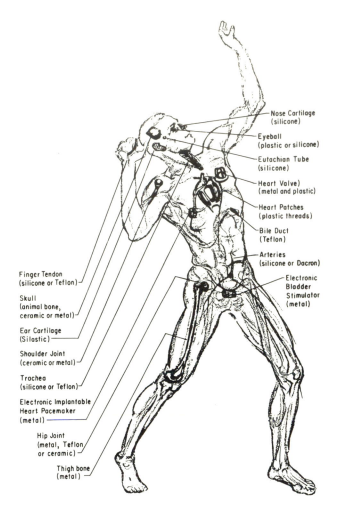

Nose Cartilage
(silicone)

Eyeball
(plastic or silicone)

Eutachian Tube
(silicone)

Heart Valve)
(metal and plastic)

Heart Patches
(plastic threads)

Bile Duct
(Teflon)

Arteries
(silicone or Dacron)

Electronic
Bladder
Stimulator
(metal)

Finger Tendon
(silicone or Teflon)

Skull
(animal bone,
ceramic or metal)

Ear Cartilage
(Silastic)

Shoulder Joint
(ceramic or metal)

Trachea
(silicone or Teflon)

Electronic Implantable
Heart Pacemaker
(metal)

Hip Joint
(metal, Teflon
or ceramic)

Thigh bone
(metal)

Man-made man. Copyright © 1971 by *The Futurist.* **Reprinted by permission.**

instant meditation will be able to achieve it. Patients who suffer from sexual impotence or frigidity will be taught by bio-feedback to achieve appropriate sexual stimulation.

Barbara Brown, former chairman of the Bio-Feedback Research Society, has speculated (in Rorvik, 1970) that bio-feedback will be used in the future in fields as diverse as athletics "to practice away from the practice field," appetite control, and the prevention and control of various psychosomatic ailments. Bio-feedback may find application in controlling a wide variety of heart troubles, "particularly tacchycardia, brakycardia, extra systoles and auricular flutter." It will find application in controlling high blood pressure and the related effects of coronary attack, strokes and kidney problems. It will be used in psychotherapy to control the disabling effects of fear and anxiety. Muscular tension can also be regulated, offering the possibility of control of muscle spasms without drugs, and perhaps the indirect control of artificial limbs by alternate feedback routes.

"Man-made man" is an illustration from the field of biomedical engineering. It indicates that broadscale replacement of defective human parts will become commonplace in the future. What of man's social progress? Harrington (1962) observed, "If there is technological advance without social advance, there is, almost automatically, an increase in human misery." The shape of the future must be different, but whether for better or worse will depend upon our capacities for devising good social or cultural fits to the technological advances we have made. In conclusion, we turn to some well informed but inspired speculation about education in the next century.

In the book's last reading selection we take a look at what might be a giant step forward in man's psychological evolution, based on a change in spirit, or, in our language, in his basic values and motivation. George Leonard discusses imaginatively many of the same developments in teaching machines, computers, and communications which have been covered in this chapter.

Leonard also examines man's attitudes, values, and motives. A prime goal that education can set for itself, he believes, is to return control of man to himself, "to encourage rather than stifle awareness," and "to help people become truly responsive and therefore truly responsible." Leonard makes a forceful case that the schools have reinforced a model of man who is narrow, cooly detached in his destructive competitiveness, eager to stockpile materialistic possessions he does not use, and mindlessly aggressive in pursuing these goals. "The first thing schools can do," he says, "to reduce narrow competition, eager acquisition, and aggression is to stop teaching them."

In "We Find Johnny," Leonard speculates about how education in the year 2001 has come to grips with these concerns.

GEORGE B. LEONARD

We Find Johnny

M Y children, I'm happy to say, are in the first generation that will feel no pressure whatever to get a college degree. As a matter of fact, after the age of ten they may never again attend a separate, formal, degree-granting educational institution. This is not to say that they will stop learning. On the contrary, they will be free to begin a lifetime of learning in a society dedicated to education.

Even in my parents' day, the distinction between college and "real life" had begun to blur, with millions of people engaged in what was then called "adult education," and millions of students dropping in and out of school. The sealed-off four years that once were college began breaking up; no longer was it possible to keep the academy separate from the community. Increasingly, the university became a study-work-recreation center for everyone. It offered various types of "membership," ranging from full-time participation to subscription to a university news service received in the home on electronic consoles. The fast, effective flow of information via computer-mediated networks made decentralization possible, and the unwieldy giants of higher education began breaking down into smaller units.

At the same time, learning environments outside the traditional university proliferated and flourished. Laymen set up their own institutes, schools, research centers. Industries and businesses realized that their real business was learning and the spread of learning. The family unit, it came clear, was basically an educational unit. Parents began consciously designing the home as an environment in which to learn.

From *Education and Ecstasy* by George B. Leonard. Copyright © 1968 by George B. Leonard. Reprinted by permission of the publisher, The Dial Press.

College degrees had become rather meaningless by the time I reached my teens: they were just too commonplace; there was so much learning going on outside of college; and the emphasis in education had turned from extrinsic to intrinsic satisfactions. The old hassles over admissions, processing and graduation had created the need for top-heavy administrative staffs. With these hassles greatly diminished, administration could be reduced, and educators and researchers could get on with education and research. Universities, unique and highly decentralized, still do exist, but not apart from the rest of the community. They are taking their place among a growing number and diversity of learning environments.

More and more communities, including Santa Fe, have begun limiting free, tax-supported education to the ages from three through ten. A sort of apprenticeship system is developing for older children. After ten, children can move from one learning environment to another, whether it be a formal school or not. Various financial arrangements are evolving, with the learner or his parents generally paying a small amount to the learning environment. After apprenticeship, the learner might receive pay for the same activity he previously had been paying for.

The Renaissance author of *The City of the Sun*, Tommaso Campanella, provided a curious piece of historical foresight when he imagined that "boys are accustomed to learn all the sciences, without toil and as if for pleasure; but in the way of history only until they are ten." If we read "history" as "all that is already known," and "science" as "research and lifelong learning," we may say that we are at last coming close to that utopian goal.

. . . We continue our casual search for Johnny. The Quiet Dome is smaller than the

Basics Dome and made of a translucent, milky-white material. Perhpas Johnny will be there, practicing the omega-form meditation he has recently been learning. We leave our shoes in one of the racks that line the entrance and push our way in through three separate sets of heavy, sound-absorbing curtains. Inside, we step onto a spongy floor that floats free from the earth on hydraulic mounts.

Just as the Basics Dome shocks the senses with an initial overload of stimuli, the Quiet Dome shocks with the lack of them. All of the interior materials absorb sound, and batteries of deep, conelike sound deadeners line the inner wall six feet up all the way around. A number of nondirectional speakers pour out a gentle flood of white sound (like that of a distant waterfall) which suffuses the space, just as does the pale, directionless light. A faint odor of balsamic incense neutralizes the sense of smell. Everything is neutral, directionless, without dimension.

We look around for Johnny, but in vain. So we sit for a while amid scores of children and a few parents, shedding the exterior world like a superfluous garment. Almost immediately, a fantasy takes form in my consciousness. It is not easy to put into words. I am in a sort of column of force, slowly ascending to another level where I move into another column and so on. It is a delicious if somewhat awesome feeling, and I simply experience it for a while. Then I shift from an experiential to a problem-solving mode of consciousness. Perhaps I can apply the fantasy to a concept of interfamily communications. *Imagine that the family members exist on different levels; that they can communicate deeply only when they join, even temporarily, on a common level; that there is only a discrete number of "columns"—maybe only one—between each level; that the members cannot communicate while en route from level to level.* I go on conceptualizing, not really getting anywhere, but enjoying myself.

And then I get a strong signal—you might call it "extrasensory"—from my wife that she wants to go on looking for Johnny. I turn to her and nod and we exchange the rather knowing smile that sometimes celebrates this particular form of intimacy. We leave, stepping past children locked in silence and contemplation. While meditation is encouraged everywhere on the school grounds, especially outdoors among the trees and flowers, the Quiet Dome is available always, good weather or bad. Kennedy [School] educators consider it necessary that the learner be free to retreat, to

take a stand within himself. He can then re-enter the world of active learning enriched by new inner connections.

We walk on to the Water and Body Domes. These domes are joined together about halfway up, creating two interconnected circular areas inside. One of the areas contains a free-form swimming pool; the dome above it slides open to the sun. The other area is a gymnasium and dance floor. The pool, we find, is fairly crowded with nude children. I comment on how many of the very youngest are in the water.

"Yes," my wife adds. "Will says that every single new three-year-old could swim by Christmas."

There are no adults in the pool—no "lifeguard," no "instructors." The older children take full responsibility for the younger, helping them learn to swim and otherwise handle themselves in the water. As Will points out, it would be practically impossible for any of the newcomers to drown. The older children have developed their empathy, their awareness of others, to a high state. There is no higher educational goal.

Over in the gym and dance area, two educators are always on hand to counsel learners about the all-important relationship between the body—its posture, tension, movements and coordination—to everything else in life and learning. A group of about ten children of various ages is dancing near the center of the floor. An educator watches as they express their feelings, in sequence, toward each member of the group, using physical movement only. When they finish, the educator will give verbal feedback on what has happened, if any child should ask. More important, he will help them pick up the feedback from their own bodies. He will help them realize how movement may alter perception.

Children at the far edge of the dome are learning to control their muscle tension, blood pressure, heart rate, peristalsis and the like. They are aided in this by quite simple Body Feedback (BF) devices that have been in use for decades. To reduce muscle tension in the neck, for example, the child sits, attaches electrodes with suction cups on either side of the neck and puts on earphones. As the tension relaxes, the tone in his earphones becomes lower in pitch. The child merely concentrates on lowering the pitch. When he does so, the muscles are relaxed. Similar sound feedback is provided for each of the body functions being educated. Two eleven- or twelve-year-old post-grads monitor the BF devices and help children attach the electrodes or other sensors. The BF devices are equipped with automatic safety cut-offs so that the children cannot reach any bodily state that might be dangerous. Within rather wide limits, however, they are encouraged to experiment freely in bringing their functions under voluntary control. They are also encouraged to control the functions *without* BF as soon as possible. We notice a cluster of children doing just that, practicing the control of respiration and pulse rate while one of the body educators watches. It is through such exercises that each child learns to read his body as accurately and easily as he reads print. When this is possible, "psychosomatic" complaints are extremely unlikely.

We walk toward the playfield. On the way we pass several Discovery Tents—structures of translucent plastic erected on skeletal frameworks over lightweight plastic floors. The tents are provided with portable air conditioners. They are easily movable or convertible to a different shape. Their character is tentative, temporary.

As we stroll past, we can make out the shapes of children inside, but can't tell exactly what they are doing. Adults rarely enter Discovery Tents. An educator is responsible for each tent (sometimes one educator handles more than one tent), but he sees his function as setting up and constantly revising educational environments that will encourage children to make their own discoveries. For example, one educator handles both of the current Matter/Energy Manipulation projects, making sure the appropriate apparatus and "instructions" are available every day. He strives to create conditions that will stretch the learners' abilities without leaving them behind.

Only a few electronic or printed reference materials are needed inside the Discovery Tents. Every learner in the school, once he has finished enough of the Basics, is given a Remote Readout device through which he can query the Central Computer at any time. The device is slightly larger than an old-fashioned cigarette pack. It has a visual display screen large enough for several lines of type at the time or for small diagrams and pictures. It is fitted with a miniature microphone, slimmer than a pencil, and an earplug. The learner thus has voice access to the computer. He can also contact the educator in charge of the project. Most of the children, however, are reluctant to do so. They have found that the real joy of learning lies in finding out for themselves, either alone or in concert with other children.

When an educator has finished setting up a new project environment, he describes its possibilities on a display at the tent's entrance. Children of various ages wander in. They are electronically recognized through their EIDs [electronic identity cards], and their names appear under "Visiting" on the display at the entrance. If they should decide to become involved in the project, they touch their EIDs to an electrode beneath the display panel, and their names then appear under "Involved." When enough children for a given project have "signed up," the display announces, "Project filled. Please try again later." Word about the ongoing projects always spreads; at particularly exciting ones you may find children checking several times daily to see if anyone has dropped out.

For several years now, one of the more popular events in the Discovery Tents has been the "Faraday Project," arranged by the Matter/Energy Manipulation educator. A tent is set up, insofar as possible, just like Michael Faraday's laboratory on the morning of August 29, 1831. All the appropriate excerpts from Faraday's notebooks dealing with the relationship between electricity and magnetism to that date are available to the children. Also provided are reports of other experiments, notably Hans Christian Oersted, who had demonstrated that magnetism could be obtained from electricity. The equipment in the tent is primitive: wire, magnets, iron cores, batteries, a galvanometer. Nothing is available that was not available to Faraday. The learners' goal is the same as was his: "conversion of Magnetism into Electricity."

Faraday, in ten inspired days, not only accomplished his goal, but also found essentially all the laws that govern electromagnetic induction and built a working model of an electric dynamo. The children of Kennedy School start out with great advantages over Faraday. They know very well that magnetism *can* be made into electricity; most of them have a pretty good idea of how it is done. What is fascinating is to see just what a group of twelve to fifteen of the young ones (six- to eight-year-olds) come up with and how long it takes them. Often their experiments lack the elegance and economy of Faraday's. After all, he was a master experimenter with a lifetime of experience. The children often build devices that seem, next to his, complex and cumbersome. They sometimes go the long way around to come to the same conclusions. But there are also those times, those ecstatic moments, when they hit upon some truly ingenious demonstration that seems to transcend Faraday. Parents, educators and other children alike eagerly await those inspired reports, put together by little children working with primitive equipment, which draw tentative conclusions beyond anything Faraday could have possibly dreamed.

As we pass the current Faraday tent, we can see the outline of children's heads bending over a table. My wife and I agree to check at the Central Dome, perhaps today, to learn what the latest Faraday projects have yielded. We walk on toward the Senoi tent, where we may find Johnny.

The Senoi project is generally filled with twenty or even more children of various ages. It is a large tent with an earthen floor, recreating the bamboo, rattan and thatch environment of a primitive tribe that inhabited the central mountain range of the Malay Peninsula. Through all the wars and horrors of the eighteenth, nineteenth and twentieth centuries, this people, the Senoi, lived without a single violent crime or intercommunal conflict. They did so by employing methods of psychology and interpersonal relations that seemed, to the people of the mid-twentieth century, nothing less than astonishing. Even today, when the absence of aggression and violence doesn't seem so phenomenal, the Senoi methods make an enjoyable and effective introduction to the control of the inner impulses, of what was once called the "subconscious."

The Senoi were a hunting and fishing people, although they practiced some agriculture. But they spent a great part of each day, starting with breakfast, in dream interpretation and the follow-up activities it triggered; this was central to the education of every child. As reported by the mid-twentieth-century psychiatrist-anthropologist Kilton Stewart, a leading student of the Senoi, when a child reported a falling dream, for example, the adult would respond with enthusiasm, congratulating the child for having had one of the most powerful and useful dreams a person can have. The adult would then ask the child where he had landed after the fall and what he had learned.

The child might answer that he had been afraid and had awakened with a start. At this point, the adult would begin his instruction, explaining that every dream-act has a purpose and a destination. The dreamer must overcome his fear. He must surrender to the spirit-world and thus get in touch with its enormous powers.

The adult would then ask the child to remember his words during his next falling dream and to find pleasure in traveling to the source of the power that caused him to fall.

To change the fear of falling into the joy of flying takes time and practice. But the entire Senoi social structure is set up to encourage such feats, and eventually every Senoi child learns to exchange hesitation and anxiety for curiosity and ecstasy. Every child learns to advance straight into the teeth of any dream-danger. He learns to travel all the way to any dream's destination or resolution and to bring back something that will be of use or delight to the entire tribe in its daily, waking life.

While in the tent, Kennedy children *become* Senoi. By so doing, they practice psychic mobility and gain control of their dreams, of a whole realm of thinking and feeling that was almost entirely ignored throughout the Civilized Epoch.

The great majority of Kennedy children have learned by the age of six, to fall asleep at will. About midmorning, everyone in the Senoi tent lies down and goes through a complete sleep cycle, including at least one dream. This takes about ninety minutes. They awaken, eat and begin their dream sessions. Older children who have been Senoi children in earlier years are now Senoi adults. For the last several weeks, Johnny has been one of them, with the added responsibility of a *halak*, a psychologist-educator. He has a "wife" and two "children," a six-year-old boy and girl. When Johnny's "son" dreams that a friend has insulted him, Johnny advises him to inform his friend of this fact. The friend's "father" then tells his child that he may have offended the dreamer without really meaning to, that he may have allowed a malignant character in the dream universe to use his image in the dream. He should therefore give a present to the dreamer (Johnny's son) and go out of this way to be friendly toward him in the future. Thus, any aggression building up around the image of the friend in the dreamer's mind becomes the basis of a friendly exchange.

When the Senoi project children are not directly involved in their dream sessions, they are preparing their meals or making gifts from the type of materials available on the undeveloped Malay Peninsula or presenting the dances, poems, drum rhythms and so on they have brought back from the universe of sleep. As a *halak*, Johnny also initiates "adolescents" into the agreement trance, or cooperative reverie, that is the mark of the adult Senoi. After adolescence, if a Senoi spends a great deal of time in the trance state, he is considered a specialist in healing or in the use of extrasensory powers. Kennedy children, because of their experience in altering states of consciousness (beginning in the Basics Dome and continuing especially in the Quiet Dome and Body Dome), probably find it much easier to enter the trance than did even the Senoi themselves.

Walking on toward the Senoi tent, we pass tents where children are playing games that join what you might call math and logic with music and the sense of touch; where children are simulating the environment of space; where they are creating an even more exotic place, late nineteenth-century America. We search the Senoi display for Johnny's name. It is not there. Though we know Johnny has pretty well mastered the Senoi environment, we speculate on what other environment could have pulled him away from it.

Perhaps the playfield. We enter it through a break in the border of flowering shrubs—a large, grassy expanse of flat and rolling ground. People from earlier times might be surprised that it is unmarked by lines or artificial boundaries of any kind. The games of limitation—which include most of the sports of Civilization—faded so rapidly after the late 1980s that the last lined area disappeared from the playfield a couple of years ago. Touch football was among the last to go. In its many permutations, football was fluid and interwoven enough to remain interesting and relevant in the new age, and some Kennedy children even now play a version of it that requires no fixed boundaries and no "officials." But the aggression it sometimes encourages leaves a bad taste in the mouths of most modern children.

Baseball, by contrast, lost its relevance long ago. Played now in four major domes across the nation before small invitational audiences, baseball may be seen on some of the lesser laservision stations. Its audience, needless to say, consists mostly of men over fifty. Suffused with sweet, sleepy nostalgia, they sit near their sets late into the night, transported back to another, more complex time. Baseball, indeed, characterizes much that has passed away. Its rigid rules, its fixed angles and distances, shape players to repetitive, stereotyped behaviors. Its complete reliance on officials to enforce rules and decide close plays removes the players from all moral and personal decisions, and encourages them, in fact, to get away with whatever they can. Its preoccupation with statistics reveals its view of human worth:

players are valued for how many percentage points, hits, home runs, runs batted in and the like they can accumulate. Everything is acquisitive, comparative, competitive, limiting.

Children who have played the games of expansion are hard pressed to comprehend baseball's great past appeal. As for these present games, many are improvised by the children themselves, then revised day by day. Refinement generally runs toward simplicity, elegance and an absolute minimum of rules. With no officials to intervene, the players themselves are repeatedly up against moral decisions.

On the flatland, several pairs of children are sailing plastic aerodynamic disks back and forth. We watch the disks spin, whirlpools of color in an ocean of blue sky, soaring, wheeling, slanting. One child throws. His co-player runs pell-mell to intercept the disk, diving, if necessary, to spear it one-handedly. It is a popular game, sort of an old standby. Rules may vary, but are generally quite simple: The two players stand about fifteen yards apart. When the thrower launches the disk, the receiver makes an all-out effort to reach it. If he cannot get close enough to touch the disk—i.e., if it is entirely out of his range—he takes a point. If, on the other hand, the throw turns out to have been within his range but he failed (through misjudgment or insufficient effort) to reach it, the receiver gives a point to the thrower. If the receiver manages to touch the disk and then drops it, he gives the thrower two points. In each case, the receiver makes the decision. There is no appeal, no intervening referee, no out-of-bounds sanctuary. Thus, the receiver is making frequent statements about his own ultimate capabilities. He is practicing moral judgment. The greatest joy comes from a perfectly executed throw and a spectacular catch. In this case no score whatever changes hands. The reward is intrinsic. There are no external standards, no statistical comparisons—only the absolute of individual ability, desire and honesty.

Over on the playfield's gently rolling area, we see a group of about ten children running wildly from one crest to another, then sitting in a circle. They creep catlike to the next crest, and again sit. I suggest to my wife that we stay for a while and try, as we sometimes do, to figure out that game's rationale or its essence. But she is more interested in Johnny, and we can see that he is nowhere on the field. So we head past the large Arts Dome on the edge of the playfield toward the Central Dome.

I ask my wife: "Are you hungry?"

"Yes, yes, yes."

We walk faster. Throughout the school day refreshments are served to parents and educators in the computer readout room. Comfortable chairs and lounges are arranged in informal clusters. Multiple stereo fills the room with music. One wall is lined with readout consoles, at which parents and educators alike can request data about Kennedy children. Parents, identified electronically through their EIDs, are granted information only about their own children, while educators can learn about any child in the school. (In another, smaller room, children can request and get the same kind of feedback about themselves.) In seconds, the computer will provide up-to-the-moment data on how much time a child has been spending in each of the environments. It will analyze a young child's "progress" in the Basics Dome or will show what kinds of information an older child has been requesting on his Remote Readout. It will also, upon request, provide a Uniqueness Profile or a number of other profiles, including Empathy, Joy of Learning, Body Development, Awareness, Consciousness Control and the like. Parents and children are cautioned, however, not to take these profiles very seriously. They are only rough guides to development, not evaluations in the old sense. The best thing about the computer readout room, most parents feel, is not the computer readout, but the happy atmosphere of relatedness between parents and educators—and perhaps the refreshments.

We don't quite make the Central Dome, however, in spite of our hunger. On the way, we pass a group of older children in a grassy clearing surrounded by shade trees. Something about the way they are sitting draws us nearer. We see at once that Johnny is among them and that all of them have been crying. My wife walks over slowly and rests on the grass near him. I follow. No words are spoken. We settle down and tune our consciousness to feel what these children feel. Gradually their melancholy suffuses us. I close my eyes and a wine-dark sea, sparkling with sapphire and gold, stretches to the horizons of my inner vision. I am overcome with a sense of waste, of utter loss. I open my eyes and meet those of children around me. Tears have made their eyes pale and bright. They meet my gaze directly and openly, and I feel my own tears welling up.

· "We couldn't go on," Johnny says softly, handing me a history-drama script, thin pages of opaque plastic bound by spiral wire. *Thucydides: The Peloponnesian Wars*.

Nodding, I say, "I know what you mean."

"We *tried* to become Athenians. We tried to stay in character. But look . . ."

He hands me the script, pointing out a passage in "The Melian Dialogue."

MELIAN: But must we be your enemies? Would you not receive us as friends if we are neutral and remain at peace with you?

ATHENIAN: No, your enmity does not injure us as much as your friendship; for your enmity is in the eyes of our subjects a demonstration of our power, your friendship of our weakness.

"And then," Johnny says, "the Athenians went on to massacre all the adult males in this—this little island—and made *slaves* out of all the women and children. It's hard to understand. It's hard to play the parts."

Tears start streaming down his face. "We tried to act out the Melian section yesterday afternoon, but we didn't do too well. And then this morning, we were in the Athenian Assembly making the decision to invade Sicily, and —in some ways they were such beautiful people—most of us know how it's going to come out—we all broke down and couldn't go on. We can't get anyone to play the part of Alcibiades. I don't know if we'll *ever* finish."

Overhearing Johnny's words, several children begin sobbing audibly. Two little girls crawl into my wife's arms.

"Don't worry about it, Johnny," I say. "Anyone who can relive the Peloponnesian Wars—or *any war*—without crying is somehow defective. Something's lacking."

"Yes, but isn't it true that people used to be able to read about wars without crying? *That* seems so sad. It seems kind of—crazy, or something."

"It would seem crazy to you. But I must remind you that even your grandmothers and grandfathers approached the subject that way. People studied wars with an attitude that *would* seem completely crazy. But I won't use that word; 'inhuman' is better. They were able to make the whole thing into a sort of chess game. They'd become 'experts' on something like our own Civil War of 1861, mapping campaigns with hypnotic fascination, never *feeling* anything except maybe an avid hope for one side to win or lose, or a captivation with strategy or tactics. Sometimes they felt 'glory,' too, which isn't so much a feeling as a substitute for feeling, programmed by Civilized societies to take the place of or even block relevant personal emotions. We have to face it, Johnny, people actually could and did read about or see movies about brutal killings and senseless destruction without most of the relevant human feelings.''

"But *why*? *How*? *How* did they do it?"

"*They were uneducated.* It's as simple as that. You know, Johnny, until very recently education was mostly nothing more than the 'teaching' of facts and concepts. Even as late as the 1960s, people could go completely through school and remain what might be called, in the words of those days, not only emotional imbeciles, but sensory ignoramuses and somatic dumbbells. That in itself, just as you said, is one of the saddest things of all. Crying over the absolute tragedy of war—and especially a war such as the Peloponnesian—is a part of learning, it seems to me, a way of practicing relevant emotions—a lot more important than remembering names and dates.''

"But we *do* remember all those things," Johnny says. "It's hard to forget, once you've *lived* it."

"Yes, and you can live it on more than one level. With psychic mobility, you can experience what you as an Athenian of 415 B.C. feel, what you as Thucydides feel (when you're working from his text), and what you living in this age feel. And isn't there a certain common ground? Don't you sense in Thucydides an irony, an outrage, even a deep personal sorrow about the events he describes?"

"Yes, I do. We all do. It adds to the sadness."

By this time several children of the history-drama group had gathered around me and Johnny.

"Why don't you stay with us today?" one of the younger girls asks, looking first at me, then at my wife.

"Why don't you be Alcibiades?" a boy, one of Johnny's friends, asks me. "And Johnny can be Nicias, and we can start over again."

"And we'll be Athenians," the girl says with determination. "We really will."

So once again, as on so many other visits, we find ourselves drawn into one of the learning projects. This tree-circled plot becomes the Athenian Assembly. I become youthful Alcibiades with all his pride and folly, instrument of an ancient male conspiracy of "honor," "power" and "glory"; while my son is old Nicias, appointed general against his will, now counseling in vain against the madness of arrogance and empire. The hours pass. We sail to Sicily, and then down that slow, agonizing whirlpool toward annihilation; the nightmarish denouement of prideful dreams; the affirmation of Thucydides' judgment in his time that unbridled human nature, finally, is "ungovernable in passion, uncontrollable by justice and hostile to all superiors."

We emerge from the past with a new sense of communion and love. We sit silently, holding hands, in a circle. We are unashamed of our tears, unmindful of differences in age and sex. In the fading sunlight we celebrate the present. By the power of our ability to feel, we are rescued from history. We know that Thucydides was wrong; human nature is what we make it. None of this needs to be said. The moment transcends words. And I cannot tell how long it is before my wife and I, descending to another state of consciousness, remember that we have forgotten to eat.

Summarizing Statements

1. Territorial behavior spreads animals out on the available territory, conserving to best advantage the food supply. It involves aggression, ritual fighting, and establishing a dominance hierarchy which minimize conflict in the long run. Male territorial behavior establishes an animal's sexual status and insures the survival of the species.

2. When animals are overcrowded on the available territory, many aspects of life may become disrupted. The main effect is for low-ranking animals to die off. When crowding exceeds certain limits, some animals become disturbed, behave irrationally, and fail to reproduce.

3. A behavioral sink developed among Calhoun's rats because the spatial arrangements for feeding fostered social eating. Eventually the behavioral sink interfered with various kinds of normal behavior, such as courting, nest building, nursing, and ordinary pup care. Mortality among newborn rats climbed to 96 percent. This study shows the basic importance of the spatial environment in controlling normal social behavior.

4. A study among humans found that in overcrowded conditions social behavior broke down, people were selfish, hoarded and stole things, and developed territorial aggression. During overcrowded conditions, people resisted attempts to organize around common goals. The people adapted easily to a great deal of pollution. Well-defined social organization is the major means of successful adaptation to overcrowded conditions.

5. Different architectural design may induce various kinds of psychological reactions. Some designs induce feelings of insecurity, which may lead to anxiety or depression, illustrating how dependent we are on buildings and places for parts of our identity.

6. The use of space is related to its function. Some classroom seating arrangements may foster learning better than others. Spatial arrangements that seem to bring people together are called *sociopetal*; those that drive people apart are called *sociofugal*. Institutions such as mental hospitals might use *sociopetal* space to further treatment goals. Libraries, on the other hand, should probably have both *sociofugal* and *sociopetal* space, depending on whether an area was designed to insure privacy or facilitate social interaction.

7. Questioning the meaning of space may lead to evaluating the part that each aspect of the environment plays toward patient recovery. Long-term residence in mental hospitals has tended to produce *institutional apathy*; in time many patients withdraw and become demoralized, dependent, and depressed. Increasingly it has been realized that some institutional routines themselves may work against the goals of recovery and release.

8. Professionalism of staff in mental hospitals can create barriers to communication with patients. Professionals are sometimes more committed to their profession than to the institution itself and its goals. Professional roles do not always correspond to job demands.

9. The doctor-nurse game is an example of a status concern of professionals that interferes with full and open communication. The game itself may be seen as a transactional neurosis, or neurotic role. People involved in such self-deception are unlikely to be able to be an effective part of a therapeutic community.

10. An institution organized as a therapeutic community sees to it that every aspect of the total institution is part of a continuous treatment program. Patients are involved in the planning of most hospital activities. Patients serve as aides, helping other patients and themselves. In a therapeutic community staff and patient roles become blurred. Patients are given the maximum opportunity to participate in decision making by investing much of the total authority in the group.

11. Computers are revolutionizing human society. Computers of the future will be able to learn from experience and program themselves, displaying "artificial intelligence" of the highest sort. Much of future education will be individualized programmed instruction controlled via computer networks. These machines will hold true dialogue with the student, and failure will be a thing of the past. Programmed instruction permits individualized, one-to-one instruction, provides immediate knowledge of results, is regulated or paced by the student himself, and employs branching (remedial) instruction to correct mistakes. Computerized teaching machines of the future will be both more flexible and adaptive. The greatest boon of widespread use of these computer-age teaching machines will be to effectively upgrade the performance of those who presently are not able to succeed educationally.

12. Wired television will probably replace broadcast for a number of reasons. In terms of communication, wired TV has numerous advantages such as two-way transmission, audience feedback, programming for small groups, and conducting group therapy.

13. Bio-feedback training has given man a beginning in developing conscious self-control over many physiological systems—for instance, alpha brain waves, blood pressure, and heart rate—formerly believed to be under involuntary control. These new feedback systems offer us striking new opportunities to better man's condition.

Reading Selection

14. Leonard speculates that education in the future will return control of man to himself. It will do this by encouraging rather than stifling awareness. It could begin by stopping reinforcement of competition, acquisition and aggression. Computer-assisted instruction will be commonplace, as will bio-feedback training.

15. At the beginning of the next century, children will be trained to develop greater empathy toward the feelings of others. Education will be less formal, more governed (controlled) by capitalizing on well-known "discovery" principles.

16. Learning environments, such as the Faraday Project and the Senoi Project, will attempt to recreate the specific conditions under which scientific discoveries were made or in which people lived. The Senoi lived in the Malay Peninsula during the 18th to 20th centuries without violent crime and conflict. Senoi children were taught to exchange fear, anxiety, and hesitation for curiosity and ecstasy, and thus to approach life in an open and expectant manner.

17. Competitive sports—the games of limitation—disappeared during the close of the 20th century. These games passed away because they stressed acquisitive, comparative, competitive values that were disappearing. Cooperative sports developed in which players, rather than officials, decided to give or withhold points to the other players for well-executed plays. The stress was on self-evaluation and practicing moral judgment.

18.   Children of the 21st century study history by acting out dramatic scripts recreating significant aspects of past events. Leonard speculates that these children will not be able to understand contemporary man's motivation for waging war. By studying such incomprehensible events they will be rescued from history and learn that man can shape human nature as he wishes. The mistakes of the past can be avoided.

Terms and Concepts

Bio-feedback device: a machine that displays information about various biological conditions, offering the possibility of developing self-control over the system. Example: alpha brain-wave training.

Computer-assisted instruction: programmed instruction regulated by a computer.

Discovery learning: a type of learning that capitalizes on the child's curiosity to govern his progress in learning.

Doctor-nurse-game: a medical status game involving mutual deception in regard to communication. Basically a transactional neurosis working against the kind of open communication needed in a therapeutic community.

Institutional apathy: A kind of sociological reaction to confinement, or institutional life, in which a patient withdraws socially, is passive and uncommunicative, and excessively dependent on the institution.

Programmed instruction: a carefully constructed program of instruction, designed to insure mastery, by delivering constant feedback about the progress of learning; the instructional material is contained in a teaching machine.

Sociofugal space: an environmental design that tends to drive people apart, such as a railway station.

Sociopetal space: an environmental design that tends to bring people together and hence facilitates social interaction.

Territorial behavior: behavior designed to spread out animals on the available territory to insure adequate food, opportunity for sex and reproduction, and security. Often involves threat, ritual fighting, and the establishment of a dominance hierarchy.

Therapeutic community: a program of treatment involving every aspect of the total environment of a mental hospital in a continuous, 24-hour program directed at patient recovery and release from the institution. Largely directed at avoiding the formation of institutional apathy.

Wired television: a type of transmission that permits two-way communication and an almost unlimited number of program sources; distinct from broadcast TV.

Bibliography

All works are listed alphabetically by author except anonymous works, which are listed chronologically. Three commission reports (Coleman, Hineman, and Kerner) are listed alphabetically.

Adorno, T. W., Frenkel-Brunswick, E., Levinson, D. J., & Sanford, R. N. *The authoritarian personality*: New York, Harper & Row, 1950.

Albert, E. M. The status of women in Burundi. In D. Paulme (Ed.), *Women of tropical Africa*. Berkeley, Calif.: University of California Press, 1963. Pp. 105–115.

Aldrich, R. A. Liquidation of the problem through research and training. In Anonymous, *The White House conference on mental retardation*. Washington, D.C.: U.S. Government Printing Office, 1963.

Allport, F. H. The J-curve hypothesis of conforming behavior." *Journal of Social Psychology*, 1934, **5**, 141–183.

Allport, G. W. *The nature of prejudice*. New York: Doubleday, 1958.

Anastasi, A. *Differential psychology*. (3rd ed.) New York: Macmillan, 1958.

Angyal, A. *Foundations for a science of personality*. New York: Commonwealth Fund, 1941.

Anonymous (1950). *U.S. census of population*. 1950, **2**, Part 1, U.S. Department of Commerce, Bureau of Census.

Anonymous (1956). *Integrated bus suggestion*. Leaflet, Montgomery Improvement Association, Montgomery, Ala., 1956.

Anonymous (1965). Screams, slaps and love. *Life*, May 7, 1965, 90A–90D, 91–96, 101.

Anonymous (1966). *The earnings gap between women and men is widening*. Washington, D.C.: U.S. Department of Commerce, Bureau of the Census, 1956–1966.

Anonymous (1967). *Prevention and control of narcotic addiction*. Washington, D.C.: U.S. Treasury Department, Bureau of Narcotics, 1967.

Anonymous (1968). *Women earn less than men in all kinds of jobs.* Washington, D.C.: U.S. Department of Labor, National Science Foundation, 1968.

Anonymous (1969a). Changing morality: The two Americas, a Time–Louis Harris poll. *Time,* June 6, 1969, 26–27.

Anonymous (1969b). Generations apart. CBS News documentary. Poll conducted by Daniel Yankelovich, Inc., 1969.

Anonymous (1969c). *Malnutrition: One key to the poverty cycle.* State of California, Sacramento, 1969.

Anonymous (1969d). Token economy plan. *California Mental Health Progress,* Sacramento, Calif.: Office of Public Information, 1969, 13–14.

Anonymous (1970a). The deceptive hitchhiker. *Life,* March 13, 1970, 61–62.

Anonymous (1970b). Racially rationed health. *Time,* April 6, 1970, 90.

Anonymous (1970d). Women's median wage or salary as percent of men's. *Current Population Reports.* Washington, D.C.: U.S. Department of Commerce, Bureau of the Census, 1970.

Anonymous (1971a). *California Women: Report of the National Advisory Commission on the Status of Women.* State of California, Documents Section, 1971.

Anonymous (1971b). Sesame Street evaluation breaks new ground. *Educational Testing Service Developments,* Winter 1971, **18**, 1–3.

Anonymous (1971c). *Social Security Bulletin,* 1971, **34**, 5. U.S. Department of Health, Education, and Welfare, Social Security Administration.

Anonymous (1971d). *Society today.* Del Mar, Calif.: CRM, 1971.

Anonymous (1971e). Teacher's desk. *Psychology Today,* September 1971, 12.

Arendt, H. *Eichman in Jerusalem: A report on the banality of evil,* New York: Viking Press, 1963.

Asch, S. E. Opinions and social pressure, *Scientific American,* November 1955, 506–509.

Asch, S. E. *Social psychology.* Englewood Cliffs, N.J.: Prentice-Hall, 1952.

Athanasiou, R., Shaver, P., & Tavris, C. "Sex," *Psychology Today,* July 1970, 39–52.

Ausubel, D. P. *Drug addiction: Physiological, psychological, and sociological aspects.* New York: Random House, 1958.

Bachrach, A. J., Erwin, W. J., & Mohr, J. P. "The control of eating behavior in an anorexic by operant conditioning techniques. In L. Ullman and L. P. Krasner (Eds.), *Case studies in behavior modification.* New York: Holt, Rinehart and Winston, 1965.

Bales, R. F. "Some uniformities of behavior in small social settings." Swanson, G. E., Newcomb, T. M., & Hartley, E. L. (Eds.), *Readings in social psychology.* New York: Henry Holt, 1952.

Bandura, A. *Principles of behavior modification.* New York: Holt, Rinehart and Winston, 1969.

Bandura, A., Ross, D., & Ross, S. A. Vicarious reinforcement and imitative learning. *Journal of Abnormal and Social Psychology,* 1963, **67**, 601–607.

Barrie, J. M. *The admirable Chrichton and other plays.* New York: Scribner's, 1930.

Benson, P., The common interests myth in marriage. *Social Problems*, 1955, **3**, 27–34.

Benson, P. The interests of happily married couples. *Marriage and Family Living*, 1952, **14**, 276–280.

Berelson, B., & Steiner, G. A. *Human behavior: An inventory of scientific findings.* New York: Harcourt, Brace and World, 1964.

Berelson, B., Lazarsfeld, Paul F., & McPhee, W. N. *Voting: A study of opinion formation in a presidential campaign.* Chicago: University of Chicago Press, 1954.

Biderman, A. D. *March to calumny.* New York: Macmillan, 1963.

Bieri, J., & Blacker, E. The generality of cognitive complexity in the perception of people and ink blots. *Journal of Abnormal and Social Psychology*, 1956, **53**, 112–117.

Binet, A. *Les idées modernes sur les enfants.* Paris: E. Flamarion, 1909.

Binet, A., & Simon, T. La mesure du developpement de l'intelligence chez les jeunes enfants. *Bulletin de la Societe Libre pour l'Etude Psychologique de l'Enfant*, 1911, **11**, 470–477.

Birren, J. E. The abuse of the urban aged. *Psychology Today,* March 1970, 36–39, 76.

Brogden, W. J., & Culler, E. Experimental extinction of higher-order responses. *American Journal of Psychology*, 1935, **47**, 663–669.

Brophy, I. N. The luxury of anti-Negro prejudice. *Public Opinion Quarterly*, 1946, **9**, 456–466.

Burgess, E. W., & Cottrell, L. S. *Predicting success or failure in marriage.* New York: Prentice-Hall, 1939.

Burgess, E. W., & Wallin, P. *Engagement and marriage.* Philadelphia: Lippincott, 1953.

Butler, R. A. Discrimination learning by rhesus monkeys to visual-exploration motivation. *Journal of Comparative and Physiological Psychology*, 1953, **46**, 95–98.

Butler, R. A. Incentive conditions which influence visual exploration. *Journal of Experimental Psychology*, 1954, **48**, 19–23.

Calhoun, J. B. Population density and social pathology. *Scientific American*, February 1962.

Cameron, N. *Personality development and psychopathology.* Boston: Houghton Mifflin, 1963.

Campbell, A. A. Factors associated with attitudes toward Jews. In T. M. Newcomb & E. E. Hartley. (Eds.), *Readings in social psychology.* New York: Henry Holt, 1947.

Campbell, E. G. Some social psychological correlates of direction in attitude change. *Social Forces*, 1958, **36**, 335–340.

Carthy, J. D., & Ebling, F. J. (Eds.). *The natural history of aggression.* New York: Academic Press, 1964.

Cartwright, D., & Zander, A. (Eds.). *Group dynamics.* (3rd ed.) New York: Harper & Row, 1968.

Cohen, J. *Secondary motivation.* Chicago: Rand McNally, 1970.

Coleman, J. C. *Abnormal psychology and modern life.* (2nd ed.) Chicago: Scott Foresman, 1956.

Coleman, J. C. *Abnormal psychology and modern life.* (3rd ed.) Chicago: Scott Foresman, 1964.

Coleman Report (anonymous). *Equality of educational opportunity.* Washington, D.C.: Department of Health, Education & Welfare, Office of Education, 1966.

Combs, A. W. Intelligence from a perceptual point of view. *Journal of Abnormal and Social Psychology,* 1952, **47**, 662–673.

Combs, A. W., & Snygg, D. *Individual behavior: A perceptual approach to behavior.* New York: Harper & Row, 1959.

Conot, R. *Rivers of blood, years of darkness.* New York: Bantam, 1967.

Coon, G., & Raymond, A. *A review of the psychoneuroses of Stockbridge.* Stockbridge, Mass.: Austin Riggs Foundation, 1940.

Coopersmith, S. Studies in self-esteem. *Scientific American,* February 1968, 96–106.

Davis, D. E. Physiological effects of continued overcrowding. In A. H. Esser (Ed.), *Behavior & environment: The use of space by animals and men.* New York: Plenum Press, 1971. Pp. 133–147.

DeRopp, R. S. *Drugs and the mind.* New York: Grove Press, 1957 and 1964.

Dollard, J. *Caste and class in a southern town.* New York: Doubleday, 1937.

Ehrlich, P. Eco-catastrophe. *Ramparts Magazine,* September 1969, 24–28.

Eibl-Eibesfeldt, I. The fighting behavior of animals. *Scientific American,* December 1961, 112–122.

Erikson, E. *Insight and responsibility.* New York: Norton, 1964.

Erikson, E. H. *Childhood and society.* New York: Norton, 1950.

Erikson, E. H. *Childhood and society.* (2nd ed.) New York: Norton, 1963.

Erikson, E. H. Eight stages of man. *International Journal of Psychiatry,* 1966, **2**, 281–297.

Fabun, D. Reward and punishment: The carrot and the stick. In *Three roads to awareness.* Beverly Hills, Calif.: Glencoe Press, 1970, 22–26.

Farm subsidies yes, welfare for poor, no. *Fresno Bee,* November 28, 1968.

Fel'berbaum, I. M. Interoceptive conditioned reflexes from the uterus. *Trud. Inst. Fiziel. Pavlova,* 1952, **1**, 85–92.

Festinger, L. Cognitive dissonance. *Scientific American,* October 1962, 93–102.

Festinger, L. *The theory of cognitive dissonance.* New York: Harper & Row, 1957.

Festinger, L., & Carlsmith, J. M. Cognitive consequences of forced compliance. *The Journal of Abnormal and Social Psychology,* 1959, **58**, 203–210.

Fiedler, F. E. Assumed similarity measures as predictors of team effectiveness. *Journal of Abnormal and Social Psychology,* 1954, 381–388.

Forrester, B. J., & Klaus, R. A. The effect of race of examiner on intelligence test scores of Negro kindergarten children. *Peabody Papers in Human Development,* 1964, **2**, 1–7.

Freeman, F. S. *Theory and practice of psychological testing.* (3rd ed.). New York: Holt, Rinehart and Winston, 1962.

Fromm, E. *The art of loving.* New York: Harper & Row, 1956.

Fromm, E. *Escape from freedom.* New York: Holt, Rinehart and Winston, 1941.

Freud, S. The ego and the id. In *The standard edition of the complete works of Sigmund Freud.* London, Hogarth Press, 1962.

Frumkin, R. M. Common interests crucial to marital adjustment. *Ohio Journal of Science,* 1954, **54,** 107–110.

Gaetanielle, J. In J. C. Coleman, *Abnormal psychology and modern life.* (3rd ed.). Chicago: Scott, Foresman, 1964. P. 378.

Gagne, R. M., & Fleishman, E. A. *Psychology and human performance.* New York: Henry Holt, 1959.

Gallup, G. 8 in 10 want limit on campaign spending. *Los Angeles Times,* November 22, 1970.

Gandhi, M. The origins of Satyagraha doctrine. In M. Q. Sibley (Ed.), *The quiet battle: Writings on the theory and practice of non-violent resistance.* Garden City, N.Y.: Anchor, 1963.

Gardner, R. A., & Gardner, B. T. Teaching sign language to a chimpanzee. *Science,* August 15, 1969, **169,** 664–672.

Geldard, F. A. Body english. *Psychology Today,* December 1968, 42–47.

Getzels, J. J., & Jackson, P. W. *Creativity and intelligence.* New York: Wiley, 1962.

Glasser, W. *Schools without failure.* New York: Harper & Row, 1969.

Glazer, N., & Moynihan, D. P. *Beyond the melting pot.* Cambridge, Mass.: M.I.T. Press, 1963.

Glueck, S., & Glueck, E. *Unraveling juvenile delinquency.* Cambridge, Mass.: Harvard University Press, 1950.

Gold, M. Punishment, guilt, and behavior in school. Ann Arbor, Mich., University of Michigan, Institute for Social Research, 1958 (mimeograph).

Gold, M. *Status forces in delinquent boys.* Ann Arbor, Mich., University of Michigan, The Research Center for Group Dynamics, Institute for Social Research, 1963.

Goldenson, R. M. *The encyclopedia of human behavior: Psychology, psychiatry, and mental health.* Garden City, N.Y.: Doubleday, 1970.

Goldstein, K. *The organism: A holistic approach to biology derived from pathological data on man.* New York: American Book, 1939.

Goldstein, M., & Rittenhouse, C. H. Knowledge of results in the acquisition and transfer of a gunnery skill. *Journal of Experimental Psychology,* 1954, **48,** 187–196.

Goffman, E. *Asylums.* Garden City, N.Y.: Doubleday, 1961.

Hall, E. Conversation with D. O. Hebb, on hocus-pocus. *Psychology Today,* November 1969, 20–28.

Hamblin, R. L., Buckholdt, D., Bushell, D., Ellis, D., & Ferriter, D. Changing the game from "get the teacher" to "learn." *Trans-action,* January 1969, 20–31.

Harlow, H. F. *Learning to love*. San Francisco: Albion, 1971.

Harlow, H. F. Love in infant monkeys. *Scientific American*, June 1959, 68–74.

Harlow, H. F., & Harlow, M. K. Social deprivation in monkeys. *Scientific American*, November 1962, 136–146.

Harris, M. One American woman: A speculation upon disbelief. In S. M. Farber & R. H. L. Wilson (Eds.), *The potential of woman*. New York: McGraw-Hill, 1963, 231–240.

Harris, T. G. To know why men do what they do: A conversation with David C. McClelland and T. George Harris. *Psychology Today*, January 1971, 35–39, 70–75.

Hartley, E. L. *Problems in prejudice*. New York: King's Crown Press, 1946.

Havighurst, R. J. *Developmental tasks and education*. New York: Longmans, Green, 1952.

Havron, M. D., & McGrath, J. E. The contribution of the leader to the effectiveness of small military groups. In L. Petrullo & B. M. Bass (Eds.), *Leadership and interpersonal behavior*. New York: Holt, Rinehart and Winston, 1961, 173–175.

Hayes, C. *The ape in our house*. New York: Harper, 1951.

Hebb, D. O. *Organization of behavior*. New York: Wiley, 1949.

Heggen, T. *Mister Roberts*. Boston: Houghton Mifflin, 1946.

Hennessy, B. C. *Public opinion*. Belmont, Calif.: Wadsworth, 1965.

Hepner, H. W. *Psychology applied to life and work*. Englewood Cliffs, N.J.: Prentice-Hall, 1941.

Herskovitz, M. J. *The American Negro*. New York, 1929.

Hess, E., & Polt, J. Pupil size as related to interest value of visual stimuli. *Science*, 1960, **132**, 349–350.

Hillsdale, P. Marriage as personal existential commitment. *Marriage and Family Living*, 1962, **24**, 137–143.

Hineman Report. *Poverty amid plenty: The American paradox*. Washington, D.C.: U.S. Government Printing Office, 1969.

Hitler, A. *Mein Kampf*. R. Manheim, trans. Boston: Riverside Press, 1943.

Hoffer, E. *The Passionate state of mind*. New York: Harper & Row, 1954.

Hoffman, L. R., Burke, R. J. & Maier, N. R. F. Participation, influence, and satisfaction among members of problem-solving groups. *Psychological Reports*, 1965, **570**, 661–667.

Horner, M. Fail: Bright woman. *Psychology Today*, 1969, 36–38, 62.

Hunt, J. M. Revisiting Montessori. In M. Montessori, *The montessori method*. New York: Schocken, 1964, xi–xxxv.

Hurley, R. L. *Poverty and mental retardation: A causal relationship*. New York: Vintage Books, 1969.

Illegitimacy and its impact on the aid to dependent children program. Bureau of Public Assistance, Department of Health, Education, and Welfare. Washington, D.C.: U.S. Government Printing Office, April 1960.

Incidence of alcoholism. U.S. Public Health Service, Bureau of Commerce, *Current Population Reports*, 1963.

Johnson, C. S. *Racial attitudes of college students*, 1934, 29–30.

Jones, M. *Social psychiatry in practice: The idea of the therapeutic community.* Baltimore, Md.: Penguin, 1968.

Jones, M. *The therapeutic community.* New York: Basic Books, 1953.

Jourard, S. M. Healthy personality and self-disclosure. *Mental Hygiene*, 1959, **32**, 499–507.

Jourard, S. M. *Personal adjustment.* New York: Macmillan, 1963.

Kagan, J., & Havemann, E. *Psychology.* New York: Harcourt, Brace and World, 1968.

Kahn, H., & Wiener, A. J. *The year 2000.* New York: Macmillan, 1967.

Karlins, M., Coffman, Thomas L., Walters, Gary. On the fading of social stereotypes: Studies in three generations of college students. *Journal of Personality and Social Psychology*, 1969, **13**, 1–16.

Katz, D., & Kahn, R. L. Morale in war industries. In T. M. Newcomb & E. L. Hartley (Eds.), *Readings in social psychology.* New York: Henry Holt, 1947.

Katz, E., & Lazarsfeld, P. F. *Personal influence: The part played by people in the flow of mass communication.* Glencoe, Ill.: Free Press, 1953.

Keezer, W. S. *Mental health and human behavior.* (3rd Ed.). Dubuque, Iowa: William C. Brown, 1971.

Kellogg, W. N., & Kellogg, L. A. *The ape and the child.* New York: McGraw-Hill, 1933.

Keniston, K., & Keniston, E. An American anachronism: The image of women and work. *The American Scholar*, Summer 1964, 335–375.

Kerckhoff, A. C., & Davis, R. E. Value consensus and need complementarity in mate-selection. *American Sociological Review*, 1962, **27**, 295–303.

Kerner Report. *Report of the national advisory commission on civil disorders.* New York: Bantam, 1968.

Klineberg, O. *Negro intelligence and selective migration.* New York: Columbia University Press, 1935.

Klineberg, O. *Social psychology.* New York: Henry Holt, 1954.

Kluckhohn, C. Have there been discernible shifts in American values during the past generation? In E. E. Morison (Ed.), *The American style: Essays in value and performance.* New York: Harper & Row, 1958, 145–217.

Kraft, A. M. The therapeutic community. In S. Arieti (Ed.), *American handbook of psychiatry.* New York: Basic Books, 1966, **3**, 542–551.

Krech, D., Crutchfield, R. S., & Ballachey, E. L. *Individual in society: A textbook of social psychology.* New York: McGraw-Hill, 1962.

Landis, P. H. *Making the most of marriage.* New York: Appleton-Century-Crofts, 1968.

Langer, S. *Philosophy in a new key: Importance of invention of language.* New York: Mentor, 1955.

La Rochefoucauld, *La Rouchefoucauld Maxims*. L. W. Tancock, trans. Baltimore, Md.: Penguin Books, 1959.

Lee, E. S. Negro intelligence and selective migration: A Philadelphia test of the Klineberg hypothesis. *American Sociological Review*, 1951, **16**, 227–233.

Le Magnen, J. Un cas de sensibilité olfactive se presentant comme un caractère secondaire féminim. *C. R. Acad Sei Paris*, 1948, **226**.

Leonard, G. *Education and ecstasy*. New York: Delacorte Press, 1968.

Levine, S. Sex differences in the brain. *Scientific American*, April 1966, 2–7.

Lindesmith, A. R., & Strauss, A. L. *Social psychology*. (3rd ed.) New York: Holt, Rinehart and Winston, 1968.

Lindsey, G., & Aronson, E. (Eds.). *Handbook of social psychology*. (Rev. ed.) Reading, Mass.: Addison-Wesley, 1968.

Lorenz, K. *On aggression*. New York: Bantam, 1966. First published in German in 1963.

Luria, A. R. *The mind of a mnemonist*. New York: Basic Books, 1968.

Macoby, E. Sex differences in intellectual functioning. In E. Macoby (Ed.), *The development of sex differences*. Stanford, Calif.: Stanford University Press, 1966, 25–55.

Martin, J. H. Freeport public schools experiment on early reading using the Edison responsive environment instrument. New York: Responsive Environments Corporation, N.D.

Maslow, A. H. *Motivation and personality*. New York: Harper & Row, 1954.

Maslow, A. H. *Motivation and personality*. (Rev. ed.) New York: Harper & Row, 1970.

McCandless, B. R. *Adolescents behavior and development*. Hinsdale, Ill.: Dryden Press, 1970.

McClelland, D. C., Rindlisbacher, A., & DeCharms, R. Religious and other sources of parental attitudes toward independence training. In D. C. McClelland (Ed.), *Studies in motivation*. New York: Appleton-Century-Crofts, 1955.

McClelland, D. C. Risk-taking in children with high and low need for achievement. In J. W. Atkinson (Ed.), *Motives in fantasy, action, and society*. Princeton, N.J.: Van Nostrand, 1958, 306–321.

McClelland, D. C. The use of measures of human motivation in the study of society. In J. W. Atkinson (Ed.), *Motives in fantasy, action, and society*. Princeton, N.J.: Van Nostrand, 1958, 518–554.

McClelland, D. C., Atkinson, J. W., Clark, R. A., & Lowell, E. L. *The achievement motives*. New York: Appleton-Century-Crofts, 1953.

McClelland, D. C. *The achieving society*. Princeton, N.J.: Van Nostrand, 1961.

MacKinnon, D. W. The nature and nurture of creative talent. In Hartley, R., & Hartley, E. L. *Readings in psychology*. (3rd ed.) New York: Thomas Y. Crowell, 1965, 426–441.

Mead, M. *Male and female*. New York: Mentor, 1949.

Mead, M. Marriage in two steps. *Redbook*, July 1966, 48–49, 84, 86.

Menninger, K. A. *The human mind*. (Revised ed.) New York: Knopf, 1945.

Milgram, S. Liberating effects of group pressure. *Journal of Personality and Social Psychology*, 1965, **1**, 127–134.

Morgan, C. T., & King, R. A. *Introduction to psychology.* (4th ed.) New York: McGraw-Hill, 1971.

Moser, D. The Nightmare of Life with Billy. *Life*, May 7, 1965, 96–101.

Mowrer, O. H. On the psychology of "talking birds"—A contribution to language and personality theory. In Mowrer, D. H. (Ed.), *Learning theory and personality dynamics.* New York: Ronald Press, 1950.

Murphy, J. V., Miller, R. E., & Mirsky, I. A. Interanimal conditioning in the monkey. *Journal of Comparative and Physiological Psychology*, 1955, **48**, 211–214.

Mussen, P. H., Conger, J. J., & Kagan, J. *Child development and personality.* New York: Harper & Row, 1969.

Mussen, P., & Distler, L. Masculinity identification and father-son relationship. *Journal of Abnormal and Social Psychology*, 1959, **59**, 350–356.

Newcomb, T. M., Turner, R. H., & Converse, P. E. *Social psychology: The study of human interaction.* New York: Holt, Rinehart and Winston, 1965.

Osgood, C. E. *An alternative to war or surrender.* Urbana, Ill.: University of Illinois Press, 1962.

Osmond, H. Function as the basis of psychiatric ward design. *Mental Hospitals* (Architectural Supplement), 1957, **8**, 23–30.

Ostwald, P. F. Acoustic methods in psychiatry. *Scientific American*, March 1965, 82–91.

Pavlov, I. P. *Conditioned reflexes: An investigation of the physiological activity of the cerebral cortex.* F. C. Anrep, trans. New York: Oxford University Press, 1927.

Petrunkevitch, A. The spider and the wasp. *Scientific American*, August 1952, 20–23.

Pettigrew, T. F. Personality and socio-cultural factors in inter-group attitudes: A cross-national comparison. *Journal of Conflict Resolution*, 1958, **2**, 29–42.

Phillips, E. L. Achievement Place: Token procedures in a home-style setting for "pre-delinquent boys." *Journal of Applied Behavior Analysis*, 1968, **1**, 217–221.

Pines, M. How three-year-olds teach themselves to read—and love it. *Harper's Magazine*, May 1963, 58–64.

Premack, D. The education of Sarah. *Psychology Today*, September 1970, 54–58.

Pressey, S. L. *Psychology and the new education.* New York: Harper, 1933.

Raab, E., & Lipset, S. M. The prejudiced society. In E. Raab (Ed.) *American race relations today.* Garden City, N.Y.: Doubleday, 1962.

Rapkin, C., & Grigsby, W. G. *The demand for housing in racially mixed areas.* Berkeley, Calif.: University of California Press, 1960.

Reiss, I. L. *The family system in America.* New York: Holt, Rinehart and Winston, 1971.

Rogers, C. R. A theory of therapy, personality, and interpersonal relationships, as developed in the client-centered framework. In S. Koch (Ed.), *Psychology: A study of science.* New York: McGraw-Hill, 1959. Pp. 184–256.

Rogers, C. R. Toward a modern approach to values: The valuing process in the mature person. *Journal of Abnormal and Social Psychology*, 1964, **68**, 160–167.

Roget's International Thesaurus. New York: Thomas Y. Crowell, 1946.

Rokeach, M. *The open and closed mind*. New York: Basic Books, 1960.

Rokeach, M. A theory of organization and change within value-attitude systems. *Journal of Social Issues*, 1968, **24**, 14–16.

Rorvik, D. M. Brain waves. *Look Magazine*, October 6, 1970, 88–97.

DeRougemont, D. The crisis of the modern couple. In R. N. Anshen (Ed.), *The Family: Its function and destiny*. New York, Harper, 1959. Pp. 451–453.

Sawrey, W. L., Conger, J. J., & Turrell, E. S. An experimental investigation of the role of psychological factors in the production of gastric ulcers in rats. *Journal of Comparative Physiological Psychology*, 1956, **49**, 457–461.

Schachter, S. Eat, eat. *Psychology Today*, April 1971, 44–47, 78–79.

Schaffer, W. E., & Polk, K. Delinquency and the schools. In Task Force on Juvenile Delinquency, *Juvenile delinquency and youth crime*, Washington, D.C.: U.S. Government Printing Office, 1967, 224–277.

Schulman, R. E., *et al*. Laboratory measurement of parental behavior. *Journal of Consulting Psychology*, 1962, **26**.

Scranton Report, *The President's Commission on Campus Unrest*. Washington, D.C.: U.S. Government Printing Office, 1970, 51–73.

Sears, R. R., Macoby, E. E., & Levin, H. *Patterns of child rearing*. Evanston, Ill.: Row, Peterson, 1957.

Senden, M. V. *Raum-und gestaltauffassung bei operierten blindgeborenen vor und nach der operation*. Leipzig, Barth, 1932, Found In D. O. Hebb (Ed.), *Organization of Behavior*. New York: Wiley, 1949.

Sherif, M. Experiments in group conflict. *Scientific American*, November 1956, 54–58.

Sherriffs, A. C., & McKee, J. P. Qualitative aspects of beliefs about men and women. *Journal of Personality*, 1957, **25**, 451–464.

Sibley, M. Q. (Ed.). *The quiet battle*. Garden City, N.Y.: 1963.

Simmons, C., Baldwin, C. L., & Hawes, P. *Welfare in California: Report to the State Senate*. Sacramento, Calif., 1970.

Simmons, J. A. The sonar sight of bats. *Psychology Today*, November 1968, pp. 50–52, 54–57.

Sivadon, P. L'espace vecu, incidences therapeutiques. *L'Evolution Psychiatrique*, 1965, **30**, 477–498.

Skeels, H. M. Adult status of children with contrasting early life experiences. *Monographs of the Society for Research in Child Development*, 1966, **31**, 3.

Skinner, B. F. *The behavior of organisms*. New York: Appleton-Century, 1938.

Skinner, B. F. Pigeons in a pelican. *American Psychologist*, 1960, **5**, 28–37.

Skolnick, P., Moss, R., Salzgeber, R., & Shaw, J. I. The effects of population size and density on human behavior. California State University, Northridge. Paper delivered at Western Psychological Association Meeting, San Francisco, Spring 1971.

Smith, C. Child development. In J. Vernon (Ed.), *Introduction to general psychology: A self-selection textbook.* Dubuque, Iowa: William C. Brown, 1966.

Sommer, R. The ecology of privacy. *The Library Quarterly,* 1966, **36**, 234–248.

Sontag, L. W., Baker, C. T., & Nelson, V. L. Mental growth and personality development: A longitudinal study. *Monographs of the Society for Research in Child Development,* 1958, **23**, whole issue No. 68.

Staats, A. W. *Learning, language and cognition.* New York: Holt, Rinehart and Winston, 1968.

Stagner, R. *Psychology of personality.* New York: McGraw-Hill, 1961.

Stein, L. J. The doctor-nurse game. *Archives of General Psychiatry,* 1967, **16**, 205–216.

Steiner, S. *The new Indians.* New York: Harper & Row, 1968.

Strang, R. *An introduction to child study.* New York: Macmillan, 1952.

Stuart, R. B. Assessment and change of the communicational patterns of juvenile delinquents and their parents. In R. Rubin (ed.), *Advances in behavior therapy techniques.* New York: Academic Press, 1969.

Stuart, R. B. Behavioral control of overeating. *Behavior Research and Therapy,* 1967, **5**, 357–365.

Stuart, R. B. Behavior contracting with the families of delinquents. Presented at the 1970 Behavior Modification Conference, Los Angeles.

Terman, L. M., & Merrill, M. A. *Measuring intelligence.* Boston: Houghton Mifflin, 1937.

Theodorson, G. A., & Theodorson, A. G. *A modern dictionary of sociology.* New York: Thomas Y. Crowell, 1969.

Thibaut, J. W., & Kelly, H. H. *The social psychology of groups.* New York: Wiley, 1959.

Thorp, R., & Blake, R. *The music of their laughter.* San Francisco: Canfield Press, 1971.

Toch, H. *The social psychology of social movements.* Indianapolis, Ind.: Bobbs-Merrill, 1965.

Trabasso, T. Pay attention. *Psychology Today,* October 1968, 30–36.

Turner, J. B. *The chemical feast.* New York: Grossman, 1970.

Udry, J. R. *The social context of marriage.* (2nd ed.) Philadelphia: Lippincott, 1971.

Verhave, T. The pigeon as quality-control inspector. *American Psychologist,* 1966, **21**, 109–115.

Washburn, S. L., & Hamburg, D. A. The implications of primate research. In I. DeVore (Ed.), *Primate behavior: Field studies of monkeys and apes.* New York: Holt, Rinehart and Winston, 1965, 607–622.

Watson, J. B., & Rayner, R. Conditioned emotional reactions. *Journal of Experimental Psychology,* 1920, **3**, 1–14.

Wattenberg, B. J., & Scammon, R. M. *This U.S.A.* Garden City, N.Y.: Doubleday, 1965.

Wentworth, R., & Flexner, S. B. *Dictionary of American slang.* New York: Thomas Y. Crowell, 1960.

Weyl, N. Some comparative performance indexes of American ethnic minorities. *Mankind Quarterly*, 1969, **9**, 106–128.

White, R. W. Motivation reconsidered: The concept of competence. *Psychological Review*, 1959, **66**, 297–333.

Whorf, B. L. *Language, thought and reality*. J. B. Carroll (Ed.). New York: Wiley, 1956.

Wilkins, L., & Richter, C. F. A great craving for salt by a child with cortico-adrenal insufficiency. *Journal of the American Medical Association*, 1940, **114**, 866–868.

Winterbottom, M. R. The relation of need for achievement to learning experience in independence and mastery. In J. W. Atkinson (Ed.), *Motives in fantasy, action, and society,* Princeton, N. J.: Van Nostrand, 1958, 453–478.

Witcover, J. '72 primary's cost per man—$10 million. *Los Angeles Times*, February 5, 1971.

Witkin, H. A. The perception of the upright. *Scientific American*, February 1959, 2–8.

Wolpe, J. *Psychotherapy by reciprocal inhibition*. Stanford, Calif.: Stanford University Press, 1958.

Yablonsky, L. *Synanon: The tunnel back*. Baltimore, Md.: Penguin, 1965.

Young, W. C., Goy, R. W. & Phoenix, C. H. Hormones and sexual behavior. *Science*, 1964, **143**, 212–218.

Yuan, D. Y. Voluntary segregation: A study of New York Chinatown. *Phylon*, Fall 1963, 255–265.

Index

Page numbers in *italic* type refer to glossary entries.

Photo Credits

CHAPTER	1	2	3	4	5
	Personality Development	Love, Work Identity	Intelligence/ Creativity	Attitudes	Learning
ISSUES	*1–27*	*28–61*	*62–87*	*88–110*	*112–143*
I Concerns of Women	Training sex roles (8–15) Stereotypes, male & female (11) Training wrong sex role (12) [illegible] Fate control, male vs female (14) Discrimination by sex (15) Life & death of Marilyn Monroe (19–23)	Meaning of divorce (41–43) Divorce & feminist progress (42) Marriage innovations (43–45) Work & identity [illegible] Woman's life (47) Woman & work (48–57)	Sex differences in IQ (76) Intellectual development of women (76–78)	Changing sex roles (98–99) Youth & counter-culture values (103–107)	
II Race and Poverty	Poverty related to discrimination against women (15)		Nursery school movement (66) Education of intelligence (67–68; 82–84) Ethnic differences in IQ (72–73) Geographic/racial factors in IQ (73–75) Fate control among minorities (75, 78) Relation between poverty & mental deficiency (75–76) Fostering intelligence & creativity (80–81)	Issues of race & poverty—one cause of student unrest (103–107)	
III Youth and Counter-Culture	Training sex roles (8–15) Stereotypes, male & female (11) Male & female traits, desirability of (14) Fate control, male vs female (14) Health values (15–17) Pursuing success—life & death of Marilyn Monroe (19–23)	Meaning of divorce (41–43) Marriage innovations (43–45) Work & identity (45–46; 48–57)	Sex differences in IQ (76) Intellectual development of women (76–78) Nature of creativity (78–81) Fostering intelligence & creativity (80–81)	Traditional values, conflict & change (99–102) Changing sex roles (98–99) Youth & counter-culture values (103–107)	Learning aggressi (131)
IV Neurosis and Psychosis	Transsexual, case of Frankie (12) Suicide, case of (19–23)	Con man (35) Dynamics of rejection (37)	Pseudofeebleminded-ness, case of (64) Nutritional mental deficiency (75–76) Education of intelligence, case study of (82–84)		Learning in psych somatic disorde (119)
V Control of Behavior	Modification of assertiveness (14–15)	Making a successful marriage (37–41)	Educating intelligence (67–68; 82–84)		Reinforcement in operant conditio (119–121) Animal training (122–124) Training kamikaz (124) Skill learning (127–129) Early reading, teaching/learnir machines (132–